DISCARD

Encyclopedia
of
OHIO
INDIANS

Encyclopedia
of
OHIO
INDIANS

VOLUME ONE

Tribes, Nations and People of the
Woodlands Areas

A to Z

Somerset Publishers, Inc
PO Box 160
St. Clair Shores, Michigan 48080

Associate Publisher
GAIL HAMLIN-WILSON

Managing Editor
DONALD B. RICKY

History
NANCY K. CAPACE

Editorial Contributors

James Clifton, R. O. Clymer, David H. Corocoran, Adolph L. Dial
Jacques Dorais, Edith M Dorian, Ernest C. Downs, Eula E. Doonkee
Phil Baer, Charles A. Bishop, Bradley A. Blake, Donald N. Brown,
Linda Ellans, Emmett M. Essin, Albert B. Elasser, Mark S. Fleisher
Mary E. Fleming, John G. Fought, Ken Harper, Arthur E. Hippler
Jean Jackson, Thelma Kimmel, Harriet E. M. Klein, Eleanor Leacock
Frank J. Lipp, Marvin K. Mayers, Mildred Mayhall, Roy W. Meyer
Jerald T. Milanch, Karen Mohr, Robert V. Morey, Kathleen A. Mooney
Jan Onofrio-Grimm, J. V. Powell, Peter G. Ramsden, Carol L. Riley
Norman D. Thomas, Janelle B. Walker

Printed in the United States of America

ISBN 0-403-09332-5

FOREWORD

After almost five centuries of contact the original Americans and those who later came to call themselves Americans remain strangers. Much was written about the original occupants, collectively called Indians, but the writing often had the impersonal character of a naturalist's description of strange fauna. Or at another extreme, the writing projected the image of a rude people waiting to be led out of darkness into the light. The Indians, for their part, having first offered hospitality only to find themselves misused, chose a course of passive noncommunication. There the matter rested through generations of sterile if not hostile coexistence. Neither learned from the other.

This condition is now changing. An obvious explanation is the change in social climate which rejects racist interpretations of historical process and fosters clinical studies of human development. Apart from the theoretical concepts emerging in this later time, the effect of which is to provide a base for understanding, a major factor in bridging the long estrangement is the massive accumulation of information about native America. Every major university in the Western Hemisphere has involved itself at one time of another in projects to recover data from the archaeological past or from living Indian communities. Public works projects devoted to the damming of streams or the construction of highways uncovered ancient settlements. Trained students recorded languages, migrations, creation stories, folk history, social systems. Museums and laboratories, some in foreign lands, were filled with material objects and their accompanying field notes. Unfortunately at first, much of the accumulation was shelved and catalogued and made accessible only to erudite specialists.

While the archivists filled their bins, the Indians in recent years have been reconnoitering on their society. Indians in unprecedented numbers are pursuing college courses, even through graduate school. Indians are going into medicine and the law. They are taking control of schools and school boards. Indian theatrical groups have come into existence. Indian poets, novelists, and playwrights are publishing. An Indian press association services local Indian publications across the country. Indian political leaders are reaching a constituency beyond tribal boundaries. Here are collective experiences finding voice and finding an audience as well.

It is not remarkable, all this considered, that the literature devoted to specific tribes, to historic periods, to official policy, and to critical evaluations of Indian-white relations has flourished in recent years. Scholarly monographs still appear in learned journals, but much of the material previously available only in technical publications, obscured further by the idiom of the technician, now finds its way into books and articles for the general reader. While Folsom Man has not yet become a household word, much of the serious Indian history now being written makes acknowledgment of an Indian past extending beyond the coming of Europeans. Some glimmering of understanding appears in print suggesting not only time depth of New World occupation, but something of the nature of that occupation, of the relationship of man and his environment, of what was valued and made holy.

It is against this background that the effort to create a state ENCYCLOPEDIA OF INDIANS is to be viewed. Here will be brought together the findings of many delvers in the past and many students who have looked critically at the impact of outlanders on native society. What can be hoped for from an enterprise of this magnitude is a further lessening of estrangement and, on the positive side, an appreciation of the variety of adaptations achieved by the Indian in his migrations. No greater service could be rendered the original occupants of these broad continents than to place them securely in their proper course among the adventuring races of mankind.

CONTENTS

INDIANS OF OHIO
and the Central Woodlands - a History

Today, the relatively few Native Americans still living in the Central Woodlands region of the United States and Canada belie their former importance in the shaping of the national experience and anthropological development in each country.

Most systematic research of the Central Woodlands Indians began with first European explorations in the sixteenth century. However, ancestors of historic tribes inhabited the region from about 10,500 BC. Studies of prehistoric and historic natives became more extensive during the seventeenth, eighteenth, and nineteenth centuries. Yet even into the present, archaeologists have often disagreed on how the Central Woodlands Indians evolved from prehistoric times to the present.

PALEO INDIANS

Initial penetration and settlement of the Central Woodlands region began about 10,500 BC - 6000 BC. Paleo Indians at that time were hunters, and their environment encompassed the tundra or park-tundra that adjoined the southern edge of the Wisconsin ice sheet. When ice began to withdraw from the terminal moraine, the tundra and spruce woodlands followed it northward. In 6000 BC, after the last of the Canadian ice disappeared, floral and faunal zones stabilized.

Some writers speculate that there were actually two stages of Paleo Indians: Early and Late. Excavation sites, tools, and implements from each stage have been studied to determine subsistence patterns and climatic changes for the region in which they were used.

Early Paleo - 10,500 - 8000 BC

Scattered evidence for Early Paleo Indians was discovered in several sites in Vermont, New York, Massachusetts, and Ohio. Tool forms, especially fluted points, exhibited consistency through most areas. Biface knives, biface preforms, end scrapers, side scrapers, flake knives, and other unifaces were also used. Very few known sites have

1

produced tools of the "rough stone" category, such as hammerstones, anvil stones, pitted stones, or abraders.

The uniformity of fluted point tools is assumed to have resulted from a highly conservative way of life, adapted to a specific subsistence pattern. Most sites are located on hills or rises where good drainage was important. Rare are rock shelters or caves, and where they have been found, they were used mostly for protection from the wind, cold, or snow and rain.

Late Paleo - 8000-6000 BC

Point tools of Late Paleo Indians were discovered at excavation sites in Michigan, the Great Lakes, Upper Ohio Valley, Wisconsin, and the Canadian side of Lake Huron. Some speculation continues about items found at these sites, since they are determined to have been used for both prairie and lake cultures.

ARCHAIC INDIANS - to 3000 BC

Sometime between 6000 BC and 3000 BC, Paleo Indian cultures disappeared, and Archaic groups came into existence. While the Paleo Indian culture has usually been equated with big game hunting in the late glacial period, Archaic groups represented a more diverse culture of hunters, fishers, and gatherers that had adapted to post-glacial climate conditions.

The big game animals of the tundra and spruce woodlands were extinct by 8000 BC. Archaic peoples depended primarily on deer, bear, elk or wapiti, smaller mammals, birds, turtles, fish, and shellfish for their subsistence. Also nuts, seeds, and other plant foods of area forests were gathered. Sites of Archaic Indians are more numerous and larger than those of the preceding era, and they reflect a larger and denser population as well as a more abundant subsistence base.

All of these changes reflect territorial and cultural diversity. Although it is assumed that Midwestern Archaic cultures evolved from Late Paleo-Indians, it is unlikely that any Asian migrations were represented. A few archeologists believe that Archaic cultures arose independently of Paleo Indians, but even those holding this view generally agree that there was probably some interaction between the two groups.

2

Eastern Archaic Indians have been divided into three sub- periods, which include Early Archaic (8000-6000 BC), Middle Archaic (6000-4000 BC), and Late Archaic (4000-1500 BC)

On the southern border of the Northeast culture area, the environment supported a number of small but widely distributed population groups. For example, the Modoc Rockshelter in southern Illinois contains 28 feet of stratified deposits and remains that were radiocarbon dated to about 8000 BC. Deposits from another site, the Koster, located on the Illinois River, have been dated as far back as 5100 BC

In New England, New York, and adjoining areas of this region, however, there are few Early or Middle Archaic remains. Some discoveries have been noted in Staten Island that date between 5310 and 7410 BC. But since they occurred together on one level, there is speculation about a mixture of components. Other sites have included Harry's Farm on the Delaware River in New Jersey, and areas in Pennsylvania and New Hampshire.

Despite new data on artifact assemblages and radiocarbon dates, most information on Early and Middle Archaic cultures comes from the southern and coastal parts of the Northeast.

Following 3000 BC, several Late Archaic phases have been defined in New England, New York, and other sections of the Northeast. Occupancy has been determined by the size and number of sites and by the amount of refuse.

Some scientists speculate that an "explosion" in population and/or stability of occupation took place. It is possible that these changes occurred in response to further environmental changes, although the Northeast had evolved to an essentially modern environment at least one or two thousand years earlier.

CULTURAL DEVELOPMENTS - 3000-300 BC

More than a century of excavations revealed important artifacts to support theories about technology and subsistence patterns of Northeast Indians from the late Archaic and Early Woodland periods (and in some areas, transitional periods between these eras). Cultural patterns were probably determined by environmental differences as well as by communication and exchange networks, which followed a number of natural features including drainage patterns and ecological zones.

One important factor in determining cultural patterns in the Midwest was the mixed prairie-hardwood forest of western Indiana, Illinois, and areas southward and westward. Extensive grasslands and stands of oak and hickory trees provided the setting for deer and elk, beaver, bear, raccoon, fox, squirrel, and other mammals. Birds, especially wild turkeys, passenger pigeons, and migratory birds, and fish and shellfish were also important. Considerable evidence supports the notion that this environment may have been present prior to 3000 BC.

Helton Culture. The Koster site in southern Illinois and several sites in Indiana have produced distinctive stone and bone components in the mixed prairie-hardwood zone. From findings at the Koster site, occupation is estimated between 5000 and 3000 BC, but it is probably closer to the end of the era. Preliminary data indicate that the Helton people from this time hunted, fished, and collected. Refuse gives evidence of subsistence and settlement patterns, but specific patterns have not yet been precisely defined.

Other evidence of the Helton culture is provided by the suggestion of wattle-and-daub houses with thatched roofs, racks for smoking or drying fish, and large roasting pits. Tools and implements were numerous and specific in their purpose.

Titterington Culture. The Titterington culture developed after the Helton culture. A variety of tools and implements used by this group were seemingly unrelated to those of the earlier culture.

Riverton Culture. Following this was the Riverton culture in the Wabash and other interior river valleys; artifacts from this complex reflect an apparent blending of midwestern and southern tradition with a lithic tradition derived from the east.

New England Coastal Area

During Late Archaic times, the coastal regions of northern New England, Maritime provinces of Canada, Newfoundland, and Labrador were regarded as a distinct culture area. The most important resources were connected with the sea, and the exploitation of these resources gave the Late Archaic culture of the coastal area its distinctive flavor.

Subsistence in the Maritime area included birds, fish, and mammals, with local variations such as swordfish harpooning in the southern region. Summers were spent on or near the coast, where sea mammals were available, and where Atlantic salmon, nesting birds, and plant foods could also be taken. At the first snow, a retreat was made from the coast to favorite hunting grounds, especially to crossing places of the caribou. During the remainder of the winter, beaver or other mammals provided red meat until spring, when a return to the coast was undertaken.

Weapons, implements, and tools implied hide- and bone- working industries. Woodworking tools were also made. Art, magic, and religion items were found in cemeteries in Maine and the Atlantic Provinces. Charms and amulets made from the feet and bills of diving birds, and claws and teeth of seals, bears, caribou, fox, and beaver were used for good luck in hunting. Burial ceremonies   was elaborate.

By 1800 BC in Newfoundland, and by 100 BC south of the Saint Lawrence River, these people were replaced by groups of interior hunters who moved along the coast and began utilizing additional resources, especially shellfish. The newcomers may have originated in the Canadian Shield and slowly spread into the open pine and spruce forest of Maine and Atlantic Provinces. Evidence suggests that the Shield Archaic tradition can be traced forward to present-day Algonquian-speaking groups of the Northeast, including the Micmac, Maliseet, and Abenaki, in an essentially unbroken sequence.

Movement to the coast of Algonquian speakers is speculated to have occurred after Maritime Archaic people vacated the area (or, alternatively, may have been partly responsible for their demise). Continuity between earlier and later inhabitants has long been recognized, although research has not yet demonstrated any "direct" relationship between Maritime Archaic and later Algonquians.

Saint Lawrence Mixed Forest Area

Flora and fauna of the Northeast are highly homogenous south of the Great Lakes-Saint Lawrence formation. Along with a mixed prairie hardwoods area, the oak, hickory, chestnut and deer-turkey environment was that of Late Archaic peoples on both Atlantic coastal and interior riverine drainages. Artifact types and varieties and adaptive patterns are similar in both major physiographic areas. Some likenesses may be the result of convergence, but others clearly show persistent contact between coastal and interior areas via rivers whose headwaters nearly meet in the Appalachian Mountains.

Atlantic Coastal Area

On the Atlantic coast, important mammals included the Virginia deer, black bear, raccoon, woodchuck, opossum, eastern and New England cottontail rabbit, otter, red and gray foxes, gray squirrel, and wolf. Also important were wild turkey, grouse, passenger pigeon, and migrating waterfowl of the eastern flyway during the fall and spring. Resident populations of sea birds and fish added variety to the diet.

Resources of this area set it apart from surrounding areas of the North, Northwest, and to a lesser extent, the West and South. Throughout the Late Archaic period, environmental differences are roughly parallel to differences in culture complexes. An increasing body of data indicates that a moderate population was already living on the northern fringes of the coastal plain during Middle or possibly Early Archaic times.

Some speculation exists as to whether a year-round coastal adaptation was present or whether coastal and inland areas represented seasonal camps of the same people. Data from "upriver" sites show a predominance of winter sites away from the coast, with summer sites surrounding the tidal marshes, ponds, and bays of the Atlantic coastal plain stretching from New Hampshire to North Carolina. People of this tradition were probably grouped in small, mobile bands. Each group likely moved seasonally within its own territory, regardless of whether coastal/inland movement was undertaken annually.

Nonperishable remains from the Late Archaic period in Middle Atlantic and southern New England states suggest a lack of elaborate technology. Many tools and implements were made from quartz and were known by various names. Art and ornamentation were virtually unknown on the coast during this period, although such crafts could have been made from easily disintegrated substances such as wood, bark, or skins. Little evidence suggests magical or religious beliefs, except for one discovery (Robbins, 1960) of a mortuary complex at the Wapanucket site in east Massachusetts.

Several local or regional cultures from the Late Archaic period in the Northeast interior had tools and implements that were similar to those of coastal complexes. Sites in Kentucky, Tennessee, New York, and Pennsylvania yielded implements and tools that are morphologically similar to eastern varieties and are probably related. Other elements show affinities with Mississippi Valley cultures.

The Riverton culture revolved around at least three seasonal camps. In the spring, riverbanks provided shellfish, turtles, and migratory birds. In fall, acorns, hickory nuts, and other vegetables were gathered. In winter, hunting camps provided deer and other mammals. Technology included sewing and weaving, and possibly hide-and-skin working. Woodworking was done, and smoking pipes, flutes, and box turtle rattles were fashioned.

The origin of this culture is unclear; it cannot be definitely traced to any earlier Archaic occupation. Similarly, there is little evidence to suggest a relationship between these people to succeeding Early Woodland peoples.

Great Lakes - Lake Forest Area

The Great Lakes drainage system, with its beech, maple, hemlock and maple-basswood forests (along with some oak, walnut, butternut, and pine,) provides evidence for the Great Lakes-Lake Forest Archaic. Two principal factors, the drainage system that was also a communication or exchange network, and the forest system, distinguish this culture from others (although some scientists believe that neither the Great Lakes Archaic or Lake Forest Archaic is entirely accurate, since the tradition is coterminous with neither).

Fauna, fish, and tools and implements found in this region show differences between northern and southern culture areas. One example is the method of fishing and the species of fish found in the Great Lakes area. While hook-and-line fishing was used throughout the Northeast in early historic times, harpoons and leisters (spears armed with three or more barbed prongs) were restricted to the Great Lakes and more northern areas, while simple spears were used in the south.

Evidence also indicates that a distinctive set of resources was attached to an equally distinctive culture type, or cultural tradition, in the Great Lakes-Lake Forest zone from about 3000 to 1000 BC. This culture was internally homogeneous yet distinct from surrounding cultural traditions. Tools and implements across a wide area suggest an actual movement of people into the Lake Forest area slightly prior to 3000 BC.

In around 3000 BC, two indigenous industrial developments took place. In the east, a ground stone industry produced axes, adzes, gouges, knives, and spears, combined with the chipped stone complex common to most of the Lake Forest area. In the western region, the copper-producing area of the Upper Great Lakes known as the "Old Copper Culture" produced objects such as spear points. Many of the copper forms appear to be functional equivalents of ground-stone artifacts.

Although there is little evidence of settlement patterns or social organization among the Lake Forest Archaic people, discoveries suggest a well-defined territory that constituted the local unit, and temporary shelters for small, mobile bands. Seasonal movements were likely determined by a variety of subsistence resources, including mammals, birds, fish, and plant foods, as they became available. There are no common objects of personal adornment, decoration, or recreation in the Lake Forest Archaic, although these became increasingly more common after about 1500-1000 BC.

Lake Forest Archaic cultural history is not completely understood (and perhaps will never be) due to the destruction of sites. Eastern portions of the Lake Forest provide data to support two phases of development: the Vosburgh, dated about 2500 BC, and the Vergennes, which was dated earlier. In the west, changes reflect minor alterations in tools, but in this area there is a somewhat greater suggestion of local or regional evolution of implement styles toward the Early Woodland forms.

TRANSITIONAL CULTURES

Late Archaic transitional cultures centered on the coast of the Middle Atlantic States and radiated from there along the coast and major river systems (the Susquehanna River being one of the major systems). Sites for this culture are all located along major rivers and their tributaries.

Later Susquehanna peoples added shellfish to their diet, while red meat still comprised a major portion of their food (as it had during the earlier Late Archaic period). Artifact forms changed somewhat, yet there seem to be no profound changes in the way of life between the

8

two periods. The rapid spread of Susquehanna artifacts, however, clearly implies some adaptive advantages. There is also evidence of a more sedentary existence via discovery of heavy and not easily transportable soapstone bowls.

Although the cultural history of the Susquehanna tradition is complex and not yet completely understood, there is a strong indication that it arrived in the Northeast via the coastal plain during about 2000 BC. It flourished until after 1000 BC, while adopting or inventing the use of ceramic vessels, which marked the transition from Archaic to Woodland cultures.

Late Archaic-Early Woodland Cultures

Recent studies by pre-historians have attempted to distinguish Archaic cultures from Early Woodland cultures, with perplexing results. It seems the only clear criterion has been the presence of ceramics in the latter. However, even this is not a clear indicator, since many Early Woodland sites are cremation burials and contain no ceramics as part of its mortuary offerings. Distinctions between Early and Middle Woodland cultures have been more numerous, yet no less confusing.

Two indigenous cultures seem to be part of the Early Woodland. (Additionally, there is a somewhat different development in northern New England and the Maritime area of eastern Canada.) The two evolved cultures appear to have had separate origins. Yet they held certain elements in common: an elaborate ritual system with lavish burial practices, and the making of thick, plain ceramics. Some scientists have called these cultures "transitional," since they represent people who produced the first ceramics in this area.

The first of the Late Archaic-Early Woodland cultures is speculated to be indigenous to the Lake Forest area, and presumes a lineal descendant of the Lake Forest Archaic. Living sites are very rare, but burial sites were found in the Lake Forest and Prairie Peninsula zones. The sites may represent a religious "overlay" on existing cultures. Artifacts from this time represent a positive link between this and the presumably later Meadow Wood culture of the Early Woodland in New York, Quebec, and Ontario.

The second of these cultures (and probably the one most clearly demonstrative of continuity during the second and early first millennia

BC) is the so-called Old Copper culture in the western Great Lakes. Most sites of this complex are cemeteries, and offer little information about the lifeway of these Late Archaic-Early Woodland people.

Artifacts from sites in New York State, Montreal, Ontario, southern Quebec, and Upper Great Lakes indicate that the economic pursuits of these cultures was not vastly different from the Archaic. It is doubtful if there was any change from the small bands that characterized the Late Archaic peoples in the same area, and evidence is lacking for year-round habitation.

While developments from an Archaic base were discovered in the Lake Forest area, influences from the south were found in other parts of the Midwest. A limited amount of plant cultivation may have begun, especially in connection with the Adena culture, although this culture is known primarily as a mortuary complex.

Daily life in the Midwest during the Early Woodland period reveals some changes in subsistence and settlement. Yet none suggests that there was wholesale migration of new peoples to the area. Instead, new traits became incorporated from north and south into existing cultures in the river valleys of the Midwest. The result was a somewhat more stable and productive hunting and gathering subsistence base.

More or less permanent villages were comprised of circular houses with out-sloping walls and conical roofs, suggesting settled villages. However, the hunting-collecting base as well as Adena material from rockshelters and other camping sites suggest considerable movement.

Artifacts from this time period include spear or dart points, flat-bottomed ceramics of several varieties, chert end and side scrapers, drills, cigar-shaped or blocked-end-tube smoking pipes, and a number of ornamental and ceremonial items.

In a number of additional sections of the Northeast, other local developments took place. These sections included cultures in New York, southern Ontario, and southern Quebec, which developed from the earlier Meadow Wood phase. The Atlantic coast also had vaguely related assemblages. These cultures shared many technological elements with the Adena, and also with one another and with their local Archaic predecessors.

The invention or introduction of ceramics is evident in several places, including the Lake Forest area, the Middle Atlantic coast, and the Midwest, although here there were no drastic changes from earlier

Archaic subsistence and settlement patterns. In some Midwest river valleys, cultivation may have become increasingly important and set the stage for religious belief that centered around treatment of the dead. This may have persisted in the Northeast for as long as two millennia.

Northeast Mortuary Ceremonies

Since the time of first Late Archaic occupation in the Northeast, special treatment was accorded to the dead. A "basic case of religious belief" persisted through several millennia and culminated in the Hopewell religion.

Burial cults were evident in several regions of the Northeast, in Maine, New England and Long Island, the Great Lakes area, northern New York, Michigan, and Ontario. Each was distinctive, but all seemed to express a similar underlying set of beliefs that could be related to a burial cult that began before 3000 BC.

Excluding a late Paleo-Indian site in Wisconsin and early burial mounds on the Labrador coast that dated before 5000 BC, burial ceremonies did not become important in the Northeast until the third millennium BC. The first unquestionably dated "red paint" cemeteries (so called because red ocher was often sprinkled at the burial site) were between 2000 and 1200 BC.

The Maritime Archaic tradition has the strongest expression of these ceremonies. The ritual included flexed or bundle burials often located on high east-facing hills or bluffs; the site was covered with red ocher and contained tools, ornaments, weapons, charms, amulets, and medicine bundles. Because graves of newborn infants were also filled with such artifacts, it is speculated that these articles were not personal possessions, but rather intended for use in the afterworld.

In Later Maritime Archaic burials, ground slate spears and bayonets were exclusively made as funeral offerings. Objects were often deliberately broken, probably done to release the spirit of the artifact.

South of the Maritime area (and at least partly contemporaneous with this complex), indigenous groups from New England, Long Island, and the Middle Atlantic coast practiced their own version of the Northeast burial cult. Elements of the Susquehanna tradition figure prominently in ceremonies. The presence of red ocher, ritually broken

11

artifacts, and choice of east-facing burials all seem to show a northern origin for basic elements of mortuary ceremonies. Cremation was an additional feature that may have begun in New England or along the Mid- Atlantic coast, and persisted until well into the Christian era.

In the Great Lakes area, similar rituals surrounded death and burial. However, cremation was the most common form. Bones and artifacts were burned either in place or in separate crematory basins; the residue was then collected and placed in a deep grave with red ocher and, occasionally, also with unburned offerings. Graves were on an east-facing slope or hill. Grave offerings included weapons, gorgets, copper tools, and ornaments.

In the west and south, other developments were taking place. Early Woodland ceremonies in southern Ohio was of the Adena complex. Theories have abounded concerning the origins of this group, from lost tribes or Meso-american migrants to much less exotic explanations. Numerous specific "traits" of the Adena have been widely studied, yet the most accepted explanation is that the Adena were closely related to, and probably derived from, the ancient Northeastern burial cult.

The means by which the Adena ceremonies were subsequently dispersed remains controversial. One suggestion is that the Adena people migrated from Middle West to the Atlantic coast. Others suggest diffusion or trade as the most reasonable explanation. Carbon-14 dating favors the former theory, while evidence of coastal Mid-Western interaction throughout the Archaic period favors the latter. Whatever theory best fits, the recurrence and elaborate elements of mortuary rituals demonstrate the only real unifying factor among otherwise varied aspects of Northeast cultures.

WOODLAND CULTURE, 300 BC - AD 1000

Around 300 BC, quantitative changes were taking place in the prehistoric Northeast. The stability of Late Archaic and Early Woodland periods moved into the dynamic phase of the Middle Woodland, which made a relatively smooth transition into the Late Woodland period. In the several centuries preceding AD 1000, a new level of energy efficiency began to be achieved. Small climatic changes in the Northeast shifted environmental and cultural patterns. These changes were small, yet they eventually necessitated a change in the entire culture.

Climatic changes during the period of 300 BC to AD 300, called the Hopewell episode (or Sub-Atlantic episode), may have been mild to more severe, although the variation may have meant greater rainfall or a different distribution rather than temperature variation. The sea level changed dramatically along the Atlantic coast, and many coastal Middle Woodland sites eventually became submerged, which could account for the difficulty in defining cultural components during this period.

Following the Hopewell episode was the Scandic episode, which lasted from AD 300-400 to AD 800-900. In the Northeast, there seemed to be a generally colder period, and this may have placed stress on earlier Woodland adaptive patterns.

After the Scandic episode was the period from AD 800 to about AD 1300, called the Neo-Atlantic episode. The period was agriculturally favorable and helped with development of the first efficient agricultural systems in the Northeast. Following the Neo-Atlantic was the Pacific, lasting from AD 1300 to AD 1450. A return to Neo-Atlantic conditions came at AD 1450, and another cooling period occurred between AD 1550 and AD 1880.

Middle Woodland Culture

The Hopewell culture covers a wide geographical area that ranges from western New York to Kansas City and from the Gulf of Mexico to Lake Huron. The characteristics that define this time period include mound burials and earthworks, distinctively marked ceramic vessels, platform pipes (often carved), cut animal jaws and teeth, pan pipes, and other artifacts.

Grave offerings in the Hopewell period led early investigators to group this culture with Adena as Mound Builders, whom they believed were genetically different from, and culturally superior to, the Native Americans who lived during the time of European contact. Recent work demonstrates that Hopewell, like Adena, was part of a local developmental sequence in the area in which it was found; all seem to be the work of prehistoric American Indians.

In spite of widespread similarities in the style of artifacts, each region of Hopewell is distinctive; it appears to be wiser to interpret the culture in terms of local sequences than as part of a broad cultural horizon. One major aspect of Hopewell in the Northeast is the evidence of widespread exchange networks. Long distance trade was carried to its peak during the Middle Woodland Period, evidenced by conch shells from the Gulf coast discovered in Michigan and Wisconsin. Also, shark's teeth were found in Illinois, and an effigy alligator pipe dated to the period was found in western Michigan. The distribution of these and other goods strengthens the notion that some exchange network, whether social or religious or both, existed at the time.

Before 1950, most archaeologists viewed Ohio as the source of Hopewell developments in other areas; more and larger sites, with better quality grave goods, were found here than in any other area.

After 1950, however, it became clear that many things that had been called Hopewellian outside of Ohio were different than were those in Ohio. Ceramics and burial mounds in the Great Lakes-Riverine area and other complexes differed from those in the Ohio region. A number of archaeological writers created elaborate divisions and distinctions to explain the complex differences. Adding to the confusion were developmental trends in different regions.

Presently, several patterns seem to have emerged from the study of the Middle Woodland period in the Northeast. First, in the Middle Woodland (and to a lesser degree, in the Late Woodland era), there seems to be a division between southern and northern cultures in adaptive strategies, economic base, social organization, and material culture.

Second, climatic trends seem to have affected the Middle Woodland culture throughout this time period. Thus, a cause and effect relationship is indicated, and both cultural and environmental factors need to be considered. In the northern section, for example, agricultural innovations were implemented at a later time than in southern regions.

Third, within a single time frame, elements of cultural developments interacted at different times. Next, the Middle Woodland cultural climax spread to the north from the south along the same channels as did earlier agriculture and ceramics. However, in spite of a lag in origin, northern and southern cultures reached their peak of development at approximately the same time.

The change from Middle Woodland to Late Woodland was primarily an artistic emphasis, and this was also a trend that moved from south to north. The subsequent Middle Mississippian influence was weaker and more varied in northern cultures than in southern, due to the northern economic base being essentially the same for Middle and Late Woodland periods, while establishment of an efficient agricultural system in southern areas had tremendous social and demographic impact.

It is clear that the cultural history of the Northeast remains to be completely understood. Radiocarbon dating provides some clues; however, interpretations continue to differ, and the mystery remains for future scientists to unravel.

LATE PREHISTORY CULTURE PATTERNS

During late prehistory, native groups from three distinct cultural areas in the Northeast lived and maintained their separate cultural traditions. They included the Coastal, St. Lawrence, and Great Lakes Indians.

Coastal Region

It was primarily river drainage systems that determined the economic shift from generalized hunting and gathering, to more specialized exploitation of natural resources. This shift seems to have taken place earlier in the southern than in the northern region of the Northeast.

On the East Coast, drainage basins of rivers and streams that flow into the Atlantic and into the southern part of the Gulf of Saint Lawrence were occupied by Eastern Algonquian tribes. Extremely south were Iroquoian groups of the upper drainages of the Neuse, Tar, Roanoke, and Chowan rivers.

Given the ecological differences between Newfoundland at the one extreme and coastal North Carolina at the other, the cultural pattern of the Coastal region has three separate patterns. At the southern extreme lived Virginia and Carolina Algonquians; their pattern was one of well-developed farming. Villages were small, and had anywhere from several to a few dozen houses. Although this group had essentially permanent dwellings, depletion of soil and other resources required relocation within intervals of 5 to 20 years.

Their houses were elongated bark-or-mat covered, and barrel-roofed with straight or rounded ends. Population density was higher than in northern drainages, and strong cultural influences were affected from the greater Southeast. On the same rivers, but upstream, lived various Iroquoian and Siouan tribes who combined hunting, farming, and fishing.

In the middle drainage systems, from the Delaware to the Merrimack, farming was also important. However, it was of greater importance to those inhabiting the lower coastal portions of the drainages, where fishing and shellfish gathering supplemented agricultural pursuits. Upstream and downstream groups were closely related, but hunting and gathering were more important to the latter. Within each drainage, regular interactions took place between upstream and downstream communities, and it is likely that economic exchange also took place.

In both areas, houses were large enough to accommodate extended family groups, although none were as large as the communal dwellings of the Iroquoians. Nonetheless, studies have shown that dwellings were larger in areas where Iroquois influence was greater. Villages were sometimes palisaded, and settlements were permanent for a decade or more in areas where agriculture was possible. Settlements in the interior uplands were less so. The Algonquians of the middle drainages were influenced by Iroquoians in the interior.

In the area of the Eastern Abenaki to the Beothuk of Newfoundland, on the other hand, farming was of little importance. Settlements were less permanent toward the northeast, and houses were smaller in the northern drainages. The settlements were probably abandoned during the season when shellfish collecting or interior hunting were done, which differed from farther south where some of the young and old probably stayed behind to protect crops during the summer.

The economic importance of shellfish decreased northward. In northern drainages, hunting and fishing were more important than they were in the south. There is some evidence for division of local tribes into upstream and downstream groups, and it is likely that this was for economic reasons. On some rivers, it seems that there was a tendency for some groups to specialize in exploitation of marine resources, while others exploited resources of interior forests and streams.

Although conflicts apparently sometimes arose between local Eastern Algonquian communities, there seems to have been some general feeling of common culture between them. Frequent trade and inter-marriage likely diffused the groups somewhat.

Since about 6000 BC, prehistoric cultures of the coastal plain have differed from those of upland oak-chestnut-hickory forests. Archaeo-logical sequences suggest that the coastal area was characterized by a steady development without any notable discontinuities, and implies that prehistoric traditions that led to historic cultures extend back sev-eral thousand years. Archaeology does not support origin myths that say that most tribes were relatively recent arrivals from distant and nonspecific regions. Rather, it seems generally that many parallel se-quences were part of a broader pattern of development, and each diverged somewhat from the mainstream in response to local condi-tions.

The late prehistory of East Coast cultures appears to be a smooth outgrowth from earlier periods. Each local sequence reflects a long-term stability, and there are a number of in- place developments, each of which was contained within a natural drainage unit. Innova-tions moved from south to north through the area as local cultures adapted to conditions. Stronger waves of change moved northward over time as such economic activities as ceramic manufacture, agri-culture, and shellfish gathering were extended.

HISTORIC NORTHEAST INDIANS

It is difficult to determine when the first meetings between Europe-ans and Native Americans took place. Limited definitive information, along with distortions by European ideas and interpretations, raise questions about the accuracy of information obtained from this time period. Generalizations abound, and differences between northern and southern groups were often not addressed. However, it is clear that European contact greatly affected changes in aboriginal cultures.

The earliest recorded European contacts seem to have been of brief duration and were largely insignificant to natives in the areas of con-tact. However, by the fifteenth and sixteenth centuries, economic interests motivated further exploration by Europeans. Increasingly, dependence on importation of expensive goods from Asia by an over-land route to Venice forced Europe to consider finding a shorter route. Nautical knowledge was increasing, especially in Portugal, and merchants were willing to give financial support to transoceanic explorations.

In the late 1400s, Spain and other western European nations began to move forward with maritime adventures across the Atlantic. In 1497, five years after Christopher Columbus discovered the Bahamas, John Cabot took possession of Newfoundland in the name of the English crown. Although he probably made no real contact with local natives, he did discover their fishing nets and other tools.

Portuguese interests focused on the southern route to India, but also included a concern with the North Atlantic. In 1500 and again in 1501, Gaspar Corte-Real explored coastal Newfoundland. Upon return from his second voyage, he kidnaped 57 Indians. With their capture and enslavement, a new aspect of commerce was introduced. More frequently, a few Indians were kidnaped in order to be used as interpreters in later contacts, or to be displayed in European cities, or to become slaves.

In the early years of the sixteenth century, many European fishermen began entering the Newfoundland region. Their activities centered mainly around the coast, and by about 1530, fisheries had expanded along the entire coastline from Labrador to south Nova Scotia. By 1550, about 30 French ships were sailing into Newfoundland. Reports in 1578 listed 50 English, 150 French, and 100 Spanish fishing boats in the general area.

Most early fishermen salted their catches at sea and sailed for home. After the middle of the sixteenth century, it was decided that "dry-fishing" was more economical. Camps were established on the shores, particularly along the east coast of Newfoundland and in Labrador. Although no specific exploration was done in the interior, contacts with the natives were likely frequent.

Limited data from the period reveal that the Indians were apparently at ease with Europeans, as they sometimes worked as fishermen for European captains, and they freely boarded the ships in nearby harbors. Such relationships provided the basis for satisfactory trade.

However, this was not the case everywhere. Clearing the lands around harbors on Newfoundland resulted in forest fires that lasted for weeks. Native food sources were often wasted. Kidnapings and other experiences caused some Indians to move further and further into the interior, which was the case of the Beothuk. Relationships with the Europeans continued to deteriorate. An extremely unfavorable stereotype was developed by the Europeans, and it was clear that the Beothuk were considered by them to be merely a nuisance and of no economic value.

In North America, it was not fishing but development of the fur trade that became historically and economically important. The potential of adding profits by trading furs with the Indians was seen by fishermen before 1519. There was strong incentive for Europeans to explore the coasts before returning home, and Maine Indians had already become acquainted with Europeans' desire for furs by 1524. Jacques Cartier was offered furs by Chaleur Bay Indians in 1534, and Indians from the Saint Lawrence came up the coast to trade with Europeans and hunt for seals as early as 1540.

The coastline between Nova Scotia and Florida appeared on European maps as a result of Spanish and French explorations. Spanish slave hunters were conducting raid along the coast of South Carolina after 1520, and on one trip they captured some 150 Indians to ship to the West Indies. News of these excursions spread far and wide to coastal tribes.

Giovanni de Verrazano's voyage in 1524 is the earliest known continuous voyage along the eastern coast of North America. According to his writings, he found the natives to be friendly and as curious as was he himself. However, when he met Indians in Maine, it was clear that they had had previous unpleasant contact with Europeans. They were less friendly, and there was no hospitality between the groups after they were done exchanging goods.

In the latter decades of the century, the fur trade changed from a subsidiary activity of many fishermen to a major occupation. Rivalry increased between the French and English in North America for the fur trade, and many early traders stereotyped the Indians they met as a result of manipulations and distortions about the native society.

Colonization Efforts

By the first quarter of the sixteenth century, slave raids had made the local Indians in New England suspicious about Europeans, and the growing prospect that these cruel strangers intended to become neighbors may have caused even further hostility.

Some early attempts at colonization met with failure. In 1585, 100 English colonists and two Indian guides came to Roanoke Island on the coast of North Carolina with the idea of colonizing. Of their initial contact with the natives, no information is recorded. However, trouble began when a silver cup was found missing. The English burned the Indians' corn and destroyed the village. They killed the Indian chief and left for home. In 1587, another group of English attempted colonization, but the natives had not forgotten the earlier destruction. When supplies arrived for the colonists at the settlement, there was no one left to receive them. Although some have speculated that the colonists joined the Croatoans, the tribe of their loyal Indian guide and interpreter, no definite explanation has been given.

During the sixteenth century, all attempts at colonization were dismal failures. However, northern areas remained favored for trading, as hunting and fishing were more profitable here than further south and on the coast.

English interests brought about an increasing desire by the French to realize their own claims in the New World. In 1604, a group of French colonists settled on the Sainte Croix River in Maine. From there, Samuel Champlain explored the New England coast south to Cape Cod in search of a better location for the French colony. The influence of the French was strong, and some of the Indians along the coast began to sport European clothing or speak some French and Basque words.

In 1607, when the French colonists temporarily gave up their coastal enterprise and left for home, some 120 English settlers and two Indian guides arrived on the Kennebec River to begin another colony. It was also doomed to fail. The first Indians they met spoke some French, and conflicts ensued. After a severe winter in which a fire also burned most of the English supplies and lodgings, the colonists returned to England in 1608. Coastal Maine remained a source of conflict between English and French throughout the seventeenth century.

On the Chesapeake Bay in Virginia, a group of 144 English colonists arrived in 1607. The next year, another 190 joined the group. The colony survived despite quarrels, starvation, and hostility with the Indians, mostly because of the dealings of Captain John Smith. His success began the start of a new phase in relationships between Indians and whites along the central East Coast.

Increasing numbers of Europeans arrived, and the Indians were introduced to a range of new cultural aspects. The newcomers differed from fur traders primarily in their interests: they were less interested in the furs of the Indians than they were in their land.

Henry Hudson explored the New England coast in 1609 while searching for a passage to China. He found a cheaper way to obtain furs than trading with the Indians: He and his crew drove the Indians from their homes and took their goods. He then sailed up the river that bears his name. One month earlier, Champlain had defeated a group of Mowhawks on Lake Champlain, north of the Hudson River.

Amsterdam merchants had heard about Hudson's bartering with the Indians and, by 1610, Dutch ships were also entering the Hudson River to engage in fur trade. They operated as far as Narragansett Bay, where they maintained a trading post long after the English had tried, without success, to take the local fur trade away from them.

In 1624, the first colonists arrived to settle the town of New Amsterdam on Manhattan Island; trading posts were established on the Connecticut and Delaware rivers. But the beaver population was soon depleted, and furs here became more difficult to obtain. The Dutch began to treat the coastal Indians with scorn, while attempting to establish friendly relationships with Indians of the interior. They desired to divert some of the trade from the French in the Saint Lawrence valley to the Hudson.

Although the fur trade brought many outsiders into the lands of the Native Americans, no proper settlement was established until 1620, when the Pilgrims arrived in Massachusetts. After landing on Cape Cod, they soon settled in former Pawtuxet territory (the tribe was earlier decimated by an epidemic of European origin). All of this activity began an era of grave importance to North American Indians. It was the onset of major cultural and environmental changes, and forced the natives to face a number of new challenges.

Native Americans after Contact

It is difficult to establish an accurate history of the Indians after European contact. The natives did not have any significant writings, and their accounts of contacts with whites were scanty at best. The full nature of events after contact with European traders and colonists is essentially one-sided, and only the main points can be understood.

The first reaction of the Indians to contact with whites was probably curiosity; some may have believed that the newcomers were supernatural. However, after only a short time, they became suspicious and hostile. As the whites began the widespread depletion of their food sources, their economy was severely disrupted. Even more destructive were the diseases that the Europeans unknowingly introduced, such as measles, smallpox, and typhus, for which the Native Americans had no immunity.

As epidemics began to ravage many coastal communities, the populations of the natives dwindled severely. A particularly devastating epidemic in 1617 decimated thousands of Indians between the Penobscot River and Cape Cod. In 1622, and again in 1631, whole communities south of the Merrimack River were exterminated. In 1633, 700 Narragansetts of Rhode Island died from smallpox. On the Connecticut River in 1634, four Dutch traders spent the winter among the natives. After an epidemic broke out, the population of some 1,000 Indians dwindled to 50 survivors. Hudson River Indians reported in 1640 that their numbers had dropped to less than one-tenth of their original population due to disease. Wampanoag, Abenaki, and Micmac natives reported similar losses. In addition, syphilis was determined as the cause of death in skeletons found along the Potomac River, and it is speculated that the promiscuous behavior of some of the fishermen and traders spread such venereal diseases through native lands.

Liquor was another cause of the decline of native populations. Early Basques and other fishermen apparently used it freely in their fur-trading negotiations with Indians. By the time the first French settlers had arrived in some regions, many Indians were already addicted to alcohol. Drunkenness reached incredible proportions among some groups. By the early decades of the seventeenth century, the Montagnais were highly addicted, and at some point, brandy became the only item of trade with which the French could compete with English and Dutch, who could sell it for less.

All of these elements had serious repercussions in the life of the Indians. Fear affected the attitude of the natives toward the Europeans. Especially with regard to disease, some tribes believed that European diseases required special European curing rituals. For the Micmac, religious rituals became altered; they believed that baptism from French missionaries could affect a cure from virulent European diseases.

The most profound changes were experienced in the fur trade and in intertribal relationships. The ancient trails and waterworks of the Native Americans were traveled by the white newcomers, and some Indians provided information regarding access to remote areas along the coast. Archaeological discoveries have revealed that pottery, shell beads, and copper were used for trade, as well as more profitable goods. Some tribes began to produce specialized trading items, such as the Nanticoke who made beaded items, and the Iroquois who fashioned pipes.

Of all the Indians involved in this new enterprise, only the Beothuk of Newfoundland refused to trade with the Europeans. In horticultural areas, groups were often passively resistant to the changes. However, the lure of new commodities proved to be irresistible. To obtain more of the white man's goods, the Indians needed to devote more and more time to hunting and trapping fur-bearing animals. In general, the fur trade upset and unbalanced the entire annual cycle of traditional aboriginal activities.

In Maine, where agriculture was less abundant, hunting and trapping increased to the point that interest in agricultural cultivation decreased even further. In some areas, particularly in Nova Scotia and coastal Quebec, adjusting to the fur-trade economy took its toll in the decrease of seashore activities; reliance on traders to bring European foods sometimes resulted in famine.

Another important change was in the hunting itself. Because it took more time and effort to trap sufficient numbers of small fur-bearing animals, larger mammals were not hunted as often, and their food and skins were less utilized. In addition, because any specific fur-trapping area was frequented more often than previously, the size of Indians' bands changed; larger bands became less common. Territoriality among native groups increased and became more defined.

Initially, many regional Indians welcomed the selection of specific bays as trading centers. But rivalry for access to trade areas sometimes resulted in intertribal warfare. An example is the friction that developed between Iroquois Indians and the Montagnais along Quebec's East Coast. It did not take long for more remote groups to realize that they were being cheated by coastal natives, and intertribal conflicts grew. In the course of these wars, political alliances were strengthened; by conquest or incorporation, local units merged into tribes, and tribes entered into confederacies.

Economic dependence, less reliance on making one's own tools and ceramics, and a weakening interest in other traditional activities frequently resulted in a decline of material culture traits. Poverty and malnutrition were often experienced after the loss of the fur trade.

Seventeenth Century Indian Wars

While powerful inland tribes in the Southeast and in interior New York did not become involved in warfare with the English until the eighteenth century, coastal tribes with whom the Europeans were in direct contact in the seventeenth century eventually became involved in full-scale warfare.

Early conflicts between New England natives and Plymouth leaders were resolved by means of a treaty of friendship. By the terms of this agreement, both sides were to keep peace, and offenses of one side to the other were punished. This peace lasted for more than one half century, although some Plymouth colonists' and Pilgrims' assaults on Indian groups raise questions.

New England's first great Indian war did not take place until 1637 against the Pequot tribe. Although one can only assume the motives of the participants, both the established colony of Massachusetts and the newer colony of Connecticut sought to profit from destruction of the powerful tribe. The occasion of the first major conflict was the murder of an Englishman, Captain John Stone, by Western Niantics allied with the Pequots. Retaliation was averted for a time by a treaty signed on November 1, 1634. In 1636, another ship captain, John Oldham, was killed on Block Island by a group of Narragansetts.

Orders were given to John Endecott and an expedition of 90 volunteers to kill the native men, capture the women and children, and take the island. The expedition was then to go to Pequot country to demand the murderers of Captain Stone and others, and collect 1,000 fathoms of wampum for damages. If the Pequots refused, force was to be used.

The expedition failed miserably. The tactic destroyed what little peace still existed between the English and the Pequots, and put in grave peril the Saybrook fort at the mouth of the Connecticut River.

Indian raids on outlying settlements increased. The Pequots sought to heal their breach with their former enemy, the Narragansetts, to fight the English. Roger Williams was able to interrupt the council that was to meet for this purpose, and the English offered to aid the Narragansetts in their efforts against the Pequots. The Narragansetts agreed to the alliance with the English. However, this agreement also brought about the later destruction of the Narragansetts.

On May 1, 1637, the General Court of the colony of Connecticut declared war on the Pequots. Both Connecticut and Massachusetts sent expeditions against the tribe, and both seemed to anticipate advantages that would be gained by being the first to destroy them. Captain John Mason of Connecticut, with 90 Englishmen and hundreds of Indian allies, torched one of the Pequot villages on the Mystic River and slaughtered all the inhabitants, a total of 300 to 700. The Narragansett allies of the English were appalled by their ruthlessness, and by their murder and enslavement of Pequot survivors.

This conflict is closely related to the creation of a league uniting the Puritan colonies of Massachusetts, Connecticut, New Haven, and Plymouth under Articles of Confederation in 1643. However, Roger Williams' Providence Plantations colony was excluded from the league. Seeing a threat to his colony and to the Narragansetts, he sought protection against the English. Intertribal wars and retaliations, agreements and breaking of agreements became part of the chaos that developed between tribes, sachems, chiefs, and their English allies. The Narragansetts soon became pawns in the conflicts, and the confederated colonies declared war on the Narragansetts.

While numerous causes have been alleged in justification of the declaration, the principal reason seems to be the Narragansetts' desire to maintain control of their own affairs in making war and making agreements. Although the tribe sought to avoid violence against the English and to meet reasonable demands, they were strongly opposed to the destruction of their position as an autonomous nation. However, a treaty was agreed upon on August 28, 1645 that made all the sachems acknowledge guilt for various misdeeds. They were to pay 2,000 fathoms of wampum and an annual tribute for each Pequot living among them, cede the whole Pequot country to the English colonies, and give hostages to the English as a pledge of good behavior.

Relations between the Narragansetts and the colonists continued to be marked by conflicts, rumors of conspiracies, and occasional punitive expeditions.

Further conflicts included King Philip's War, a bloody battle in 1675 between the Plymouth colonists and the Wampanoag Indians based on the issue of land. King William's War (1689-1697) and Queen Anne's War (1702-1711) were part of an international struggle between Great Britain and France, and the Indians played a secondary role to the two nations.

In Virginia, conflicts between the Indians and the colonists were similar to those in New England. Suspicion, violence against the natives, and broken trade agreements escalated until war was inevitable. Destruction wrought retaliation, and further attacks were carried out by both factions. Bacon's Rebellion in 1675-1676 was a terrible battle fought over the Indians' fear of losing control and the English desire to dominate trade and land ownership.

In analyzing the process by which wars developed between Indians and whites in New England, there appears to be no single explanation. It is possible that war was inevitable considering the expansiveness and aggression of white settlement, and the decline of population of the Indians due to epidemics and other problems introduced by Europeans. Another cause might be the passions and misunderstandings that were created by particular individuals at particular times. Still another may be the questionable legal status of the colonists and Indians in their relationships to one another regarding trade and land ownership.

A more ethnocentric reason might be the hatred the Puritans bore toward the native culture that contradicted with their system of beliefs, and by other European whites who did not and would not accept the natives as equals. Whatever the final analysis, the wars of the seventeenth century changed the life of the Northeast Indians irrevocably.

SAINT LAWRENCE LOWLANDS PATTERNS

In the area that runs from Schoharie Creek west of Schenectady to the Genesee at Rochester lived the Iroquois Indians. The Adirondacks and Lake Ontario were the northern border of this region, and the headwaters of the Delaware, Susquehanna, and Allegheny flanked to the south. The Iroquois comprised the Five Nations of New York (Mohawk, Oneida, Onondaga, Cayuga, and Seneca) and after 1772, the Six Nations that included the Tuscarora. Their way of life was not unique, but was shared by other local groups, especially the Hurons.

Iroquoia, the territory south of Ontario that was the early Longhouse of the Five Nations, lay just north of Lake Ontario and Lake Erie and southeast of Lake Huron. The Trent waterway connected Iroquoia via the Thousand Islands with Huronia. Southeast of Lake Ontario was the Mohawk River, whose broad valley cut through the uplifted plateau and the higher Adirondack mountains to the north, and this was the only water route through the Appalachian chain. These were the communication routes of the Iroquois and neighboring tribes, and they were the natives' corridors for trade, war, and peace. This was also the area that, for Europeans, became the avenue of exploration and expansion.

Deciduous birch-beech-maple-elm trees and coniferous pine and hemlock grew in the forests of this region, along with fir and spruce to the north. In the Appalachian area, oak, chestnut, and yellow poplar reached toward eastern Iroquoia via valleys tributary to the Hudson. However, the sugar maple, American elm, and white pine were the trees most important to Iroquois technology.

Elm bark was important for shelter, containers, and vessels. Deer, bear, and small mammals were hunted in the forests about one day's travel from Iroquois settlements. Turkey, partridge, and a large number of migratory game birds also provided food for the group. Freshwater fish in lakes and streams were caught, and turtles, especially the snapper, were trapped.

Of all the Eastern Woodland Indians, the Iroquois were the best known as horticulturists. Slash-and-burn agriculture was practiced by women, and fishing and hunting were done by men. After a harvest, hunting parties would abandon villages, leaving the old natives, pregnant women, and children to tend the crops. Bows and arrows, knives, traps, and later, guns were used to obtain meat and skins.

Among the Iroquois, food taboos were almost nonexistent. Diet consisted of most things that walked, crawled, swam, or flew. However, although they were in theory conservationists, in practice they often contributed to the decline of species, especially in the eighteenth century when beaver and deer populations dwindled.

Maple was harvested, although this industry was later taken over by Europeans of New York and New France. Salt was not exploited until after European contact, when some tribes became heavy users. Berries were picked and dried for winter use, and nuts from a variety of trees were gathered.

"Indian tobacco" was grown for ceremonial and social smoking. Maize, beans, and squash, the "three sisters" of Iroquois ceremonial, were cultivated. Settlements had up to 1,500 people. Iroquois women grew and harvested the crops, and their work operated on a principle of mutual cooperation. Rituals, songs, and drama were part of the growing cycle; Green Corn and harvest festivals were celebrated.

Iroquois life moved in an ecological cycle. Hunting and gathering were keyed to a lunar calendar and divided into four seasons, each marked with special ceremonies and rituals. Although it is believed that the Indians were earlier primarily hunters and gatherers, crop-growing later became more important, with far less dependency on meat and gathered foodstuffs.

Material Culture

The technology of the Iroquois showed a great capacity to use available materials. One example is the grotesque wooden masks that were worn by members of the Society of Faces, known commonly as false faces. (These masks are now exhibited in many major ethnographical museums throughout the world and in contemporary shows of American Indian art.) After the introduction of steel tools, the art evolved considerably, but all are related to a specific type of woodworking.

Many items from the nineteenth century were embroidered with moose or deer hair and porcupine quill. The Iroquois knew how to bend and shape wood for house frames, pack frames, toboggans, snowshoes, basket rims, handles, and lacrosse sticks. Their understanding about the principle of gravity was apparent in their deadfalls and corn pounders. Their war clubs and pump drills showed an understanding of centrifugal force, and they moved and erected timbers by way of levers. Blow and dart guns utilized the principle of the piston.

Structures were highlighted by the longhouse. A typical dwelling had from three to five fires, each shared by two nuclear families of five or six members. Houses averaged about 25 feet in width, and length was determined by the number of families to be sheltered. The longhouse was the most conspicuous feature of Iroquois settlements. It was synonymous with residential units, the household or maternal lineage, and was their symbol of identity. The Iroquois called their confederacy "The People of the Longhouse."

Settlements typically had from 30 to 150 longhouses surrounded by a palisade, and were situated on high land accessible to drinking water and near a navigable waterway.

The Iroquois were travelers, and they covered vast distances over forested trails quickly. In contrast, the Hurons were primarily traders and canoeists.

Museums do not have many exhibits of Iroquois and Huron clothing. However, both seemed to favor black-dyed buckskin. The Iroquois wore twined cornhusk slippers in summer. Decoration included face painting. In general, black was used for war or mourning. Northern Iroquoians, especially Mohawks, were tattooed with geometric designs, double-curl motif, and clan crests, which were pierced with bone awl and rubbed with charcoal on the chest, shoulders, and face.

Social Organization

One of the primary patterns of social structure of the Iroquois was based on the division of labor between the sexes. Although towns were built and governed by men, men owed their offices to female succession, and the village and its environs were the domain of women. Men were active in the council and in the forest where they hunted, warred, and maintained peace and trade.

Each tribe was divided into villages and longhouse families. These were divided into two moieties; each moiety comprised two or more clans. Clans were segmented into one or more maternal families or lineages. Each maternal family traced its home to some longhouse of which it once formed the household. Lineages were the building blocks of the entire social system.

The "fireside" or nuclear family was the simplest unit of Iroquois society; within it were the husband and wife and their children. From the fireside family stemmed the siblings of the wife's mother, the wife's siblings, the wife's children and her daughter's children, and descendants of the preceding women in the female line. The senior woman was the matriarch and presided over the household. A lineage of per-

29

sons traced from a common mother. Some call this the "maternal" family, and it was the primary unit of Iroquois government. In time, it might occupy several longhouses in several villages, and give rise to segments of a clan.

A clan was composed of two or more maternal families that behaved as if the members of each generation were siblings, or as if they constituted a single maternal family. One or more clans constituted a moiety, and acted together as if they were siblings. Usually two moieties existed in any Iroquoian community. Political structure extended the basic pattern of social structure.

Warfare

Although the message of peace was inherent in the longhouse society, Iroquois men revered war above all else. After introduction of the fur trade, this became a powerful force that threatened the very structure of Iroquoian society. Much energy was expended in training, preparation, and travel for war, and heavy losses of manpower were only partly compensated by the adoption of captives. The native population of Iroquois towns steadily dropped during the seventeenth century, and from the middle of that century, there were more outlanders than natives in Iroquoia.

Early Iroquoian Contact with Europeans

By AD 1500, Iroquoian-speaking peoples of the Northeast had evolved a cultural pattern with most elements that had characterized them in the historic period. Their subsistence was based primarily on horticulture and fishing. Extended families lived in longhouses. Clan segments joined together in villages with 1,000 or more inhabitants. Neighboring villages were linked together to form tribes.

The age of the Iroquois confederacy is uncertain, but it appears that the five tribes that formed the Five Nations were joined together in the sixteenth century. There is no evidence that membership in the confederacy at this time involved more than an agreement among tribes to avoid blood feuds and cease raiding one another.

Iroquoian-speaking peoples lived in tribal cluster areas, each of which had several thousand people located in one or more nearby villages. Clusters were separated from one another by extensive tracts of hunting and fishing territory spread out over a large area that centered on Lake Ontario. Between this and the shores of Georgian Bay lived four Huron tribes and the Petun. West of Lake Ontario and in the Niagara Peninsula were various Neutral tribes. The Erie, Wenro, and possibly other groups lived southeast of Lake Erie.

Beyond the Niagara River, the five tribes of the Iroquois stretched across upper New York State as far as the Mohawk River valley. Along the Susquehanna River was one or more Iroquoian tribes, and the Saint Lawrence lowlands were occupied by more groups that became known as the Saint Lawrence Iroquoians.

The late prehistoric period was one of local self- sufficiency. Intertribal warfare was common, and long-distance trade was limited in volume and restricted to luxury items such as native copper and marine shells. A notable exception was the Hurons living in Simcoe County, Ontario, who appear to have traded tobacco, fishing nets, and other items for skins and dried fish and meat produced by hunting tribes to the north. Some evidence points to a similar trade between Iroquoian tribes in the upper Saint Lawrence Valley and Algonquians and Montagnais north of them.

When the northern Iroquoians first encountered Europeans in the first half of the sixteenth century, their history and cultural development became inseparably linked with the newcomers. The first recorded contact between Europeans and Iroquoians was in the Baie de Gaspe on July 16, 1534. French explorer Jacques Cartier was sailing north when inclement weather forced him to take shelter in this bay. The French met some 300 men, women, and children who had come down the Saint Lawrence River from Quebec City to fish for mackerel.

The Native Americans welcomed the French with songs and dances. They desired some small articles the French had brought, including combs, knives, and other items. In fact, the French later described the natives as being great thieves. However, the French showed themselves to be greater thieves, for they kidnaped two sons of the fishing party's leader, Donnacona, and took them back to France in hopes that they might serve as guides and interpreters on future voyages.

Cartier returned to Canada the next year, directed by Donnacona's sons, and sailed up the Saint Lawrence to visit Iroquoian villages in Quebec and on Montreal Island. While spending the winter in Quebec, Cartier heard accounts of a wealthy kingdom called Saguenay where native copper existed. Wishing for King Francis I to hear these stories firsthand, he kidnaped Donnacona and took him and nine other natives back to France. None of the Indians ever saw their homeland again.

Donnacona's interview with Francis I eventually led to two short-lived colonies becoming established a few miles upriver from Quebec City, in 1541-1542 and 1542-1543. Both were abandoned, in part because of the hostility of Saint Lawrence Iroquoians toward the French due to kidnapings and intrusion into their territory. For many years, the opposition of the tribe ruled out further attempts by Europeans to travel upriver from Tadoussac, which became the main trading center.

The fur trade had a great impact on Iroquoian-speakers of the Northeast. By 1534, European fishermen were earning extra money by trading furs with Indians in the Gulf of Saint Lawrence. By the middle of the century, Basque whale hunters had penetrated up the Saint Lawrence to Tadoussac. By the latter decades, the demand for beaver pelts had increased significantly.

Around 1580, the expanding fur trade on the Saint Lawrence gave ship owners the impetus to again hazard up the Saint Lawrence. The main center of trade was still the port of Tadoussac.

In the early part of the seventeenth century, the Montagnais and Algonquians attempted to break the power of the Iroquoian Mohawks who had overrun the area. The growing fur trade in Tadoussac probably gave both northern Algonquians and remaining Saint Lawrence Iroquoians a great advantage over Iroquois tribes living further to the south.

The Mohawks seem to have begun raids on the Saint Lawrence Valley in order to plunder trade goods from Saint Lawrence Iroquoians and Algonquians. It is possible that they attempted to drive the groups from the valley so that they might gain control of the nearest center of trade goods in Tadoussac. In fact, it has been speculated that the need to obtain European goods and resist northern tribes might have been influential in the formation of the Iroquois confederacy.

Failure to gain access to trading ports drove the Mohawks to remain dependent on warfare for obtaining a supply of iron tools. When Champlain discovered them in 1609, this was the situation that existed.

SEVENTEENTH CENTURY INDIANS

Tribal life became very complex and difficult after the Europeans established trade in the Saint Lawrence-Lowlands region. In the early part of the seventeenth century, the Montagnais at Tadoussac were middlemen in any trade between the French and the Indians living further inland. Tribal etiquette made it an offense for one group to travel across the territory of another without permission; to protect their trading interests, the Montagnais would not allow tribes living in the interior to visit Tadoussac, nor would they permit Frenchmen to travel up the Saguenay River.

In about 1603, in order to fight the Iroquois who threatened their trade monopoly, the Montagnais enlisted the aid of Algonquians who lived west of them. As allies, Algonquians were allowed to come to Tadoussac and trade with the French. It was during this period that many peoples living north of the Saint Lawrence became allied against the Iroquois, and this played an important role in the historical development of the time.

The Hurons also began to obtain some European trade goods about 1580, but only in very small quantities. Algonquians probably increased their trade with the Hurons for corn. For the Hurons, the impact of receiving trade goods was significant; most of what they obtained was not utilitarian, but luxury items. They increased their numbers by allowing the Arendaronon and the Tahontaenrat to join the Huron confederacy and move into Simcoe County. The four Huron tribes continued to live in close proximity to the only supply of trade goods they could obtain.

The Hurons also began to supply trade goods in limited supply and at high prices to the Iroquoians living in southwest Ontario. A growing demand for trade goods from the south led the Hurons to have contact with other tribes, especially the Susquehannocks.

Possession of trade goods provided the impetus for Seneca and other neighboring Iroquois tribes to attack the Hurons. It was at this time that an important transformation took place. The largely ritual warfare of prehistoric times gave way to economic warfare.

The Hurons sought to establish their own trading relationship with the French. This action opposed the self- interests of the Algonquians

33

who, like the Montagnais, wished to preserve their role as middlemen. As Iroquois raiders began increasing attacks on Algonquians in order to steal trade goods, Algonquians were forced to look for military allies. Soon they enlisted their Huron trading partners to become allied with them, and together they began to fight the Mohawks in the Saint Lawrence Valley.

French traders realized that a coalition of northern tribes would greatly increase the volume of furs from the interior. They sought to develop new trading posts upriver from Tadoussac, and make the Saint Lawrence River a main artery of trade. In 1608, Samuel de Champlain built a fortified trading post at Quebec, and the following summer, the French sought to intervene in the struggle to control the Saint Lawrence. They joined the Montagnais and Algonquians in an expedition against the Iroquois.

The French and their allies made the Mohawks' attacks on the Saint Lawrence Valley dangerous. The Mohawks were forced to abandon their quest for a time, but they soon found another source of obtaining goods by establishing a trade exchange with the Dutch who had begun to develop trading relationships in the Hudson valley and along the Saint Lawrence.

The Dutch, however, had their trading agenda. They sought to establish good relations with Algonquians and Montagnais in hopes of diverting rich furs away from French trading centers to their own. Since the Dutch also controlled sources of wampum in the vicinity of Long Island, they could offer the Indians this as well as European goods.

The Mohawks were aware that they had less to offer the Dutch than did their northern rivals, and their fear of again being prevented from trading with Europeans drove them to seize control of the area around the Dutch trading post, then called Fort Orange. Although the struggle lasted four years, the Mohawks were finally victors and gained control of the route to Fort Orange.

The Dutch had no choice but to comply with the Mohawks, and since the Mohawks would not allow the Algonquians, Montagnais, or any other northern group to trade with the Dutch except with themselves as middlemen, Dutch trading ambitions became severely crippled.

French-Huron Alliance

The first contact between Hurons and French was through Arenda-ronon warriors who accompanied the expedition by Champlain against the Mohawks in 1609. Two years later, Huron council chiefs sent an expensive present to Champlain and expressed their desire to have a trade alliance that was independent of their alliance with the Algonquians. The Algonquians naturally protested this threat to their role as middlemen, and Champlain was prevented from further visits with the Huron for several years.

In 1615, Champlain offered to assist the Hurons and Algonquians in raiding central tribes of the enemy Iroquois confederacy. Although the raid was a failure, it opened the door for Champlain to meet Huron headmen and create an alliance with them. The Algonquians were too few in number and too dependent on the Huron for corn and military assistance to prevent this trade alliance.

From 1615 to 1629, the Hurons traded with the French, and also traded with the Nipissings and Ottawas to obtain additional furs for the French. Hurons also traded with Algonquians in Ottawa Valley to obtain corn that was traded for furs, as the expanding fur trade required that Hurons have corn to exchange. The wealth from trade activities did not cripple the social system of the Hurons, but instead continued to strengthen it.

Because the lands of the Huron were remote from areas of European settlement, the number of Europeans who visited their region was small. Jesuit missionaries began their work in the area sometime after 1629, and their attempts at conversion of the Indians had enormous impact. One proof of this was in 1627, when a Huron trader allowed his son Amantacha to travel to France, where he remained for two years and learned to speak, write, and read French. After his return to Huron country, he became important as an intermediary between the Huron people and French.

Jesuits gained more strength in Huron country after 1634. Their goal was to convert whole communities rather than individuals, and ultimately to convert the entire confederacy. Although they did not succeed in their quest, they were eventually successful in upsetting the balance of the Huron social culture. After 1640, about 100 Hurons per year were converted. However, it is important to remember that the primary reason was not religious belief, but the fact that Christians were better treated than non-Christians in trading with the French, and they were paid a higher price for their furs.

The Jesuits created new factions within the Huron culture. The group was now separated into Hurons for and against one another, the French, and Christianity. The growing division within the Hurons came at a very disastrous time because the confederacy was fighting for its very survival.

Epidemics

Epidemics plagued all the Saint Lawrence tribes. A number of severe outbreaks left many groups in this region with declining populations. In 1634-1635, a number of Mohawks died from smallpox. Between 1635 and 1640, epidemics reduced the population of the Hurons from 20,000 to 10,000. In 1646-1647, another smallpox epidemic swept through the Iroquois country and killed over 1,000.

Not only were the deaths from epidemics horrific and devastating, but they also changed the structure of Indian society. Some of the tribes' great leaders died, and many of the groups suffered severely from a weakening or lack of effective leadership.

Iroquois Wars

Throughout the first half of the seventeenth century, all of the Iroquois tribes in the Northeast grew increasingly more dependent on European trade goods. This was especially true for the Mohawks and the Susquehannocks, as they lived closest to European trading posts. By the 1630s, Hurons were also greatly dependent on trade goods.

By 1640, beaver populations were dwindling. In that year, Iroquois furs were also being diverted by traders from New England, that had gained the Mohawk market by offering to sell them guns. The Iroquois became increasingly more militant, and began to steal skins from parties traveling with trade goods. Conquering whole villages of other Indians, they would plunder them before burning them to the ground.

It is speculated that by this time, Iroquois men were split into two factions. While half of the men were waging wars, the other half was hunting beaver for trade. Although the Iroquois were highly effective warriors, they did not cultivate any entrepreneurial skills in order to compete with other tribes for resources. They did not form alliances as middlemen, nor did they cultivate any trading relationships with tribes to obtain trade goods.

Only the Mohawks sought to secure French neutrality in trading. By 1642, western tribes of the Iroquois confederacy were attacking Huron villages to obtain furs. Many tribes of the Huron confederacy were attacked in a methodical matter, beginning with more remote communities on the eastern border and moving inward. Village by village, the Huron were forced to disperse.

By 1650, Iroquois warriors had dispersed many of the tribes they sought to destroy, and they now moved more westward and into Erie country. The Erie had gained strength by adopting many of the Huron who had been dispersed, and also by adopted many Neutral refugees. The Erie region inhibited the Iroquois from raiding and hunting in the Ohio Valley where beaver was plentiful.

In 1651-1652, the Mohawks attempted to attack the Susquehannocks, hoping to disperse them as they had the Huron. However, they failed because the Erie and Susquehannocks had become powerful and strong in number. In 1653, the Seneca led the Iroquois confederacy into the first general peace between themselves and the French. This peace lasted until 1658. However, their war with the Erie continued until 1657.

After 1650, the Mohawks became extremely aggressive in dealing with other tribes of the Iroquois, and the western tribes sought an alliance with the French. The conflict led to hostilities resuming between the Iroquois and the French.

In 1663, the power of the Susquehannocks was broken. But this did not come as a result of victory by the Iroquois, but by an attack by European backwoodsmen from Maryland and Virginia. The defeat of the Susquehannocks was the last of the Iroquoian groups that had surrounded the Five Nations Iroquois. The Iroquois victory did not, however, bring them the peace or prosperity they sought. The French were now able to trade not only in the north, but also to extend their trade routes into the lower Great Lakes and Illinois country.

Although the Iroquois launched a full-scale war with the Illinois in 1680, the attack not only brought them into conflict with their Indian enemies but also with Frenchmen who were competing with them for furs. The Iroquois were forced to enter into a new era, one in which they would have more direct involvement with European powers now establishing them selves in North America.

Rising mortality rates among Iroquois males due to war brought about social changes as well. Women had begun to play a greater role in village management and political activities than ever before. In a generally sense, women's political importance rose dramatically during this period.

GREAT LAKES-RIVERINE REGION PATTERNS

The societies that were established in the upper Great Lakes and in the valleys of Ohio and upper Mississippi were mostly Algonquian, along with some Siouan-speaking Winnebagos. Native Americans in this region were organized into two primary types of social and political organization.

The first type included the Shawnee, Illinois and Miami tribes, Sauk, Menominee, and Potawatomi; the Winnebagos reflected strong post-European Algonquian influence. All shared a maize agriculture economic base, and all tribes did seasonal hunting and gathering. Settlement patterns alternated between semi-permanent riverine villages in the summer months, and large camps during the winter. In spring and fall, camps would disperse.

Each tribe had a system of patrilineal clans that emphasized rituals and extended into political organization. Outsiders were integrated into the society. Each group was organized as tribes, and had a dual political structure that consisted of organizations for peace and war, and different officials associated with each.

The second type included the Ottawa and Chippewa who lived along the northern fringe of the region. Their settlement patterns were not primarily agricultural, but instead included fishing sites in the summer and dispersal the remainder of the year. Settlements were generally small. Patrilineal clans were present but weak. Political organization was of the band type, with some sporadic tendencies toward integration.

For the the Potawatomi tribe, most members fell into Type 1, but some northern groups fell into Type 2. Several features suggest that this tribe was unique in that it shifted from the second type to the first at a relatively late date, probably during early historical time.

Although there were a vast number of differences between societies, each group within the two types shared significant features.

Type 1 Systems

Groups in this society were organized into patrilineal clans. Clan names were most often derived from animals or mythical beings, such as Wolf, Bear, Elk, Fox, Deer, Thunder, Water-Spirit, or Panther. Bird and fish eponyms were less common and more likely to be specific to a particular tribe. Plant eponyms were very rare.

At one time, clan and lineage relationships were equivalent, but after post-contact, the functions of lineages became somewhat eroded. However, lineage still determined political office and ceremonial leadership. Although members could punish infringements of some rights, lineages had no functions connected with landholding and ownership of nonritual property. There is some evidence that lineage determined residence, but this appears to have been strongest in the Menominee and Winnebago.

Clan systems of the group may be divided into several defined types. The first included the Sauk, Fox, Kickapoo, and Potawatomi. They had primarily group and cult names, and contact with the supernatural was achieved through the vision quest. Each clan was founded through a vision in which the clan ancestor was blessed by a spirit in the form of the eponym. The vision included instructions for ceremonies, and the person who received the vision was directed to assemble such ceremonies. Ritual societies consisted of persons blessed by the same spirit, and sometimes assumed certain clan traits such as inheritance of membership. Each clan owned a stock of personal names, which was given to each member shortly after birth, and reverted back to the clan stock at its holder's death. These names carried with them a degree of power derived from the vision in which the clan was founded. Clan names also were used for horses and dogs.

The Winnebago system had some differences, especially in the concept of descent from the eponym and a much stronger association of specific political functions with particular clans.

The Shawnee apparently restructured their clans during the nineteenth century, and many features of their earlier structure are uncertain. Instead of name stocks owned by clans, they obtained per-

39

sonal names from the dreams of name-givers that were called upon shortly after a birth. Positions in warfare, government, and ritual that were given to individuals or clans were based on qualities considered appropriate for the action required. Shawnee clans were not cult groups, and major ritual units comprised divisions or communities, each presenting annual ceremonies in which positions were given according to clan affiliation.

Among the Illinois and Menominee, only scanty information is known. It appears that Miami clans controlled names through a system similar to the Shawnees, and that they had a similar role in the organization of ritual and ritual aspects of warfare.

The Menominee clan system broke down before pre-contact, and thus little of it is known. However, it appears that they contrasted strongly with preceding tribes in that an elaborate origin legend described the formation of the clan system, and each clan owned a few eponymous names. However, these were primary titles given to certain adults. Ordinary names were derived from dreams of shamans or parents, and these were given without reference to clan affiliation. Individuals could obtain supernatural power through their eponyms or with their aid on an individual basis. There appears to have been some association between clans and political organization.

Type 2 Systems

The political organization of Type 2 tribes appears to have been loose and informal, although the use of ritual strongly parallels similar functions as Type 1.

Formal offices were usually held by men. There are occasional references to female chiefs; however, it is unclear whether these women actually held the office or whether they dominated their communities through ability. Potawatomi women were apparently an exception, as women were among those who signed several treaties with the United States. One Shawnee report states that a widow of a divisional chief would take over his functions until his successor was appointed.

Political Organization

For all tribes in the Great-Lakes Riverine region, political organization seems to have become more decentralized after contact. From large villages, many groups divided into smaller units. In general, a major division separated the institutions centering on peace from those centering on war.

Peace organizations were headed by a tribal chief and lesser chiefs of similar type who may have been clan heads. These officials had assistants who were called criers, ceremonial runners, and speakers. Peace organization chiefs were expected to show behavior appropriate to their role and avoid any display of anger or aggression. Participation in warfare was generally forbidden.

On the other hand, war organizations were based on hierarchy. The office appears to have been achieved through consistently successful leadership of war parties. War organizations were also headed by a chief and lesser chiefs, as well as a group of warriors who sometimes also carried out police functions and could enforce tribal regulations.

A third organization, called the tribal council, probably included both war and peace officials. All aspects of political organization were highly ritualized. War organizations enforced regulations on specific occasions, and the men who were charged with this duty were chosen by the war chief. Tribal councils were convened by the chief, who presided; although these were classed with peace organizations, war officials were apparently present and discussions included issues such as war.

As was true in many other areas of North America, the political and social organization of local natives of the Great Lakes-Riverine region changed considerably and irrevocably after European contact.

White Exploration of Great Lakes Region

The first record of white exploration on Lake Huron was by Samuel de Champlain in 1615, while he was traveling in the Nipissing-Huron area. In his reports, he made many scattered comments about Indians to the west and north of Georgian Bay. From his accounts as well as those in the *Jesuit Relations,* generalizations have been drawn about the Indians of the Great Lakes during the early decades of the seventeenth century.

Ottawa and Chippewa tribes dwelled here. Many European reports also mentioned a system of exchange between the Nipissings and Hurons in which they traded fish and furs for corn. Intertribal bands

41

and relationships were not determined by cultural or linguistic affinity. An Algonquian band would go to war against another group of Indians for a variety of reasons, but would fight against other Algonquians as easily as Iroquoian or Siouan groups.

Semi-nomadic hunting and fishing tribes of Algonquians dominated the Upper Great Lakes early in the century. Siouan groups (Dakota and Assiniboin) controlled the western edge of Lake Superior; other Siouans (Winnebago) lived along the western side of Lake Michigan. After 1650, scattered Iroquoian bands came to the Michigan side of the present Michigan-Ontario border.

Until the Huron-Iroquois war of the late 1640s, European contact had little impact on the area. However, Upper Great Lakes groups were familiar with French trade goods after their introduction by the Huron in exchange for furs. The Hurons were important middlemen in the French fur trade during the 1630s and 1640s, and although tribes from the area participated in the trade, no real evidence shows their culture or material possessions being affected significantly by their participation.

Native Americans After Contact

By the middle of the seventeenth century, the Neutral and then the Iroquois had begun attacks on indigenous tribes of southern Michigan in order to seize furs and expand their hunting grounds. Sauk, Fox, Mascouten, Miami, Kickapoo, and some Potawatomi retreated west into the prairie and wild-rice areas of Illinois and Wisconsin, where they encountered Menominee and various Siouan groups.

The contacts between tribes led to major cultural changes and created economic and political conflicts that led all the groups to become involved in the fur trade. Before this process was complete, Hurons and other Ontario Iroquoian groups (Petun and Neutral) experienced great difficulty with the French. In a major Indian war between 1648 and 1650, Iroquoian warriors burned five Huron villages, and many other villages were abandoned. The blow scattered the Hurons, and survivors were absorbed by Petun, Neutral, and other groups. Huron and Petun who sought refuge in the Upper Great Lakes region came to be called the Wyandots.

After dispersal of the Hurons and through the 1690s, further economic and social upheaval took place as the French founded missions, forts, and trading posts. By the late 1660s, small French groups had penetrated from Quebec to Hudson Bay, West Lake Superior, and Green Bay. Key Jesuit missions had become established before 1670 in Western Lake Superior, Sault Sainte Marie, and Green Bay. An important mission was built in 1671 at present Saint Ignace, Michigan, by Jesuit Father Jacques Marquette.

Before 1649, the Ottawas played a subsidiary role, while Hurons were the key middlemen in trade with the French. After the Huron-Petun dispersion, the Ottawa assumed a dominant role in trade exchange. For the next century, Ottawa and Wyandot villages were established side by side, especially in Chaquamegon Bay, Mackinac, and Detroit. The Wyandot became part of an uneasy arrangement with the Algonquian Ottawa, who were hunters and fishermen as well as agriculturalists.

European Alliances

The European presence on the Native Americans became overwhelming. Beaver areas determined trade routes and tribal locations, and this led to the French establishing Jesuit missions. The missions became social and economic centers, encouraged by French traders and missionaries. Before long, military posts and mission centers attracted other bands. Such tribes as Nipissing, Fox, Sauk, Potawatomi, and Chippewa began to gather, along with the Ottawa and Wyandot, and considerable interaction took place. Native settlement patterns became altered, to the advantage of the economic and religious interests of the French.

As the distinct cultural and geographic identity of the Indians weakened, the French economic, religious, political, and military influences became stronger, and soon French interests were a major determining factor of the natives' activities. The Indians were aware of these changes, and sought the most advantageous alliances with Europeans to meet their own needs. In return, Europeans sought to ensure support of the tribes by giving gifts of trade goods and supplies.

Several important French centers were established in the late 1600s to discourage English encroachments, including Fort de Buade at Saint Ignace, Michigan; Fort Saint Joseph at Port Huron, Michigan; and Fort Saint Joseph at Niles, Michigan. North of Lake Superior, the

French also built Fort La Tourette and Fort de Francais, both constructed to threaten British interests on Hudson Bay.

Warfare activities of Upper Great Lakes tribes also became greatly influenced by French interests. Smaller groups who, just a few decades earlier, were involved in local hunting, fishing, and warfare were now forming large groups from many tribes to travel in a large war party and pursue the goals of French powers.

In 1697, the French government ordered the closing of posts in the Upper Great Lakes region. By this time, the Mackinac center had become a key site for houses of worship and trading activities, for obtaining brandy, and for tribes and bands to meet. The Jesuits were blaming the army and traders of degrading the Indians, and said that many Indian women were experiencing major problems with the French. The Jesuits recommended closing the posts, and Fort de Buade at the Straits of Mackinac was abandoned in the late 1690s.

Cadillac convinced the French government to build a post at Detroit to prevent English penetration and to aid the Indians and French to establish a settlement. Fort Ponchartrain was built in 1701, and many Great Lakes Indians came to settle. Villages included those of Chippewa, Huron, Fox, Potawatomi, Sauk, and Miami. Mississauga, Shawnee, and other tribes sometimes came to trade. Detroit soon became a major center for both Indians and French.

After the Treaty of Utrecht in 1713, which ended Queen Anne's War, the French attitude changed. The treaty made the Iroquois English subjects, and the French logically feared that this would weaken their trade interests, since the treaty permitted both English and French to trade with western Indians. Also, the Indians were aware that English trade goods were less expensive and of better quality than those of the French.

A string of military and trading posts in the Upper Great Lakes region was established by the French in response to the treaty. They included Michilimackinac in 1715, Fort Saint Joseph at Niles in 1715, and Fort Beauharnois in Minnesota in 1728.

French interests were not always harmonious. Intertribal disputes began being resolved by French and Indian allies, sometimes with fatal consequences on both sides. Many expeditions were sent out, and many of them failed. But they created even more hostility between Indians who were allies of the French and those who were not.

The French increased gifts and supplies to Indian allies in the 1740s in response to a series of minor revolts. The prestige and success awarded to Great Lakes Indians was closely related to French aims during the era. By the mid-1750s, Indian tribal and band names were used with less frequency as settlement patterns shifted and cultural differences between Indian groups decreased. Many village warriors of different groups now had muskets, iron hatchets, tobacco, knives, clothing, and other goods provided by the French. Cultural differences became subordinate to political and economic considerations.

The French and Indian War in 1756-1760 created a major change in Indian life. The event, a further extension of hostilities in Europe, forced Indians into yet another alliance with whites. Although most of the fighting took place in the eastern region of the country, many Upper Great Lakes warriors aided the French in expeditions at Pennsylvania and New York. After the English won the war, they seized control of the Saint Lawrence valley, and terminated all French military activity in North America. Algonquian tribes of the Upper Great Lakes were forced to make major adjustments as the primary political and economic policies affecting them were now British, enforced by British military operations.

British Regime, 1760-1796

Most of the major hostilities of the French and Indian War ended in September 1760 after Montreal and the French colony of Canada were surrendered to British forces. All French military posts in the Upper Great Lakes region transferred to British control. Although the end of the conflict did not produce immediate dramatic changes in the existing relationships between the French and Indians, due in part because the French civilian population remained, a new political system was implemented in which the British philosophy, objectives, and methods of administration would alter the life of the Indians in further ways.

The British victors were interested in pursuit of the fur trade. However, they also sought to expand colonization and settlement in North America, and to develop new resources and products such as mining interests, and agricultural and forest products. Their interest in native religions was limited.

45

At the time of Great Britain's victory, the Great Lakes region Indians had become more centralized near major forts and trading posts. The native groups had become increasingly more dependent on European trade goods for their existence, and had largely abandoned their former traditional tools and methods in response to more efficient and durable goods by the Europeans. The Indians' ability to provide for themselves had also decreased with the scarcity of important game animals and less emphasis on hunting, fishing, and agriculture for subsistence in favor of those activities that would be useful for trade.

It was now essential for the Indians to participate in the fur trade, as this was the only way to ensure continued access to European staple supplies and trade goods.

Native culture changes accelerated and diversified ever more rapidly during the several decades after 1760 due to increased adaptation of European objectives. The Indians soon felt the effects of British policy changes. Trade goods and provisions were not freely dispensed to the natives as a means of securing alliance and cooperation, as they had been during French control. Instead, these goods and provisions were distributed only in exchange for commodities valued by the British, especially furs. Fraudulent trade practices, a fear of losing their lands, and the denial of guns and ammunition resulted in an Indian rebellion against the British in 1763, led by Ottawa Chief Pontiac. Fort Michilimackinac and other western posts were taken.

In response, the British imposed changes in Indian policies that were supposedly designed to benefit the natives, including one that reserved all lands west of the Alleghenies for the Indians, and one that prohibited Indian land purchases except by royal agents. European traders were required to have licenses to conduct trade, and trade could only be done at major military posts, regulated by the officer in charge.

Although this initially seemed to allow more freedom than had the French monopoly, since anyone could obtain a license, in reality it increased the number of traders, and fur-trade interests led to more competition in a now rapidly diminishing resource, with the result that fur-trade practices became more fraudulent. Although proposed new land policies had some positive results early in the era, after 1776 colonial land interests and the American Revolution caused a loss of any benefits.

Indian support and alliances were again promoted during the American Revolution. Native Americans were called upon by the

British to assist in putting down the colonial rebellion, and most Upper Great Lakes groups, excluding the Sauk and Fox, aligned themselves with the British because they believed they were less a threat to their lands than the expansion-oriented American colonists. On the opposing side were the American revolutionaries, along with French and Spanish allies. Ironically, the Indians had again become allies with the losing side in a major conflict of European powers.

Although the primary battles of the American Revolution were fought in the East, major effects were experienced in the Great Lakes area as well. British forts were strengthened by Indian warriors, and the Indians left their homes to participate; trade became more difficult because a license and a pass were needed to enter the Great Lakes area; restrictions on ship passage into the area also slowed trade. The decrease in trade activity put severe hardship on the Indians.

After the Americans won the war, and especially after 1783, land policies presented more critical problems for the Indians. Western lands were viewed by Americans as conquered and, thus, available for development and settlement. Although the Indians were allotted reservations, and American settler encroachment was forbidden, much of their former lands were ceded to the American government to compensate for their part in the revolutionary conflict. The ceded land was eventually sold to American settlers, and the lands reserved for Indians was ultimately claimed by Americans. Indian rebellions were begun, and put down by American forces.

Although the British lost title to most of the Upper Great Lakes at the close of the American Revolution, they remained for a time at western posts and continued to control the fur trade and their Indian allies until 1796, when the posts were turned over to the Americans. Trading establishments such as the North West Company and the Mackinaw Company, established in the 1780s, introduced new trade patterns for the Indians.

Specific Indian bands and tribes during the period were relatively stable. Most of the Ottawas, Chippewas, and Hurons were in southeastern Michigan and adjacent Ohio. Smaller bands of Chippewa were living in Mackinac, Chaquamegon, Sault Sainte Marie, Saginaw, and along the western shore of Lake Superior. A group of Ottawas also had a settlement at L'Arbre Croche on the northeast shore of Lake Michigan below Mackinac. The Potawatomi were located in southwestern Michigan near Fort Saint Joseph, and the Sauk and Fox were living in Wisconsin, although they had now moved farther north and west along the Mississippi.

American Regime, 1796-1800s

After the establishment of the American Fur Company in 1808, which was centered in Mackinac, the fur trade reached its peak. Subagents were scattered through the area, and this lessened the need for Indians to gather at central points. They now delivered their furs to settlements such as Grand Haven, Milwaukee, and Green Bay, where they would receive trade goods in return. Until the decline of the trade in the 1830s and 1840s, their annual cycle changed to one of trapping in the winter, delivering furs in the spring, and gearing up for the next winter's trapping activities.

Half-breeds, called Metis, became a strong force in fur trade and Indian life. In the villages around the Upper Great Lakes and west of Lake Superior, their numbers ranged in the thousands, and many had settlements of their own. Most Metis were French and Indian, although a considerable number were of Scotch or Irish ancestry. The Metis commonly held a higher position in the fur trade than did the Indians, as they were socially and culturally more European than Indian.

European conflicts continued to plague the American frontier. In the War of 1812, the Indians again were forced to choose between two foreign nations. Most sided with the British, assuming that if the Americans won the war, the country would soon be teeming with American settlers. Indians aided in successful attacks at Fort Mackinac and Detroit. Shawnees, led by Chief Tecumseh, were the most notable.

However, after this war ended, problems for the Indians intensified enormously. Once again, they had backed the side of the loser. In a series of treaties from 1814 to 1825, primarily controlled or encouraged by Michigan territorial governor Lewis Cass, they were reminded of their error of participating with the wrong side during the war.

The Indian Removal Act of 1830 resulted in some of the Upper Great Lakes tribes joining other tribes and finding new homes west of the Mississippi. Potawatomis from southwest Michigan, along with

Ottawas and Wyandots from Southeast Michigan, were removed to Kansas and Indian Territory. Some fled to Canada.

Periodically, pressure was put upon the government to remove large bands of Ottawa and Chippewa. Some Winnebagos were removed from Wisconsin to Minnesota. A comment from the *Minnesota Pioneer* dated December 29, 1853, states the position of most citizens who sought Indian lands and allegedly wished to protect the natives: "It is a fact, well established by experience, that the Indian and the white man cannot 'dwell together in unity,' and in nothing has the philanthropic justice of our Government been more apparent than in the removal of Indians from land to which the Indian title has been extinguished, before they become contaminated by intercourse with the whites on the ceded lands."

From the 1790s to 1870, a number of treaties were created by the United States Government to deal with the Indian problem. Many tribes sold their lands in Wisconsin, Michigan, and Minnesota. They were assigned reservations that slowly but surely diminished in area by later treaties. Americans were eager for the copper, lead, iron, and timberlands of the region, and in some cases, land surveys were already in progress at the time the treaties were ratified.

The federal government made some token efforts in the treaties that were meant to "civilize" the Indians; occasionally a blacksmith, carpenter, or farmer was placed at a reservation. The government also provided funding for Protestant and Catholic missions for reservation schools. The American Fur Company usually favored Protestants, and the Indians were frequently forced to take sides with beliefs and powers that they did not understand in order to conduct trade.

During most of the nineteenth century, superintendents and agencies handled Indian issues. Superintendents were responsible for specific geographic areas, while agents had responsibility for individual tribes or reservations. In Michigan, the superintendent operated in Detroit, while agents functioned in Mackinac Island, Traverse Bay, Sault Sainte Marie, L'Anse, and Saginaw Bay. As white settlements increased, the influence of agencies decreased. After the Treaty of 1836, most Indian title to land in northwestern Michigan was ceded to the government.

By the middle of the nineteenth century, most tribes of the Upper Great Lakes region had experienced a common fate. Most were shifted from place to place, and many tribes were removed to areas in which they were ill equipped to adapt, such as the forest-dwelling Winnebagos who were moved to the Dakota plains. Multi-cultural activities were common, such as as the Green Bay Agency, where Ottawas, Menominees, Chippewas, Winnebagos, and Potawatomis lived; all were Algonquian speakers except for the Siouan-speaking Winnebago.

Indians of different linguistic and cultural backgrounds changed their lifestyles to adapt to a new way of life. They were now far removed from their former hunting-trapping-gathering traditions, and were exposed to the problems of inadequate living conditions and influences by religious and social foreigners. Some of the agents attempted to end the old traditions, such as the traditional hatred the Chippewa and Sioux had for one another. Most efforts were unsuccessful.

By the late nineteenth century, most tribes had sold their best lands, and many were removed far from their traditional homes. Others were placed on small reserves.

Some of the Great Lakes Indians received a more favorable fate. In the 1830s and 1840s, many Ottawas and some Ojibwa left the midwest and were settled on Manitoulin Island, Parry Island, and other parts of Ontario under British control. Because land pressures were not as intense in Ontario and Manitoba, many of the natives were able to maintain their traditional practices for a longer time than did those in the United States, where lumbering, mining, farming, and manufacturing continued to develop on lands that once belonged to the Indians.

History of Ohio Valley Region

The Ohio Valley was inhabited by a number of little-known tribes who were apparently sedentary. After the so-called Beaver Wars in 1680, this area became hunting lands. As the fur trade changed, the region underwent further alterations and was repopulated by groups whose original homes had been beyond its borders.

European contact affected some Ohio groups earlier than others. The Susquehannocks traded with the Dutch and the Swedes on Delaware Bay, and the southern area Shawnee appeared to have had early commerce with Spaniards. It may be assumed that epidemics introduced by Europeans spread along routes of native communications far beyond actual contact areas. Epidemics may have played a part in depopulating the region.

The dispersal of early Ohio Valley natives is generally attributed to the Iroquois, although there is some evidence that the Susquehannock also had a hand before their defeat in 1675. European exploration of the Ohio section came at a relatively late date, and its geographical location contributed to this. A mountain barrier of the east delayed entry by the coastal colonies, and the Great Lakes and Ottawa River further north provided easier access from Canada to the interior of the country and to the Mississippi. It was by this route that French explorers first reached the mouth of the Ohio.

Information about the people living in the Ohio Valley began with the Erie. They were mentioned in 1635 as one of a number of groups who spoke Iroquoian languages. According to reports by Jesuits in 1647-1648, they were forced to retire far inland to escape their enemies further to the west. (These enemies were apparently not the Iroquois, since they did not defeat and disperse the Erie until 1654.)

The French learned about the Ohio River in about 1670. Two years earlier, La Salle was in Montreal and learned from some visiting Iroquois that the river was a three-day journey from Seneca. The following year, La Salle visited the Seneca and was told that descending the river would be dangerous because both the Touguenha and Antastoez (Susquehannock) dwelled there.

In 1673, Louis Jolliet and Jacques Marquette descended the Mississippi and passed the mouth of the Ohio, where the Shawnee lived in great numbers. From Indian informants it was learned that the people of the Ohio spoke languages of the Algonquian and Iroquoian families. (Other languages may also have been spoken.)

To the west, Iroquois Indians had begun attacks on the Illinois beginning in 1680. They were slowed by distance and by the beginning of French-supported opposition. To the south, after dispersal of the Shawnee, raids and retaliations had begun with the Cherokee. All of this warring activity was called the Beaver Wars, and it provided the basis for official English and French official claims to the area.

The English claimed that the Iroquois had submitted their lands to the British crown in 1701, after their conquest of the Ohio country, and by the Treaty of Utrecht in 1713 were acknowledged as being under British dominion. At the same time, the French claimed the country on the grounds that La Salle had taken possession of it when inhabited by the Shawnee.

The Iroquois wanted possession of the Ohio Valley region not for habitation, but for hunting. After gaining possession through raids, they did not attempt to resettle the area. The French as well as other Indians challenged the Iroquois' right to these lands because they had been obtained through forcible possession.

In 1681, La Salle met a party of 40 Algonquians from the Hudson-Delaware area near the southern end of Lake Michigan. In 1686, a Miami war party was seen near Rochester, New York. Indians came into the area from two major directions: from the north, where the French were establishing posts along the lakes; and from the east, where the British had settled or acquired coastal colonies. It was this that set the stage for the later Anglo-French struggle of the fur trade.

The first of the new settlers from the north were the Wyandot (Huron) and Miami. Illinois, Ottawa, and others operated as French auxiliaries in the colonial wars. Kickapoo and Potawatomi tribes also came at a later date. From the east came Iroquois, especially Seneca, Delaware, and Shawnee tribes, along with some other small bands. Southern warriors included Cherokee, Catawba, and others who were British auxiliaries in the Upper Ohio region in 1757-2758.

The Wyandot and Ottawa were the first two groups settled at Detroit, aided by the French who operated a post there in 1701. Under French protection, the Wyandot hunted toward the Ohio.

In 1732, when the French encouraged the Shawnee to the upper Ohio, the Wyandot rejected any settlement in fear that this would upset their hunting rights. Trouble with the Ottawa led to Wyandot chiefs seeking to move elsewhere. Some located at Sandusky Bay under the influence of English traders and English- affiliated Indians. The Wyandot also had a small village or post on the Tuscarawas River.

In 1747, England and France were at war. The Wyandot broke with the French under Chief Orontony, who burned the village at Sandusky Bay and withdrew to Ohio country. About 100 warriors settled near Coshocton, Ohio at Conchake. Orontony and 30 others fled to the Beaver River. It is assumed that the Wyandot abandoned the Beaver River area in 1750 after Orontony's death. Those at Conchake returned to Sandusky Bay at the outbreak of the French and Indian War.

The first contact between the Miami and the French was in Wisconsin before 1670, but in 1680, a part of the tribe was at the south end of Lake Michigan. In the next 20 years, war and hunting parties of this group ranged into New York, Pennsylvania, and Maryland.

Fox refugees were marginal in the Ohio area. In 1712, two bands joined the Iroquois after being defeated by the Wyandot and Ottawa. Others joined the Seneca after problems with the French in 1730. Most settled on the border of Seneca country in New York; one group moved further down the Allegheny River.

Reentry into Ohio country from the east was made under Iroquois supervision, and involved groups interested not only in hunting but also in residence. Although these groups were classified as hunters and were unqualified to sit on council or negotiate with their neighbors, the Iroquois desired to settle dependent groups around their borders and create a buffer zone. They extended permission to the Ohio, where refugee Fox, Shawnee, and Delaware were allowed to settle on and near the Allegheny River.

For the Seneca, possession of Ohio country had specific advantages. They had the readiest access to the new hunting territory, and they also had the greatest opportunity to increase their numbers by adopting refugees and captives. However, they were badly situated for trade, since the Susquehannock banned them from any trade on Delaware and Chesapeake bays.

In 1690, the defeat of the Susquehannock allowed the Seneca to build a town called Conestoga in the Susquehannock Valley for trade with the south. A French post at Niagara in 1720, and later establishment of English trading activities to the Ohio further reduced the importance of this town.

Iroquoian settlements in Ohio were primarily family-sized settlements. Iroquoian families were also scattered among other populations.

In 1692, refugee Shawnee arrived in Maryland. One band received permission from the Iroquois to settle on the upper Delaware; the move became the start of a long and respected relationship between the Delaware and the Shawnee. Another group received Iroquois permission to live on the lower Susquehanna in 1701.

However, the Iroquois kept a close watch over their former enemies, and after a small disturbance in 1728, they ordered the groups to leave the area and go back to Ohio. By 1731, the Shawnee had established three towns on the Kiskimintas River, and later settlements were established on the lower Allegheny and upper Ohio rivers.

In 1734, a Shawnee division from the south killed a Seneca chief. The French sought out the Shawnee in order to offset the work of English traders, but the French were unsuccessful until 1745, when Martin Chartier's half-breed son Peter persuaded the tribe to plunder traders of Pennsylvania and decamp down the Ohio. Instead of remaining on the Wabash where the French had allowed them to settle, they divided and part followed Chartier to Alabama, while the remainder settled at the mouth of the Scioto River. Along with other Shawnee on the Ohio, this group enlisted Iroquois aid in 1748 for renewed friendship with Pennsylvania. A French minister in charge of the colonies at the time wrote that these Shawnees had formed a kind of republic that was dominated by Iroquois of the Five Nations.

British colony traders who were active in the Ohio country, along with resident Indians, were finding it difficult to negotiate with the Iroquois Council at Onondaga. Without permission, they began direct negotiations with one another. The trading post at Logstown became the site for treaties between Pennsylvania and Virginia officials with the Indians. The colonies and a Seneca spokesman designated Shingas (a Delaware) as the ruler of these people. The trade republic was added to by Wyandot and Miami that had defected from the French in 1747. However, it was disrupted by French occupation of the Forks of the Ohio in 1754. Logstown was torched and pro-British followers retired to eastern Pennsylvania and then to Iroquois country in New York.

The Shawnee defected to the French, and a new village was built for them at Logstown. Ohio Iroquois who accepted French occupation lost their status after the British were victorious in 1758; some who remained formed detached, roving bands that were later identified as Mingo. The Iroquoian League retained considerable prestige and influence. However, the British had no further need to support claims to the Ohio country, and the Iroquois were not in any position to repeat warlike activities of the previous century.

Delaware migration to the Ohio country was sporadic and piecemeal. By 1737, the Delaware had sold all their land in Pennsylvania and were primarily living on lands assigned to them by the Iroquois. Some Delaware later settled as far upriver as present Warren. Others moved down the river to and below the Forks of the Ohio; by 1751, their farthest boundary was a town on the Scioto a few miles above its mouth. These Delaware became part of the Logstown trading complex. Lacking any unified tribal organization, they accommodated themselves to the French military occupation of 1753-1759 in a variety of ways that ranged from retirement to attacks on English settlements. The war and subsequent British occupation accelerated the western movement of the Indians. Scattered Delaware groups contributed in the 1760s to a resurgence of the "Delaware nation" under leadership of King Netawatwees. Although he did not succeed in uniting all the Delaware, his influence survived his death in 1776.

Shawnee bands around the Scioto River were less successful. The fugitive band in Alabama returned from the south and moved to Illinois. They may have rejoined those living on the Scioto River after the French defeat in 1760. A group was involved in hostilities with Virginia in 1774.

American Revolution

At the onset of the American Revolution, the Delaware underwent a difficult time; along with their western neighbors, the Miami, they shifted their settlements westward; some small parties broke away and crossed the Mississippi.

The second dispersal of Indians from the Ohio Valley was final. Pontiac's War in 1783-1784 was a somewhat planned but partly spontaneous uprising. It involved most British groups of the area but failed in its attempt to end British occupation and halt English settlement. At the first Treaty of Fort Stanwix in 1768, the Iroquois surrendered claims to lands south of the Ohio to the Kittanning. The eastern section of this area was the first part of the Ohio Valley that the Indians lost to white settlement.

After the American Revolution, the new nation handled the claims of the Indians of Ohio in two treaties. The first was with the Iroquois at Fort Stanwix in 1784, and the second was with the western tribes at Fort McIntosh in 1785. The Iroquois surrendered to the United States all their claims to lands west of New York and Pennsylvania. In separate negotiations, they released to Pennsylvania all land claims within that state. The settlement at Fort McIntosh was repudiated by the Indians, but eventually the Delaware and Wyandot also released their holdings. The Treaty of Greenville in 1795 was a further loss of Indian lands that included almost all of the Ohio Valley in the present state of Ohio. Other tribal cessions, both individual and collective, followed, and by 1818, the Indians had released almost all of Ohio and most of Indiana south of the Wabash.

The government sought to expedite white settlement and began to move the tribes to reservation lands beyond the Mississippi River. However, the final cessions of Ohio Valley lands were delayed until 1840, at which time the Miami surrendered their tract around Kokomo, Indiana. In 1842, the Wyandot released their land at Upper Sandusky in Ohio.

History of Illinois Region

The Illinois region was early occupied by a group of 12 related villages or tribes that were later referred to as the Illinois Confederacy. Included were the Kaskaskia, Maroa, Cahoka, Tamaroa, Peoria, Tapouaro, Coiracoentanon, Moingwea, Chinkoa, Espeminkia, Michigamea, and Chepoussa. This confederacy was never as politically organized as the Iroquois Confederacy.

In about 1673, when Europeans first extended into the Illinois region, the Illinois occupied a roughly triangle section; the base extended from the Chicago River westward into western Iowa, the eastern boundary extended southward through eastern Illinois along the Mississippi-Wabash watershed, and the apex was located in northeastern Arkansas. The French referred to this area as the "Illinois country." Until 1717, it was under the authority of New France, and afterward the portion south of a line eastward from the mouth of the Illinois River became part of Louisiana.

During the late prehistoric period, the Miami lived immediately to the east of the Illinois; this group included the Wea and Piankashaw, who later were regarded as distinct groups. The Shawnee were further to the east. The Sauk, Kickapoo, Fox, and Mascouten lived on the lower Michigan peninsula, and to the north of them were the Potawatomi. All groups were linguistically related to the Illinois. However, traditional mistrust and inherent differences discouraged any close or lasting alliances. All took up residence in Illinois country at different times throughout the historic period.

North and northwest of the Illinois was the land of the hostile Chiwere Sioux and their linguistic kin, the Winnebago. South of the Ohio River and southwest were unfriendly Dhegiha Sioux. Beyond the western limits and the Mississippi River lived the Pawnee and Arikara, Caddoan-speakers who were traditional enemies of the Illinois.

During the mid-seventeenth century, a westward thrust by the Neutral and then the Iroquois exerted strong pressure on tribes to the east and northeast of the Illinois. By mid-century, the Miami and their related tribes had moved westward and settled in northwest Illinois and adjacent sections of Iowa and Wisconsin from which the Chiwere Sioux had earlier withdrawn. Tribes in Lower Michigan had withdrawn around the head of Lake Michigan into northern Illinois and southeastern Wisconsin. From the Straits of Mackinac, the Potawatomi had moved westward to Washington Island and the Door County peninsula of Wisconsin. For reasons still unknown, the Dhegiha Sioux abandoned the lower Ohio River during this same time.

History of Upper Great Lakes Region

The Iroquois first attacked the Illinois about 1655. Periodic raids as far as the Chicago River and upper Illinois were to plague the Illinois throughout the next half-century. When the Illinois were not being directly threatened by the Iroquois, their warriors often waged battles against the Quapaw, Osage, and northern Sioux.

About 1667, the Illinois became firmly associated with the French. When a mission was established at Saint Esprit and the nearby trading post near La Pointe, small groups of Illinois became frequent visitors to the post and mission. They also visited the French trading center at the Miami-Mascouten village about 1670.

In 1673, Louis Jolliet and Father Jacques Marquette visited three villages of Peoria and Tapouaro on the Iowa River. A rumor that the two visitors intended to set up a trading post and mission on the Illinois River resulted in bands and villages of Illinois coming to the Kaskaskia village the following year. The mission of the Immaculate Conception of the Blessed Virgin was established among the Kaskaskia. By 1680, La Salle found some 11 tribes of Illinois living in lodges at Grand Kaskaskia Village.

The threat of an Iroquois war party in September 1680 caused most of the Illinois to abandon the Grand Kaskaskia village and move to the Mississippi. After destroying the village, the Iroquois pursued, and the Tapouraro, Maroa, and Espeminkia tribes who had chosen to remain at the mouth of the Illinois were attacked and suffered heavy losses.

The Illinois reassembled on the Ohio River after Henri Tonti constructed Fort Saint Louis at the top of Starved Rock in 1682. Shawnee, Miami, Wea, and Piankashaw were also present, as were some 18 Eastern Algonquian warriors and their families. A new village was established across the river, and some 4,000 warriors represented a population of about 18,000 people. However, the community was plagued by intertribal distrust and jealousies, and the Miami elected to abandon the area in 1688. The Shawnee left the following year.

The Kaskaskia village site was abandoned in 1691, and a new village called Pimiteoui was established lower on the Illinois River. Tonti relocated the fort and trading post close to the area. The mission was also moved. The community had 260-300 lodges and a population of over 3,500 in six groups that included the Peoria, Coiracoentanon, Kaskaskia, Monngwena, Maroa, and Tapouaro.

As Kaskaskia Indians became more Christianized, their relationship with the Peoria became strained. Two events led to the community's eventual demise; England's restriction of trade to the Illinois River, and Pierre Le Moyne d'Iberville's arrival at the mouth of the Mississippi. The Kaskaskia left the village in 1700 after hearing about d'Iberville's plan to relocate the upper Mississippi. They traveled as far as the Des Peres River across the Mississippi from where the Tamaroa settled. The two tribes joined together the next year and, in 1703, they moved the village to the mouth of the Kaskaskia River. In 1714, an epidemic reduced the community by about one-fourth.

The Mission of the Immaculate Conception, under direction of Father Gabriel Marest, went with the Kaskaskia to the Kaskaskia River, and missionary influence continued until the Jesuits were banned from the Mississippi in 1763.

Other tribes in Illinois country also relocated: The Tamaroa moved to the eastern side of the Mississippi River and established a village near the present village of Cahokia. The Cahokia tribes also moved near the Tamaroa. In 1700, the two villages had about 90 lodges. The Moingwena remained with the Peoria.

To the south, Chepoussa and Michigamea were forced to withdraw up the Mississippi due to hostility with the Quapaw. By 1693, they had settled on both sides of that river near the mouth of the Kaskaskia. Many of the smaller tribes were generally absorbed into larger ones, resulting in a loss of a clear individual identity for some groups.

In the next six decades, three Illinois populations existed. Michigamea and Kaskaskias on and near the Kaskaskia River totaled some 250 warriors; Cahokias and Peorias at Cahokia had 200; Peorias on the Illinois River totaled 50; altogether there were more than 2,500 individuals.

Soon after 1710, the arrival and development of a French agricultural-based society in Illinois country created a situation in which previous trade-mission-garrison relationships waned. Contentions now arose over land ownership and social discrimination. In a move to alleviate tensions in 1719, the commandant at Kaskaskia requested that the Indians remove from the French settlement. All the existing tribes moved away from the settlement, but in close proximity to their former communities.

Despite some harsh treatment from the French, the Illinois remained constant in their loyalty and continued to deal with them after English possession of Canada. They harassed the British during their 10-year occupation of Fort de Chartres. They also supported the colonies in the American Revolution, and during subsequent confrontations with British.

Due to their loyalty, the Illinois were attacked by the Fox and other pro-British followers to the North, and occasionally by the Shawnee and Chickasaw from the South. The Cahokia suffered heavy losses when their village was destroyed in 1752, and survivors settled near the Michigamea.

Peorias were forced to withdraw from the Illinois River valley on several occasions, the last in 1769. After the Peoria killed Ottawa chief Pontiac, a combined force of Ottawa, Potawatomi, Chippewa, Fox, Winnebago, and others attacked and forced the Peoria to withdraw. Abandoning their traditional homeland, they settled on the western side of the Mississippi.

In the last three decades of the century, Illinois tribes were confined to the waters of the Kaskaskia and Big Muddy rivers. Struggles with Piankashaw, Kickapoo, Potawatomi, and Shawnee ensued, with heavy losses for all tribes. The Kaskaskias ceded their land south of a line drawn eastward from the mouth of the Illinois River, with two small tracts reserved on the Big Muddy. The remnants of the Illinois in the state established their last village in their traditional homeland on one of the tracts.

In 1832, the Peoria (including the Tamaroa, Michigamea, and Cahokia) ceded their land north of the line, and the Kaskaskia ceded their two remaining tracts. The last of the Illinois thus withdrew permanently from the Illinois county.

Miami, Wea, and Piankashaw. The Miami tribes included the Atchatchakangouen, Kilatika, Mengakonkia, and Pepikokia, and sometimes also included the Wea and Piankashaw, although both these groups maintained political independence until the nineteenth century.

After they withdrew from the Wabash-Saint Joseph region in mid-seventeenth century, the main body of the Miami settled in central and southwest Wisconsin. Some went to northwestern Illinois. The Wea and Piankashaw settled in western Wisconsin, and some went into northern Iowa.

In 1679, Green Bay traders aided a group of Atchatchakangouen, Mascouten, and Wea to settle on the Saint Joseph River to prevent La Salle from gaining access to the Illinois on the Illinois River. After attacks from Iroquois, they accepted La Salle's invitation in 1682 to make peace with the Illinois and move near Fort La Salle on the Illinois River. The combined population of villages near the Iroquois River and Fort Saint Louis was about 7,500.

However, the Miami found it difficult to overcome their traditional distrust of the Illinois, and in 1688 they abandoned the area. Some settled on the Mississippi, and some returned to the Saint Joseph River. A few years later, they moved down to the Wabash. The Wea occupied the area of Chicago until 1698, when French trade was restricted. In about 1717, they moved to the Wabash River, where they established the village of Ouiatonon. A French post was also established nearby.

Shortly after 1700, the Miami of the Maramek and Miami in Wisconsin moved to the east side of the Wabash between the Wea and

Piankashaw. In time, their range extended eastward into Ohio. The Miami established a firm attachment to the British, along with Wea and Piankashaw.

In about 1800, small bands of Miami, Wea, and Piankashaw moved to the western side of the Mississippi. Treaties beginning in 1803 ceded their land to the government. In 1828, the last of the Piankashaw left Illinois. The Wea left Indiana in 1832. The Miami made a last Indiana land cession in 1840.

Sauk and Fox Tribes. After moving from Michigan, the Sauk (Sac) settled on the lower Fox River of Wisconsin, and the Fox (Masquaki) removed to the upper Fox River southeast to the Chicago River.

Loyalty of the Sauk vacillated between the British and the French. Fox warriors defended the French until their tribe was almost destroyed in 1712 at Fort Ponchartrain. The incident began the "Fox War," a retaliatory effort in which Fox were joined by Mascouten and Kickapoo. In 1730, some 300 Fox left the area and moved to New York to join a band that had settled with the Seneca some 20 years previously. They were intercepted in central Illinois and suffered heavy losses. They eventually returned to the Fox River.

In 1733, the French determined to settle the problem with the Fox by destroying them. The Fox sought sanctuary with the Sauk, but eventually both groups were forced to abandon the fort and remove to the banks of the Mississippi. In 1743, the French persuaded some Sauk to return to the Fox River.

The Sauk and Fox continued to vacillate during the French and British conflict. At the conclusion of the war, they promised loyalty to the British, but continued a close contact with French traders who had moved across the Mississippi into Spanish territory. At the outbreak of the American Revolution, the two tribes were again split in their loyalty.

After an American attack on Rock River villages, the tribes turned against the Americans and supported the British through the War of 1812. (A negotiation in 1804 by Governor William H. Harrison of Indiana Territory had already relinquished claims of Sauk and Fox to all land lying east of the Mississippi.) Although the main body of both tribes denounced the treaty, it was ratified by each near the close of the War of 1812.

61

By 1829, most Sauk and Fox had moved to the western side of the Mississippi. Black Hawk eventually accepted the treaty of 1804 and moved into Iowa, but he refused to abandon the ancestral burial ground on the Rock River and continued to visit annually. He visited the site in 1832, in defiance of an agreement made in 1831, and General Henry Atkinson defined this as an invasion of the United States. A subsequent military campaign resulted in a defeat of Black Hawk and his followers at Bad Axe Creek, and the Sauk and Fox left Illinois.

Kickapoo and Mascouten. The Kickapoo and Mascouten moved from Michigan with the Sauk and Fox. In 1679, a band of Mascouten joined in the effort to cut off La Salle's approach to the Illinois country. After the failure of the effort, they later reoccupied their old village on the Fox River. Internal conflicts resulted in some Mascouten joining the Miami, while others joined the Fox. The main body joined with the Kickapoo.

In 1702, a band of Mascouten moved to the mouth of the Ohio, but the following year, smallpox decimated this community. Survivors settled on both sides of the Wabash, and were joined by other groups. Eventually they lost their individual identity and were absorbed by their neighbors, especially the Kickapoo.

The Kickapoo were the most conservative tribe in the Illinois region, and thus they maintained a general anti-European position throughout the early historical period. They became attached to Nicolas Perrot, an Indian agent and trader, in 1685. They were a small tribe, and some joined with the Wea during the early 1700s, and some with the Fox. By 1717 they had been reduced about one-third. Internal conflicts within the group were strong until they turned against the Americans who were moving into the Wabash valley. Some of their villages were destroyed. They joined with Tecumseh and in 1811 suffered in the defeat of Tippecanoe, and the following year some of their towns were destroyed on the Sangamon and one at Peoria.

After 1800, small bands began moving to the west of the Mississippi, with an acceleration of emigration after destruction of the Prairie towns. In 1819, two groups in separate treaties ceded their lands in Illinois and Indiana, providing they could still hunt and live on the land. In 1832, the government ordered their removal to Kansas.

Potawatomi, Ottawa, and Chippewa. Potawatomi tribes moved into the Green Bay area from the Straits of Mackinac about 1641. They became allies of the French until 1699, when restricted trade caused relationships to deteriorate. Several bands moved to the Saint Joseph River and sought contact with the British, but they were unable to establish a relationship with the Iroquois. In 1712, they resumed friendly contact with the French at Fort Ponchartrain.

After the Peoria were driven from the Illinois valley by the Three Fires group, the Potawatomi occupied the whole of the upper Illinois River valley. They remained loyal to the French through the French and Indian War. After the conflict ended, they continued to trade with the French. However, conflict with American colonies caused them to support the British, which continued through the War of 1812. Although some Potawatomi leaders retained a friendship with American settlers, especially Shabonee, the majority continued an anti-American movement.

The economy of the Potawatomi, based on fur-trading, lasted into the first quarter of the nineteenth century. The increasing density of white settlers denied them access to beaver ponds, and buffalo and wapiti had diminished in number. Small bands were forced to move west of the Mississippi. Land cessions began in 1816, with others in the 1820s and 1830s. After each cession, populations were displaced and groups moved west of the Mississippi. By 1834, there were few Potawatomi left in Illinois and Indiana.

Shawnee and Delaware. The Shawnee spoke Algonquian, and were often victims of Iroquois attacks. Groups on the upper Ohio River sought security with the French, and began to appear in large numbers in Illinois in 1683.

When relationships with the Illinois became strained, and after the Miami withdrew from the Fort Saint Louis community in 1688, the Shawnee also withdrew the following year. Joining neighbors on the Cumberland River in Tennessee, they became attached to the British. They began more frequent attacks against the Illinois.

After 1759, the Shawnee returned to the Scioto River. The Delaware also moved down the Ohio and settled among the Shawnee on the Scioto and westward into Indiana. A large body settled in Missouri in 1787, and Illinois became a thoroughfare between the Scioto and the Mississippi. Shawnee again occupied the Shawnee- town site, and Delaware settled nearby, along the western bank of the Wabash and on Saline Creek.

Although the Delaware established a relationship with the Kaskaskia who were their neighbors, the Shawnee did not attempt to establish villages in the area. They encroached on Illinois hunting grounds on the eastern side of the Muddy River, and strong resistance from Kaskaskia resulted in a final confrontation in 1802, when Shawnee warriors took a heavy toll on a Kaskaskia village. The Shawnee continued to pass through southern Illinois until the nineteenth century was underway, but they did not claim the region.

Winnebago. The Winnebago's traditional lands were in the Lake Winnebago-Green Bay region. However, reduced by warfare and disease, they became dependent on their newer neighbors, the Potawatomi, Sauk, and Fox. They were allies of the French, and enemies of the Illinois. Their intent to destroy the Illinois resulted in the expulsion of the Peoria from the Illinois River valley.

Before 1770, the Winnebago began moving onto the headwaters of the Rock River. After the Middle Rock valley was abandoned by the Kickapoo, they moved into the region and had direct contact with the Sauk and Fox on the Mississippi River.

Some Winnebago were actively involved against the Americans during the War of 1812. Most of the tribe declared themselves at peace with the government in 1816. In 1829, the group ceded the region in Illinois that the government had designated as Winnebago land, but they were granted fishing and living rights. When Black Hawk defied the government in 1832, the Winnebago Prophet was still living at Prophetstown 40 miles up from the mouth of the Rock River. The Prophet aided his nephew Black Hawk, and then joined him in the retreat up the Rock River. Later in the same year, the Winnebago ceded their remaining lands in Illinois and left the area.

Menominee. The Menominee intermarried with many of their native neighbors in later historic times, and many small groups attached themselves to Potawatomi, Fox, Miami, Sauk, and Winnebago, often only temporarily. However, these relationships account for the fact that Menominee families still live in northern Illinois, especially on the Fox and Rock rivers, and also in mixed villages identified as Menominee that are located in the area.

CONTEMPORARY NORTHEAST INDIANS

Of all the large and populous groups that once inhabited the Northeast, few remain today. Although a number of small tribes became decimated by epidemics, wars, and by dispersal, others became absorbed into larger groups and lost their individual identity. For some tribes, the only evidence of their former existence remains in the place names of locations where they once dwelled.

Some Indians of the Northeast have lived in relative isolation and poverty since their removal to federal or state reservation lands. In many cases, allotted lands have slowly but surely diminished in size. However, some groups have sought to reestablish tribal rights and gain economic independence. A number of large Northeast tribes, along with the tribes who were adopted by them, have recently fought for additional lands and resources.

The Micmacs, with a population of 482 residents, now live in northern Maine. The group has established tribal and intertribal councils and political groups, and has revived traditional arts, organizations, and language. In 1991, they gained recognition of their tribal status and together with 28 other bands in Canada formed part of the Micmac Nation. In 1982, the Aroostook Micmac Council was incorporated, and established its headquarters in Presque Isle.

Another Coastal tribe that has somewhat overcome adversity is the Delaware, who now live in scattered communities of Ontario and Oklahoma. Although many were formerly unskilled laborers, increasing numbers have sought to become professionals. In recent years, scheduled events have gathered together leaders from scattered communities, and increased efforts to renew contacts between all Delawares have been aided by such organizations as the Delaware Nation Grand Council of North America, incorporated in Ohio in 1992.

The Huron-Wyandots of the Saint Lawrence region have also gained political and economic strength by making scholarships available, providing daily meals for elder residents, creating a health center, and purchasing land in Park City, Kansas for the purpose of building a gambling casino. They have begun efforts to preserve and maintain their heritage, including establishing a library of archives.

Mohawk communities and lifestyles have undergone major changes in the twentieth century. Former farming, dairy cattle raising, and sport fishing activities have been replaced primarily by ironworking activities, which is considered a source of pride and self-esteem by many Mohawks. However, political differences between traditionalists and more acculturated members have continued to plague some Mohawk communities.

Seneca-Cayuga Indians maintain reservation lands in Oklahoma. Their population of 2,460 continues to practice tribal rituals, and many are involved in ranching. Many members of the Tuscarora tribe who live in Lewiston, New York are employed in industrial plants and in structural steel work.

Of the large population of Shawnees who formerly dwelled in the Great Lakes area, three bands currently reside in Oklahoma: the Absentee Shawnee, the Eastern Shawnee, and the Loyal Shawnee. Each group has derived income from a number of industries including farming, livestock, small businesses, and other mainstream American jobs. Most members also maintain their tribal culture, including seasonal dances.

The Sauk and Fox tribes today are federally recognized as the "Sac and Fox of the Mississippi in Iowa." They are known as the Mesquaki Nation (Red Earth People) and live near their tribal-owned settlement on the Iowa River. Many grow corn and soybeans, and others work in surrounding communities. In the 1980s, the group established the Economic Development Zone and opened a bingo facility. Plans for other businesses, including a hotel and restaurant, are underway. These economic opportunities have not weakened Mesquaki kinship ties or their sense of family. Religious ceremonies and powwows continue to dominate their cultural life.

A number of other reservations have also established health centers, funding for homes, scholarships, and cultural centers. Many formerly unskilled laborers have increased job skills and are now employed in skilled positions, especially in iron working. Many of today's steel bridges and skyscrapers have been built by Indians from a variety of groups. In addition, educational dropout rates have been reduced significantly in some groups.

Although it is true that a few tribes from the Northeast have maintained their traditional hostilities towards other groups and non-natives, many have instead focused their energies toward reestablishing their own tribal customs and maintaining their unique cultural identity.

Educational opportunities, self-sufficiency, and employment advances continue to help some Native Americans gain a sense of pride. Celebrations and rituals, once such a large part of Indian societies and later abandoned, are again being practiced. Some groups hold annual events. A few groups, such as the Mohawks, now travel across the United States to perform their native ceremonies, allowing Indians and non-Indians alike to share in their unique cultural heritage.

INDIANS OF OHIO
A to Z

ADARIO

Adario (Tionontati, ? - August 1, 1701), was a chief whose sabotage of a peace effort between the French and the Iroquois Confederacy led to a massive Iroquois attack on settlements in New France, now Canada.

In 1688, the French enlisted Adario's support against his hereditary enemies, the Iroquois. Early in his mission against the Iroquois, Adario stopped at Cataracuoy, now Kingston, Ontario, Canada, where the French Commandant told him to halt his expedition because an Iroquois embassy soon was expected in Montreal to negotiate a peace.

However, Adario, fearing that his people would be abandoned to the Iroquois for the sake of French self-interest, ambushed the Iroquois delegation.

Adario told the Iroquois that the French had commissioned him to kill the party. When the Iroquois stated their mission, Adario feigned surprise and outrage at the alleged French treachery. He released all but one of the Iroquois, the one remaining to replace one of his own men who had been killed in the ambush, and urged them to take revenge on the French.

Adario took his single captive to the French at Michilimackinac, who had not yet heard of the plans for peace with the Iroquois, and who therefore put the prisoner to death. To be certain that the confederacy learned of his act, Adario released a long-held Iroquois prisoner from his own village and bade him tell the confederacy that Adario had been unable to save the man.

The Iroquois, believing Adario's representations, were enraged. On August 25, 1689, some 1,200 Iroquois attacked Montreal, where they killed hundreds of French and burned their houses. They also raided other settlements on the Saint Lawrence River. The French were saved from extinction only by their strong forts.

Adario was later converted to Christianity and became a friend of the French. In 1701, while part of a delegation concluding a peace treaty at Montreal, Adario became ill and died. The French buried him with military honors.

AHATSISTARI, EUSTANCE

Eustance Ahatsistari (Huron, ? - August, 1642), was a chief who distinguished himself in warfare against the Iroquois Confederacy, the traditional enemy of the Huron.

In 1641, Ahatsistari and 50 Huron warriors defeated about 300 Iroquois. Earlier, under his leadership, the Hurons had routed a large party of Iroquois in war canoes on Lake Ontario. In August 1642, while leading a small party of Huron and French up Lake Saint Peter, Ahatsistari and his group were ambushed by a band of Mohawk Indians. He was killed several days after the ambush.

ANNAWAN

Annawan (Wampanoag, ? - August 12, 1676), was a sachem who served as chief counselor and captain under King Philip (Metacom). He had earlier served under Philip's father, Massassoit, in wars against other New England Indian nations. Even among his enemies, Annawan was recognized as a great and valiant soldier.

When Philip was killed in an attack on his swamp fortress, Annawan rallied the surviving warriors. They escaped and continued to attack settlers of Swansea and Plymouth, constantly moving their camp to avoid detection.

Later that year, a captive Indian led a small party under Captain Benjamin Church to Annawan's retreat, (now known as Annawan's Rock), a hill set in a swamp near the Reheboth River. There they surprised and captured Annawan and his chief counselors. The main party of warriors was deceived into surrendering when Church told them that that his army had surrounded them. Annawan, correctly believing his party to be the last to resist the English, gave Church a deerskin bundle containing Philip's wampum belts, symbols of his office and other effects.

Although Church pleaded for Annawan's life, his confession that he had tortured and killed several English captives led the Plymouth authorities to behead him while Church was away.

ASPINET

Aspinet (Wampanoag, ? - 1623?), was a sagamore (tribute chief over two or more subtribes) and chief of the Nauset tribe on Cape Cod at present-day Eastham, Massachusetts. Although a small group of

Nauset warriors ambushed an initial scouting party sent out from the Mayflower, Aspinet always gave the appearance of being a firm friend of the Plymouth colonists. In 1621 he assisted in returning young John Billington to the Plymouth settlement after the boy was found lost in the woods. During the winter of 1622, Aspinet's people gave beans and corn to the starving colonists. Although Miles Standish's intemperate outbursts often might have provoked Aspinet to act against the colonists, he seemed to prefer peace.

Aspinet died about 1623 in a hiding place in the swamps after being driven there from threat of attack by the colonists. In spite of the friendship he displayed toward the English, Aspinet appears to have been one of the leaders of a conspiracy of other Wampanoag sagamores and Massachuset and Narraganset Indians to destroy Plymouth. The plot was discovered by Massassoit, principal chief of the Wampanoag.

ATTIGNAWANTAN

One of the largest tribes of the Huron Confederacy, The Attignawantan at one time comprised about half the Huron population, and formerly lived on Nottawasaga Bay, Ontario, Canada. In 1638 they were settled in 14 towns and villages. Collectively, the Huron called themselves *Quendot* (Wendat). The Attignawantan (Bear) among the Huron, had tribal names that were also names perhaps taken from main area clans.

The Jesuit missions of Saint Joseph and La Conception were established among them. The Jesuits wrote that the Attignawanton and Petun Huron spoke the same language, and had similar customs, even extending to female hairstyles. Vague tribal oral tradition says that the Attignawantan formed the nucleus of the Huron Confederation in about A.D. 1400.

The Arendaronon were indicated as the first of the Huron confederacy to establish trade with the French in about 1609, control of this trade was effectively seized by the Attignawantan, who apparently dominated the confederacy in many ways. Late in the 1630s the Jesuits described the Huron Confederacy as consisting of the Attignawantan, Attigneenongnahac, Arendaronon, Tahonaenrat, and Ataronchronon. By the late 1640s, The Jesuits had made many conversions to Christianity among the tribe, which was also the most hostile among the Huron to their long-standing enemy, the Iroquois.

71

Their diet was about 85 percent vegetables, mostly corn, 15 percent fish, and five percent meat. They were quite healthy and showed no nutritional deficiencies, records indicate.

Eventually, the Iroquois pushed many of the Huron, now generally referred to as Wyandotte, west to Ohio and Michigan. In 1843 the United States moved them by force to Kansas. They were pushed further west and settled in southeastern Oklahoma in 1857.

They moved deeper into the Indian Nation to avoid the opposing factions of the United States Civil War. Their reservation was broken up by allotment in the 1890s. Those arriving too late to receive lands returned to Kansas, Ohio, Michigan, or Quebec.

In 1937 they officially formed the Wyandotte Tribe. They were singled out for extinction as a tribe in 1956, but after twenty years' struggle, regained federal recognition. A recent count showed over 3600 tribal members in Oklahoma. In the 1990s they owned 192 acres in common, plus individually held allotments.

AXION

The Axion were a division of the New Jersey Delawares formerly living on the east bank of Delaware River, between Rancocas Creek and the present Trenton. In 1648 they were one of the largest tribes on the river, being estimated at 200 warriors. Brinton thinks the name may be a corruption of Assiscunk, the name of a creek above Burlington. They disappeared as a distinct band before 1700.

BLACK BEAVER

Black Beaver (Delaware, 1806 - May 8, 1880), also known as Se-ket-TuMa-Qua, distinguished himself as an intelligent and trustworthy guide for United States explorers crossing the continent, and also as a remarkable Indian scout and faithful friend of the United States Army and early pioneers. He was born at the present site of Belleville, Illinois, probably during his family's move west to a new home.

In February 1824, when the Delawares were being relocated on White River in Arkansas, white men stole almost all their horses, worsening the Indians' already desperate situation. William Anderson, the head chief, Black Beaver, Natacoming and other Delawares sent this letter to General William Clark requesting aid, "Last summer a number of our people died just for the want of something to live on

... We have got in a country where we do not find all as stated to us when we was asked to swap lands with you ... Father. We did not think that big man would tell us things that was not true ... Father, you know it is hard to go hungry, if you do not know it we poor Indians know it ... We are obliged to call on you once more for assistance in the name of God ..."

Black Beaver again came to the attention of the United States government in 1834 when he served Colonel Richard Irving Dodge as interpreter at a conference with the Comanche, Kiowa and Wichita tribes on the Upper Red River. Black Beaver's skills as a translator earned the admiration of military and scientific explorers who were embarking upon transcontinental expeditions. Black Beaver was among thirty-two Indians hired for the Dragoon expedition of 1834, commanded by General Henry Leavenworth, and from that time on Black Beaver was in constant demand as a guide and interpreter.

He served on many expeditions, helping to push the frontier American settlement steadily westward from the Plains to the Rocky Mountains. Black Beaver also served as a Captain in 1846 during the war with Mexico, commanding a company of Delaware and Shawnee Indians.

In April of 1849, Captain Randolph B. Marcy was ordered to escort five hundred emigrants to California from Fort Smith, Arkansas, and to find the best route. At Shawneetown he was fortunate to meet Black Beaver and enlist him for the journey. Describing Black Beaver's qualifications, the impressed Marcy wrote, "He has traveled a great deal among the western and northern tribes of Indians, is well acquainted with their character and habits, and converses fluently with the Comanche and most of the other prairie tribes. He has spent five years in Oregon and California, two years among the Crow and Black Feet Indians. (IIc) Has trapped beaver in the Gila, the Columbia, the Rio Grande, and the Pecos; has crossed the Rocky Mountains at many different points, and indeed is one of those men that are seldom met with except in the mountains."

"He had for ten years been in the employ of the American Fur Company, and during this time had visited nearly every point of interest within the limits of our unsettled territory. He had set his traps and spread his blanket upon the headwaters of the Missouri and Columbia; and his wanderings had led him south of the Colorado and Gila, and thence to the shores of the Pacific in Southern California. His life is

that of a veritable cosmopolite, filled with scenes of intense and star-
tling interest, bold and reckless adventure."

Black Beaver had been to California before, along with Jesse
Chisholm and other guides, and their experience and counsel was regarded by all with great respect. Most of Captain Marcy's success and
reputation as a pathfinder in the Southwest was due to Black Beaver.

On October 7, 1849, a lieutenant from Captain Marcy's party left
camp to examine a ravine about two miles ahead. Lieutenant Montgomery Pike Harrison, the grandson of President William Henry
Harrison and an older brother of President Benjamin Harrison, never
returned. Captain Marcy sent Black Beaver and Lieutenant Joseph
Updegraff to search for him.

They followed his tracks to a place about a mile and a half past the
ravine, where it appeared that Harrison had met a party of Indians and
gone on with them. His body was found further up the trail near a
small branch of the Colorado River, by Lieutenant Delos B. Sacket.
According to Marcy, Black Beaver studied the tracks and grass and
reconstructed the crime: "The murder was committed by two men.
They had two mules and one horse with them. They came down upon
their victim at a full gallop, but finding that he was not disposed to fly,
but ... walked his horse towards them, they also pulled up to a walk ...
They rode a short distance together, then dismounted, and seating
themselves on the grass, smoked together. Here they got possession of
his rifle to examine it."

After they had taken his only weapon, they overpowered him, tied
him up on his horse and led him into some timber where one of the
Indians shot him in the head. They stripped and scalped the lieutenant, then threw his body into the ravine where it was found later by the
search party. When the identity of the Kiowa murderers was discovered, Black Beaver's reconstruction was found to be correct.

Black Beaver worked two seasons as a guide for Captain Marcy,
who wrote in his book *The Prairie Traveler*, that he always found
Black Beaver "perfectly reliable, brave, and competent. His reputation
as a resolute, determined, and fearless warrior, did not admit of question, yet I have never seen a man who wore his laurels with less van-
ity."

Marcy also recorded Black Beaver's description of his marital relationship: "One time he catch 'um wife. I pay that woman, his modder,
one hoss-one saddle-one bridle-two plug tobacco, and plenty goods. I

take him home to my house. Got plenty meat, plenty corn, plenty everything. One time me go to take walk, maybe so three, maybe so two
hours. When I come home, that woman he say, 'Black Beaver, what
for you go away long time?' I say, 'I not go nowhere; I just take one
littel walk.' Then that woman he get heap mad, and say, 'No, Black
Beaver, you go to see nodder woman.' I say, 'Maybe not.' Then that
woman cry long time, and all e'time now he mad. You never see
'Merican woman that a-way?"

In his Journal of Army Life, Doctor Rodney Glisan described a
small band of Delaware Indians, under the leadership of Black Beaver,
occupying the deserted army camp near the Canadian River in the
spring of 1851. "They make the most trustworthy and useful guides of
any Indians in the country-from the fact of their exact knowledge of all
parts of the West ... having traded, hunted and trapped among nearly
every tribe of wild Indians in the United States."

In 1853-1854, Lieutenant A.W. Whipple mentioned Black Beaver
in his journal several times. Black Beaver was also noted in Baldwin
Milhausen's Diary of a Journey from the Mississippi to the Coasts of
the Pacific during this same time period. Whipple was exploring for a
railway from Fort Smith to Los Angeles and tried to engage Black
Beaver as a guide several times by messenger. When Whipple's expedition reached Fort Arbuckle, Whipple and several men visited Black
Beaver's log house where, "under a simple corridor, on a rough
wooden settle, an Indian sat cross-legged smoking his pipe, and
awaiting his visitors in perfect tranquility. He was a meager-looking
man of middle size, and his long black hair framed in a face that was
clever, but which bore a melancholy expression of sickness and sor-
row, though more than forty winters could not have passed over it."
Black Beaver was approximately 47 years of age at that time. He
spoke fluent English, French, and Spanish, and about eight separate
Indian languages .

For three days Whipple attempted to persuade Black Beaver to join
his expedition and though more tempting offers were made to him,
Black Beaver sadly declined, saying, "Seven times I have seen the Pacific Ocean at various points; I have accompanied the Americans in
three wars, and I have brought home more scalps from my hunting expeditions than one of you could lift. I should like to see the salt water
for the eighth time. But I am sick, you offer me more money than has

ever been offered to me before, but I am sick. But if I die, I should like to be buried by my own people."

It seemed to Whipple that each time Black Beaver was almost persuaded, Black Beaver's wife, who was sitting nearby playing with their only son and a black bear cub, spoke to him in her native tongue and Black Beaver declined Whipple's offer.

Baldwin Millhausen, in his Diary, explained that the abandoned post had been given to the Delaware chief "named Si-ki- yo-ma-ker (the Black Beaver), who had done the United States good service in the Mexican war as a hunter and guide. The position was quite in accordance with his wishes; others of his race settled near him, and they now live very happily under the protection of the astute and experienced 'Black Beaver.' The fort itself is such as one might expect to find in these wild regions, consisting of a number of log-houses built in a right angle at the edge of the forest, about a mile from the Canadian, which formerly served as barracks for soldiers; and there is also a separate court surrounded by a high palisade, that is intended as a place of refuge for cattle in case of attack. Several Delaware families have now taken possession of the abandoned barracks, and are continuing the cultivation of the rice fields laid out by the former garrison..."

The Delaware and Caddo Indians lived with the Wichitas on the North side of the Washita on Sugar Tree Creek. Matthew Leeper, the new agent in Indian Territory, included Black Beaver in his first report on September 26, 1860: "The best improvement found on the reserve is a private enterprise of Black Beaver, a Delaware Indian located here. He has a pretty good double log house, with two shed rooms in rear, a porch in front and two fireplaces, and a field of forty-one and a half acres enclosed with a good stake-and-rider fence, thirty-six and a half of which have been cultivated ."

On April 16, 1861 at the beginning of the Civil War, Fort Washita was abandoned and the troops there joined with Colonel William H. Emory's forces at Fort Cobb. They captured the advance guard of the Confederate Texas troops and Emory marched to Fort Leavenworth. Meanwhile, Black Beaver led the command into the Cherokee Outlet, near where the Chisholm Trail later crossed Kansas' southern border.

Israel Yore recorded, "General Emory, then in command of the United States troops in that section of the country, learning that the rebels were marching directly upon him, urged Black Beaver to act as a guide, to enable him with the combined commands of Forts Smith, Cobb, and Arbuckle, to elude the enemy, and, by seeking the open prairies, to reach Fort Leavenworth, Kansas. He, Emory, states that, 'of all the Indians upon whom the Government had lavished its bounty, Black Beaver was the only one that would consent to guide the column.' To do so he abandoned his property, which appears to have been seized and destroyed by the enemy. The command reached Leavenworth in safety, and several officers certify to the great value of his services and his unflinching patriotism."

According to historian George Rainey in *The Cherokee Strip*, when Black Beaver led the Federal troops from the Indian Territory forts to Fort Leavenworth, Kansas, they arrived at "Fort Leavenworth in fine condition without the loss of a man, horse or wagon, although two men deserted on the journey." Years later, Black Beaver filed a claim with the United States Government to be reimbursed for his property, including 600 head of cattle, 300 hogs, horses, mules, wagons, harness, farming implements,tools, 4,500 bushels of corn, household equipment and a four-room hewed log house with a passageway through the center. The committee on Indians Affairs granted him $5,000, less than one-fourth of his claim.

In *The Trampling Herd*, Paul I. Wellman wrote, "Led by the celebrated old Delaware Black Beaver ... Emory ... marched his 750 soldiers and 150 non-combatants north across the best fords of the Canadian, Cimarron, Chiaskia, Ninnescah to the Arkansas River to the site of the present Wichita from where he dispatched his first message to military headquarters announcing the finish of his march ..."

In July 1867, Black Beaver was summoned to Lawrence, Kansas by Superintendent James Wortham, who employed him as interpreter for the Indian relocation to the Leased Lands west of the Chickasaw Nation. For his services as guide in preparation for and during the removal of the tribes from Kansas to the Leased Lands, Black Beaver was promised one thousand dollars a year.

F.A. Rector left the following record, "... while en route the cholera made its appearance among the Indians, causing the immediate stampede of every white Man accompanying the expidition (sic) except C.F. Garrett and the deponent -- That had it not been for the presence of Black Beaver, it would have been impossible, (in his opinion), to have kept the Indians together and affected their removal to the Leased Lands at that time ... after their arrival ... Black Beaver was left in charge of them for several months without an Agent, or Government official of any kind."

In the fall of 1867, many prominent Indians and army officers, Indian agents and newspaper correspondents attended the Medicine Lodge Peace Council, which was called in an attempt to end a three-year war started by the Chivington massacre in Colorado. Black Beaver, then 61 years old, was in attendance.

Black Beaver was a delegate to the International Indian Council held at Okmulgee on August 1, 1870, where an inquiry was made into the Kiowas who had been raiding in Texas. Black Beaver criticized the mild speeches from the Five Civilized Tribes and proposed to speak plainly and brutally to the wild Indians. He prepared a speech in English with the aid of Cyrus Bede, representing the Indian superintendent, delivered it in English and it was translated for the different tribes.

A new teacher among the Caddoes on the False Washita River, Thomas C. Battey wrote in his diary that on February 18, 1872, he first saw the farm of Captain Black Beaver. "In conversation with him at one time," wrote Battey, "he told me of having visited, on two different occasions, among the mountains of Arizona, the remnant of a white race, who lived in a walled town, or rather a town built on a kind of peninsula, being nearly surrounded by a canon, or impassable ravine, so that there was but one way of approach and that by a narrow neck of land, across which they had built a wall, which effectually excluded the wild tribes by which they were surrounded ... He described them as living entirely at peace, being kind and hospitable to strangers whom they admit to their town. The second time he visited them, they recognized him and his party while at a distance, and a deputation carrying fruits were sent out to offer them the hospitalities of their town.

"Captain Black Beaver has a large farm under cultivation, and lives in a very comfortable manner, having good, substantial frontier buildings. He commenced life as a wild Indian trapper, until, becoming familiar with almost all the unexplored regions of the west, and being a remarkably truthful and reliable man, he was much sought after as a guide, and accompanied several expeditions in that capacity. His life has been one of bold adventure, fraught with many interesting incidents, which, if properly written out, would form an interesting and entertaining volume."

Stanley Pumphrey, in his *Indian Civilization, A Lecture*, saw Black Beaver as a true Christian when he saw him at the Wichita Agency. "The Quakers are your friends," said Black Beaver of the Delawares in 1872. "Their fathers and ours bound themselves to be friends forever. Their treaty was never broken. The Indians have never taken any Quaker's blood, and the Quakers have always been true friends to the Indians. Our Grandfather at Washington knew this, and for this reason has sent them among us. He knew that they would do right by his red grand-children."

Still trying to get the Kiowas to "make one road and travel in it", the International Council was held at Anadarko in August, 1872, and featured speeches by Captain James Vann of the Cherokee Nation, John Jumper of the Seminoles, and Captain Black Beaver who said, "I am mighty glad that all we red people meet here together this pleasant morning. That shows for our brethren our good part that we feel for one another. I wish it had been sooner that we meet together.

"Now I am an old man, I know all these people, my red brethren. I have traveled all over this country but I have never been over the waters ... all this western country I know it, and it knows me. I have been in it. The reason I do that, I want to know how many nations of my red brethren are in this country. I know them all. I have had pretty hard troubles, sometimes I see hard times, but I would not give up ... Sometimes I have to eat mule for a month. I did not want to, but I have to, to save my life ... I traveled five years for that suffering I got. When I come home I was not satisfied and traveled south.

"I find here lots of Indians, just my color; Wichitas, Ionies, Pen-e-tethcas, also some others of my brethren. Then my brethren just like the wild ones (here pointing to Cheyennes and Arapahoes). Then they make treaty with the United States. The first one they break up before I got in; second treaty I was in. Then I see Pen-e-teth-cas, Caddoes, &c., and they say here is my war hatchet; no more war.

"We planted an ear of corn in the ground, and promised to go to raising corn. At that time Indians had mighty good chiefs; they are all dead now, but the young chiefs are all here to carry out the same provisions; 'Keep the war hatchet buried ...' We all want peace among ourselves and with the United States. We want our country; we love it all here together. Well, now after we make friends, all of us, no more bad, then we are no more afraid to go anywhere; go all over the United States; meet white man, he asks what tribe you belong to; we tell him;

he say that is mighty good Indian. We like that. I hope we are all united together, all chiefs, that's what we want - peace. That much I talk to my brothers." Black Beaver then encouraged the attending wild Indians to help the Kiowas get out of trouble and persuade them to make peace with the government.

In October, 1872, Black Beaver was part of a delegation of plains Indians that Special Indian Commissioner Captain Henry E. Alvord took to Washington and New York. The tribes represented were Delaware, Kiowa, Comanche, Apache, Arapaho, Caddo, Wichita, Waco, Tawoccaro, and Kichai. The New York Herald reported on October 31, 1872 that "The Red Men were on a tour to learn Fraternity and Christian Virtues." Black Beaver was introduced as a former guide to Audubon.

Israel G. Yore, Black Beaver's old friend, spent the winter of 1873-1874 at his home and during this time convinced Black Beaver to dictate his memoirs, which he then recorded. For several years, Black Beaver acted as an interpreter for various Baptist missionaries and preachers and, in September of 1876, he and several other Indians were baptized in Sugar Creek. In later life, he became a Baptist minister. He also attended the Grand Council held at Okmulgee in May, 1878, still in demand as an interpreter.

On June 2, 1880, Indian Agent P.B. Hunt of the Kiowa, Comanche & Wichita Agency in Anadarko, Indian Territory, wrote to the commissioner of Indian affairs in Washington, "On the 8th day of May, Black Beaver, a Delaware, and the most prominent of all the Indians belonging to the old Wichita Agency, died suddenly of heart disease, in the 72nd (74th) year of his age.

"He was many years ago a noted guide and acted in that capacity for Fremont, Auderbon (sic) and Marcy; had acquired a fair knowledge of English & delighted in speaking it, when occasion offered; was a good friend of the white men, had professed religion, had consented to two of his daughters marrying white men, & set his red brethern (sic) a good example by his tiring industry & earnest desire to follow the white man's road to the end. His burial took place the day following his death, and more than 150 persons showed the esteem in which he was held, by following the remains to their last earthly resting-place. The coffin was borne by Agency employees and other white residents, and the burial services were conducted by the Delawares led by their Seminole preacher."

80

He was buried a short distance southwest of his farm. His daughter Lucy married an Osborne who died tragically. In 1871, she married H. Pat Pruner. Black Beaver's four grandchildren were John R. Osborne, Charles Beaver Pruner, Margaret Osborne McLane, and Mattie Pruner Sturm, who married Jesse Sturm, son of J.J. Sturm.

Black Beaver's skills as a scout and interpreter earned the Delaware Indian a reputation as one of the best guides in the United States. His friend Israel Yore called him one of God's noblemen, honest and truthful.

BLACKSNAKE

Blacksnake (Seneca, 1760 - December 26, 1859), also known as Thaonawyuthe (variant spellings: Thaowanyuths, Tenwaneus, or Twyneash), a name meaning the "Chain Breaker," and Dadgayadoh, "The Boys Betting", was an important Seneca chief during the turbulent period following the American Revolution. Born about 1760 at Cattaraugus, New York, about a mile north of Cold Spring, he was a nephew of Cornplanter, the great Seneca chief of the later 1700s and the early 1800s, and of the prophet Handsome Lake. As a young man Blacksnake took part in many major tribal meetings, largely due to his oratorical skills. He received the Wolf Clan name Thaonawyuthe when he became a war chief.

During the American Revolution Blacksnake served on the British side, as did most of the Iroquois. He figured prominently in many battles, including those at Oriskany and in the Wyoming Valley. He is said to have taken part in the Wyoming massacre of 1778.

After the war Blacksnake and other Indian leaders met with officials of the newly formed United States government in an attempt to establish firm boundaries and obtain better treatment for the Indians of the frontier. Washington and other white leaders were sympathetic, but the tide of settlers continued to flow westward. While there were no more full-scale battles between whites and Indians in Iroquois country, there were many local incidents of violence.

The Indians were aware that their traditions and heritage were threatened by the advancing white civilization. In 1799 Blacksnake's uncle, Handsome Lake, had a series of visions that led him to found a new religion that was, in essence, a return to the old tribal culture. The religion also had elements of a social reform movement. Blacksnake was so impressed that he became an early disciple of Gaiwlio, the "Good Word." Like many other people, he believed that indulgence in drink and other aspects of the white man's culture had to be eliminated from Indian life. He remained a believer even when he disagreed with Handsome Lake's often-dictatorial methods of dealing with political problems.

In the War of 1812, Blacksnake fought on the side of the United States. He took part in the Battle of Lake George in 1813. After the war, when he became the principal leader of the Seneca people, he was popularly known as Governor Blacksnake. From his home on the Allegheny River he continued efforts to secure justice for the Iroquois from both the state and federal governments. He also took a leading role in preaching the religion of Handsome Lake following the latter's death in 1815.

Although Blacksnake remained a staunch traditionalist and leader of the so-called "pagan party," his became a strong voice in favor of improved education for tribal youths, the use of modern agriculture, and other changes in Indian life, but in a way that would not mean the end of the traditional life style. His oral version of the Code of Handsome Lake found acceptance among many of the Senecas. He is remembered today as having kept the Seneca people together in the critical period following the death of Handsome Lake. At that time the religion, once so effective as a force binding the people into a single group, could have collapsed, thus destroying their unity and vitality.

Blacksnake died at Cold Spring, New York on December 26, 1859, at the age of 99 years.

BRANT, JOSEPH

Joseph Brant (Iroquois, 1742 - November 24, 1807), also known as Thayendanegea, from the Iroquois thayendane-ke, "He Places Two Bets," was an important Mohawk chief who was born while his parents were on a hunting trip along the Ohio River in 1742. His father was Tehowaghwengaraghkwin, a Mohawk Wolf Clan chief, and his mother a full or half-blooded Indian. Because his mother was apparently not a Mohawk, Brant never became a sachem even though his father bore that title. He did, however, become a Mohawk chief.

When his father died, grant's mother remarried. Her second husband, Nicklaus Brant, gave Joseph his English name. Young Joseph grew up at Canajoharie Castle, the family home in the Mohawk Valley. His older sister, Molly, married Sir William Johnson, an English trader who later became the British Superintendent of Indian Affairs. After his marriage to Molly, Johnson adopted the boy and assumed the responsibility for his education. When he was 13, Brant accompanied Johnson in the campaign of 1755, an episode in the French and Indian War of 1754-63. During the campaign he was present at the Battle of Lake George. In 1759, he took part in the Niagara campaign, becoming known for his outstanding bravery.

Brant was educated for a year at Eliazer Wheelock's Indian Charity School in Lebanon, Connecticut, the forerunner of Dartmouth College. At the Charity School he became a Christian convert, learned to read and write English, and began translating the Bible into the Mohawk language. That project occupied him intermittently for the rest of his life.

In 1763, shortly after leaving school, Brant fought with the British in the war against the Ottawa Indian Chief Pontiac. He married the daughter of an Oneida chief in 1765. By the 1770s he was recognized as a prominent leader in the Iroquois League.

As the American Revolution began, Brant became secretary to Guy Johnson, appointed to the post of British Superintendent of Indian Affairs following the death of his uncle, William. Accompanying Guy Johnson to England in 1775, Brant was presented at court and had his portrait painted by the British artist George Romney. He came home more devoted than ever to the British cause; ironically, his influence contributed to the disunity of the Iroquois League during and after the American Revolution. After lengthy debate, the Six Nations of the league divided; the Seneca, Cayuga, Onondaga, and Mohawk factions joined Brant while the Oneida and Tuscarora sided with the Americans.

Brant became a British colonel and participated in devastating raids throughout the Mohawk Valley. A commander of Indian forces at the Battle of Oriskany on August 6, 1777, he displayed desperate courage.

Afterward the Six Nations Indians, fighting with the British, harried the Mohawk Valley, southern New York, and northern Pennsylvania, attacking sometimes alone, sometimes with British sympathizers in the colonies.

Brant is believed to have directed the Cherry Valley massacre of 1778 as well as many others. Brant's defenders have claimed that he tried to protect women, children, prisoners, and wounded. If so, he was not always successful. He is known to have taken part in the massacre at Minisink in July 1779.

After the Revolution, he used his influence to establish peace on the Mohawk frontier and to protect his people from American reprisals. He also tried without success to resolve the Iroquois land claims against the new American government. In 1786, while still a British officer on half-pay, Brant returned to England for a visit. The British rewarded him for his efforts in the war with a land grant at Anaquaqua, along the Grand River in Ontario, Canada. He retired to that area with his Mohawk followers. Other Indians from the League joined the group and the area became the Six Nations Reserve.

Brant built the first Episcopal Church in Upper Canada at Brantford, a town that was named for him. He devoted his remaining years to missionary work and translations of sacred texts. He had helped establish "the Old Mohawk Church;" his translations into Mohawk included the Book of Common Prayer and Saint Mark's Gospel. In July 1793, at the request of George Washington, he helped bring peace between the Miami Indians and the United States.

Brant became a strong believer in evangelical Christianity. His first wife died, leaving him two children; he married her half-sister, who was childless. His third wife gave him seven children. He died on his own Ontario estate and was buried near the church he had built.

The American Revolution helped bring about a split in the Iroquois League that was never healed. Brant nonetheless followed the course in which he believed, and his loyalty to the British never waned. A complex man of many talents, he was a scholar, translator, man of religion, highly respected leader of the people, and a courageous, ferocious warrior. In 1886 the Canadian government donated 13 bronze cannons for a statue to be erected in Brant's memory.

BUCKONGAHELAS

Buckongahelas (Delaware 18th Century), was a war chief during the Indian uprisings of the 1790s who won the admiration of his enemies for his candor and humanitarian principles. Born in the mid-18th century, probably in western Ohio, Buckongahelas became Chief of the Delaware on the White and Miami rivers. Although he eventually fought for the British in the American Revolution, he distrusted the white man and evacuated as many of his people as would follow him to the upper Miami River in April 1781, where he hoped they would find sanctuary. Almost all of the Christian Delaware at Gnadenhutten and Salem Ohio, declined his invitation as he passed through, and nearly 100 of these peaceful Indians were massacred 11 months later by the Pennsylvania militia.

In the 1790s Buckongahelas was prominent among the leaders of the Indian uprising against the United States. The Delaware, Shawnee, Miami, and other tribes destroyed the force of General Arthur Saint Clair on November 4, 1791, north of Hamilton, Ohio, but were conclusively defeated themselves on August 20, 1794, by General Anthony Wayne at the Battle of Fallen Timbers. The retreating Indians were denied entrance to Fort Miami, Ohio, a sanctuary that had been promised by the British who incited the uprising.

This treachery ended Buckongahelas' alliance with England. He pledged allegiance to the United States in the Treaty of Greenville on August 3, 1795, but by December 1802 he found it necessary to confront President Thomas Jefferson in Washington, D.C., with what he believed were illegal land appropriations by the government. Later, probably under pressure from General William H. Harrison, he ratified the cessions in treaties signed in Indiana at Fort Wayne on June 7, 1803, and in Vincennes on August 18, 1804.

Buckongahelas died in 1804 or 1805, probably in Buckongahgelas' Town on the White River near present-day Muncie, Indiana. He never retracted his words to the Delaware at Gnadenhutten before their massacre: "I admit that there are good white men, but they bear no proportion to the bad, for the bad rule."

CANARSEE

The Algonquian-speaking Canarsee were formerly a leading tribe of present-day Long Island, New York, living in what is now Kings County, centered near Flatlands. According to Ruttenber they were connected or subject to the Montauk. This is doubtful, however, as those Indians on the western end of the island, at the time of the Dutch settlement, appear to have been paying tribute to the Iroquois.

Canarsee, their main village, was most likely near Flatlands; in addition to which they had others at Maspeth and Hempstead. The site of present-day Brooklyn was originally theirs. After the Dutch appeared, they became independent of the Mohawk, and were nearly exterminated in an attack by them. During the war of the Long Island tribes against the Dutch, the Canarsee suffered greatly.

Their supposed last survivor died in 1800. Any possible survivors may have descendants now living in small communities in the area, including the Poosepatuck and Shinnecock Reservations and the Montauk Indian Village.

CANONCHET

Canonchet (Narraganset, ? - 1676) was a 17th Century chief, son of Miantonomo, and a leader in the war of King Philip (Metacom), chief of the Wampanoag, against the English in 1675-76. The Narraganset at first refrained from an active part in the war, but probably provided refuge to the Wampanoag and perhaps a few warriors for Philip's forces. In October 1675, Canonchet signed a treaty with the English in which he agreed to surrender refugee Wampanoag. Apparently, Canonchet never intended to deliver the refugees for he is reported to have said: "Not a Wampanoag will I ever give up. No, not the paring of a Wampanoag's nail!"

On December 16, 1675, a force of more than 1,000 men from the New England Confederation attacked the swamp fort of the Narraganset. The Indians suffered heavy losses, but Canonchet escaped and actively fought in the war against the whites. He led several raids against the English settlements, and in March 1676 he defeated English troops under Captain Michael Peirse.

In April 1676, while on a mission to obtain seed corn for planting, Canonchet, surprised by an English force, was captured. When he was sentenced to death, Canonchet stated, "I like it well; for I shall die before my heart is soft, or I have spoken anything unworthy of myself."

At Stonington, Connecticut, Canonchet was shot, beheaded, and his body burned by representatives of the English allies: the Pequot, the Mohegan, and the Niantic. His head was sent to Hartford as a trophy. Canonchet's death was a serious blow to Philip's movement, and because it left the Narraganset with no other leader as capable as Canonchet, it probably shortened the course of the war.

CAYUGA

The Cayuga (*Kwenio-gwe*, "The place where the locusts are taken out"), was a tribe of the Iroquois Confederation, formerly living on the shores of Cayuga Lake, New York. Their local council had four clan phratries. This became the pattern of the confederation of the Five Nations of the Iroquois, in which the Cayuga had 10 delegates. There were some 1,500 Cayugas in 1660. When the American Revolution began, most of the tribe went to Canada, never to return.

The remainder were scattered among other confederacy tribes, and soon sold their lands to New York. Some Cayuga went to Ohio, joining other Iroquois in the "Seneca of the Sanduskey". Their descendants are now in Oklahoma. Other Cayuga joined the Oneida reservation in Wisconsin, while about 200 went with the Iroquois of New York, their descendants living on the Allegany, Cattaraugus, Tonawanda, Onondaga, Oneida, and Saint Regis reservations in that state. The Majority, however, some 700 or 800 in 1900, were relocated to the Grand River Reservation in Ontario, Canada, and are now represented on the Six Nations, Caughnawaga, and Tyendinaga (Bay of Quintes) reserves in Canada.

They had three villages in 1670: Kiohero, Goiogouen, and Onondare. Up to the early to mid-1800s, their main village was Gayagaanha. Lesser villages, according to Morgan, were Ganogeh, Gewauga, and Neodakheat. Others were Chonodote, Gandaseteiagon, Kawauka, Kente, Nuquiage, Ondachoe, Owego, Onugareclury, Sant Joseph, Sannio,, Skannayutenate, and Swahyaawanh. Their clans were Iroquoian. The Canadian Iroquois recently numbered about 20,500, while the United States Iroquois numbered some 22,000.

CHEESHATEAUMUCK, CALEB

Caleb Cheeshateaumuck (Wampanoag, ? - 1666), was the first American Indian to receive a degree from Harvard College (1665). The son of a chief, he was born in the area of Martha's Vineyard, Massachusetts.

CHOPTANK

The Choptank were apparently an Algonquian-speaking tribe consisting of three subtribes, the Ababco, Hutsawap, and Tequassimo, formerly living on the Choptank River in Maryland. Choptank was also a village name, and Abaco was one of their chiefs. They lived along the Choptank River in Dorchester County on the Eastern shore.

The Choptank were among the signers of the Treaty of 1659, and were lone signers of a similar treaty in 1705. Such treaties failed to protect the Indians from the encroachment of white settlers.

The Indians typically complained of the destruction of fences around their corn fields by the English and their livestock, while the

English claimed the Indians were killing their hogs. Increasing white pressure by whites and the Five Nation Iroquois led the Choptank and other scattered groups in Southern Maryland to consolidate on reservations in the 1680s. Choptank lands were greatly reduced by a series of more or less forced land sales.

Scarcity of deer in the area made a greater reliance on fowling and fishing. They greatly relied on crops, planted by women on patches cleared by the men, and included corn, beans, and pumpkins. The men hunted deer, bear, squirrel, turkeys, partridges and other game and fowl with bows and arrows, whose wood or reed shafts bore glued-on tips of stone, antler, or bone, and were fletched with turkey feathers. Guns soon replaced bows and arrow, as did metal trade tomahawks for wooden clubs. Trapping increased with the developing beaver pelt trade. Along the coast, fishing and shellfishing was also important.

Corn meal was baked into bread, and whole corn was boiled into hominy. Meat was spit-roasted, or stewed with oysters. Food was served in wooden bowls, with shells for spoons. Women made baskets of yucca fiber or reeds. Their boats were dugouts or bark canoes. Skin clothing was worn by adults, while children often went naked in fair weather. European clothing was accepted early, especially by Indians of high status.

The Choptanks, closely associated with the Nanticokes, had several chiefs, perhaps representing villages, but central authority was weakly developed. There is evidence of Choptank independence, but they are variously mentioned as if part of the Nanticokes or Assateagues, reflecting temporary shifts in location between 1684 and 1694.

Seventeenth population estimates say of the Choptank, "tis almost impossible to have the exact number of men or towns". A few members of mixed Native American and Black blood remained along the Choptank River as late as 1837. Their remnants lost their tribal status and became known as "free Negroes". Close association with blacks is reflected in a 1740's word list that identified several words as Mandingo, a West African Language. This black element may account for early reports about the dark complexion of most of the tribes of southern Maryland.

COCKENOE

Cockenoe (Montauk, 1630-1700), taught John Eliot, the Puritans' "Apostle to the Indians," the language of the Massachusetts Indians and assisted Eliot in translating the Bible into Algonquian. Captured in the Pequot War of 1637, Cockenoe soon was helping Eliot preach to local Indians in their native tongue. Eliot's Bible, the first complete Bible printed in the colonies, probably would not have come into existence were it not for Cockenoe's translation. Cockenoe later served as interpreter for the civil authorities in New York and New England.

CONESTOGA

The name "Conestoga" comes from the word *Kanastoge*, "at the place of the immersed pole." The Conestoga were an important Iroquoian tribal group that formerly lived on Susquehanna River and its branches. When first met by Captain John Smith, in 1608, and until their conquest by the Iroquois Confederation in 1675, they were allied with the Algonquian tribes of the east shore of Chesapeake Bay and at war with those on the west shore. They were described as warlike, with a physique far superior to that of neighboring tribes. By conquest, they claimed the lands on both sides of Chesapeake Bay, from the Choptank and Patuxent Rivers north to the territory of the Iroquois.

In 1675, after their defeat, they established themselves on the east bank of the Potomac, in Maryland, immediately north of Piscataway Creek, below which the Doag (Nanticoke) were then living. They formed a close alliance with the Dutch, Swedes, and the English of Maryland. The Iroquois had carried on relentless war against them, with varying success, which finally reduced them from about 3,000 in 1608 to about 550 in 1648, while their allies brought the aggregate to about 1,250. Champlain says that in 1615 they had more than 20 villages, of which only three were then at war with the Iroquois, and that their town of Carantouan alone could muster more than 800 warriors. The Iroquois of the north drove the Conestoga down on the tribes to the south and west, which were allies of the English, a movement involving the Conestoga in a war with Maryland and Virginia in 1675. Finding themselves surrounded by enemies on all sides, a portion of them abandoned their country and took refuge with the Occaneechi on Roanoke River, while the rest remained in Pennsylvania.

A quarrel occurred soon with the Occaneechi, who joined the whites against the fugitive Conestoga, who were compelled to return to Susquehanna River and submit to the Iroquois. According to Colden they were all finally removed to Oneida country, where they remained until they lost their language. They were later allowed to return to Conestoga, their ancient town. Here they wasted rapidly, until, at the close of the year 1763, the remnant, numbering only 20, were massacred by a party of rioters inflamed by the accounts of the Indian war then raging along the Pennsylvania frontier.

Around 1675 their stockade, where they were defeated by the Maryland forces, was on the eastern side of Susquehanna River, three miles below Columbia, Pennsylvania. Herman's map of 1676 located it at nearly the same point on the river, but on the western bank, The Swedes and Dutch called them Minqua, from the Delaware name applied to all tribes of Iroquoian stock. The Powhatan tribes called them Susquehannock, a name signifying "roily river," which was adopted by the English of Virginia and Maryland. The names of their villages are Attock, Carantouan, Cepowig, Oscalui, Quadroque, Sasquesahanough, Testhigh, and Utchowig. The Meherrin on the river of that name in southeast Virginia, were officially reported to be a band of the Conestoga driven south by the Virginians during Bacon's Rebellion in 1675-76. (See SUSQUEHANNA and SUSQUAHANNOCK.)

CONOY

An Algonquian tribe, the Conoy (Piscataway) were related to the Delawares, from whose ancestral line they apparently sprang, but their closest relations were the Nanticoke. The Conoy were probably united with them in late prehistoric times. The two formed a single tribe, while their language is supposed to have been allied to that spoken by the Powhatan in Virginia. Heckewelder believed them to be identical with the Kanawha, who gave the name to the chief river of West Virginia. Along with the Nanticoke Indians, they lived on the eastern and western shores of Chesapeake Bay and the Potomac River in Maryland, and in southern Delaware.

Thirteen generations would carry back the date of their first "emperor" to the beginning of the 16th century. Lord Baltimore's colonists in 1634 established a mission among them, and the Emperor Chitomachen, otherwise known as Tayac, said to be ruler over a dominion extending 130 miles east and west, was converted, with his family. They were, however, so harassed by the Conestoga that a few years later they abandoned their country and moved farther up the Potomac.

Rapidly decreasing, they were in 1673 assigned a tract on that stream, which may have been near the site of Washington, District of Columbia. The Conestoga, when driven from their own country by the Iroquois in 1675, again invaded the territory of the Conoy and forced that tribe up the Potomac and into Pennsylvania. This was gradual, unless it took place at a much later period, for Baron Graffenried, while searching for a reported silver mine in 1711, found them on the Maryland side of the Potomac about 50 miles above Washington, and made a treaty of friendship with them. He calls them "Canawest".

About then the Iroquois assigned them lands at Conejoholo on the Susquehanna, near present Bainbridge, Pennsylvania in the vicinity of the Nanticoke and Conestoga. Here they first began to be known as Conoy. Some of them were living with these tribes at Conestoga in 1742.

They gradually made their way up the Susquehanna River, stopping at Harrisburg, Shamokin, Catawissa, and Wyoming, and in 1765 were living in south New York, at Oswego, Chugnut, and Chenang, on the east branch of the Susquehanna. At that time they numbered only about 150, and, with their associates, the Nanticoke and Mahican, were dependent on the Iroquois. They moved west with the Mahican and Delawares, and soon became known only as a part of those tribes. In 1793 they attended a council near Detroit and used the turkey as their signature.

The customs and beliefs of the Conoy may best be given by the following quotation from White's *Relatio Itineris*, 1635, although the author's interpretations of customs often go far astray, "The natives are very tall and well proportioned; their skin is naturally rather dark, and they make it uglier by staining it, generally with red paint mixed with oil, to keep off the mosquitoes, thinking more of their own comfort than of appearances. They disfigure their countenances with other colors, too, painting them in various and truly hideous and frightful ways, either a dark blue above the nose and red below, or the reverse. And as they live almost to extreme old age without having beards, they counterfeit them with paint, by drawing lines of various colors from the extremities of the lips to the ears."

"They generally have black hair, which they carry round in a knot to the left ear, and fasten with a band, adding some ornament which is in estimation among them. Some of them wear on their foreheads the figure of a fish made of copper. They adorn their necks with glass beads strung on a thread like necklaces, though these beads are getting to be less valued among them and less useful for trade. They are clothed for the most part in deerskins or some similar kind of covering, which hangs down behind like a cloak. They wear aprons round the middle, and leave the rest of the body naked. The young boys and girls go about with nothing on them."

"The soles of their feet are as hard a horn, and they tread on thorns and briers without being hurt. Their arms are bows, and arrows three feet long, tipped with stags horn, or a white flint sharpened at the end. They shoot these with such skill that they can stand off and hit a sparrow in the middle; and, in order to become expert by practice, they throw a spear up in the air and then send an arrow from the bow string and drive it into the spear before it falls. But since they do not string the bow very tight, they can not hit a mark at a great distance. They live by means of these weapons, and go out every day through the fields and woods to hunt squirrels, partridges, turkeys, and wild animals. For there is an abundance of all these, though we ourselves do not yet venture to procure food by hunting, for fear of ambushes."

"They live in houses built in an oblong, oval shape. Light is admitted into these through the roof, by a window a foot and a half long; this also serves to carry off the smoke, for they kindle the fire in the middle of the floor, and sleep around the fire. Their kings, however, and chief men have private apartments, as it were, of their own and beds, made by driving four posts into the ground, and arranging poles above they horizontally."

According to the same authority, they acknowledged one god of heaven, yet paid him no outward worship, but strove in every way to appease a certain imaginary spirit, which they called Ochre, that he might not hurt them. They also worshiped corn and fire. The missionary probably here alludes to the use of corn and fire in certain religious ceremonies. The Conoy villages were Catawissa, Conedogwinit, Conejoholo, Conoytown, Kittamaquindi, Onuatuc, Opamemt, Peixtan.

Their descendants now live in the Nanticoke Community in Sussex County, Delaware and numbered about 400 in a recent count.

CORNPLANTER

Cornplanter (Seneca, 1732 - February 18, 1836), also known as John O'Bail, (his Indian name was Gayentwahga), was a chief who fought against the Americans during the United States War of Independence, but who later concluded treaties that ceded substantial tracts of Indian land to the United States. Born at Conewaugus, New York, Cornplanter was of mixed parentage. He derived his exalted position among the Seneca from his mother, a descendant of the tribe's ruling family.

Cornplanter's father was a white trader of either English or Dutch ancestry named John O'Bail or O'Beal who lived in Albany, New York. Little is known of his early life, although it is generally believed that he was present at the defeat of General Edward Braddock near Fort Duquesne, present-day Pittsburgh, Pennsylvania, in 1775. Also as a young man he visited his father in Albany.

Although he was reluctant to join the other tribes of the Iroquois League on the British side during the American Revolution, Cornplanter finally went along with the tribes in the confederacy which pledged allegiance to the crown. He was one of the two Iroquois war chiefs named by the British.

Throughout the hostilities, Cornplanter participated in raiding parties that terrorized white settlements throughout New York and Pennsylvania. When General John Sullivan invaded Seneca country in 1779, Cornplanter fought valiantly, but his hated rival, another Seneca chief named Red Jacket, fled upon catching sight of Sullivan's troops at Lake Canandaigua. Sullivan defeated the Seneca, inflicting heavy losses, burning the villages, and destroying the crops.

Nevertheless, the Seneca, as well as the other Iroquois tribes, never felt that they had been conquered by the Americans. Therefore, when Cornplanter participated in the treaties of 1784, 1789, 1797, and 1802, all of which ceded substantial Indian territory in western New York to the United States, his stature among the Seneca went into eclipse. Meanwhile, Red Jacket seized upon the tribe's sense of humiliation at this time to promote his own power and popularity. He protested the land cessions to which Cornplanter signed his name. In fact, Cornplanter became so despised that for a time his life was in danger by members of his own tribe. Cornplanter, however, an eloquent orator, continued to work to assure that the United States Government would

93

live up to the provisions of the treaties. In 1790 he sent a message to President George Washington in Philadelphia, laying before him the grievances of the Seneca.

The white inhabitants of New York and Pennsylvania began to look upon Cornplanter in a different light. Far from the terrifying enemy he had been during the Revolution, Cornplanter was later considered to be a "good Indian." On March 16, 1796, therefore, the State of Pennsylvania granted the Seneca chief a 640-acre tract of land "for his many valuable services to the whites." By 1816 Cornplanter owned 1,300 acres along the banks of the Allegheny River, and he received a pension of 250 dollars annually from the United States Government.

About 1820 Cornplanter experienced a series of visions which he claimed were confrontations with the Great Spirit. Instructed by the Great Spirit to sever all ties with white people, Cornplanter suddenly renounced Christianity and burned all the mementos (flag, medals, belt, hat, sword, etc.) of his warrior days. Moreover, his favorite son, Henry O'Bail, who had been carefully educated, became a drunkard, adding to the trials of Cornplanter's later years. He was still an impressive figure at the time of his death in 1836. A monument was erected in his honor by the State of Pennsylvania at the site where he was buried on his land near the Allegheny.

DEKANAWIDA

Dekanawida (Huron, 16th Century), was a prophet, statesman, and lawgiver who determined to unite the entire human race into a confederation based upon the principles of equity and righteousness, and succeeded in laying the moral and political foundation for the Iroquois Confederacy. A mystic being during his lifetime, Dekanawida has been shrouded in mystery. No doubt a real person, he ranks as a demigod in Iroquois legend. In fact, stories about him often confuse Christian theology with Iroquois tradition.

Dekanawida, says tradition, was born near present-day Kingston, Ontario, the son of a virgin. After his birth, however, the mother and grandmother attempted to murder Dekanawida, fearing that the child had an evil destiny. The grandmother learned in a dream that the child would indirectly cause the destruction of the Huron people. The Iroquois Confederacy that Dekanawida helped establish did in fact destroy the Huron Confederacy. Mother and grandmother tried three times to kill the newborn infant, pushing him through a hole in the ice

94

of a frozen stream; but in each instance the baby was found alive and unharmed in its mother's arms when she awoke the following morning.

Dekanawida grew up an outcast, shunned by the Huron. No doubt his alienation from the tribe contributed greatly to his inability to speak without stammering. Nonetheless, he was convinced that he had a divine mission, a conviction reinforced by his vision of all mankind united, living in peace and brotherhood. Three sets of double principles formed the constitutional framework for his unification of all tribes throughout the world: 1. Equity and justice, and righteousness in conduct, thought, and speech. 2. Physical strength and civil authority, plus inner spiritual power. 3. Sanity of mind and physical health, and peace among individuals and groups. Dekanawida, sure of his destiny, set out from the land of the Huron to go to Iroquois territory. There he won converts to what would come to be called "The Great Peace."

The exact circumstances are buried deep in mystery and obscure legend, but in some way Dekanawida joined forces with Hiawatha, who had been trying to unite the Iroquois. Although well intentioned, Hiawatha had lacked specific principles to construct a lasting confederation. Dekanawida converted Hiawatha to his code for the unification of all people under the three sets of double principles, and the two embarked upon winning over the main stumbling block to the Iroquois Confederation, the Onondaga chief Wathatotarho. Dekanawida was the prophet; Hiawatha was the spokesman. Together they converted Wathatotarho and aligned the five Iroquois nations, (Onondaga, Mohawk, Cayuga, Seneca, and Oneida) into a powerful league that would last for more than two centuries.

The league was ruled by a council of 50 peace chiefs, known as sachems, which were chosen from specific clans. Since he was not an Iroquois by birth, Dekanawida became a chief on the basis of merit, and he forbade the appointment of a successor to his office.

Believing that this great triumph was merely the beginning of the realization of his divine mission, Dekanawida left the Iroquois to take his message to the world. As legend has it, he paddled out on Lake Ontario in a canoe made from brilliant white stone, and disappeared into the sunset.

DEKANISORA

Dekanisora (Onondaga, ? - 1730), was an Iroquois chief and an a noted orator who tried to maintain peace with both the French and the English. Dekanisora (Teganessorens) is first mentioned as a leader of an Iroquois peace embassy to Montreal in 1682. In 1688 he was one of the deputies captured and then released by Adario, in his successful effort to reopen hostilities between the French and the Iroquois.

In 1694 Dekanisora arranged a truce with the French at Quebec, but insisted that English allies be included in the peace negotiations. At Albany, Dekanisora found the English opposed to any reconciliation between the Iroquois and the French. He reaffirmed his loyalty to the English but asserted the Iroquois right to act independently. Nevertheless, the Iroquois could not come to terms with the French, and general peace failed. In 1701, however, Dekanisora represented the Indians in a lasting peace treaty with the French.

In 1726 Dekanisora was again an ambassador to Albany, where he helped to execute an agreement that placed Iroquois hunting grounds under the protection of the king of England. He died about 1780 at an advanced age.

Because of his reputation as a speaker among the Iroquois, Dekanisora took part in most of their negotiations with the French and English. He was described by his contemporary Cadwallader Colden as having "a great fluency in speaking and a graceful elocution that would have pleased in any part of the world. "He may have been a Christian convert. Dekanisora helped to preserve, so far as was possible, the independence of the Five Nations from both European powers.

DELAWARE

The Delaware are an Algonquian-speaking group whose ancestors inhabited the lower Hudson River valley and the entire Delaware River drainage when Europeans first came to North America. With a native population variously estimated at between 10,000 and 40,000, the traditional Delaware homeland extended throughout the Middle Atlantic coastal plain and adjacent highland interior of southwestern Connecticut, southeastern New York, western Long Island, all of New Jersey, southeastern Pennsylvania, and the State of Delaware.

The Delaware called themselves as the Lenni Lenape, "common, original, or real people." The English named them after the Delaware

River, which in turn had been named in honor of Sir Thomas West, Lord de la Warr, the first colonial governor of Virginia.

Known among their Eastern Algonquin brethren as "grandfathers," their Iroquoian-speaking neighbors to the north and west called the Delaware "nephews." The Algonquin and Siouan peoples who shared their long westward exile knew them as *Wapanachki,* "easterners, or people of the dawn." The Delawarans, on their part, knew the European colonists that streamed upon their lands as *Swannekens,* "salt water, or bitter people." Long years of struggle led the Delaware to name the American successors to the Europeans *Kwun-nah-she-kun,* or "long knives."

Never politically united, the Delawarans did share a common tongue. The Algonquian linguist, Ives Goddard, has identified two closely related Delaware languages, Munsee and Unami. Goddard stated that Munsee was spoken by the Lower Hudson and upper Delaware River Valley groups, while Unami was used by the Delawarans of the lower Delaware River watershed. Each language was further divided into a presently unknown number of dialects. Most closely related to Mahican, the relationship between Delaware and other Algonquian languages is poorly understood.

The Dutch merchant-explorers who first visited the Delawarean homeland during the seventeenth century came upon a neolithic farming, fishing, hunting, and gathering people, whose settlement was thickly lined the watercourses, lagoons, and beaches along their territories. Those who lived near the coast drew their lives from the sea. They hooked, speared, netted, and trapped cod, salmon, herring, sturgeon, and many other kinds of fish. Hard clams, oysters, mussels, crabs, lobsters, and other forms of shellfish were also very important parts of the coastal Delaware diet.

Sharp fish bones were used as needles and awls, while the cracked shells of mollusks provided keen cutting edges. The shells of hard clams and periwinkles were ground into tubular white and purple beads. These became a species of currency known as sewan or wampum. The flesh and eggs of seabirds, a myriad of berries, many forms of seaweed, and the meat and oil from seals and stranded whales were other major coastal Delawarean food sources.

Wetlands supported luxuriant stands of tall grasses that provided mats that served as floor, wall, and roof for the coastal Delaware roundhouses and longhouses. Grasses were also woven into bags and

97

baskets that served as furniture and luggage. Rimless conical pottery, bark and skin containers, and hollowed logs further furnished their homes and lined their cooking fires. They expertly plied low, sleek dugout canoes on, bringing people and resources together. White-tailed deer, bear, and smaller mammals were hunted and trapped.

Corn, beans, and squash contributed modestly to coastal Delaware-ans, who had large villages located in sheltered bays and sounds during blustery winters. These settlements broke up during the spring, when the villagers moved to small fishing, shellfishing, and hunting camps. Many inland people were hosted in turn by their coastal relatives, from late spring through fall.

The Delaware of the highland interior made their living from the upland fields, forests, and streams. Gardens yielded large amounts of corn, beans, squash, sunflowers, and other crops. Spawning anadromous fish such as shad, salmon, and herring added to the substantial catch of pike, bass, pickerel, catfish, carp, and other lake and river fish. Individual and group hunts brought an abundance of white tailed deer, elk, black and brown bear, forest bison, beaver, and many other forest animals. Extensive mineral outcrops of argillite, jasper, and quartz furnished the raw materials for a wide range of cutting and piercing tools and weapons.

An extensive selection of tubers, greens, fruits, and berries were available during warmer months. Passenger pigeons, ducks, geese, turkey, and other birds rounded out the interior Delawaran diet. The bark of elm, hickory, and birch trees provided building materials for longhouses, cooking utensils and containers, and skins for frame canoes. The deep forests of oak, hickory, maple, pine, and other trees furnished fuel, house frames, tool handles, and a multitude of other necessary utensils. Clays from riverbeds and lake bottoms were transformed by Delawaran craftswomen into globular pots with high, elaborately decorated, castellated rims.

The interior Delawaran groups had small, scattered hunting camps located in sheltered upland valleys during the winter months. Families gathered by river falls and rapids to harvest massive fish runs in early spring. The matriclan segments then moved into the large agricultural villages located along the fertile river bottoms during the late spring and early summer. Lower Delawarean villages were strung out along sections of large river valleys. Upper Delaware agricultural villages were more concentrated, with many larger settlements fortified with timber palisade walls during hostilities.

Inland and coastal Delaware people exchanged visits following spring planting and fishing. Summer was the time for trading and raiding, and the able-bodied, accordingly, roved widely throughout the region, while the very young and very old tended the fields and gathered wild plants.

The people returned to the agricultural villages for the fall harvest and its attendant festival. They then went back into the forests for the annual communal hunt. Parties up to several hundred surrounded a section of woodland, set it afire, and then drove the game within the circle of flame. The game killed was preserved for winter. The families then returned to hunting camps until spring.

Little is known about Delawarean religion. Early European observers noted that they followed an extensive round of religious dances and feasts. Guardian spirits obtained through dreams and visions played an important part in daily life and medicine people of both sexes were active in Delaware society.

All were lightly clad during the warmer months. Men generally only wore skin breechcloths, while the women dressed in skin kilts. Both sexes wore moccasins made from tanned deer hide. The people normally applied clarified bear grease mixed with onion grass to their bodies as protection from the sun and insects. Both sexes adorned themselves with paint, ear and nose ornaments, and tattoos. Successful warriors and gifted medicine persons sported particularly elaborate tattoos over their entire bodies. Men and women usually wore their hair long, in a wide variety of styles. Warriors shaved their heads and wore a small scalp lock decorated with feathers, wampum, and fur. Both sexes wore leggings, loosely fitted shirts, and bearskin robes during winter.

The longhouse was the predominant Delaware house type. Ranging in length from thirty to sixty feet and from ten to fifteen feet wide, the longhouse was constructed of thick saplings joined together to form a series of arches. These arches were connected by supporting branches, and the frame was covered with grass mats or bark. Fireplaces were located along the central corridor, and families occupied cubicles on their side of the hearths. The center portion of the roof was left open to let out the smoke from fires, and access to and from the structure was through doors at either end of the long central corridor. Goods were stored in baskets below the family sleeping compartments, and matrilineage possessions were kept in storage rooms located at the ends of the longhouse. Dried foodstuffs and other perishables were hung from the ceiling, kept in caches above ground, or buried in pits near the settlements.

Each Delaware house sheltered a matrilineal-matrilocal kinship group. The Delaware traced descent through women. Groups of related women and their male kinsmen made up a matriclan segment. These segments were parts of a larger matriclan whose members resided at various locations throughout the Delaware homeland. Later sources suggested the existence of three Delaware matriclans: the wolf, the turtle, and the turkey. Such a division of lineages was not confirmed in the seventeenth century record, and aboriginal Delaware society was probably organized into a larger number of matriclans.

The Delaware practiced matriclan exogamy, which required people to select marriage partners from other lineages. The rule of matrilocal residence saw to it that Delaware husbands moved into their wife's households. Important or wealthy men were permitted more than one wife, but these were usually from the same matriclan. When wives were of different lineages, the man either lived with the senior wife, a favorite, or divided his time among the households of his various spouses.

The matriclans owned all rights to land. Lineage members were free to use any matriclan lands not used by other relatives. The cooperative efforts of women living in the same household on the land assured continued control over the lineage territorial holdings. The marriage of men into other matriclan groups further insured the benefits of foreign resources and assistance from other groups. Seventeenth century Delawares never acted as a distinct political entity. Though they shared significant linguistic, kinship, and ethnic ties, locality was always the single most compelling aspect of Delaware political life. Family ties claimed the strongest allegiance in aboriginal Delaware society. Organization above the clan level was flexible and largely voluntary.

Four levels of Delaware socio-political integration beyond the matriclan have been identified. The village consisted of one or more dwellings, each housing a matriclan segment containing a population of a few dozen to several hundred. The village was the most important international agent of seventeenth century Delaware society.

Districts were a flexible combination of villages and separate matri-clan organizations in a relatively limited territory. The district area permitted a number of loosely affiliated social groups to cooperatively exploit the resources of a given area.

Delaware tribes were a fluid combination of matriclan, village, and district organizations that generally held jurisdiction over a portion of river drainage and its surrounding lands. The tribal level of so-cio-political integration was only convened during periods of interna-tional stress.

Confederacies were the short-lived highest-level response to so-cio-political problems of the Delaware. The confederacy usually con-sisted of a group of tribes, and was generally only invoked during ma-jor wars. Confederacies were usually disbanded immediately follow-ing the end of the conflict. The Esopus of the Mid-Hudson River val-ley, however, appear to have been organized as a confederacy both before and after the bloody Esopus Wars and Iroquoian Five Nations. The threat of sustained hostility with these groups may have caused the Esopus to confederate to an extent unparalleled by other Delaware societies. It should be noted that the Delaware never united into a sin-gle confederacy at any time in their history.

Each level of Delaware sociopolitical organization was led in peace by a civil chief, known as a sachem or sagamore, and by a war captain in times of war. Both chiefs were supported further by respective councils. The office of civil chief was transmitted hereditarily and de-scended through the matriclan. War captains achieved their rank through battlefield successes. Councils were constituted of chiefs of the same approximate rank, and council leaders were very much "first among equals." War captains could compel absolute obedience during military operations. Sachems, however, were not permitted to arbi-trarily order any action. All civil decisions were made by consensus, and a leader's authority depended upon diplomatic ability rather than coercive power.

Just as Delaware settlement-subsistence patterns could be under-stood in terms of interior and coastal types, the socio-political life was organized into the Munsee-speaking Upper Delawaran and Unami-speaking Lower Delawaran culture provinces. The major Up-per Delawaran groups included the Wappinger, Nochpeem, Kichta-wanck, Sint Sinck, Wieehquaesgeck, Manhattan, Canarsee, Nayack, Rockaway, Massapequa, and Matinecock of western Long Island; the five confederated Esopus tribes; the Haverstraw, Tappan, Hackensack, Raritan, and Neversink to the west of the Hudson River; and the Minisink and Forks of the Delaware groups of the north reaches of the Delaware River. The major Lower Delawaran peoples were the San-hican of the Trenton, New Jersey area; the Atsayonck of Crosswicks Creek; the Remkokes, Armewamex, Mantaes, Naraticonck, Little Si-conese, and Sewapois of the eastern shores of the tidewater Delaware River; and the Quineomessinque, Minguannan, and Big Siconese of the western banks of Delaware Bay.

The coastal Delaware were first contacted by European exploratory voyages during the 1500s. The first sustained contacts occurred during the Dutch and English expeditions of the opening decades of the seventeenth century. The Dutch West India Company established their colony of New Netherland in the heart of the Delaware homeland during the 1620s, and major Dutch trading posts were built at the mouths of the Hudson and Delaware Rivers, and 160 miles up the Hudson River near modern Albany, New York, by the early 1630s.

The Dutch post on the Delaware River was destroyed by the Lower Delaware Indians shortly after it was built, and the upriver post, known as Fort Orange, exclusively catered to the Mahican and Mohawk trade. The Dutch desired furs, and paid for them with iron tools, kettles, textiles, alcohol, and firearms all strongly desired by the native groups, and competition over trade soon followed the first contacts. The Delaware quickly exhausted their local fur resources, and were denied access to interior sources by the powerful Susquehannock to the south and the Five Nations and Mahican to the north.

These inland groups repeatedly attacked their Delaware competitors during the early years of the trade, and Dutch refusal to trade muskets to the Delaware put them at a serious disadvantage. They did manage to secure firearms from clandestine Dutch traders and from the Swedish trade forts established along the lower Delaware River during the 1640s.

Massive smallpox and measles epidemics, combined with warfare against the Dutch, the interior groups, and each other, killed over 90 percent of the Delaware. Exhausted by their losses, they eagerly allied themselves with the English following the fall of New Netherlands to a British fleet in 1664. The Delaware groups pursued a policy of peaceful trade with the English, and paid for their alliance both by providing small parties of warriors and guides for the wars between the English and the French, and by the gradual sale of their land holdings at low prices. The Delaware slowly withdrew into the upper reaches of their river valley domains as the English acquired the more desirable lowland tracts. Population losses, coupled with land sales, caused most of the Delaware groups to merge in their upriver retreats scattered throughout the traditional Delaware homeland during the last decades of the seventeenth century.

By 1700, most of the Delaware were concentrated in the Esopus country, the Minisinks, the Forks of the Delaware, the Falls of the Delaware, and in the Schuylkill and Brandywine River valleys. Smaller concentrations were located in the lower Berkshire Mountains, Rockaway, Long Island, the upper reaches of the Passaic and Raritan valleys, the interior of southern New Jersey, and the eastern branch of the Susquehanna River. Parties of Delaware moved among the Miami in the Ohio country, and others settled along the Allegheny River in western Pennsylvania.

Eighteenth century Delaware had undergone profound changes during the preceding century. They had fully adapted to an interior woodland settlement-subsistence-pattern, and had further been fully incorporated into the European economy. They lived in large permanent villages, and their men were absent throughout the winter, tending their traplines. Furs and military service provided the European trade goods that the Delaware had become dependent upon. Relocation onto heavily forested lands favored hunting and trapping and discouraged farming. Agriculture had furnished the greater part of the traditional diet, and the de-emphasis on cultivation increasingly forced them to depend upon white foodstuffs.

Sociopolitical power was fast moving from the matriclans into the hands of powerful chiefs. The steady centralization of Delaware society further saw the rising importance of confederacies.

Extensive land sales, including the notorious fraudulent "Walking Purchase" of 1737 that alienated most of the upper Delaware River valley, forced most Delaware to the Susquehanna and Allegheny valleys under the sponsorship of the Five Nations during the 1730s and 1740s. These groups swiftly affiliated with, and absorbed elements of, the Mahican, Nanticoke, Conoy, and other Algonquin refugees settling under Iroquoian auspices. These communities, located at Shamokin, Wyoming, Otsiningo, Chugnut, and Kancstio in Pennsylvania, were governed by representatives of the Five Nations, who gradually sold

103

these lands from under them, forcing them to move into the upper Ohio River valley by the 1750s.

Many Coastal Algonquins who remained in their homeland came under the influence of missionaries during the 1730s and 1740s. Mission communities at Stockbridge, Schagticoke, Shekomeko, Cranberry, Crosswicks, and the Forks of the Delaware, attracted large numbers of Delaware people. Most of these mission stations collapsed during the 1750s, but in the Moravian Brethren community at the Forks, the Delaware persisted. The Moravian settlements contained a high percentage of Delaware converts, and both the communities and their missionaries shared the gradual Delaware westward exile into the lower Great Lakes during the next half century.

Embittered and directly threatened by the consequences of a complete English victory, the Susquehanna Delaware sided with the French during the opening years of the Seven Years War (1755-1762). Both sides suffered heavy losses during the conflict, and most Delaware groups signed a separate peace with the English at Eaton, Pennsylvania in 1758. The bulk of Delaware groups relocated in the upper Ohio drainage after the war, and many fought against the English during the Pontiac War of 1762-1764.

An uneasy peace followed the end of the Pontiac War, and the Delaware prepared for future conflicts by establishing strong ties with their Miami, Shawnee, Chippewa, Ottawa, and Wyandot neighbors. The Delawaran groups largely attempted neutrality when the American Revolution against England broke out in 1775. By 1778, the Delaware were promised entry into the Union as a separate Indian State in return for their continued non-involvement in the conflict. The Delaware were strongly divided by the struggle, however, and the pro-English faction finally won support following the American massacre of the Delaware-Mahican mission community of Gnadenhutten in 1782.

Most Delaware withdrew deeper into Ohio after the end of the American Revolution. Other Delaware groups settled the upper White River valley of Indiana during the 1780s. They fought in the resistance against the American armies during the 1780s and 1790s, and large Delaware contingents were present during the defeats of the armies of Generals Harmar and Saint Clair in the Indiana country. The defeat of the Native Coalition at Fallen Timbers in 1794 finally forced them to abandon the Ohio, and most Delaware withdrew into Indiana.

The English continued to support them and their allies against the Americans during the next decades, and many Delaware followed Tecumseh and his brother, the Shawnee Prophet, during the first decade of the eighteenth century. Defeat during the War of 1812 caused many Delaware to migrate to Ontario, Canada, where their descendants continue to reside at Munceytown, Newfairfield, and Grand River.

Those who remained in Connecticut, New York, and New Jersey, joined the Oneida and Seneca of upstate New York by 1810. Most of these groups followed the Oneida west to their reservation near Green Bay, Wisconsin between 1821 and 1825. Others assimilated into the Seneca, and either remained on the Allegany reservation in New York or joined the Seneca reservation in Oklahoma. Delaware descendants who joined the Oneida live today on the Stockbridge-Munsee reservation in Wisconsin.

The main body of the Delaware gradually moved from the Indiana country to southern Missouri in 1815. Continual pressure for their lands forced them to settle on a reservation in eastern Kansas in 1829. The reservation was liquidated by 1854, and the bulk of the Delaware Nation settled among the Cherokee and Creek in northeastern Oklahoma, where their descendants live today.

The long century of westward exile worked profound changes upon Delaware society. Repeated removals and continual military defeat by white armies and hostile native groups impoverished the Delaware. The end of the fur trade and their use as allies for the contending European forces forced them to depend upon federal annuity payments for their lands. Prophets rose among them, and the rise of the Big House religion allowed the Delaware to continue their traditional cultural life while making drastic adjustments to changing economic conditions.

The Tribe gradually turned to farming, ranching, and wage labor. The clans lost their importance, and the Delaware languages began to disappear. Participation in the white economy devalued women, and the shift to patrilineal-neolocal kinship organization was virtually completed by the end of the nineteenth century. Most Delaware were sent to white schools, at least nominally adopted white religion, wore white clothing, and spoke English. The last Big House ceremonies were "brought in" during the 1920s.

Modern Delaware largely assimilated into white culture, with only a few very old people speaking the language or following old ways.

Most Delaware in the United States and Canada still live on reservations. The Oklahoma Delaware received twelve million dollars from the Indian Lands Claims Commission for lands taken from them during their western exile. The economic success of the Stockbridge-Munsee and the relative success of the Ontario Delaware clearly demonstrated that the Delaware showed every sign of continuing their four-century old tradition of cultural persistence in the face of the most damaging attempts to eradicate them as a cultural entity.

Today, most of the Delaware still reside in a number of widely scattered communities in Ontario and Oklahoma. A group of Munsis live in the Stockbridge-Munsee area of Wisconsin, and a small group of Chippewa live in Kansas; however, most Munsi live in Ontario, where they share the Six Nations or Grand River reserve under sponsorship of the Cayuga. Unami Delaware are living in eastern Oklahoma. Delaware in western Oklahoma, who moved from Missouri into Texas and lived with the Caddo until 1859, are the only federally recognized Delaware community in the United States. In a recent count, enrollment included some 1,000 defined as one-quarter or more Delaware. A recent entire Delaware tribal roll, which recognizes descendancy, not blood quantum, included about 10,000.

In the twentieth century, several cultural features ended. Munsi and Unami languages were almost extinct, men no longer wore earloops, and women gave up puberty observances. Most became Christian, and some became active in the Peyote Religion.

Communities still host powwows, however, and ceremonial costumes in Woodland style are still worn for the events. Naming ceremonies continue to be held, but lack the ancient supernatural sanction of a personal vision to enhance seniority of the name giver. A few members of the tribe still organize and study the Delaware culture and teach others the language.

Although many Delaware have formerly been unskilled laborers, an increasing number have become profesionals. Those who live near urban centers are better employed and paid more than those in rural areas. Cattle and oil industries have employed many Delaware workers. A tribal or band Business Council governs each community, and in Oklahoma, tribal income has been generated from bingo and tobacco product sales.

Self-pride has been strengthened by events held by many communities who have come together for the purpose of reestablishing cultural, political, and social traditions. In 1987, a group of Delaware leaders gathered in New York to rebury the bones of an ancestor found during the renovation of Ellis Island. Civic leaders have held academic and social gatherings of the Delaware to foster contacts among all groups.

DOCKSTADER, FREDERICK J.

Frederick J. Dockstader (Oneida-Navajo, February 3, 1919 - ?), a distinguished anthropologist, author, and expert on Indian arts, was born at Los Angeles, California, and spent much of his early life on the Navajo and Hopi reservations in Arizona. After an early teaching career, Dockstader became a staff ethnologist at the Cranbrook Institute of Sciences (1950), and later became the curator of anthropology at Dartmouth College (1952). He joined the staff of the Museum of the American Indian, Heye Foundation, in New York City as assistant director (1955) and became director in 1960.

Dockstader, a practicing silversmith, was named the commissioner of the Indian Arts and Crafts Board of the United States Department of the Interior in 1955. His publications include Great North American Indians (1977), Indian Art in America (1961), Indian Art in Middle America (1964), Indian Art in South America (1967), and Pre-Columbian Art and Later Indian Tribal Arts (1968).

ERIE

Now extinct, the Erie were a populous, sedentary Iroquoian tribe. In the 17th century, their territory extended south from Lake Erie to the Ohio River, east to the lands of the Conestoga along the Allegheny River, and the Seneca along the Genesee River, and north to those of the Neutral of Lake Erie.

Historically, little is known of the Erie and their political and social organization, but it was similar to that of the Huron. The Jesuits gave a few glimpses of their lives, while describing their last wars with the Iroquois Confederation. The Erie had many towns and villages, and were organized into several divisions; they cultivated the soil, and spoke a language resembling that of the Huron.

It is not known which four of the five Huron dialects, usually called "Wendat" (Wyandot) by them selves, was actually spoken. From the same sources comes a rough estimate of the population of the Erie at the period of final war. At the taking of the Erie town of Rique in 1654, it is claimed that the defenders numbered between 3,000 and

4,000. But since it is not likely that all warriors of the tribe were present, 14,500 would probably be a conservative estimate of the population of the Erie at the time.

The years 1655-56 were the last for the Erie. Thirty ambassadors of the Cat Nation were sent to Sonontouan, the Seneca capital, to renew the existing peace. Through an accident, one of the men of the Cat Nation killed a Seneca. The incensed Seneca massacred all except five of the ambassadors, which led to the final war between the Erie and the confederated tribes of the Iroquois, especially the Seneca, Cayuga, Oneida, and Onondaga.

The Erie were brave and warlike, employing only bows and poisoned arrows. Following the rupture of relations between the Erie and the Iroquois in 1653, the Erie burned a Seneca town, pursued an Iroquois war party returning from the Great Lakes, and slaughtered 80 men, while Erie scouts had come to the very gates of one of the Iroquois palisaded towns and captured Annenraes (Annencraos), "one of the greatest captains." All this, of course, roused the Iroquois, who raised 1,800 men to punish the Erie.

After stubborn resistance, the Erie were overrun and the Onondaga "entered the fort and so many women and children were killed that blood was knee-deep in certain places." This was at the town of Rique, which was defended by between 3,000 to 4,000 Indians, and was assailed by the 1,800 Iroquois. This devastating war lasted until about the close of 1656, when Erie power was broken and its members were destroyed, dispersed, or captured. Six hundred surrendered at one time and were led to the Iroquois country to be adopted as one of the constituent people of the Iroquois tribes. The defeat at Rique forced the Iroquois to remain in enemy territory for two months, caring for the wounded and burying the dead.

FIVE NATIONS IROQUOIS

(See IROQUOIS and IROQUIAN FAMILY) When Europeans first encountered Indians in what is now upstate New York, they met the Five Nations Iroquois. This confederacy was to play an important role in the struggles among Europeans and Americans for control of the northeastern woodlands.

The Iroquois got their name from their Algonquin Indian enemies; Iroquois is thought to mean "real adders." The five tribes called themselves the *Ongwanonhsioni,* meaning "longhouse builders," or *Hodi-*

nonhsioni, "people of the longhouse," in reference to their confederacy. The five tribes of the confederacy were the Seneca, Cayuga, Onondaga, Oneida, and Mohawk. These names were applied to the tribes by themselves, as well as by other Indians, the French, the Dutch, the English, and the Americans over several hundred years. Each tribe had a name for itself, meaning the "people of" a particular town or place. The Seneca were Onondewagano, the Cayuga were Gayokwehono, the Onondaga were Onontaga, the Oneida were Oneyotdehaga, and the Mohawk were Kanyengehaga. The Iroquois are believed to have descended from hunters and gatherers who lived for thousands of years in upstate New York. The actual date of the formation of the League of the Iroquois is not known. Most estimates fall between AD 1400 and 1600. The Iroquois generally stated that the league was formed before European contact. In Iroquois oral tradition, two men, Deganawida and Hiawatha (not Longfellow's Hiawatha), founded the league.

At the time of European contact, the Seneca, Cayuga, Onondaga, Oneida, and Mohawk, in that order, lived from west to east in the region between the Genesee River and Schoharie Creek.Their hunters, traders, and warriors ranged from the Mississippi River to New England.

The Five Nations spoke Northern Iroquoian languages. Each tribe's speech was sufficiently distinct to call it a separate language, but there was also enough mutual intelligibility between them that they could be called dialects of a single language. The Iroquois made pictographs, but did not develop a written alphabet.

The Iroquois believed that the world had many supernatural spirits whose goodwill was needed for a bountiful life. Therefore, everyday activities were closely interwoven with religious beliefs. The core belief for the Iroquoian-speaking confederacy was an elaborate funeral rite known as the Condolence. Through time, this rite became the vehicle for political meetings, and it brought together leaders from various Iroquois tribes and villages. Although some of the leaders were identified as peace chiefs or sachems, the real political power of the confederacy resided with the war chiefs.

The group held seasonal festivals and ceremonies to give thanks to their spiritual leaders. The Iroquois year began in the spring, and a festival was held to express gratitude to "The Creator" and "The Maple" for the sweet syrup made from sap. Spawning fish and roosting pigeons were caught.   During this season, clearings were made in the forests to replace old fields and also to build new palisaded villages.

Villages had to be moved every ten to twenty years, as firewood supplies and fields became exhausted.   By May, "The Three Sisters" of maize, beans, and squash were planted, and a festival was held to give thanks for these foods, their main sustenance.   Elm bark for long-houses, canoes, and containers, was then gathered.   Wild strawberries appeared in the woods, and a festival was held in thanks for these first fruits.   In summer, most men departed to trade or go into battle.   Women gathered wild plants for food and medicine, worked in the fields, and harvested and stored the crops.   Festivals were held to honor "The Corn Mother" and to celebrate the harvest.

In the fall, deer were hunted, nuts were gathered, and fish were caught in preparation for winter.   Councils were held during this time, as snow confined them to their villages for the most part.   Winter was a time for socializing, storytelling, and the manufacture and repair of tools and clothing.   Raw products, including stone, clay, plant fibers, and animal products were made into knives, axes, drills, bows, arrows, clubs, jars, bowls, mortars, mats, baskets, fishhooks, needles, snow-shoes, lacrosse sticks, dolls, and much more. The New Year came after winter solstice, and Midwinter, another important festival, was held to strengthen "The Creator" after his winter struggle with his evil twin.

Iroquois children were free of responsibilities, and all played to-gether until the age of eight or nine, when the boys and girls were separated and began to acquire adult skills through observation and mimicry.   After marriage, the husband usually went to live in his wife's longhouse.   Their children belonged to the mother's clan.   Each longhouse held several families, which belonged to a single matriclan, tracing descent through the women.

Villages contained at least three of twelve different clans. The clans had ceremonial duties towards each other in various games and rituals.   The clans were the basis of political organization at all levels.   Clan chiefs and other elders determined village policy.   The clan matrons selected the fifty hereditary sachems representing the tribes at the confederacy's councils, Other leaders, such as war chiefs, were selected on the basis of merit.

Contact with white culture brought many changes.   The Iroquois adopted western technology, but their rich cultural traditions survived, as shown in their art forms, including pottery, basketry, bead and por-

110

cupine quill decoration, silversmithing, and carving. They are best known for false facemasks used at healing ceremonies.

After European contact, the Iroquois fell into competition with surrounding Indian groups for hunting territory in order to obtain furs for trading for French, Dutch and, later, English goods, such as cloth, beads, guns, metal axes, knives, and kettles. Between 1638 and 1675, the Iroquois defeated the Wenro, Huron, Petun, Neutral, Erie, and Susquehannock confederacies. Many of the defeated Indians moved among the victorious Iroquois.

Throughout most of the seventeenth and eighteenth centuries, the Iroquois maintained their position between the British and the French by a combination of warfare and skillful diplomacy. French Jesuits began missionary activities among the Iroquois after 1653. Their missions were soon closed, but were resumed in 1668. Relations with the French became strained and the missions were abandoned in the early 1680s. The Iroquois raided the French, who attacked the Seneca in 1687, the Mohawk in 1693, and the Onondaga and Oneida in 1696.

Smallpox and warfare reduced the Iroquois population during the seventeenth century, though some of their loss was made up by the adoption of other Indians. In 1660, the Iroquois tribes were believed to have had less than 2,200 warriors.

Starting in the latter part of the seventeenth century, a number of Iroquois left their traditional homeland. During the 1660s, some Cayuga settled along the Saint Lawrence River in Canada, and by the mid-eighteenth century, they had established large settlements at Saint Regis and Caughnawaga.

Cayugas, Onondagas, and Oneidas also moved to the Saint Lawrence area and, in the 1750s, a number were living at Oswegatchie (now Ogdensburg, New York).

The Five Nations Iroquois added the Tuscarora to their confederacy in the 1700s, and the name was changed to the Six Nations Confederacy. In 1753, the Cayuga adopted the Tutelo and Saponi, who established a village south of Cayuga Lake. After the British defeated the French at Montreal in 1760, the Iroquois could no longer control the balance of power. When the American Revolution broke out, the Iroquois attempted to remain neutral. Eventually most of them were drawn in on the side of the British, though some Oneida sided with the Americans. In 1779, an American army destroyed the homeland of the Iroquois, who fled to western New York and Canada.

111

The American Revolution destroyed the power of the league. The Americans made treaties with the Iroquois, forcing them to sell their remaining lands in New York, except for a few reservations. Many Iroquois moved to reserves in Canada and some went west. Two councils were formed, one in Canada, and one in the United States. After the last treaty was signed in 1842, land continued to be sold or leased to whites.

The change to reservation life was a difficult one. Drinking and fighting became serious problems. However, the teachings of Handsome Lake, a Seneca, reconciled traditional religious beliefs with white material culture and helped the Iroquois adapt to their new lives. Constitutional governments replaced the hereditary chiefs on the Allegany and Cattaraugus reservations in 1848, and in 1924, the Canadians forced an elected council on the Grand River Reserve. By the late 1980s, the Iroquois population on reservations in Canada and in the United States was conservatively estimated at about 30,000 people.

Today the Iroquois live both on and off the reservations. Except for garden plots, farming in general has decreased in importance, as individuals seek wage labor. For example, Mohawks from the Saint Regis and Caughnanwaga Reserves have achieved prominence as high steelworkers. On reservations, many old practices and beliefs are maintained by traditional members of the community, though most Iroquois are Christians. Ceremonies for traditional foods, healing rituals, and the Midwinter Festival are still held. The League of the Iroquois continues in existence, and clan mothers wield their influence in selecting chiefs. The Iroquois genius for survival has kept their cultural heritage alive through the present.

The underlying myth of the present-day Six Nations Confederacy was the journey of a cultural hero named Deganawidah, who brought forth a plan of peace and harmony to the five warring tribes. From this reformation came a confederacy calling for establishment of a hereditary council of fifty sachems from the five tribes, appointed by clan matrons, and a ceremonial and political protocol that is rooted in kinship structure and traditional world view of the people.

The Code of Handsome Lake, by which the hereditary councils still function, is a formalized belief system set forth in 1799 by Seneca sachem, Handsome Lake, after he had a series of visions that called upon the Iroquois to return to their former ways. The code provides an ideological and political link to all the reservation communities.

Although today there is less than a full complement of sachems in the Canadian and New York reservation confederacies, chiefs and titles are often "borrowed." Neither confederacy is officially recognized by its respective state, provincial or federal government, but both have considerable political influence. The New York confederacy seeks to extend authority over all Iroquois communities and replace remaining elective systems with hereditary councils.

The New York confederacy today is strengthened and sustained by its nativistic beliefs, assertions and expressions of sovereignty, and a small corp of leaders who are both skilled politicians and information managers. Activities are focused onstate and federal governments. Recently, the confederation intervened in the Seneca lease issue and land claims, though not without opposition from other Iroquois. In 1989, after years of negotiations and demands, the State of New York returned 12 wampum belts to the Onondaga, who now hold them in their traditional role as wampum keepers of the confederacy.

New legislative efforts have resulted in introduction of an Indian burial protection bills, and passage of a measure exempting Indians from the oath of allegiance to New York. Over the last several years, the confederacy has sought to control land claims and to prevent gambling casinos from operating on reservations.

HACKENSACK

The Hackensack consisted of a number of Munsee Delaware-speaking groups which inhabited the coastal lowlands of northeastern New Jersey to the east of the Watchung Hills from the Hackensack-Passaic River drainage south to the lower reaches of the Raritan River. The Hackensack, who were no longer identifiable as a tribe by the mid-1700s, are today known almost exclusively through the surviving documentation of the successive Dutch (1609-1664), English (1664-1782), and American (1782- present) regimes. Archaeology has failed to establish a connection between any known site and a historically known Hackensack settlement.

The first documentary record of aboriginal occupation in Hackensack territory occurred in a 1616 Dutch reference to a group located along the west bank of the Hudson River opposite Manhattan Island. Identified as the Machkentiwomi, this group may have had people "dwelling over against the Manhattans," who were decimated

113

by epidemic disease and dispersed by the Wappinger sometime before 1628.

A number of "aboriginal proprietors" later identified as Hackensack sachems, or leaders, participated in a series of land sales to the authorities of the Dutch colony of New Netherland in 1630.

Among the native signers were a number of "Virginians." The terms "Virginian" and "Southern Indian" referred to native people from groups that inhabited lands to the south of the Delaware River and the southern boundary of New Netherland. The presence of Virginians, along with the dispersion of the earlier native population of the Hackensack Valley, clearly point out the enormous changes that were occurring among native groups during the opening years of European intrusion. This also indicates that the group later known as the Hackensack was made up of a number of different peoples from several regions.

The 1630 land sales conveyed the Bayonne Peninsula and Staten Island to the Dutch. The Dutch soon established trading posts and plantations on these lands, which were located close to the centers of Hackensack settlement. The major Hackensack communities of the period were Ahasimus, on the Bayonne Peninsula, Hespatingh, in the city of the same name, and the Hackensack Castle, situated in the highlands to the northwest of Hackensack.

The Dutch settlements became a source of friction between the Hackensack and the Dutch soon after their establishment in the early 1630s. Sharp trade deals, defective trade goods, and liquor defrauded many of the Indians. The fatal shooting of a Dutchman by a "Hackingsack" man at Pavonia, now New Jersey City, in 1642, marked the first time the Hackensack were mentioned by name in the Dutch records. This and other incidents led the Dutch to consider retaliation against the lower Hudson River Native groups. The Dutch got their opportunity when a large Mahican war party attacked the Wiechquaeskeck of the east bank of the lower Hudson River during February 1643. The Wiechquaeskeck claimed and received refuge from the Mahican under the walls of Fort Amsterdam in lower Manhattan and at Pavonia across the river in Hackensack territory. Both camps were simultaneously subjected to Dutch surprise attacks during the night of February 25-26, 1643. The lower Hudson River groups were outraged by this massacre. Many Hackensack reportedly perished, along with some 120 Wiechquaeskeck people at Pavonia. The lower Hudson

River groups immediately burned the outlying Dutch settlements throughout the region and drove their inhabitants to the shelter of Fort Amsterdam.

The conflict was ruinous for both sides, dependent as they were upon each other. New Netherland was a trading colony, and the native people of the area provided the furs that were the raw material of the commerce. The Dutch, on their part, supplied the metal tools, cloth, muskets, and other trade goods that had become an indispensable part of aboriginal life. The Hackensack sachem, Oratam, accordingly agitated for peace, and succeeded in arranging a truce with the Dutch on April 22, 1643 on behalf of "the savages living at Ackinkes hacky...and...Tappaen, Rechgawawanc, Kichtawanc, and Sinsinck."

Oratam continued to play a major role in negotiations between the remaining native rebels and the Dutch. Two years later, on August 30, 1645, Oratam signed the general peace treaty that ended the conflict, known thereafter as "The Governor Kieft War," after the Director of the Colony of New Netherland. The Wiechquaeskeck and their allies did not participate in this treaty. Finally, following pressure from the powerful Susquehannock group, and under Hackensack sponsor, the last remaining hostile groups pledged to keep the peace with the Dutch on July 19, 1649.

The Hackensack were again split into pro and antiwar factions during the brief "Peach War" of 1655-1656. A report dated November 10, 1655 noted that the Hackensack and Tappan groups did the most damage to the Dutch; Oratam's speaker, Pennekeck, served as a key intermediary between the warring groups, and assisted in ransoming a large number of white captives during the conflict.

These wars resulted in extensive changes in native life. Large numbers of native people living near the center of the Dutch settlement immigrated to more hospitable regions. The Hackensack accepted a substantial number of Western Long Island, Staten Island, and Wiechquaeskeck immigrants. The nature of the Hackensack settlement also changed at this time. The natives of the region found that their large fortified towns were easy targets for Dutch armies.

Population losses caused by wars and epidemics made such large settlements even more vulnerable. The Hackensack and their neighbors accordingly chose to settle in small hamlets scattered throughout their territories. These were more difficult to surprise, easier to escape from, and gave the impression of a sizable native presence in their territories.

Oratam and the Hackensack served as intermediaries between the hostile Esopus groups of the mid-Hudson valley and the Dutch during the "Esopus Wars" of 1659-1664. Favoring the Esopus pro-peace faction, Oratam secured asylum for their sachems, ransomed white captives, and gave the Dutch information of Esopus activities. Other Hackensack sided with the hostile Esopus, and supported their operations. Dutch military successes and Hackensack diplomacy brought the contending parties to the conference table, and a treaty was signed by the Esopus and the Dutch on May 15, 1664.

The Hackensack swiftly allied with the English following the capture of New Netherland by the forces of the Duke of York on September 6, 1664. The English quickly embarked on a series of land purchases that increasingly crowded the Hackensack out of their traditional territories along the lower reaches of the Hackensack and Passaic rivers. Relations with the English remained peaceable, however, and the Hackensack submitted to English jurisdiction.

The Hackensack responded to English territorial demands by selling small parcels and demanding the right to remain in their small settlements. Relentless English pressure gradually drove them northward to the headwaters of the northeastern New Jersey River drainage by the turn of the eighteenth century. The records indicate that the Hackensack increasingly became involved with the Tappan, their northern neighbors. Sachems like Mindawassa and Jan Claes came to represent both groups, and the Hackensack and Tappan effectively merged by 1700.

The Hackensack and Tappan were last mentioned by name on April 19, 1693. The people that made up these groups did not, however, disappear along with their name. They remained in small communities scattered throughout the upland portions of the Passaic watershed during the first half of the eighteenth century. Their leaders, Memshe, Memerescum, Taphow and others, signed documents as sachems, "of all the nations on Romopuck, Sadie, Pasqueek, Narashunk, Hackensack rivers and Tappan."

The northern New Jersey Indians became increasingly connected with their Minisink neighbors to the west along the upper Delaware River Valley. Most of them either joined the Minisink or moved further south to settlements at the "Forks of the Delaware" at Easton,

Pennsylvania. Both groups finally sided against the English during their last war with the French over control of North America, known as the Seven Years', or French and Indian War (1755-1762).

Not all of the native people of the region chose to oppose English dominion, however, and most of the remaining groups still in New Jersey signed a treaty with the English at Crosswicks on January 8-9, 1756. A number of otherwise unidentified "Indians in the County of Bergen," the heart of traditional Hackensack territory, claimed English protection under the provisions of the Crosswicks Treaty on March 16, 1756. They and other natives living north of the Raritan River were confined to an area between the Hudson River and the western limits of the Passaic and Raritan valleys for the duration of the conflict. The "Bergen County Indians" and their neighbors were unable to wait the conflict out, however.

On October 23, 1758, the Minisink sold their last claims to land in northern New Jersey from the Raritan River north to the New York-New Jersey line. They and their allies then moved into the western Susquehanna and Allegheny River valleys of Pennsylvaniaby June 15, 1759. It was reported that "the Indians in the northern parts of the Province (of New Jersey) have entirely exited it and are going to Sesquehannah." The descendants of the Hackensack were among those westward immigrants, and today they reside in the surviving Munsee communities in Wisconsin, Oklahoma, and Ontario, Canada.

HALF KING

Half King (Huron, late 18th Century), was a Wyandotte chief in the area of Sandusky, Ohio, who joined the British during the War of Independence to fight against American encroachment on Indian territory west of the Allegheny Mountains. During the Revolution he commanded Ottawa, Chippewa, Shawnee, and other tribes of warriors in addition to his Huron followers. He won particular recognition for the firm discipline he enforced on this unusual composite force. To assure the good behavior of his warriors, Half King took special pains to prevent their access to alcohol. The result was that Half King's Indian army behaved well in combat and avoided the temptation to spill white blood indiscriminately.

The primary beneficiaries of Half King's efforts were the Moravians of Lichtenau, an evangelical Protestant sect that settled in Ohio. At times during 1777 as many as 200 warriors camped immediately out-

117

side of Lichtenau, and since it was largely anti-settler sentiment that motivated many of the Indians to fight on the British side, the Moravians could easily have been massacred. Half King kept the mixed assemblage of warriors from making the Moravians the victims of their wrath.

Nevertheless, Half King did insist upon the removal of Christianized Indians from the Sandusky area. This was done not so much out of hostility to Christianity as from concern that such Indians were not safe among their unconverted brethren. He continued to protect the Moravians and their converts after the Revolution, even when the Protestants abandoned his domain and went to Detroit.

On March 6, 1782, two Indian families were killed by settlers' militia. The northern Ohio area tribes, even those supporting the colonies, arose to seek revenge. On June 4, about two miles from his village, Half King met the militia under Colonel William Crawford. With the aid of Butler's Rangers (British reinforcements), and warriors sent from the Delaware and Shawnee tribes, Half King overwhelmed the colonial militia and caught and executed Crawford. After the Revolution, Half King signed the Treaty of Fort McIntosh on January 2, 1785.

HANDSOME LAKE

Handsome Lake (Seneca, 1735 - August 10, 1815), also known as Ganiod'yo, was a chief and a religious elder who developed an ethical code which became the basis of a new religion for the Iroquois people, known as the Handsome Lake religion, or the Longhouse religion.

Handsome Lake, was born at Ganawaugus, New York, at the end of the era of power and prosperity for the Seneca nation. During his youth and early manhood, he watched his society and his culture disintegrate while he fought as a warrior against the British in Pontiac's Conspiracy, then against the Cherokee and Choctaw, and during the Revolution against the Americans. At the council with the British at Oswego, New York, in the early summer of 1777, Handsome Lake supported the position of his brother, Cornplanter, that the Iroquois should remain neutral in what was a civil war among white people. However, the warriors voted to go to war and Handsome Lake fought with his people.

He took an active part in the drawn-out negotiations between the Iroquois and the Americans following the war. After several disastrous treaties, the Seneca sold all their lands, with the exception of a few reservations, at the Treaty of Big Tree in 1797.

After a period of prolonged whiskey drinking, Handsome Lake became seriously ill in 1799 and was near death. He recovered and declared that he had been visited by three spirits, which had revealed to him the will of the Creator. More visions followed, and from 1800 Handsome Lake became an itinerant preacher of the religion that he called Gaiwiio ("good message").

His message was predominated by three apocalyptic themes: the imminence of world destruction, the definition of sin, and the prescription for salvation following the practices he recommended). He condemned the drinking of whiskey and the practice of witchcraft and magic, and he urged his people to confess their sins and abandon their evil ways. His message was a combination of traditional Iroquois beliefs and Christian ethics. It provided the Iroquois with a faith that revitalized their civilization at a time when it was threatened with extinction.

In 1801 Handsome Lake accused Red Jacket of witchcraft. The confrontation was precipitated by an argument over land. Red Jacket favored selling to the State of New York a strip of land along the Niagara River, which was a favorite fishing place of the Seneca. Handsome Lake was a leader of the opposition, and his "slanders" against Red Jacket for a time cost him his position of sachem.

Beginning in the fall of 1801 and increasingly in the years thereafter, Handsome Lake emphasized a social message: temperance in daily life, peace, land retention, domestic morality, and acculturation. In the winter of 1801-02, he led a delegation of Seneca to Washington and met with President Thomas Jefferson. Although his political power waned in later years, Handsome Lake always remained a triumphantly successful evangelist. He died on a visit to Onondaga, New York, and was buried there in the center of the council house.

HAVERSTRAW

The Haverstraw tribe was also known as the Remahenonck and Rechgawawanck. They were a small group speaking Munsee-Delaware, that lived on a stretch of shoreline along the western banks of the Haverstraw Bay reach of the Hudson River, in southeastern New York. Closely hemmed in by the steep walls of the northernmost escarpment of the Palisades Highlands, the Haverstraw settlements were bounded on the south by the territories of the Tappan group, and by the slopes of the Hudson Highlands to the west and north. The village of Haverstraw today occupies the central portion of the traditional Haverstraw country.

The Haverstraw were named after a prominent sachem, or peace leader, as were many Delaware groups. A manuscript dated March 6, 1660 documented the fact that their chief was named "Rumanchenanck, alias Haverstroo." This practice has long contributed to the misidentification of the Rechgawawanck as the Manhattan Indians of central Manhattan Island and the adjacent southwest Bronx. The Reverend Robert Bolton, a prominent early nineteenth century student of local native ethno-history in Westchester County, New York, first made this connection.

He noted that a sachem named Rechgewac signed over a number of tracts of land in Manhattan and the Bronx to Dutch purchasers. He further noted that several place names on Manhattan, most notably Rechewas Point and Rechewanes, seemed to suggest a relationship with Rechgewac. It only took a small leap to name the otherwise un-located Rechgawawanck of the colonial literature after this sachem.

The problem with this interpretation is the fact that many place names based upon the Delaware words *lekau,* "sand" and *lechauwaak,* "fork, branch" occur widely throughout this region by virtue of the extensive presence of sand and complex river systems. Further, the Rechgawawanck were repeatedly mentioned in company with the Tappan and Hackensack, neighbors of the Haverstraw.

The Hudson River was a formidable boundary, and the other ethno-historic data does not support extensive connections between the downriver groups fronting its shorelines. Finally, the only known Rechgawawanck sachem was listed as Sesekemu, which was another spelling for Sessikout, an influential Haverstraw paramount sachem.

The Haverstraw first appeared in Dutch documentation of their New Netherland colony in 1642, when some chiefs from "Ackinghsack and Rechawanck" reported that the murderer of a Dutchman in the Hackensack area had fled into the interior. A number of them were later victims of a Dutch massacre of fugitives from the Mahican raid on Manhattan and at Pavonia, now Jersey City, New Jersey, on the night of February 25-26, 1643. They were among the groups represented by the Hackensack sachem, Oratam, in subsequent peace negotiations with the Dutch. Oratam concluded the peace on April 22,

120

1643 on behalf of his own people and for "the savages of Tappaen, Rechgawawanc, Kichtawanc, and Sintsinck."

The latter two groups lived along the eastern banks of the Tappan Zee and Haverstraw Bay reaches of the Hudson River, opposite the Tappan and Haverstraw groups. The sachems Sesekemu (Sessikout) and Willem of "Tappaens and Rechgawawanch" signed the final peace treaty of August 30, 1645 that ended the Governor Kieft War (1640-1645) on behalf of their people. These friendly relations were reaffirmed on July 19, 1649 by the group, then identified as the Remahenonck.

The Haverstraw were first mentioned by that name on the 1656 Adriaen van der Donck map of New Netherland. Documents related to the events of the Esopus Wars (1659-1664) indicated close relations between Haverstraw neighbors. On July 10, 1657, a Haverstraw chief named Keghtackcean sold out his land holdings to the Dutch. He then moved north among the Esopus of the lower Wallkill River Valley. On March 15, 1664, it was revealed that Sessikout was the brother of an Esopus sachem. An earlier document, dated March 6, 1660, noted that Corruspin, often mistaken for the chief sachem of the Haverstraw, was actually the brother of Sessikout. Both citations clearly demonstrate the principle of matrilineal descent commonly found among native peoples of the mid-Atlantic Coast. This kinship held that leadership was inherited not by a person's son, but by brothers and sisters, and then by sisters' children.

Many Haverstraw chose to support the Esopus and their allies in the struggle against the Dutch. Confused by Haverstraw intentions, and lacking direct evidence of their participation in the war, the Dutch attempted to obtain confirmation of war or peace from their sachems on April 21, 1664. The Dutch were put off at that time, but "Ses-Segh-Hout, chief of the Rewechnongh or Haverstraw" placed his mark upon the May 16, 1664 treaty that ended the Esopus War.

The English takeover of New Netherlands on September 6, 1664 did not immediately affect the Haverstraw. Corruspin signed the April 13, 1671 deed to lands along the Palisades in Hackensack territory as "Croppun, sachima of Haverstroo." This land conveyance did not, however, concern any part of the traditional Haverstraw homeland. It did serve to emphasize the connections between the Haverstraw and the Hackensack.

English interest finally focused directly upon the Haverstraw territory during the following decade, and two land cessions, dated July 13, 1683 and September 10, 1684, completely sold off their homeland. A number of Haverstraw families moved north to the Esopus, though most moved among their Tappan- Hackensack neighbors in the upper Ramapo and Pequannock River drainages in northern New Jersey.

Known during the following century as part of the River Indians, descendants of the Haverstraw may today reside on two reservations in Ontario, Canada; on the Stockbridge-Munsee Indian Reservation in Wisconsin; and on the former Cherokee, Wichita, and Caddo Reservations in Oklahoma.

HENDRICK

Hendrick (Mohawk, 1700 - September 8, 1755), also known as Tee Yee Neen Ho Ga Row (Christianized Hendrick), was an influential chief and one of the "Four Indian Kings."

HIACOOMES

Hiacoomes (Wampanoag, 1610 - 1690), was allegedly the first Indian in North America to be converted to Christianity and the first to be ordained a Christian clergyman. Information about his life is largely unsubstantiated, but apparently he lived on Martha's Vineyard, Massachusetts, near Thomas Mayhew, Junior, who settled there in 1642. Hiacoomes was Mayhew's first convert in 1643. He began preaching in 1646, and was ordained in August, 1670. For some years before his death, he was unable to preach.

HIAWATHA

Hiawatha (Mohawk or Onondaga, 1525 - 1590), also known as Teharonhiawagon, was an apostle of peace and brotherhood, who according to tradition, devoted his life to ending the bloodshed among the Mohawk, Oneida, Cayuga, Seneca, and Onondaga, and to uniting these five tribes into the League of the Iroquois (the Confederation of Five Nations).

Possessing exceptional oratorical powers, Hiawatha was a medicine man and magician among the Onondaga, and like them, he probably practiced cannibalism. Distressed at the constant warfare and never-ending feuds among the five tribes, though, Hiawatha emerged as a reform leader, advocating the unification of the tribes and the cessation of blood revenge. His bitter opponent, the Onondaga chief Wathatotarho, did all he could to prevent the reformers from achieving their objectives, including having one of Hiawatha's daughters murdered. Unable to overcome Wathatotarho's opposition, Hiawatha left the Onondaga to preach his message of peace and brotherhood to the Mohawk, Oneida, and Cayuga, all of whom agreed to unite and abandon bloodshed among fellow Iroquois on the condition that Wathatotarho and the Onondaga did likewise.

Apparently defeated in his reform efforts once again, Hiawatha was about to abandon hope when he fell under the influence of a mystical peacemaker and prophet named Dekanawida. He converted Hiawatha from cannibalism and convinced him that the obstinate and evil Wathatotarho could be won over to what would later be called The Great Peace. Together, Hiawatha and Dekanawida persuaded the Onondaga chief to join the League. During the negotiations Wathatotarho won certain concessions, but the League of the Iroquois became a reality, cannibalism was outlawed except in times of war, and blood revenge was ended among the five tribes.

Hiawatha now turned missionary, carrying Dekanawida's confederation ideas and moral principles to other tribes. He roamed far from his home territory, traveling as far away as Lake Superior and the Mississippi River. Although he had some success in winning converts to the Great Peace, no other tribes joined the confederation until the white man had advanced so far that various tribes were forced to seek sanctuary on the lands of the Five Nations. The remnants of the conquered Tuscarora, for example, became the sixth nation in the league about the year 1715.

Meanwhile, the Iroquois were committed to warring against tribes who rejected their overtures of peace of brotherhood, with the ironic result being that the whites came to know the Confederation of Five Nations only as cruel and bloodthirsty warriors, the antithesis of the pacifist principles to which Hiawatha had devoted his life. The apostle and missionary himself probably spent his last days as an elder statesman among the Mohawk. The confederation he had helped to forge, however, lasted until the American Revolution, inspiring the colonists in their dream of creating a stable federal union.

In the second quarter of the 19th century, Henry R. Schoolcraft, an early United States ethnologist, collected some of the Iroquois legends and published them in such a way that Hiawatha became identified as the greatest of the Iroquoian gods, Teharonhiawagon ("The Master of Life"), which Schoolcraft apparently assumed was just another way of spelling Hiawatha. He went on to identify this same god with the chief deity of the Chippewa (Ojibwa) Indians, who lived farther west in the Great Lakes region. The ethnologist referred to the Chippewa deity Manabozho as Hiawatha in a series of Chippewa myths which he published. This error was compounded by Henry Wadsworth Longfellow. Fascinated by Schoolcraft's Chippewa legends, Longfellow based his famous poem, written in 1855, on them, and the name Hiawatha became identified with a fictionalized Chippewa god and hero.

HOPOCAN

Hopocan (Delaware, ? - 1794), also known as Chief Captain Pipe, known by his own people as Konieschguanokee, was a hereditary sachem and a tribal war chief who fought with the British during the American Revolution, but later became a signer of the first peace agreement on September 17, 1778. Hopocan fought with the French during the French and Indian War and participated in Pontiac's Conspiracy (1763-64) to throw the English from their outposts west of the Appalachians. In the attempt to overtake Fort Pitt, however, Hopocan was captured and never took arms against the British again.

Following the failure of Pontiac's Conspiracy, Hopocan moved to the upper Muskingum River in Ohio. He had been a prominent member of councils held at Turtle Village and at Fort Pitt, and he enjoyed a reputation for possessing wisdom and superb oratory. When the colonists declared their independence from the British, the Delaware chief accepted a position on the side of the crown fighting against the Americans and their Indian allies. Hopocan foresaw, however, what might happen to him and his tribe when the conflicting whites patched up their differences. Therefore, he made a point of informing the British commander at Detroit that the Delaware would not act cruelly.

His people had no interest in the struggle for independence and sought only to maintain their own wellbeing. Nevertheless, Hopocan did violate this pledge once during the Revolution. In retaliation for a party of whites killing a group of Indians, Hopocan had United States Colonel William Crawford tortured after Crawford was captured during a rout of his regiment in May 1782. Well before the war was over, though, Hopocan signed a treaty with the United States. On September 17, 1778, at Fort Pitt, the Delaware chief endorsed the first treaty between the new government and an Indian nation. Later, he signed additional treaties, including those at Fort McIntosh, Ohio, (January 21, 1785), and at Fort Harmar, Ohio (January 9, 1787). During the early 1780s Hopocan moved to what was called Captain Pipe's Village near the Upper Sandusky River in Ohio.

HURON

During the first half of the 17th Century, French soldiers, explorers, and missionaries observed and described a confederation of several tribes living in a small region of southern Ontario between Lake Simcoe and Georgian Bay, which they referred to as the Hurons. These people were sedentary farmers, living in semi-permanent stockaded towns, and spoke a language belonging to the Iroquois language family. They were similar in culture and language to the Five Nation Iroquois of New York State, with whom they probably shared a biological ancestry. They had even closer affinities with other Iroquoian peoples in the Great Lakes area: the Saint Lawrence Iroquois, the Neutrals of southwestern Ontario, and the Petun of the Blue Mountain region, just west of the Huron.

NAME: *Huron* is a French word that was applied to people in all the tribes of the Huron Confederacy. The word itself means a "a wild boar," and may refer to the hairstyle of Huron men at the time; it was also used more generally as a name for rough or rustic people. The name used by the Hurons themselves to refer to the whole confederacy was *Wendar.* This is often interpreted to mean "people living on an island," and could refer to the fact that the Huron territory in the 17th century was almost surrounded by water. It has also been translated as "people who speak a common language." This receives some support from the fact that the Hurons referred to neighboring Iroquoian groups, such as the Neutrals, as Attiwandaronk, "people who speak a slightly different language," and this was the same name by which these neighbors referred to the Hurons themselves.

HISTORY: Huron culture can be traced archaeologically to approximately AD 1200, at which time the Hurons can be recognized as occupying several "tribal" areas, each comprising a few villages, in a triangle bounded by Hamilton, Kingston, and Penetanguishene. These local groups appear to have been relatively independent. At approximately AD 1500, European trade goods were introduced to the Hurons from the Saint Lawrence Iroquois, who were in contact with Portuguese, Basque, and Breton people exploiting the Gulf of Saint Lawrence.

This led to competition among the Hurons for access to this trade, resulting in new patterns of intertribal alliances, warfare, and migrations. At approximately 1550, probably because of a depletion of furs in the southern regions as well as hostilities, there was a gradual movement away from Lake Ontario towards the upper Trent River Valley and "historic" Huronia. Following the intensification of hostilities between the Hurons and the New York Iroquois at the end of the 16th century, the Hurons all moved into Huronia, forming the Huron Confederacy.

Hurons were first met by the French at Quebec in the opening years of the 17th century, after which an alliance was forged between the French and the Hurons involving trade agreements, and commitments of military aid against their respective enemies. The most intensive contact between the Hurons and the French resulted from the establishment of Jesuit missions in Huronia in the 1630s and 1640s. During this time, the Huron continued to trade with French commercial interests at Quebec. As a result of competition for the fur trade, the Hurons were attacked and dispersed by the New York Iroquois in 1649, and many Hurons became captives of the Iroquois.

Others fled to neighboring tribes such as the Neutrals, only again to be attacked by the Iroquois. One group fled westward with the Petun, and spent the next 150 years in a series of movements throughout the western Great Lakes. In 1815 they settled in Ohio and Michigan, only to move a few years later to Oklahoma. A small group of Hurons made it to Quebec in 1656, and were later known as the Hurons of Lorette. An average estimate for the total population of Huronia, around 1630, is between 25,000 and 30,000. Within the ensuing 20 years, warfare and disease had reduced the population to 10,000 or less.

CULTURAL BOUNDARIES AND SUBDIVISIONS: By the early 17th century, when first coming into contact with the Europeans, all the Hurons lived in a small region referred to now as historic Huronia, extending from the town of Orillia on Lake Simcoe to the Penetang Peninsula on Georgian Bay. This is a region of rolling sandy terrain which, at that time, would have been covered with areas of maple-beech forest and open country. There were uninhabited areas adjacent to Huronia, such as the valley of the Trent River system, which the Hurons controlled and used as hunting territories. The Huron country was divided into five areas, each occupied by a tribal nation, whose names were Attignawantan (Bear), Arendahrenon (Rock), Attigneenongnahac (Cord), Tohontaenrat (Deer, or One-White-Lodge), and Ataronchronon (People of the Fens). They all shared a common language and essentially the same culture. The number of towns and villages comprising each nation ranged from one to fourteen.

TERRITORY: In the 17th century the Hurons were crowded into a territory measuring approximately 35 miles by 15 miles, in a band from Orillia to the Penetang Peninsula. It is clear from archaeological evidence that prior to AD 1600 the Hurons inhabited a much broader region than this. Pre-contact Huron village sites are known not only from historic Huronia, but all over an area bounded on the west by the Niagara escarpment, on the south by Lake Ontario, and on the east and north by the Canadian Shield. Villages appear to be concentrated in the region from Toronto northward to Huronia, along the shore of Lake Ontario, and in the valley of the Trent River system.

LANGUAGE: The Huron nations spoke a common Iroquois Family language. The Petun, just to the west, spoke the same language, while the Neutral to the southwest apparently spoke a language that was somewhat different. Huron is more distantly related to the languages of the League Iroquois, suggesting that the two groups have been linguistically separated for some time, perhaps more than 2,000 years. The Iroquois language family also includes Cherokee, and the family as a whole is related to the Siouan family.

CULTURE [Subsistence and economy]: Huron subsistence was based upon farming, hunting, fishing, and gathering of wild plants. Plants cultivated by the Huron included maize, beans, squash, pumpkins, sunflowers, and tobacco. While men cleared the fields of trees and brush, women took on the task of planting, tending and harvesting the crops. After harvesting, corn was dried and pounded into a meal and stored for use during the winter, when it served as a staple food. During the fall and early winter, Huron men hunted mostly whitetail deer, beaver, and bear. Other animals that were eaten included rabbits, ground hogs, squirrels, raccoons, skunks, turtles, and birds. Hunting techniques made use of traps, snares, spears, and bows and arrows. In at least some villages, substantial numbers of domestic dogs were raised for food.

Fish formed an important part of the Huron diet, and were used in soups as well as eaten fresh, dried or smoked. Fishing was a communal activity, carried out primarily in Spring and Fall. Fish were caught in lakes and streams, by nets, weirs and lines. In wintertime, some icefishing was done with nets or lines.

Wild plant foods used by the Huron included several kinds of berries, nuts, plums, cherries, grapes, apples, beans and peas, and a few roots. Many of the fruits were dried for winter use. An important aspect of Huron economy was trade, particularly in the historic period.

During their involvement in the fur trade, the Hurons traded corn and other items to the more northerly Algonquians for animal skins and fish. The animal skins, particularly beaver, were taken to Quebec, where they were traded to the French for European goods.

SETTLEMENT AND EARLY VILLAGE LIFE: The focal point of Huron life was the semi-permanent village. Most villages were enclosed and might occupy over 20 acres. These villages were relocated every 10 to 30 years, when soil and firewood had been exhausted. Huron houses were of the longhouse type, and accommodated several related families, being approximately 25 feet wide and anywhere from 30 to 200 feet long. Houses were constructed of poles that were bent over and tied together to form a roof, and covered with bark. Down the center of the house was a common passageway that contained cooking fires shared by individual families, who occupied compartments down each side of the house. On the average, a longhouse might accommodate about 10 families, or roughly 50 to 70 people.

A small village might contain just a few such houses, while the larger ones might contain as many as 100. One large Huron village on the early 17th century was reported to have 200 longhouses. The Huron population spent the winter in the villages, living on preserved and fresh game, and crops and other foods stored during the summer and fall. During this season, much time was spent at games, ceremonies, and feasts.

In spring, many people left the village for varying periods, the men spending the summer in fishing and hunting, warfare, and trading. The women grew crops, and many of them built houses and lived in the cornfields during the growing season. During the fall, people gathered at favorite fishing places, after which men were busy hunting. The population finally reassembled in the village during December.

128

TECHNOLOGY: Prior to the introduction of European materials in the 16th century, Hurons had what could be termed a neolithic level of technology. Metallurgy was virtually unknown; most tools, weapons and utensils were made from wood, bone, antler, shell, stone, or pottery. Native copper was sometimes used for implements such as awls, or for beads. Household utensils included pottery vessels for cooking and storage, wooden bowls, spoons and forks, and other containers of wood and bark. Women's tools included flint knives, flint scrapers and bone fishers for preparing animal hides, and bone awls and needles for piercing and sewing leather.

Hunting implements included arrows tipped with flint, bone or antler, harpoons with barbed bone or antler points, and spears tipped with stone. Axes and adzes of ground or polished stone were used for felling trees, and dressing poles for houses and palisades. Principal war weapons were bows and arrows, and wooden clubs. Also used were shields of leather or bark, and armor made of wooden slats laced together. Following contact with the French, native technology was quickly replaced by the use of European copper kettles, iron axes, knives and awls.

SOCIAL AND POLITICAL ORGANIZATION: The basic economic and social unit of Huron life was the family, which had the responsibility for providing for its members. A household accommodated a number of families related through the female line, thus approximating a matrilineally extended family. The families sharing a house customarily cooperated in many ventures, and were expected to share and to help each other when necessary. The village seems to have enjoyed a high degree of autonomy, but was tied to other villages by common concerns and activities.

Village affairs were governed by a council of older men. Among these councilors were chiefs of two kinds: those concerned with the government of the village, including such things as feasts, games and funerals; and those concerned with war. Chieftainship was largely hereditary, so that when a chief died, the successor was selected from among his sisters' sons. Certain of the chiefs were recognized as being preeminent by virtue of their personal qualities of wealth, and their influence was corresponding greater than that of the other chiefs. Above the village level, tribal affairs were governed by a council composed of the most respected chiefs from all the villages in that tribe.

Of this council, one member was recognized as being the principal chief of the nation. This chief and his council had the responsibility for making treaties with other nations, declaring war, and giving permission for foreigners to cross the tribal territory. The entire confederacy of the Huron was likewise governed by a council, which probably consisted of a combination of the various tribal councils.

RELIGION: The Huron believed that every object, as well as people and animals, possessed souls or spirits. Some of these spirits had the ability to affect human affairs, and were propitiated by offerings. Among the most important spirits were those of the sky, and of certain geographical entities such as lakes, islands, large rocks, etc. Some people, such as shamans, were believed to have a familiar spirit who was acquired in a vision or dream, and whose aid they could enlist. The most important function of shamans was curing the sick. This was accomplished by extracting an offending object from the patient's body, breaking a sorcerer's spell, or interpreting and fulfilling the patient's dreams. Other shamanistic functions included the controlling of weather, and the bringing of good luck in hunting, fishing, or warfare.

The Hurons regarded dreams as the means whereby the soul made its thoughts and desires known; to let such desires go unfulfilled could bring sickness and death. Thus, if a man dreamed that he would die if he were not presented with certain gifts, the required items would be found and given to him. Charms were objects found and collected by Huron men which were believed to bring luck in hunting, war, and other activities. They were held in awe, and feasts might be given to maintain their power.

LIFE CYCLES: For the first two or three years of its life, a Huron baby was breast-fed and fed meat previously chewed by its mother. During this time, the infant spent the day in a cradleboard, was wrapped in fur, or roamed the floor of the house. At night it slept between its parents. The period between infancy and adulthood was spent in games that anticipated adult activities. Boys spent their time shooting bows and arrows or playing games of physical skill, while girls engaged in play imitating the grinding of corn or other household activities.

Relations between the youth of different sexes seem to have been generally uninhibited, and girls apparently competed for the greatest number of lovers. When a girl became pregnant, her lovers would all claim that the child was theirs, and she would choose from among them the one she liked best for a husband. When a young man and woman decided to marry, the man asked for the permission of the woman's parents. If he was an acceptable suitor to both the woman and her parents, a wedding feast was held for the couple's friends and relatives, at which their marriage was announced. A man's own children were not his heirs, but rather the heirs of his wife's brother. Similarly, his own heirs were his sister's children; to them he would pass on his titles and possessions, and they, in turn, supported him in his old age. The elderly were respected, and their opinions were sought on matters of importance.

Death was approached calmly by the Hurons. If a man was dying of natural causes, he might give a farewell feast for his friends and, as his death approached, he was shown the clothes and finery in which he would be buried. Immediately following death, the body was wrapped in a robe, and covered in furs and bark. The death was announced through the village, and feasts were held. Three days after the death, the body was carried to the cemetery just outside the village, where it was placed in a tomb made of bark. Sometimes bodies were buried in the ground, and a small hut of bark was erected over the grave. Every 10 years, several Huron villages cooperated in holding a Feast of the Dead, at which the bodies of those who had died since the last feast were removed from their graves and reburied in a common pit, amid a great deal of feasting and exchanging of presents.

CONCLUSION: The available information on the Hurons depicts a relatively large aboriginal group being profoundly affected and disrupted by the complex events surrounding the arrival of Europeans in the eastern part of North America. Traditional Huron patterns of settlement, subsistence, and politics were greatly modified by the effects of the European presence. Huron involvement in European politics in North America helped to weld them into a confederacy, allied with the crown of France.

It also led to, a scant 50 years later, their destruction as a social and cultural entity at the hands of the League of the Iroquois. Most Hurons today are called Wyandotte, although the name Huron is still used by members of the tribe living in Quebec. Some contemporary Hurons still live on the Saint Lawrence River. The Wyandotte Tribe of Oklahoma was established in 1937 after the Oklahoma Indian Welfare Act of 1936.

131

The constitution provides for a tribal government composed of a chief, a Tribal Council that meets each month, and elected representatives. During the Eisenhower administration in 1956, the Wyandotte were one of the tribes singled out to lose its tribal identity. After a twenty-year struggle, in 1978 the tribe successfully regained federal recognition. In Oklahoma, a recent count showed 3,617 members. Significant social, educational, and cultural advances have been made, including tribal government scholarships, daily meals for elders, a health center, new homes for tribal members, a preschool facility, and a tribal center and meeting hall. Funding has been granted for establishment of the Wyandotte museum and Cultural Center, and money has been made available for locating, purchasing, and cataloguing material culture.

Oral interviews with elders have helped to renew the Wyandotte heritage and language, and a library and archives have recently received funding. The tribal historical committee has published a book that provides a brief history of the tribe, and a series of paperbacks is forthcoming. The tribe today remains diverse; its members are employed in nursing, teaching, ranching, art, farming, labor, clerking, and secretarial positions. The group in Oklahoma, as well as elsewhere, maintains pride in its Indian identity and cultural heritage.

IROQUOIAN FAMILY

(See FIVE NATIONS IROQUOIS and IROQUOIS) The Iroquoian Family is a linguistic stock of the following tribes and tribal groups: the Hurons were composed of the Attignaouantan (Bear people), the Attigneenongnahac (Cord people), the Arendahronon (Rock people), the Tohontaenrat *Atahontaenrat* or *Tohontaenrat*, White-eared or Deer people), the Wenrohronon, the Ataronchronon, and the Atonthrataronon (Otter people, an Algonquian tribe); the Tionontati or Tobacco people or nation; the Confederation of the Attiwendaronk or Neutrals, composed of the Neutrals proper, the Aondironon, the Ongniarahronon, and the Atiragenratka, *Atiraguenrek*; the Conkhandeenrhonon; the Iroquois Confederation composed of the Mohawk, the Oneida, the Onondaga, the Cayuga, and the Seneca, with the Tuscarora after 1726; and in later times, the incorporated remnants of a number of alien tribes, such as the Tutelo, the Saponi, the Nanticoke, the Conoy, and the Muskwaki or Foxes; the Conestoga or Susquehanna of at least three tribes, of which one was the Akhrakouaehronon

132

or Atrakouaehronon; the Erie or Cat Nation of at least two allied peoples; the Tuscarora Confederation composed of several leagued tribes, the names of which are now unknown; the Nottaway; the Meherrin; and the Cherokee composed of at least three divisions, the Elati, the Middle Cherokee, and the Ataii, and the Onnontioga consisting of the Iroquois-Catholic seceders on the Saint Lawrence.

Each tribe was an independent political unit, except those which formed leagues in which the constituent tribes, while enjoying local self-government, acted jointly in common affairs. For this reason, there were no general names for themselves common to all tribes. In 1534, Jacques Cartier met people of the Iroquoian stock on the shore of Gaspe Basin; the following year, he again encountered their home on the site of the city of Quebec, Canada. Both banks of the Saint Lawrence River above Quebec, as far as the site of Montreal, were occupied by people of this family.

He visited the villages of Hagonchenda, Hochelaga, Hochelayi, Stadacona, and Tutonaguy. This was the first known habitat of an Iroquoian people. Champlain found these territories entirely deserted 70 years later, and Lescarbot found people roving over this area speaking an entirely different language from that recorded by Cartier. He believed that this change of languages was due to "a destruction of people," because, he wrote, "some years ago the Iroquois assembled themselves to the number of 8,000 men and destroyed all their enemies, whom they surprised in their enclosures." The new language that he recorded was Algonquian, spoken by bands that passed over this region on warlike forays.

The early occupants of the Saint Lawrence were probably the Arendahronon and Tohontaenrat, tribes of the Hurons. Their lands bordered on those of the Iroquois, whose territory extended westward to that of the Neutrals, neighbors of the Tionontati and western Huron tribes to the north, and the Erie to the south and west. The Conestoga occupied the middle and lower basin of the Susquehanna, south of the Iroquois. The northern Iroquoian area, which Algonquian tribes surrounded on nearly every side, therefore embraced nearly the entire valley of the Saint Lawrence, the basins of Lake Ontario and Lake Erie, the southeastern shores of Lake Huron and Georgian Bay, all of the present New York State, except the lower Hudson Valley, all of central Pennsylvania, and the shores of Chesapeake Bay in Maryland as far as the Choptank and Patuxent rivers. In the south, the Cherokee area, surrounded by Algonquian tribes in the north, Siouan in the east, and Muskhogean and Uchean tribes in the south and west, embraced the valleys of the Tennessee and upper Savannah rivers and the mountainous parts of Virginia, the Carolinas, and Alabama.

Separated from the Cherokee by the territory of the eastern Siouan tribes was the area occupied by the Tuscarora in the eastern part of North Carolina and by the Meherrin and Nottoway north of them in southeastern Virginia. The northern Iroquoian tribes, especially those of the Five Nations, were second to no other Indian people north of Mexico in political organization, statesmanship, and military prowess. Their leaders were astute diplomats, as the wily French and English statesmen with whom they dealt soon discovered. In war, they practiced ferocious cruelty toward their prisoners, burning even their unadopted women and infant prisoners.

However, far from being a race of rude and savage warriors, they were a kindly and affectionate people, full of keen sympathy for kin and friends in distress, kind and deferential to their women, exceedingly fond of their children, anxiously striving for peace and goodwill among men, and profoundly imbued with a just reverence for the constitution of their commonwealth and for its founders. Their wars were waged primarily to secure and perpetuate theirpolitical life and independence. The fundamental principles of their confederation, persistently maintained for centuries by force of arms and by compacts with other peoples, were based primarily on blood relationships, and they shaped and directed their foreign and internal policy on consonance with these principles.

The underlying motive for the institution of the Iroquois League was to secure universal peace and welfare among men by recognition and enforcement of the forms of civil government. This was to be done through direction and regulation of personal and public conduct and thought, in accordance with beneficent customs and council degrees; by stopping bloodshed in the blood feud through tender of a prescribed price for killing a co-tribesman; by abstaining from eating human flesh; and, lastly, by maintenance and necessary exercise of power, not only military, but also magic power, which were believed to be embodied in the forms of their ceremonial activities.

The tender for a homicide, or the murder or killing by accident of a co-tribesman, was twenty strings of wampum, ten for the dead person, and ten for the forfeited life of the homicide. The religious activities of these tribes expressed themselves in the worship of all environing elements and bodies and many creatures of a teeming fancy, which, directly or remotely affected their welfare. They were regarded as man-beings or anthropomorphic personages endowed with life, volition, and peculiar individual "orenda," or magic power. In the practice of this religion, ethics or morals did not have a primary consideration, but only a secondary one, if any.

The status and personal relations of the personages of their pantheon were fixed and regulated by rules and customs similar to those in vogue in the social and political organization of the people, and there was therefore, among at least the principal gods, a kinship system patterned on that of the people themselves. The mental superiority of the Hurons over their Algonquian neighbors was frequently mentioned by the early French missionaries.

A remainder of the Tionontati, with a few refugee Hurons among them, fled to the region of the upper lakes (along with certain Ottawa tribes) to escape the Iroquois invasion in 1649, and maintained among their fellow refugees a predominating influence. This was largely because, like other Iroquoian tribes, they had been highly organized socially and politically, and were therefore trained in definite parliamentary customs and procedures.

Although they were a small tribe, the Hurons claimed and exercised the right of lighting the council fire at all general gatherings, showing the esteem in which they were held by their neighbors. The Cherokee were the first tribe to adopt a constitutional form of government, embodied in a code of laws written in their own language, in an alphabet based on the Roman characters adapted by one of them. Although in weighing these facts, the vast influence of their commingling with white settlers must be considered The social organization of the Iroquoian tribes was, in some respects, similar to that of other Indians, but much more complex and cohesive, and there was a notable difference in regard to the important position accorded the women. Among the Cherokee, the Iroquois, the Hurons, and probably among the other tribes, the women performed important and essential functions in their government.

Every chief was chosen, and retained his position, and every important measure was enacted by the consent and cooperation of the child-bearing women, and the candidate for the position of chief was nominated by the matrons of this group. His selection by them from among their sons had to be confirmed by the tribal and federal councils, respectively, and finally, he was installed by federal officers. Lands and houses belonged solely to the women. All the Iroquoian tribes were sedentary and agricultural, depending on the chase for only a small part of their subsistence. The northern tribes were especially noted for their skill in fortification and housebuilding. Their so-called castles were solid log structures, with platforms running around the top on the inside, from which stones and other missiles could be hurled down upon attackers. The population of tribes composing the Iroquoian family is detailed in the entry for the Iroquois Confederacy, and the descriptions of the various Iroquoian tribes.

IROQUOIS   (See FIVE NATIONS IROQUOIS and IROQUIAN FAMILY) The tribes known in history (among other names) as the Five Nations, comprising the Cayuga, Mohawk, Oneida, Onondaga, and Seneca. Among the Iroquoian tribes, kinship was traced through the blood of the woman only.

Kinship meant membership in a family, and this in turn, constituted citizenship in the tribe, conferring certain social, political, and religious privileges, duties, and rights which were denied to persons of alien blood; however, by a legal fiction embodied in the right of adoption, the blood of the alien could be figuratively changed into one of the strains of the Iroquoian blood, and thus citizenship could be conferred on a person of alien lineage. In an Iroquoian tribe, the legislative, judicial, and executive functions were usually exercised by one and the same class of persons, commonly called chiefs in English, who were organized into councils.

There were three grades of chiefs. The chieftainship was hereditary in certain of the simplest political units in the government of the tribe. A chief was nominated by unit matrons, and the nomination was confirmed by the tribal and federal councils. The functions of the three grades of chiefs were defined in the rules of procedure. When the five Iroquoian tribes were organized into a confederation, its government was only a development of that of the separate tribes, just as the government of each of the constituent tribes was a development of that of the several clans of which it was composed. The government of the clan was a development of the several brood families of which it was composed, and the brood family, strictly speaking, was composed of

136

the progeny of a woman and her female descendants, counting through the female line only.

Therefore the clan could be described as a permanent body of kindred, socially and organized politically, who traced actual and theoretical descent through the female line only. The simpler units surrendered part of their autonomy to the next higher units, and as such, the whole was closely interdependent and cohesive. The establishment of the higher unit created new rights, privileges, and duties. This was the principle of organization of the confederation of the five Iroquoian tribes.

The date of the formation of this confederation (probably not the first, but the last of a series of attempts to unite the several tribes in a federal union) was not earlier than about the year 1570, which was some 30 years earlier to that of the Huron tribes. The Delawares gave them the name of Mingwe. The northern and western Algonquians called them Nadowa "adders." The Powhatan called them Massawomekes. The English knew them as the Confederation of the Five Nations, and after the admission of the Tuscarora in 1722, as the Six Nations. Moreover, the names Maqua, Mohawk, Seneca, and Tsonnontowan, by which their leading tribes were called, were also applied to them collectively.

The League of the Iroquois, when first known to Europeans, was composed of the five tribes, and occupied the territory extending from the eastern watershed of Lake Champlain to the western watershed of Genesee River, and from the Adirondacks southward to the territory of the Conestoga. The date of the formation of the league is not certain, but there was evidence that it took place about 1570, occasioned by wars with Algonquian and Huron tribes.

The confederated Iroquois immediately began to make their united power felt. After the coming of the Dutch, from whom they procured firearms, they were able to extend their conquests over all the neighboring tribes until their dominion was acknowledged from the Ottawa River to the Tennessee and from the Kennebec to the Illinois River, and Lake Michigan. Their westward advance was checked by the Chippewa. The Cherokee and the Catawba proved an effectual barrier in the South, while in the North, they were hampered by the operations of the French in Canada.

Champlain, on one of his early expeditions, joined a party of Canadian Indians against the Iroquois. This made them bitter enemies of the French, whom they afterward opposed at every step, to the close of the French regime in Canada in 1763, while they were firm allies of the English. The French made several attempts through their missionaries to win over the Iroquois, and were so successful that a considerable number of individuals from the different tribes, most of them Mohawk and Onondaga, withdrew from the several tribes and formed Catholic settlements at Caughnawaga, Saint Regis, and Oka, on the Saint Lawrence.

The tribes of the league repeatedly tried, but without success, to induce them to return, and finally, in 1684, declared them to be traitors. In later wars, Catholic Iroquois took part with the French against their former brethren. Upon the outbreak of the Revolutionary War, the League of the Iroquois decided not to take part in the conflict, but to allow each tribe to decide for itself what action to take.

All the tribes, with the exception of the Oneida and about half of the Tuscarora, joined the English. After the revolution of the Mohawk and Cayuga, (with other Iroquoian tribes that were in the English interest), they were finally settled by the Canadian government on a reservation on Grand River, Ontario, where they continued to reside, although a few individuals emigrated to Gibson, Bay of Quinte, Caughnawaga, and Saint Thomas, Ontario.

A large number of the Iroquois population within the United States resided on reservations in New York with the exception of the Oneida, many of whom settled near Green Bay, Wisconsin. The so-called Seneca of Oklahoma were composed of the remnants of many tribes, among which may be mentioned the Conestoga and Hurons, and of emigrants from all the tribes of the Iroquoian Confederation. It was very probable that the nucleus of these Seneca was the remnant of the ancient Erie. The Catholic Iroquois of Caughnawaga, Saint Regis, and Oka, although having no connection with the confederation, supplied many recruits to the fur trade, and a large number of them became residents among the northwestern tribes of the United States and Canada.

The number of the Iroquois villages varied greatly at different periods and from decade to decade. In 1657 there were about 24, but after the conquest of the Erie, the entire country from the Genesee to the western watershed of Lake Erie came into possession of the Iroquoian tribes, which afterward settled colonies on the upper waters of the Allegheny and Susquehanna, and on the northern shore of Lake Ontario, so that by 1750, their villages may have numbered about 50.

The population of the Iroquois also varied much at different periods. Their constant wars greatly weakened them. In 1689, it was estimated that they had 2,250 warriors; that numbers, which was reduced by war, disease, and defections to Canada, dropped to 1,230 by 1698. Their losses were largely made up by their system of wholesale adoption, which was carried on to such an extent that at one time their adopted aliens were reported to equal or exceed the number of native Iroquois.

Due to the defection of the Catholic Iroquois and the omission of the Tuscarora from the estimates, it is impossible to get a statement of the full strength of the Iroquois until much later. Around the middle of the 17th century, the Five Nations were supposed to have reached their highest point, and in 1677 and 1685, they were estimated at about 12,850, but in the next nine years, they lost more than half by war and by desertions to Canada.

The most accurate estimates for the 18th century gave the Six Nations and their colonies between 10,000 and 12,000 members. In 1774, they were estimated at 10,000 to 12,500. In 1904, they numbered about 16,100, including more than 3,000 mixed-bloods, as follows: In Ontario, Iroquois and Algonkin at Watha (Gibson), 139 (about one-half Iroquois); Mohawk of the Bay of Quinte, 1,271; Oneida of the Thames, 770; Six Nations on the Grand Reservation, 4,195 (including about 150 Delawares). In Quebec: Iroquois of Caughnawaga, 2,074; of Saint Regis, 1,426; of Lake of Two Mountains, 393. The total in Canada was about 10,418.

The Iroquois of New York in 1904 were distributed as follows: Onondaga and Seneca on the Allegany Reservation, 1,041; Cayuga, Onondaga, and Seneca on the Cattaraugus Reservation, 1,456; Oneida on the Oneida Reservation, 150; Oneida and Onondaga on the Onondaga Reservation, 513; Saint Regis Reservation, 1,208; Cayuga and Seneca on the Tonawanda Reservation, 512; Onondaga and Tuscarora on the Tuscarora Reservation, 410. Total, 5,290. In 1905, there were also 366 Indians classed as Seneca under the Seneca School in Oklahoma. The Algonquian and other Indians included with the Iroquois were probably outnumbered by the Caughnawaga and others in the Canadian Northwest, who were not separately enumerated.

139

The following villages were Iroquois, but the particular tribes to which they belonged were either unknown or were collective: Adjouquay, Allaquippa, Anpuaqun, Aquatsagana, Aratumquat, Awegen, Blackleg's Village, Buckaloon, Cahunghage, Canowdowsa, Caughnawaga, Chartierstown, Chemegaide, Chenango, Chinklacamoose, Chugnut, Churamuk Codocoraren, Cokanuck, Conaquanosshan, Conejoholo, Conemaugh, Conihunta, Connosomothdian, Conoytown (mixed Conoy and Iroquois), Coreorgonel (mixed), Cowawago, Cussewago, Ganadoga, Ganagarahhare, Ganasarage, Ganeraske, Ganeious, Gannentaha, Glasswanoge, Goshgoshunk (mixed), Grand River Indians, Hickorytown (mixed), Janundat, Jedakne, Johnstown, Jonondes, Juniata, Juraken (2), Kahendohon, Kanaghsaws, Kannawalohatta, Kanesadageh, Karaken, Karhationni, Karhawenradon, Kayehkwarageh, Kaygen, Kente, Kickenapawling, Kiskiminetas, Kittaning, Kuskuski (mixed), Lawunkhannek, Logstown, Loyalhannon (?), Mahusquechikoken, Mahican, Mahoning, Manckatawangum, Matchasaung, Middletown, Mingo Town, Mohanet, Nescopeck, Newtown (4 settlements), Newtychaning, Octageron, Ohrekionni, Onaweron, Onkwelyede, Opolopong, Oquaga, Osewingo, Oskawaserenhon, Ostonwackin, Oswegatchie, Otiahanague, Otskwirakeron, Ousagwentera, Owego, Paille Coupee, Pluggy's Town, Punxatawney, Quinaouatoua, Runonvea, Saint Regis, Sawcunk, Schoharie, Schohorage, Sconassi, Scoutash's Town, Seneca Town, Sevege, Sevickly's Old Town, Shamokin, Shannopin, Shenango, Sheshequin, Sheoquage, Sittawingo, Skannayutenate, Skehandowa, Solocka, Swahadowri, Taiaiagon, Tewanondadon, Tioga, Tohoguses Cabins, Tonihata, Tullihas, Tuscarora, Tuskokogie, Tutelo, Unadilia, Venango, Wakatomica, Wakerhon, Wauteghe, Yoghroonwago, Youcham. Catholic missions among the Iroquois were: Caughnawaga, Indian Point, La Montagne, La Prairie, Oka, Oswegatchie, Saint Regis, and Sault au Recollet. For the other Iroquois settlements, see under the several tribal names.

Disregarding the extraordinary estimates of some early writers, it is evident that the modern Iroquois, instead of decreasing in population, have increased, and number more at present than at any former period.

JAMES THE PRINTER

James The Printer (Nipmuc, 1643 - 1728), also known as Wowanus, aided the Reverend John Eliot to translate and print the Saint James

English Bible into the Indian language. The first edition was completed in 1663. A member of Eliot's second "praying band," the Hassanamisco, James attended Cambridge Charity School and then, beginning in 1659, was apprenticed for 16 years to the printer Samuel Green. He left Green in 1675 to join King Philip's forces and fight the English. He was later given amnesty and returned to present-day Grafton, Massachusetts, to teach both Indians and colonials to read and write English. It is assumed that his brother, Tukapewillen, died on Deer Island while imprisoned by the English during King Philip's war. James' name appears as the printer of a psalter published in 1709.

JOHNSON, EMILY PAULINE

Emily Pauline Johnson (Mohawk, March 10, 1861 - March 7, 1913), also known as Tekahionwake or "Double Wampum," was a critically acclaimed poet. Born near Brantford, Ontario, Canada, she was the daughter of a Mohawk Chief, Henry Martin Johnson, and an English woman, Emily S. Howells. Her love of the written word started early on and by the age of 12, she had read most of the classics, such as the work of Shakespeare, Longfellow, Byron and others. It was around that time that she began writing poetry.

While still a teenager, she sent a poem to a local newspaper whose editor advised her to send it to publications with a larger audience. Soon she began having her work published in such periodicals as Harper's Weekly, Smart Set, and The Atheneum.

In 1892, she attended a program sponsored by the Young Liberals Club of Toronto devoted to the presentation of Canadian literature. Attending in full Mohawk regalia, she read a poem entitled, "A Cry From an Indian Wife," about the Northwest Rebellion from the Native point of view: "O! coward self I hesitate no more; Go forth, and win the glories of the war. Go forth, nor bend to greed of white men's hands, By right, by birth, we Indians own these lands.

She made an impression on her audience and her performance was written about in the newspaper on the following day. She then began to give solo readings of her work, one of which included the famous, The song, My Paddle Sings. In 1889, she had her first book published, entitled *Songs of the Great Dominion*, and soon began to travel throughout Canada and to London to give her readings. She continued to meet with critical acclaim and in 1895 wrote *White Wampum*. She toured extensively for the next fifteen years, adding the United

141

States to her itinerary, and in 1903 she published her third book, *Canadian Born*, which was quite successful.

When she stopped touring, she settled in Vancouver, British Columbia. Her next book was a collection, called *Legends of Vancouver*, published in 1911. It was described by one critic as "an imaginative treatment of Indian folklore...the beginning of a new literature." During 1913, a short time before her death, she published *The Shaganappi* and *Flint and Feathers*. She died of cancer on March 7 of that year. In 1961, the Canadian government honored her with the issue of a 5-cent postage stamp celebrating the hundredth anniversary of her birth. It was the first time both a Canadian author and an Indian had been honored in that manner.

LAPPAWINZO

Lappawinzo (Delaware, 18th Century), was one of several to sign the notorious Walking Purchase Treaty in Philadelphia in 1737. He refused to leave his land after signing the treaty, claiming fraud, but was finally forced out by pressure from the Six Nations, and remained bitter lifelong over the English deceit. Lappawinzo was one of several noted Delaware chiefs, including Nutimus and Sassoonon, who lived in the Forks region west of Philadelphia, probably between the Lehigh and Delaware rivers.

Lappawinzo's home may have been the village of Hockendocqua. The chief signed the Walking Purchase on August 25, in Philadelphia, but was outraged by the English use of trained runners to pace out boundaries far in excess of the Delawares' intent and refused to make way for the English settlers.

It is said that when Edward Marshall, one of the runners, stopped by Hockendocqua to ask Lappawinzo for an Indian to accompany him, the chief said, "they had got all the best land, and they might go to the Devil for the bad, and he would send no Indian with them." In July 1742, Pennsylvanians James Logan and Governor George Thomas persuaded the chiefs of the Six Nations, overlords of the Delawares, to rebuke their rebellious subjects for not adhering to the treaty. The chiefs sent their famous orator Canasatego to tongue-whip Lappawinzo and the other chiefs, and after their conference on July 12, 1742, the Delawares departed for land set aside for them by the Six Nations chiefs on the Susquehanna River at Shamokin and Wyoming. Bitter to the, Lappawinzo was overheard to remark in reminiscence about the

English runner's "walk: "No sit down to smoke, no shoot a squirrel, but fun, fun, fun, (sic) all day long."

LOGAN, JOHN

John Logan (Cayuga, 1725 - 1780) was a leader of the Iroquois tribes living along the Ohio and Scioto Rivers during the middle of the 18th century. He led a retaliatory attack upon white settlers after whites had massacred members of his family. Logan was born in Shamokin, Pennsylvania. Although his father was white, in all probability Logan took his English name from his friend James Logan, secretary and later acting governor of Pennsylvania.

The Cayuga leader lived near Reedsville, Pennsylvania, for many years, acquiring a reputation for being a staunch friend of the white settlers. He hunted and sold skins to support himself and his family. Around 1770, Logan moved to the banks of the Ohio River, and by 1774 he was living at Old Chillicothe. During that year, a group of white settlers attacked and killed a large number of Indians at the mouth of Yellow Creek in Ohio.

Among the natives murdered were several of Logan's relatives, including his sister. In retaliation, the formerly friendly Cayuga chief led bands of warriors in raids upon nearby white settlements. During the several months that Logan was on the warpath, many frontier families were butchered. Finally, Governor Dunmore established a treaty meeting to make peace with Logan and put a halt to the killing.

Logan's speech at the time he laid down the tomahawk was so eloquent that Thomas Jefferson was moved to compare it with the orations of Demosthenes and Cicero. Sadly, Logan had begun to drink about the time he first settled along the Ohio and, after peace was reestablished with the whites, he became a notable drunkard.

The remainder of his life was undistinguished, six years after he had taken up the tomahawk, John Logan was killed by his nephew during a quarrel that took place on a return trip from a visit to Detroit. A monument has been erected at Auburn, New York, to honor his memory.

MASSACHUSETTS

The Massachusetts (*Massa-adchu-es-et*, "at or about the great hill") tribe was a confederacy that occupied the territory around Massachusetts Bay, including the present site of Boston. In their heyday the tribe had thirty villages, and since warfare was chronic, especially with the Mohican and the Narragansett, each village was fortified with palisades of heavy logs. Their homes were the dome-shaped structures called wigwams, each with a smokehole cut into the ceiling. Poles or saplings, birch bark, bulrushes, cattails, cedar bark, and grass mats went into the house. Men ordinarily prepared the poles and the framework, and women then fastened the mats or other coverings over it.

To make the homes sturdier, women frequently made ropes of woven fibers long enough to extend across a wigwam and finally be fastened down to stakes on either side. Since a wigwam was big enough for two or three families, a walled village often had a population of eight or nine hundred. The Confederacy spoke Algonquian, one of the largest linguistic stocks in native North America. From well beyond Hudson's Bay on the west, to Newfoundland on the east, the tribes were all solidly Algonquian. The Algonquians moved down through New England and Virginia, crossed to include all states north of Tennessee, and traveled down the eastern side of the Mississippi Valley.

There was one additional though small pocket of Algonquian: in the prairie states, both the Cheyenne and the Arapaho spoke Algonquian. These Algonquian villagers were corn-growers and hunters. In winter, men strapped on snowshoes and went on the "long hunt" to add fresh deer, bear, and turkey to the smoked fish, dried clams, and jerky already on hand.

When planting time arrived, the Algonquians left their villages for favorite fishing streams and planted their crops nearby. The men used the slash-and-burn process to prepare the fields, and even planted some of the corn. Then the women took over with hoes of shell or bone, hoping that their mysterious power of producing children would be magically transferred to make the earth yield abundantly.

Like most hunters, Algonquians counted descent in the male line, but the fields generally went to the women. They planted pumpkin, eight varieties of squash, corn in a variety of colors, and between the rows, sixty varieties of beans. When berries ripened, and nuts began to fall, they were added to the larder. Spring was the time to tap the sugar maples and use the syrup, or even make candy by pouring boiled syrup in the packed snow. It was the Algonquian who taught the settlers about succotash, hominy, cornpone, planked shad, clambakes, and New England's specialty, beans cooked for twenty-four hours in a warm place without a fire. Male clothing consisted of skin leggings, breechcloths or skin trousers and shirts, especially in winter, plus soft-soled moccasins. Female clothing included wrap-around skirts and poncho-type blouses; some one-piece dresses, occasionally soft-soled moccasins, robes woven in rabbit skin, and feather cloaks. Household items included birch bark, elm bark, and wooden dishes and vessels; bed frames and cornhusk mattresses; pottery; mats of reed and cedar bark and cornhusks; bone and shell utensils; woven bags; quill and later bead decorations on many household containers; hairbrushes of stiff grass or of porcupine quills; and baskets of rush coils, splint plaiting, or sweetgrass.

Transportation included birch-bark canoes, which a man or woman could create in two weeks. They were quite light and could be carried by one person over several miles of portage, and were easily repaired. The Native Americans also used snowshoes, which the settlers also called snow racquets. Except for his scalp lock, a warrior's hair was pulled out by mussel shell tweezers.

For war and ceremonies, the Brave's face was painted, and he often wore a crown of upright feathers, a turkey-feather cloak, necklaces of bone or shell, and sometimes a string of wampum. War weapons included bows and arrows; wooden shields and some slat armor; warclubs, knives, and tomahawks (which meant a ballheaded club with a triangle of bone or shell in its knob). Algonquian tribes who were constantly at war used quick commando raids, and took scalps and tortured prisoners, as did their enemies.

The Algonquians invented wampum, calling it *wampompeag* (the settlers shortened it because it was easier to say), and no ceremonial was complete without a wampum record.

A man, wise in years, learned the wampum belts by heart, and saw to it that his successor would do exactly as well. Making and drilling wampum, which was white beads from clamshells and purple ones from mussels or quahogs, took great skill and was usually done by women experts. Once settlers brought in steel awls, the women could work faster, and the English and Dutch soon accepted wampum in trade either loose, on strings, or woven into belts. However, by 1640, the Dutch already had an ordinance against wampum, which white counterfeiters were turning out. To the settlers, both English and Dutch, wampum was money used in trade, whether used by Indians or themselves.

145

To the Algonquians, however, wampum always had a sacred quality. One use of wampum was to pay the medicine man (shaman) for his services. Indian medicine was closely allied to religion, and most internal diseases were attributed to supernatural causes. Rattles and sleight-of-hand tricks characterized the Massachusetts medicine men or "Pow-wows," as the settlers called them. Nor did they resort only to the sweat bath, profuse sweating in a confined space followed by a plunge into cold water. There was an incredible amount to be learned about folk medicine, but there was too wide a gap between the "Puritan Saints" and the "Savage Hounds" to accomplish much.

John Josselyn, in his *New England's Rarities*, had Indian cures for scurvy and fevers, among a dozen others, and Cotton Mather, in *The Angel of Betheseda*, the earliest medical treatise to be written in this country, claimed that "our Indians cure consumption with a Mullein-Tea."

Even in 1920, thirty drugs used by New England Indians were still official in the United States pharmacopoeia. By the time the Puritans were well settled, the Massachusetts tribes were already on the verge of extinction, hit by the same plagues that struck the Algonquians on the northeast coast from Narragansett Bay to the Kennebec River, and inland for twenty or thirty miles.

The Indian had no immunity to the white man's diseases, but if this one disease was an attack of bubonic plague, neither had the white man. Almost all of the 17th century writers say the plague killed nineteen of every twenty Indians. Thomas Morton, in his *New English Canaan* (1637), vividly described the results of the plague: "For in a place where many inhabited, there hath been but one left alive, to tell what became of the rest, the living being (as it seemed) not able to bury the dead, and they were left for crowes, kites, and vermin to prey upon. And the bones and skulls upon the several places of their habitations, made such a spectacle after my coming into those partes, that as I travailed into that Forrest, near the Massachusetts, it seemed to me a new found Golgotha."

Once again, in 1622, the Massachusetts led a conspiracy to exterminate the whites nearby, and once more "a great sickness fell upon them." This time the illness may have been smallpox, but from all accounts by people who saw the results, it was "not unlike the plague, if not the same." Since the Puritans, early on, had classified the Massachusetts' beliefs as devilish, there has only been a vague picture of their real beliefs. Some of them included the Great Spirit, or Manitou, the thunder-beings; a huge bird armored in wampum, the sun and the moon as Manitous. An age-old theory of the hunting people was that a slain animal did not die, but sent its spirit back to its own village in human form to see if man had enough gratitude to return the bones of water animals to water, and to hang up the skulls of land animals with a prayer for forgiveness and an offering of tobacco. Finally, John Eliot (pastor and Cambridge graduate) conceived the idea that the heathen beliefs of the natives could not be expected to yield to Christian doctrines, nor could they be converted, until they heard these in their own tongue.

Cotton Mather was horrified "to think of raising these hideous creatures into our holy religion." Could Eliot "see anything angelical to encourage his labors? All was diabolical among them." Just the same, Eliot took a Natick Indian into his home so he could learn the language. He translated the Bible (the first edition in the New World), and by 1675, he had 1,150 "praying Indians" in fourteen villages.

Unfortunately, 1675 was the year when King Philip of Mount Hope and Cononclet of the Narragansett led their warriors against the whites. Most of Eliot's converts joined the Indians.

Those who did not were deported by the whites, who feared them. Population figures for the Massachusetts were probably 2,500 or 3,000 in their heyday. If any are left, they probably have been thoroughly mixed with whites. Between the plague and the aftermath of King Philip's War, when most of them were sold into slavery, the Massachusetts seem to have become extinct as a separate tribe.

MASSAPEQUA

Massapequa ("Great Pond", from *massa*, "great", and *peag* or *pequa*, "pond", the term frequently occurring in dialectic forms in New England and on Long Island). The Massapequa were an Algonquian tribe formerly of the South coast of Long Island, New York, near Seaford and Babylon, extending from Fort Neck to Islip. Massapequa, their chief village, was most likely at Fort Neck.

According to Flint, "Under constant fear of attack from their more warlike neighbors, the Indians at each end of the island had built at Fort Neck and Fort Pond, or Konkhongauk, a place of refuge capable of holding 500 men". This stronghold was destroyed in 1653 by a Captain Underhill, in the only great Indian battle fought on Long Island. Squaw Island was a refuge for women and children during the conflict.

The remains of the quadrangular building, with 90 foot sides, were evident until the late 1800s. The Massapequa sachem Tackapousha exasperated the white settlers in his vicinity, being forced to pay tribute to him repeatedly. He was one of the most turbulent of Long Island Indians. The Massapequa were a farming and fishing people who inhabited several settlements on necks of land surrounded by low marshy hummocks and protected from the ocean by the barrier island of Long Beach.

They further resided in smaller settlements in the interior to the south of the Ronkinkoma Moraine, a highland ridge that ran lengthwise along Long Island from Great Peconic Bay on the east, to the westernmost tip of present Brooklyn. Their settlements generally consisted of one or more longhouses or roundhouses covered with a combination of grass mats and sheets of bark.

The Massapequa also constructed large fortified villages surrounded by palisades of closely spaced timbers during times of war. Their principal fort was located at Fort Neck near Rockville Center, Long Island. The Massapequa took their life from the sea. Their villages bordered the calm shallow lagoons and rich beds between the main island and the barrier beaches. They netted, speared, trapped, and gathered large quantities of fish and shellfish from those waters. Across the barrier islands they cast nets and spears into the surf to harvest the open ocean.

They traveled throughout their territories in lithe dugout canoes. Small groups paddled into the interior during the colder months to live in hunting and trapping camps, stalking deer and bear. These increased in importance during the early years of Dutch colonization in the early seventeenth century. The fur trade brought metal tools, firearms, cloth, and alcohol in exchange for animal skins. The Indians of New Netherland quickly became dependent upon these trade items, and the pace of hunting, trapping, and processing furs was stepped up accordingly.

The Massapequa were first mentioned in the Dutch records of January 15, 1639. On that date, "Mechoswodt, chief Sachem of Marossepinck" put the entire Massapequa territory under Dutch protection. The document further stipulated that the Massapequa would only sell their lands to the Dutch, and that they would retain the rights to dwell, plant, fish, and hunt at their accustomed places. This manuscript confirmed the special relationship between the Massapequa and Dutch.

Part of the price for this special relationship was Massapequa military service whenever the Dutch requested it. The Dutch called in that debt in 1641, when they asked that the Massapequa send war parties against the Raritan of central New Jersey. The Raritan had retaliated against a Dutch attack upon their settlements in Staten Island, New York in 1640 by burning Dutch plantations there during the summer of 1641. The Massapequa, accordingly, sent their warriors to the Raritan country, and they returned with many scalps.

The Massapequa were horrified by the unprovoked massacre of the refugee lower Hudson River Delawaran groups by the Dutch, near Fort Amsterdam on the night of February 25-26, 1643. They did not, however, make immediate moves against the Dutch as did most of their Native allies and relations. Most of the Massapequa moved, along with many other Long Island Native groups, to the remote village of Rechqua Akie, near modern Far Rockaway, to await events and avoid Dutch attack.

On March 5, 1643 a one-eyed sachem, later identified as Mechoswodt, received a party of Dutch diplomats headed by David de Vries at Rechqua Akie. These negotiations led to the signing of a peace agreement between them on March 25, 1643. On November 13, 1643, the natives of "Masepeage, Merriack, or Rockaway" sold what was apparently the western half of their territories around Hempstead, Long Island. The deed was signed by "the Sagamore or Maespeage" and a number of other persons. The Governor Kieft War increased in intensity during the winter of 1643-1644. A number of Dutch attacks against native settlements caused the deaths of hundred of Native people on the mainland and on Long Island. Those desiring neutrality were forced to renegotiate with the Dutch.

The Matinecock sachem, Gauwaroe, accordingly entered into a new peace agreement with the Dutch on behalf of his people and for the "villages" of Marospinc and Siketeuhacky (Setauket) on April 15, 1644. Gauwaroe further promised that his people would not support the still hostile Rockaway, Jamaica Bay, and Marechkawieck groups.

A final peace treaty signed on May 24, 1645, ended the war for all of the Long Island groups. Tackapousha, the successor of Mechoswoldt, renewed his people's friendship with the Dutch during the opening days of the Peach War on November 7, 1655. Two years later, on July 4, 1657, "Takaposha, sachem of Mersapeage" confirmed the November 13, 1643 sale of Hempstead. Witnessed by the Montauk sachem, Wantaugh, the sale was reconfirmed by Tackapousha and his followers on May 11, 1658. These reaffirmations did not succeed in determining the precise boundaries of the sale, and the English of Hempstead repeatedly claimed that the 1643 deed sold all of the Massapequa lands, while the Massapequa claimed they had only the western half of their domain.

This dispute continued until March 24, 1685, when Tackapousha and his followers conveyed all of their lands to the English, reserving the right to remain at their main settlement at Cow Neck. On March 6, 1660, during the Esopus Wars, "Tapousah, chief of Marsepingh and Rechkawyck (Rockaway)" renewed the peace with the Dutch and pledged warriors to join their forces in the Esopus country in the Mid-Hudson River Valley. Many men were sent, and Massapequa forces numbered some forty-six men by October 1663. These warriors served as scouts and were effective soldiers against the Esopus villages.

Somewhat ill-treated by the race-proud Dutch, the Massapequa contingent repeatedly complained that they were not given a fair share of the booty. On May 15, 1664, Siejpekenouw, the brother of Tackapousha and leader of the warriors, signed the peace treaty ending the Esopus Wars on behalf of the Massapequa and their Long Island allies. The threat of the Massapequa involved in the King Philip's War, which had engulfed the adjacent English colonies of New England, renewed European interest in them during 1675-1676.

The English, who had conquered New Netherland in 1664, were gratified to hear on October 21, 1675 that "Tackerparis of Marsepeake and Marricoke" had moved closer to the English settlements some three to four years earlier. Living near the English and under direct surveillance, the English authorities were able to discount rumors spread by the Hempstead settlers that the Rockaway and "Masha-Peage" were contemplating an attack against them. The close connection between the Massapequa and the Rockaway sachems was identified as Tackapousha's son.

A year earlier, Tackapousha reaffirmed a friendship with the English on behalf of the "Rockaway, Mashepeage, Maricock, Vinchechauge, and Sequetalke." Two years later, on April 2, 1678, he renewed their alliance for all these groups. Most of the Massapequa moved east among the Unchechauge near Patchogue, Long Island, following the final sale of their traditional homeland on March 24, 1685. They were joined by a large number of western Long Island Native people. This community became known as the Poosepatuck group during the early 1700s.

The group gathered around the nucleus of the Unchechauge Reservation first established in 1666. These people lived by whaling, fishing, shellfishing, peddling their baskets and other handicrafts, and by selling herbal cures to their white neighbors. A large number of Poosepatuck left the reservation in 1775 to join the Native missionary, Samson Occum, in Connecticut. Only three old women spoke the old language when Thomas Jefferson visited the community in 1791.

Ten families were recorded as residents on the reservation toward the end of the nineteenth century, and their last sachem, Elizabeth Joe, died at Poosepatuck in 1832. The Poosepatuck reservation continues to exist today as a state reservation. Its inhabitants, many of them intermarried with blacks and other Native groups, still live on ancestral land.

MASSASOIT

Massasoit (Wampanoag; 1600 - 1661), was also known as Woosamequin), the chief of the Wampanoag in southeastern New England at the time of the Pilgrims' landing, opted for the friendship of the whites at the price of enormous tracts of tribal lands. Massasoit, born near present-day Bristol, Rhode Island, felt threatened by the Narraganset Indians who lived across the bay from the Wampanoag, and was quick to appreciate the advantages of the alliance with Plymouth colonists. There were other reasons for Massasoit's desire to fulfill the Pilgrims' image of "the good Indian." From his first visit in 1621, Massasoit was treated as royalty by the struggling colonists.

Introduced to the Europeans by Samoset, who led the chief and 60 Wampanoag warriors from their Rhode Island villages to the whites' crude cabins, Massasoit made his mark on a treaty of alliance between the Wampanoag and King James I of England. In December 1621, Massasoit made another journey to Plymouth, this time to help the Pilgrims celebrate a day of thanksgiving for their having survived the first year in the wilderness. Two years later, in 1623, a group of settlers traveled to the Wampanoag village upon hearing that Massasoit was dying.

To the Indians' amazement, the Puritans nursed the sachem back to health, thereby creating an even closer relationship between Massasoit, his people, and the colonists. The close bond between Massasoit and the whites, though, veiled the growing animosity on the part of the Wampanoag and the increasing anxiety on the part of the Pilgrims. The 40-year period between Massasoit's first meeting with the settlers in 1621 and his death in 1661 saw the steady expansion of white towns into what had been Wampaneag territory. Massasoit ceded major portions of the tribe's other manufactured goods. The guns and factory goods, of course, entranced Massasoit's personal power and prestige vis-a-vis the neighboring Narraganset Indians, but he sold his tribe's birthright in exchange.

The Europeans even seized lands that had not been granted to them, and then jailed Indians who dared to trespass on what the settlers considered to be private property. Massasoit seldom supported the rights of his people when those rights came into conflict with the colonists' expansionist desires.

His aping of white ways even went so far as his request that the General Court in Plymouth provide English names to his two older boys, Wamsutta and Metacom. They became Alexander and Philip, but following Massasoit's death in 1661, the policy of friendship at any price came to an end; the Wampanoag sachem called Philip launched a war of revenge in 1675, a war to regain all that his father had given away so cheaply.

MATINECOC

The Matinecoc, a Delaware-Munsee speaking group, were an Algonquin tribe that formerly lived on the northwest coast of Long Island, New York, from present Newton, Queens County, to Smithtown, Suffolk County. There were Matenecoc villages at Flushing, Glen Cove, Cold Spring, Huntington, and Cow Harbor, but even before whites intruded, they had been greatly reduced. This was most likely from wars with the Iroquois, to whom they paid tribute. After the war of 1643, most Matinecoc survivors moved to their settlement at Nissequaque, on the Nesaquake River, near present Smithtown, in Suffolk County, Long Island, New York.

Records indicate that by 1650 there were only about 50 families of this once important tribe. Ruttenberger includes the Matinecoc as having melded with his Montauk group, which is about equivalent to Metoac; but the interrelationship of the tribes in the western part of Long Island was not definitely determined. In 1628, Isaak de Rasieres reported that on Long Island "many savages dwell, who support themselves by planting maize (corn) and making sewan," or wampum, a form of shell money.

He further reported that "the tribes are held in subjection by, and are tributary to, the Pyquans," also known as the Pequot, an Algonquian-speaking group that lived in eastern coastal Connecticut. The Pequot were scatered by the English in 1637, and many of their survivors settled among the natives of Long Island.

On January 15, 1639, Mechoswodt "Chief Sachem of Marossepinck, Sintsinck (otherwise called Schout's Bay) and its dependencies" conveyed the entire western half of Long Island to the Dutch of New Netherland. This was not an outright land sale, however.

Mechoswodt, "with his people and friends" reserved the right "to remain upon the land, plant corn, fish, hunt, and make a living." He further placed himself and his followers under Dutch protection. This document was clearly meant to seat an alliance between the western Long Island groups and the Dutch by granting the latter rights to unclaimed lands in the area.

On May 13, 1640, the sachem Penhawitz notified the Dutch that a number of English settlers were squatting on unpurchased lands of Schout's Bay. By August 9, 1640, Natives at Martin Gerritsen's Bay tore down the coat of arms of the State General of the Netherlands and replaced it with a fool's head. This open act of defiance of Dutch authority resulted in a Dutch resolution to attack and subdue the perpetrators. War with the Raritan of central New Jersey diverted Dutch attention, however.

A number of Matinecock probably joined the war parties that attacked the Raritan, due to their alliance with the Dutch throughout 1641. Many Matinecock and their relations were killed in the Dutch massacre of the refugee villages near the walls of Fort Amsterdam on the night of February 25-26, 1643. Mechoswodt and Penhawitz signed a peace agreement with the Dutch on March 25, 1643.

A substantial number of western Long Island Indians refused to honor this treaty, and their warriors harassed the Dutch and English settlements repeatedly during 1643. The Dutch attacked the village of Matsepe, and a smaller settlement during the winter of 1643-1644. Over one hundred and twenty men and an unknown number of women and children were killed in both assaults. These actions brought the Matinecock and their allies to the conference table. On April 15, 1644 "Gauwarowe, sachem of Matinecock, Marospinc and Siketeuhacky" signed a peace agreement with the Dutch.

He further agreed not to support the still hostile "Indians of Reckonhacky, the bays and Marechkaqieck." On May 24, 1645, the sachems of the eastern Long Island Montauk and Shinnecock groups signed a final peace agreement with the Dutch that ended their participation in the Governor Kieft War.

They acted on both their own behalf and for the villages of "Onheywichkingh, Sichteyhacky, and Reckoouhacky", the latter of which was reported as being under Native eastern Long Island protection. This document also noted that the "Matinnekoncx" were living at Nisinckquehacky during the conflict. Disputes between the English settlers at Hempstead and their Matinecock and Massapequa neighbors became more frequent toward the end of the war.

English cattle and hogs overran and destroyed unfenced Native gardens and fields. The lucrative liquor trade demoralized and defrauded the Native people. They responded by shooting marauding animals, and alternately calling for prohibition of the liquor trade and increasing consumption of alcohol. On August 23, 1647 the Hempstead settlers accused the Massapequa sachem, Tackapousha, of plotting an attack against the Europeans. These repeated accusations were denied by the Western Long Island groups. The Hempstead settlers felt that the January 15, 1639 deed entitled them to the Matinecock land, an assumption the Matinecock strenuously contested. War scares were only part of the Hempstead strategy to dispossess the Matinecock from their lands.

The Dutch speculator, Cornelis van Tienhoven, wrote in his land promotion pamphlet of March 4, 1650 that the "Martinne houck" had their plantations along the smallest of three streams that flowed into Martin Gerritsen's Bay. He further wrote that "this tribe is not strong, and consists of about 30 families. They were formerly in and about this bay, great numbers of Indian Plantations, which now lie waste and vacant." This grim testimony gave witness to the toll of a half-century of epidemic diseases and wars with the Dutch and their own traditional native enemies. The outbreak of the Peach War (1655-1657) cast suspicion on all of the Native groups of New Netherland.

On September 30, 1656, a delegation of Massapequa men reported that "the savages of Matinecogh of the tribe called Sicketawagh" had stolen some clothing from them and that they were further sympathetic to the Wappinger, a group at war with the Dutch. This complaint was accomplished by an expression of Tackapousha's anger at this act, his assurance that he would control the Matinecock, and a reaffirmation of his support of the Dutch in the war. Several Matinecock were included among the 26 warriors furnished by Tackapousha to serve with the Dutch against the Esopus of the mid-Hudson River Valley in 1659.

This contingent, which swelled to include 46 Long Island warriors by 1663, gave crucial support to the Dutch during the Esopus War (1659-1664). On September 6, 1664, New Netherland passed into English hands. This event signaled an increased tempo of Hempstead demands for the eviction of the Matinecock. On March 14, 1667, the Matinecock refused to sell their lands to the Hempstead settlers. They did, however, permit the seven families already living on their lands to remain.

On June 8, 1669, the Governor of New York advised the Hempstead men to prove that the Matinecock were party to the 1639 conveyance. Evidently unable to show that the Matinecock were subjects to the Massapequa, the Hempstead settlers nevertheless continued to litigate for the Matinecock lands. Finally, on May 17, 1676, the Matinecock sold "three parcels of land one mile square each about Muskitoe Cove" to the Hempstead men for 600 guilders of wampum. A final sale of all of the disputed lands on western Long Island on March 24, 1685 completely cleared the English title to the Matinecock territory. The majority of the Matinecock moved east to the Poosepatuck Reservation near Patchogue, Suffolk County.

A portion of the group chose to remain in their homeland. These settled in small hamlets along the north shore near the sites of their earlier villages. Many of their number became expert harpooners on the ships of the burgeoning whaling fleets that sprang up in many north shore ports during the latter years of the 17th century.

Other Matinecock worked on the English plantations, sold medicinal herbs, acted as midwives and surgeons, and sold homemade handicrafts. Many Matinecock served among the 150 Long Island Indians who fought for the English against the French in the Queen Anne's

War (1702-1713). On September 12, 1711, it was reported that they were "being of great use for managing batteus (long boats) and canoes and all other hard labour."

The Long Island people also provided warriors for the English during the Seven Years War (1755-1762), and the Americans during the American Revolution (1775-1783). The Matinecock have continued to live in their ancestral territory. A number of families claiming Matinecock heritage today live near Glen Cove in Nassau County, New York. Other descendants of the Matinecock groups may be found in the modern Poosepatuck, Shinnecock, and Montauk reservation communities in Suffolk County, New York.

METOAC
Metoac, according to Gerard, is from "*metau-hok*", "the periwinkle, from the columella of which beads were made". It is also a collective term embracing the Indians of Long Island, New York, who seem to have been divided into the following tribes, subtribes, or bands: Canarsee, Corchaug, Manhasset, Massepequa, Matinecoc, Merric, Montauk, Nesquake, Patchoag, Rockaway, Secatoag, Setauket, and Shinnecock. There were some minor bands or villages that received special designations. They were all closely connected linguistically and politically, and were probably derived from the same ethnic system. Ruttenber classes them as branches of the Mahican.

The Montauk, who formed the leading tribe in the eastern part of the island, are often confounded with Metoac, and in some instances the Canarsee of the West have also been confounded with them. The eastern tribes were at one time subject to the Pequot and afterward to the Naraganset, while the Iroquois claimed dominion over the western tribes. They were numerous at the first settlement of the island, but rapidly wasted away from epidemics and wars with other Indians and with the Dutch, disposing of their land piece by piece to the Whites. About 1778 a large part of the survivors joined the Brotherton Indians in Oneida County, New York.

The rest, represented chiefly by the Montauk and Shinnecock, dwindled to perhaps a dozen individuals of mixed blood. The Indians of Long Island were a seafaring people, mile in temperament, diligent in the pursuits determined by their environment, skilled in the management of the canoe, seine, and spear, and dexterous in the making of Seawan or Wampum, according to Flint. The Chieftancies were hereditary by lineal descent, including females when there was no male representative. Metoac villages were Canarsee, Cotsjewaminck, Cutchogue (Corchaug), Merric, Mirrachtauhacky, Mochgonnekonck, Montauk, Nachaquatuck, Nesaquake, Ouheywichkingh, Patchoag, Rechquaakie, Setauket, Sitchteyhacky, Wawapex (Matinecock). Descendants of the Metoac now live on the small Poosepatuck and Shinnecock Reservations in the area, or in the Montauk Indian Village.

MOHEGANS

Popularly memorialized in James Fenimore Cooper's novel, *The Mohegans* (also known as Mahicans, from *maingan*, "wolf") were decimated by a plague in 1616-17. This tribe, of Algonquian stock, had originally ranged from New York into the upper portions of the Housatonic Valley in Massachusetts. In 1664, their council moved its fire from Albany to Stockbridge, Massachusetts. From Stockbridge, some of the Mohegans migrated to the Susquehanna River, but the remnants of these people were gathered into a mission at Stockbridge, with a forlorn hope for perpetuation.

In winter, the men wore a costume later adopted by white hunters: leggings, dressed buckskin shirts, breechcloths and moccasins, and sometimes fur caps. In summer, the breechcloths and moccasins formed a complete costume. Women wore leggings and long gowns. Garments were decorated with fringes and sometimes painted with simple designs. Both sexes painted their faces. Tattooing was confined to the cheeks, upon which totemic figures were permanently placed by the insertion of black pigment beneath the surface of the skin.

The men plucked their beards, and hair was dressed in various styles according to the sex, age, and station of the individual. The primary weapon was the wooden bow strung with moose sinew, and wooden arrows tipped with stone or bone and carried in quivers of skin. In warfare the usual offensive weapon was the tomahawk, with bark shields serving to some extent for defense. Communities were built on hunting and agriculture.

The members of the tribes or communities were the recognized proprietors of certain hunting, fishing, and agricultural lands, held as a rule in common. The winter villages were usually situated in warm, thickly wooded valleys near a lake or river. The early spring was spent on the fishing grounds, and when the planting season arrived, the tribe moved to its summer fields. Each family had its garden of corn, beans, pumpkins, squash, artichokes, and tobacco, cultivated with hoes of stone, wood, or clamshells, and fertilized by herring and shad.

Wild berries, roots, and nuts furnished other sources of food, supplemented by fish and by the meat of the larger mammals preserved by cutting in strips and smokedrying. The Indians divided themselves very strictly into three social classes: those of royal blood, including the sachems, shamans, elders of the council, and subordinate chiefs; commoners or freemen with rights to the tribal lands; and "outsiders" of alien blood, usually captives, with no tribal rights.

Descent was through the female line, and the office of head chief or sachem was hereditary. If tribes were large and important they might be governed by several underchiefs, and each tribe had a council of elders of noble blood. The shamans possessed great influence. They were partly seers and partly physicians. When, as occasionally happened, the offices of sachem and shaman were combined, the person vested with this dual authority held tremendous power. Polygamy was fairly common, and divorce was frequent, the right being exercised as freely by women as by men. Justice was a simple matter. If any tribesman was wronged, all related to him were bound to see that proper restitution was made. Murder was avenged or suitably punished by the kinsmen of the victim.

Their descendants may now be among Indians now living on the Western Pequot Reservations, and the Schaghticoke Reservation, and in the Mohegan Community in Connecticut, and the Narraganset Community in Rhode Island. A recent count showed about 1000 on the tribal roll.

MONTAUK

The meaning of *Montauk* is uncertain, and has been used in different senses, sometimes limited to the particular band or tribe known by this name, but in a broader sense including most of the tribes of Long Island, excepting those about the west end. It is occasionally used incorrectly as equivalent to Metoac. The Indians of Long Island were closely related to the Indians of Massachusetts and Connecticut. The dialect of the Montauk was more nearly related to the Natick of Massachusetts than was the Narraganset. The Montauk, in the limited sense, formerly occupied Easthampton Township, Suffolk County, at the East End of Long Island, and controlled all the other tribes of the island, except those near the west end. That these so-called tribes were but parts of one group, or tribe, or the loosely connected elements of what had been an organized body, seems apparent.

Ruttenber, speaking of the Montauk in the limited sense, says: "This chieftaincy was acknowledged by both the Indians and the Europeans as the ruling family of the island". They were indeed the head of the tribe of Montauk, the other divisions named being simply clans or groups, as in the case of other tribes. Wyandance, their sachem, was also the grand sachem of Paumanacke, or Sewanhackey, as the island was called.

Almost all land deeds were confirmed by him. His younger brothers, Nowedonah and Poygratasuck (Poggatacut), were respectively sachems of the Shinnecock and the Manhasset." The Rockaway and Cannarsee at the West End were probably not included. It is doubtful whether he is correct in including the west-end Indians in the confederacy. The principal Montauk village, which probably bore the name of the tribe, was about Fort Pond, near Montauk Point. The Pequot made them and their subordinates tributary, and on the destruction of that tribe in 1637, the Narraganset began a series of attacks which finally, about 1659, forced the Montauk, who had lost the greater part of their number by pestilence, to retire for protection by the whites at Easthampton.

Since 1641 they had been tributary to New England. When first known they were numerous, and even after the pestilence of 1658-59, were estimated at about 500. Then began a rapid decline, and a century later only 162 remained, most of whom joined the Brotherton Indians of New York, about 1788, so that in 1829 only about 30 were left on Long Island, and 40 years later these had dwindled to half a dozen individuals, who, with a few Shinnecock, were the last representatives of the Long Island tribes. They preserved a form of tribal organization into the 19th century and retained their hereditary chiefs until the death of the last "king," David Pharaoh, about 1875.

Only a few mixed-blood Montauk now remain. Montauk descendants may be found among the approximate 400 Indians now living in

small communities in the area, including the Poosepatuck and Shinnecock Reservations, and the Montauk Indian Village.

MORAVIANS

Mahican, Munsee, and Delawares who followed the teachings of the
Moravian brethren, were gathered by them into villages apart from
their tribes. The majority of "Moravian Indians" were Munsee. In 1740
the Moravian missionaries began their work at the Mahican village of
Shekomeko in New York. Meeting with many obstacles there, they
moved with their converts in 1746 to Pennsylvania, where they built
the new mission village of Friedenshuetten on the Susquehanna. Here
they were more successful and largely recruited from the Munsee and
Delawares, almost all of the former tribe not absorbed by the Delawares finally joining them.

They made another settlement at Wyalusing, but on the advance of
the white population, removed to Beaver River in west Pennsylvania,
where they built the village of Friedensstadt. They remained here
about a year, and in 1773 removed to Muskingum River in Ohio, in
the neighborhood of the others of their tribes, and occupied the three
villages of Gnadenhuetten, Salem, and Schoenbrunn. In 1781, during
the border troubles of the American Revolution, the Hurons moved
them to the region of the Sandusky and Scioto, in north Ohio, either to
prevent their giving information to the colonists or to protect them
from the hostility of the frontiersmen.

The next spring, a party of about 140 were allowed to return to their
abandoned villages to gather corn, where they were treacherously attacked by a party of border ruffians. Most were massacred, and their
villages burned. The remaining Moravians moved to Canada in 1791,
under the leadership of Zeisberger, and built the village of Fairfield on
the Thames River. The village was burned by the Americans during
the War of 1812, so the Indians rebuilt on the opposite side of the
river, in Orford Township, Kent County, Ontario, Canada. The tribe
numbered 275 in 1884, but had increased to 348 in 1906. There were,
until recently, a few in Franklin County, Kansas.

NARRAGANSET

The Narraganset were first mentioned by Giovanni da Verranzano in 1524. The name and tribal identity have persisted to the present with no alternate nomenclature, but with various spellings. The name may mean "people of the place crossing over." This Algonquian-speaking tribe, along with the Mohegan, Pequot, and Niantic long lived in the region. The Narraganset occupied the land surrounding Narrangansett Bay on the southern shore of Rhode Island and westward through the present town of Charleston, Rhode Island, off their southern coasts.

The aboriginal culture of the Narraganset people, including their tributaries and near neighbors, was a combination of hunting, fishing, gathering and farming. Living close to the ocean and saltwater inlets, the Indians had readily available sources of fish and shellfish. Freshwater fish from the many ponds and rivers was also abundant.

Ocean fishing and shellfish gathering were activities of the spring, summer, and early autumn. At these times, families camped near the salt water. In early and midsummer, family groups settled further inland and cultivated garden plots of maize, beans, squash and tobacco. Wild plant foods were also gathered, such as berries, ferns and mushrooms. In late autumn and throughout the winter the family groups lived inland and hunted deer, bear and small animals.

Their housing was the wigwam; a bowl shaped structure of pole supports covered with bark siding and further covered with woven reed mats. These were single nuclear family homes built in villages of at least 10 such houses of related families. There were at least 20 such villages between Providence and Westerly, Rhode Island. Clothing was made mostly of animal skins. Women wore a wraparound skirt topped by a sleeveless jacket with removable sleeves. Men wore a tunic of deerskin, loincloth and leggings.

Both wore soft-soled moccasins and winter robes of woven strips of rabbit skin or bearskin. Garments were decorated with dyed porcupine quills embroidered in geometric designs. Also, wampum beads were used for decoration as well as for symbolism of states of friendship or war. There were well-established foot-trails, some of which have become modern roads.

On water the dugout canoe was used, and some were reputed to hold 60 people, able to transverse the Long Island Sound and go as far as present Martha's Vineyard and Nantuckett Islands. Their religion was largely shamanistic. The shaman or "medicine man" cured the sick by supernatural means. It also included seasonal ceremonies related to planting and harvest. An important divinity was Cautantowit, a creator of mankind, and Chepi, who was involved with the spirits of the dead. There was also a belief in "spirits" in natural things.

Strange and inexplicable things were given the term "manitoo" and thus, in a way, deified. The raven was believed to have brought maize from the south. The earth was the mother of all things and the winds of the four directions shared in deification through their separate beneficences. The dead were buried with their heads toward the west or southwest. At first slow to accept Christianity, by the mid-eighteenth century the tribe had built a Protestant Church on their reservation and all of its ministers have been Narragansett.

Social life centered about the extended family. Most authorities contend that family relationship and inheritance was passed down through the female line for non-sachem families. Polygamy was practiced. Women performed most of the farm work and shellfish gathering, while men made dugout canoes, hunted, fished in the ocean, fought other tribes, and raised tobacco. Genealogies and recorded history reveal that the sachem position was inherited through the male line and that chief-based families were linked through marriage with such families of neighboring tribes. Concerning political organization, three early accounts mention dual sachems, with the two of them being related in the male line and about a generation apart, but not father and son.

These were the great sachems with tributary sachems of lower degree, who knew the bounds and landmarks of their territories and composed a council that advised the great sachems, but were not expected to join them in wars. The sachems had the responsibility of providing for orphans and dependent people. The strength of the Narragansetts was continuously being lost through sales of land to European colonists, some of whom were honest, some fraudulent. For the Narragansett tribe, the King Philip's War, (1675- 1676) was a major disaster. The officially neutral Narragansetts sheltered neighboring Wampanoags as well as their own women, children and elderly in their territory.

This shelter was discovered by the colonial forces and destroyed by fire. The loss of life was speculated to be in the hundreds along with supplies of stored food. Narragansett power was broken and they were subjected to the will of the colonists. Some were taken into homes of Rhode Island colonists as indentured servants. Some, captured by other colonies, were sent to the West Indies to be sold as slaves. To save the remaining Indians from ongoing land loss through sales, some by the Indian sachems themselves, in 1709 the Rhode Island colonial legislature limited a reservation of 64 square miles for Indian occupancy only. However, sales continued.

By 1740 a school for Indian children had been built on it. In 1792 the new Rhode Island Assembly drew up a constitution for the Narragansetts. It specified regular elections of a president and 4 councilmen instead of following the old government of an hereditary sachem and his chosen advisors. In 1850 the tribe accepted a detailed constitution from the Assembly and agreed to keep a ledger and minutes of their monthly meetings. It reveals their means for providing for their elderly poor, their maintenance of the reservation schoolhouse, and their mediation of land inheritance and boundary problems within the reservation. In 1880 the tribal council voted to end the tribe as an organization, and to sell what was left of the reservation to the State of Rhode Island.

There are different opinions as to their reasons for doing so. As a result, they no longer existed as an entity in State politics. However, they never ceased to exist as a group through the institutions of their tribal organization with elected officers, regular meetings, their own church and Indian ministers, and their annual August Meeting or Powwow, on old reservation grounds. In the 1970's, the Narragansetts were encouraged to reclaim their reservation lands, and, in 1975, with the aid of non-Indian lawyers, filed a suit to reclaim some of the land that they had sold in 1880.

They won their case in 1979 in an Act of Congress that returned over 1,800 acres to them. The land was to be managed by a nine-person council, five Indians chosen by the tribe, and four non-Indians. Several hundred acres were donated to the Narragansett by Irving and Arlene Crandall in 1991. In 1833, the population was about 250.

There could have been many more uncounted. In 1880, 324 were agreed upon to receive payment for a share in the sale of the reservation. In the 1970s, the tribal membership was around 300. A recent count shows membership of some 2,400 individuals.

NASHUA

The Nashua tribe formerly lived on the upper Nashua River, and are said by some to have been connected with the Massachusetts, but classed by Potter with the Pennacook. They had a village called Nashua near the present Leominister, but their principal village seems to have been Weshacum, a few miles farther south.

The Nashua tract extended for several miles in every direction around Lancaster. At the outbreak of King Philip's War in 1675, they joined the hostile Indians and, numbering several hundred, attempted to escape death in two groups to the east and west.

Both parties were pursued and a large number were killed or captured, the prisoners being afterward sold into slavery. A few who escaped eastward joined the Pennacook, while about 200 others crossed the Hudson to join the Mahican or the Munsee, causing the Nashua to cease existing as a separate tribe. A few still remained near their old homes as late as 1701.

NAUSET

An Algonquian tribe formerly living on Cape Cod east of Bass River, The Nauset formed a part of, or were under control of, the Wampanoag. A writer noted: "The Indians in the county of Barnstable were a distinct people, but they were subject in some respects to the chief sachem of the Wampanoags." They probably came in contact with the whites at an early date, as the Cape was frequently visited by navigators. From this tribe, Hunt, in 1614, carried off seven natives and sold them into slavery with 20 Indians of Patuxet.

Champlain had an encounter with the Nauset immediately before returning to Europe. They seem to have escaped the great pestilence that prevailed along the New England coast in 1617. Although disposed to attack the colonists at their first meeting, the two groups eventually became friends, and with few exceptions, remained faithful to their friendship through King Philip's War, in some instances even lending each other assistance.

Most of them had been Christianized before this war broke out. The estimated population in 1621 was 500, but this is probably below their real strength at that time. About 1710, by which time they were all organized into churches, they lost a great many by fever. In 1764 they had decreased to 106, living mainly at Potanumaquut, but in 1802, only four were said to remain. Their principal village, Nauset, was near the present Eastham. Although their location indicates that fish furnished their chief sustenance, the Nauset were evidently farmers, as supplies of corn and beans were obtained from them by the famishing Plymouth colonists in 1622.

NEPANET, TOM

Tom Nepanet (Nipmuc, late 17th Century), one of the Christian Indians unjustly imprisoned on Deer Island in Boston Harbor during King Philip's War, nevertheless risked his life to help the English recover prisoners taken by Nipmuc warriors allied with Philip. Beginning in April, 1676, he acted as liaison between the Massachusetts colonists and the Nipmuc chiefs, carrying letters which at length won freedom for the Rowlandson family and others.

In May 1676, he helped Captain Henchman successfully ambush a party of Nipmuc near Lancaster, Massachusetts.

NETAWATWEES

Netawatwees (Delaware, 1678 - October 31, 1776), also known as Newcomer, whose name means skilled advisor, was a Delaware chief of the Turtle subtribe, appearing in colonial records as Netawatwees, Netahutquemaled, Netodwehement, Natautwhalemund, etc. Probably born in the Delaware River Valley around 1678, Netawatwees in his youth was forced to move west with other members of the tribe due to white pressures. In July of 1758, he was living in a Delaware Indian settlement at the mouth of Beaver Creek, a tributary of the Ohio below Pittsburgh, where the records identify him as "ye great man of the Unamie nation." (The Unamie was a tribal division of the Delawares along with the Munsie and Unalachtigo).

Netawatwees moved to Ohio with other migrant Delawares during the French and Indian War and established a village at present Cuyahoga Falls. From there he moved to the Tuscarawas, a tributary of the Muskingum, where he became a chieftain at the Delaware town called Gekelmukpechink, "still water". This town, which became known as Newcomer's Town, was on the north bank of the Tuscarawas on the eastern outskirts of present Newcomerstown, Oxford Township, Tuscarawas County. The Great Council met here until the Delaware population was consolidated at nearby Coshocton. In the fall of 1764, Colonel Henry Bouquet led a campaign against the Delawares, Shawnee, Mingoes, and Mahican in Ohio, who were considered hostile to the British. Because Netawatwees refused to discuss peace terms, Bouquet deposed him.

After peace was negotiated and Bouquet departed, Netawatwees resumed his chieftancy, his Delaware followers remaining loyal. Although Netawatwees was never converted to Christianity, the Moravian missionaries made a strong impression on him. Infirm in his old age, he was succeeded by White Eyes in 1776. His dying words implored the Delawares to give up teachings of the Moravian pastors. He was survived by his grandson, Captain John Killbuck, Junior.

NEUTRAL

The Neutral consisted of a group of tribes joined into a loose confederacy with a common policy towards their neighbors. Each tribe was composed of a number of largely autonomous villages who shared a common tribal history and were probably tied to each other through intermarriage. Their economy revolved around slash-and-burn farming, operated by women, of which the principal crop was corn. The men hunted, fished, and carried on warfare. Their language was a dialect of Iroquoian and their culture in almost all respects was similar to the other Iroquoian groups in the eastern Great Lakes area. The term Neutral was first used by the French explorer Samuel de Champlain when he heard about the group on his visit to the Petun country in 1616.

His reason for calling them that was their neutrality in the wars between the Huron-Petun alliance and the five New York Iroquois tribes. The Huron name for the Neutral was Atiouandaronk, Attiwanfron, or Attiuindaron. The meaning of the name, according to Jerome Lalemant, was "people of a slightly different language." Their own collective, or confederacy name is not known. As among the Huron, it is probable that the tribal names were of greater importance than the confederacy name. The number of tribes belonging to the Neutral Confederacy is not known.

The known: Aondironnon (Ahondihronnon); the Onguiarahronon (Ongmarahronon, Niagagarega); and until 1638, the Wento (Ahouenrochrhonon, Oeanohoronons, Oenroronon, Oneronon), and others. Judging from 17th century maps and tribal lists, the following may also have been Neutral tribes: Antouaronon, Kakouagogo (Rakouagega, Ohreokouaehronon), and perhaps the Atiraguenrek (Attiragenrega).

The latter name is thought by some to be a variant of Attiouandaronk, the collective term. In the first half of the 17th century, the Neutral occupied a territory which arched around the west end of Lake Ontario from the present town of Milton, Ontario, through the Niagara Peninsula into New York State as far as Oak Orchard Creek.

No villages existed west of the Grand River in Ontario and south of Buffalo Creek in New York. Of the various Neutral tribes, the Aondirononnon occupied the northern frontier in Ontario; the Antouaronon were in the lower Grand River Valley; the Onguiarahronon were on the lands adjacent to the Niagara River; the Kakouagoga were on the present site of the city of Buffalo; and the Wenro were in an area thirty miles east of the Niagara near Oak Orchard Swamp. The main concentration of Neutral villages appears to have been between the cities of Hamilton and Brantford, Ontario. This was the area occupied by the Atiraguenrek.

LANGUAGE: No specimens of the Neutral language have survived. The Jesuits considered it to be similar to Huron, in other words, a dialect of Iroquoian. The linguistic similarities between the various Iroquoian speakers led the Jesuits to speculate that at one time the Huron, Neutral, and Iroquois had been one group. On their visit to the Neutral in 1640, Fathers Chaumonot and Brebeuf were able to adjust their Huron dictionary and syntax to the Neutral dialect in only twenty-five days. The Wenro dialect may have been more similar to Seneca than to Huron.

TRIBAL CULTURE: The area occupied by the Neutral is in the northern limits of the deciduous Carolinian forest zone in Ontario. As such, it has a milder climate and longer growing season than any other part of eastern Canada, a fact noted by all the 17th century visitors. Of particular importance were the extensive stretches of oak and chestnut forest throughout the area because they attracted large concentrations of deer. Extensive areas of well-drained sandy soil, preferred by all the Iroquoian groups for their crops, were common, as were excellent fishing sites at the mouths of the many creeks flowing into Lakes Ontario and Erie.

In the opinion of 17th century visitors, the Neutral shared almost all aspects of their culture with their cultural relatives, the Huron, Petun, and other Iroquoian groups. Judging from the distribution of archaeological sites containing French trade material, the various Neutral tribes were composed of spatially separated village clusters much like the five Iroquois tribes, but unlike the Huron and Petun. Most of the villages were fortified with a palisade.

On the average, their villages seem to have been smaller than those of the Huron, although some were up to eight acres in size, housing perhaps 2,000 people. Similar to other Iroquoian groups, the Neutral formed nuclear families gathered together into closely co-operating matrilineal extended families, each of which occupied a longhouse. The length of the longhouses varied in size of the extended family, but could be well over 100 feet. In width, these homes were about 25 feet, reflecting limitations in the bent saplings and bark, bonded together, that were used as construction materials.

Similar to the Huron, it is likely that the various extended families were put into matrilineal groups according to known descent along the female line. It is also likely that the Neutral had a clan system similar to the other Iroquoian groups, which would have acted as a socio-political force giving internal cohesion to the confederacy. The main staple was corn, followed by beans and squash. Hunting and fishing were well developed, although hunting seems to have been more important than among the Huron.

All early writers mention the high densities of deer, elk, and beaver in the area. Other important animals were the moose, turkey, raccoon, and black squirrel, with the latter two being hunted for their pelts. Neutral farming technology was typical of mild latitude slash-and-burn horticulture.

As a consequence, soils became exhausted over time, sometimes contributing to village relocation. Tobacco was a major crop grown for domestic use as well as export to the Huron. Politically, the Neutral were organized into largely autonomous villages whose affairs were regulated by a village council composed of the male heads of the extended families and presided over by a chief elected from one of the prominent clan segments. The powers of the chiefs were informal. Most acted as chairmen of the councils and spokesmen for the village. None had coercive powers. The most influential chiefs were those who had proven ability as leaders in war, were liberal with gifts, and were persuasive orators. Politics at the tribal and confederacy level is not clear.

Father Daillon reported the existence of a tribal or confederacy chief who had more power than his equivalent among the Huron. The function of such a chief would have been to call meetings of the tribal or confederacy councils which were made up of representatives from the various villages. Such meetings were to discuss common problems of trade and war. It is likely that the unusual powers described by Daillon for the Neutral chief were the reflection of personal qualities rather than powers that came with his office. Like their Iroquoian neighbors, the Neutral believed in a spirit world.

All animate and inanimate things had spirits that exercised a considerable influence on human affairs. Dream interpretation was important. This required the presence of a shaman, who was an influential member of the community. Similar to the Huron, the Neutral had a winter festival called *ononharoia*, or "the upsetting of the brain."

In describing this festival, Brebeuf and Chaumonot stated that its function was to drive out demons that possessed individuals. Judging from their description, two of the prime functions of *ononharoia* were to vent pent-up emotions and to redistribute wealth. During the festival, articles were seized from non- participants and not returned. The Neutral also practiced resurrection of the dead. This seems to have been an organized attempt to pass the virtues of a great man who had just died onto a deserving individual. After the ceremony, the individual so honored proceeded to act, and was treated like, the person whose spirit he had just acquired.

The Jesuits reported only four aspects of culture in which the Neutral differed from their neighbors. The first of these was their lack of dress. Although the women were covered from their waist to their knees, most of the men wore nothing. What clothes they had were highly decorated. The second way in which the Neutral differed was their fondness for tattooing and painting their entire bodies. Thirdly, the Jesuits reported somewhat different burial customs. The Neutral and Huron practiced ossuary burial, a large communal grave that was prepared during the Feast of the Dead shortly before a village was moved. The difference between the groups concerns the disposal of the bodies before they were interred in the ossuary.

While the Hurons would place their dead in temporary graves or on scaffolds outside the village, the Neutral would keep them in their houses until the corpses were in an advanced state of decomposition. The remaining flesh would then be removed for mourners until the feast-of-the-dead. Fourthly, the Jesuits reported that although the torture of male prisoners was common among all groups, the Neutral also tortured and burned to death female prisoners. Finally, the Jesuits were under the impression that the physique of the Neutrals appeared to be "taller, stronger, and better proportioned," than the Huron. Daillon reported that on his visit he "met no humpback, one-eyed, or deformed persons."

FOREIGN RELATIONS: At the time of European contact, the Neutral were at peace with their Iroquoian neighbors. The Huron-Petun and five Iroquois tribes, protagonists in an ancient war, considered the Neutral villages to be a sanctuary in which they were secure from attack. The reasons for their neutrality are not known. It is probable that it was in the interests of both warring groups to preserve friendly relations with the Neutral. The Neutral population was greater than the Huron and larger than the combined Iroquois tribes. Neither side could afford to wage war against a Neutral-Huron or Neutral-Iroquois alliance.

The Jesuits stated that because the main route traveled by the Huron and Seneca war parties lay through Neutral territory, it was in the interest of these tribes that they stay at peace with the Neutral. The Neutral on their part were engaged in a protracted conflict with the Assistaeronnon "fire people" or Mascouten, a group of semi-sedentary Algonquian tribes in the Michigan peninsula. In this conflict, were aided by the Ottawa.

For this reason, it was also in the interest of the Neutral to keep at peace with the Huron and five Iroquois tribes. The Neutral had strong trading ties with the Ottawa, Petun, and Huron. Algonquian products filtered south to the Neutral, while exotic skins, tobacco, and perhaps chert were traded in return. The extent of Neutral trade with their other Iroquoian neighbors is not known. It is probable that they traded with the Erie, Seneca, and Susquehannock.

HISTORY: The prehistoric origins of the Neutral have been traced to archaeological cultures in Southwestern Ontario. Their first contact with Europeans was with Champlain, who was visiting the Petun in 1616. Although the Neutral invited Champlain to visit them, the Petun and Ottawa dissuaded him, saying that the Neutral would kill him in revenge for a Neutral they had killed earlier. As knowledge of the Neutral grew, some Frenchmen began to contact them directly. Best known of these men were the interpreters and traders, Brule and Grenole.

It was Brule who kindled the interest of the Recollet Order in sending a missionary to the Neutral. As a result, Father Joseph de la Roche Daillon set out from the Huron in October 1626 to spend part of the winter with the Neutral. The object of his trip was not only to spread the Gospel, but also to conclude a trade agreement with the Neutral. The Neutral showed some interest in his proposals, but were apparently unskilled in the use of canoes, and unfamiliar with the route to the Saint Lawrence River.

When the Huron heard of Daillon's proposals, they did everything to turn the Neutral against the priest. Over the years, the Huron had assumed a position as middlemen in a lucrative trade between the French and a number of inland tribes, including the Neutral. This trade would have evaporated if the Neutral had developed direct trade contacts with the French.

As a result of Huron innuendoes, Daillon was driven from the Neutral villages and considered himself lucky to escape with his life. Little was known about the Neutral until 1638, when some 600 desperately ill and starving refugee Wenro tribal members arrived at the village of Ossossane in Huronia. Earlier they had sent an embassy to the Huron requesting that they be permitted to settle there.

The original cause for the Wenro migration is not known. For some reason they had incurred the displeasure of the other Neutral tribes, who terminated their alliance with them. This placed the Wenro open to attack from their eastern neighbors, the Seneca. Unable to mount an adequate defense, and suffering from epidemic diseases, the Wenro decided to leave their territory and join the Huron. A small number of Wenro settled among the Neutral.

A possible reason for Seneca animosity towards the Wenro may have been the latter's attempts to trade directly with the Dutch and English, a prerogative that the Seneca and their Iroquois allies probably tried to keep for themselves. Evidence of Wenro occupation has been determined archaeologically in Huronia at the site of Ossossane and neighboring villages. In 1639 the Neutral were hit by a severe famine. Some fled to the Petun, while others sold their children for corn. During that year and the previous two, smallpox and other contagious diseases had gripped the Neutral as well as the Petun and Huron.

In November 1640, the Jesuits opened their mission for the Neutral under Fathers Brebeuf and Chaumonot. The Neutral had somewhat of a preconceived notion of fear concerning the priests because some Huron had claimed the latter were sorcerers who were causing the epidemics. The Jesuits, in turn, tried to allay these fears by pretending to be traders. Once the Jesuits had been tentatively accepted, they sought permission to spend the winter in the country. The confederacy council finally rendered the decision to let them remain until their chief, Souharissen, had returned from war. Only he, they claimed, could make the final decision.

The Jesuits then dropped their pretense as traders and began missionary activities. When the Huron saw that the Jesuits were permitted to remain among the Neutral, their fear of a French-Neutral trade alliance was heightened. Consequently, they began an active campaign to either have the Jesuits thrown out of the country, or have them killed. Their principal accusation was that the Jesuits wanted to kill as many Neutral as possible through their sorcery and diseases in order to gain their souls. The Huron also accused the Jesuits, principally Brebeuf, of seeking an alliance with the Seneca against the Neutral.

The result of these accusations was that the Neutral council asked the Jesuits to leave. Brebeuf and Chaumonot, however, refused and found shelter among some individuals who were better disposed toward them. Finally, in March 1642, when it seemed as if the two priests were in serious danger, the decision was made by the Order to remove them from the Neutral, thus ending the Neutral mission and direct French contact. During the next few years, the Jesuits attempted to carry on the mission by sending Huron converts to the Neutral. The success of these men appears to have been limited.

In spite of the fact that 100 Neutral came to Huronia in 1643 requesting the Jesuits to return, the mission was not reopened. During the 1640s, the Iroquois tribes were carrying their war more successfully into Huronia. In 1647, they succeeded in dispersing the Arenda-ronon, a Huron tribe on the eastern frontier of Huronia. That same year, the victorious Seneca turned on the Neutral and managed to destroy the main village of the Aondironnon territory.

Since the Aondironnon had not prevented the deaths, they had compromised their neutrality. To the surprise of the Huron and the Jesuits, the Neutral Confederacy made no effort to avenge the destruction of the Aondironnon. Instead, the Neutral tried to have their captives among the Seneca restored peacefully. The Seneca attack may have been the first phase in a deliberate plan to disperse the Neutral in order to gain access to their beaver hunting grounds.

As Seneca power declined, the Neutral probably felt that they were in a poor position to engage the Iroquois tribes militarily. In 1649, the Iroquois, largely led by the Seneca and Onondaga, managed to destroy and disperse the Huron. By the spring of 1650, the Petun were also forced to abandon their country. Many Huron and Petun fled to the Neutral, who were now seeking arms and other help from the French.

The Iroquois, however, moved swiftly against the Neutral, and in the autumn of 1650, they destroyed one of the principal Neutral villages with a force of 1,500 men. The Neutral, led by a Huron contingent, retaliated and killed 200 Iroquois. The news of this defeat caused the Seneca to move the population of their main village temporarily to the Cayuga. At about this time the Neutral concluded an alliance with the Susquehannock, with whom they had had a long-standing trading alliance.

The Iroquois were quick to avenge their losses. In the early winter of 1651, they returned with an army of 600 to 1200 men and destroyed the main Neutral village, Teotondiation. As a result of this loss the Neutral, along with the Petun and Huron refugees, began to disperse. Some were captured, and others joined the Seneca, where they were still reported as maintaining an identity as late as 1673. Others may have fled to the Erie and the Susquehannock.

In July 1653, a group of 800 Neutral were reported wintering in eastern Michigan on the peninsula between Saginaw Bay and Lower Lake Huron. Their aim was to join with the refugee Petun camped on the south shore of the Straits of Mackinac, as well as with some Algonquian bands from the Sault Saint Marie area. It is possible that this group merged with the Petun to become the historic Wyandotte.

173

POPULATION: Estimates of the total Neutral population have varied greatly. Champlain, who had never come in contact with the Neutral, considered them to be a powerful group with 40 villages, capable of fielding 4,000 warriors, while others reported 5,000 to 6,000 warriors. Father Daillon, after his 1626 visit to the Neutral, wrote that they had 28 principal villages. Probably the most accurate population estimate was made by Fathers Brebeuf and Chaumonot, after their five months sojourn among the Neutral. It was their opinion that there were about 40 villages containing 12,000 people and 4,000 warriors. The Fathers added that the original population had been greatly reduced by three years of famine, epidemics, and war.

The ten villages in which the Fathers stayed the longest had 500 fires and 3,000 people. The figures given by Brebeuf and Chaumonot represent a post epidemic population, which, of course, did not include the Wenro, most of which had left the area by 1638. Death rates among the neighboring Huron during the same period were estimated at 60 percent. A similar death rate among the Neutral would place their pre-epidemic population in the neighborhood of 30,000 people, excluding the Wenro.

A second approach to the problem is the relationship between 500 fires and 300 people. Since there were two nuclear families to a fire in an Iroquoian longhouse, these figures imply a post- epidemic family size of three people. In view of what is known about Iroquoian family structure, this figure should be doubled, implying a loss of life of at least 50 percent as a result of the epidemics.

A final pre-epidemic estimate of 33,000, including the Wenro, does not seem unreasonable. This estimate lends support to Father Le Jeune's statement, written in 1634, that the Neutral were "much more populous than the Huron," and that their numbers were roughly around 30,000; later estimates reduced the number to 18,000 or 21,000. Since the Neutral ceased to exist as a tribal entity in 1651, post-dispersal population estimates are not available.

CONCLUSIONS: From the little that is known about the Neutral, it appears that in the early part of the 17th century they were the largest of the native confederacies in the Great Lakes area. For some time, they managed to remain at peace with the other warring Iroquoian groups, but fought extensive campaigns against the Algonquian Mascouten in the Michigan area. As competition for trading rights and beaver hunting areas increased during the 1630s and 1640s, the Neutral Confederacy began to disintegrate. In 1638, the Wenro were abandoned by the Neutral and defeated by the Seneca, followed by the Aondironnon in 1647.

In spite of these setbacks, and with either an inability or unwillingness to perceive the consequences of their policy, the Neutral still tried to remain outside the Huron-Iroquois conflict.

By 1649, when the Huron were destroyed, the balance of power shifted dramatically in favor of the Iroquois. Too late, the Neutral entered the war joined by Petun and Huron refugees. In two years, the Neutral were defeated and dispersed to such an extent that there is no further mention of them after 1653. Twenty years after their defeat, the old Neutral territory was known as a beaver hunting ground of the Iroquois.

Like many northeastern native groups, the Neutral got caught in events not of their making and rivalries they thought had nothing to do with them.   Like the Huron, the Neutral failed to appreciate the changing motives and methods of Iroquois warfare until it was too late.

NIANTIC

The Niantic were an Algonquian tribe formerly living on the coast of Connecticut, from Niantic Bay to the Connecticut River. According to De Forest, they once formed one tribe with the Niantic of Rhode Island, which was cut in two by the Pequot invasion. Their main village, also called Niantic, was near the present town of that name. Another important village was Wekapaug, on the great pond near present Charlestown. They were subject to the Pequot, and had no political connection with the eastern Niantic. They were nearly destroyed in the war of 1637, with its survivors placed under Mohegan rule.

They became so closely connected with the Narragansett, they formed practically one tribe with them. By refusing to join in King Phillip's war in 1675, they preserved their territory and tribal organization. At the close of the war, the Narragansett, who had submitted to the English, were placed with the Niantic under Ninigret, and the whole body thereafter took the name of Narragansett.

They numbered about 100 in 1638, and about 85 in 1761. Many traceable Niantic members joined the Brotherton Indians in New York about 1788, with none now existing under their own name. According to Kendall, they had a village near Danbury, Connecticut in 1809, but were probably a remnant of the western Connecticut tribes, not Niantic. According to Speck, many mixed-Niantic-Mohegans lived into the early 1900s, descendants of a pure Niantic woman from the mouth of the Niantic River. Their voices were reportedly more high-pitched than their neighbors.

Today's Niantics, or their mixed-blood descendants, may live on the Eastern and Western Pequot Reservations, and the Schaghticoke Reservation, and in the Mohegan Community in Connecticut, and the Narraganset Community in Rhode Island.

NINHAM, DANIEL

Daniel Ninham (Wappinger, 1710 – August 1778), was a chief of the Mahican in Westenhuck, New York who supported the colonial settlers in both the French and Indian War, and the American Revolution, and who pressed Wappinger territorial claims all the way to England. He became principal chief of his tribe in 1740.

During the hostilities of 1740-48 Nimham supported the British forces against the French. He enlisted his warriors under Sir William Johnson in 1755 to fight for the colonial settlers during the French and Indian War, and participated in the construction of Fort William Henry and the Battle of Lake George in September, 1755. About 1762 Nimham and a group of Connecticut Mahican chiefs travelled to England to press the recovery of certain tribal lands from the colonies. Having been well received, they returned to North America and entered into court proceedings to regain their territory. Unfortunately the American Revolution began shortly, and the court claims were never settled.

Once more Nimham joined the colonial settlers, and in August 1778 was killed in battle at Kingsbridge, New York. The state of New York regarded Nimham as a loyal and steadfast citizen, and entered his name in the memorial lists of those who served in the Revolution.

NINIGRET

Ninigret (Niantic, 1600 - 1678), also known as Nenekunat, Ninicraft, Janemo and Ayanemo, was a sachem of the Narraganset Tribe. He lived in Wequapaug, Rhode Island, and found himself continually having to walk a tight wire of diplomacy, because of the always-tenuous relationship between whites and Indians. He tried to remain neutral during the Pequot-Narragansett War in 1632, but the Boston authorities were offended by his independent stance and it caused a rift in their relations. In 1637, Uncas felt that he was siding with the Pequot, claiming that he was harboring some of their warriors and Ninigret had to appear before the colonial court to defend himself against these charges.

He was also involved in a treaty situation where he was forced to abide by, as well as to pay a large annual amount of "good white wampum." Then in May of 1645, he was brought into court again on another charge, plus his failure to pay the sum of wampum from the first agreement. He was one of a whole group of Narragansett chiefs that was fined 2,000 fathoms of the wampum, which amounted to a string of handmade shell beads almost two and a half miles in length.

It was an amount that was beyond the means of the tribe to pay and was a constant source of contention between them and the whites. Until this amount was settled, the Natives were not allowed to leave Boston. When Ninigret finally left Boston for a short time in 1652, he visited the city of Manhattan, spending the winter with the Dutch. Uncas once again leveled accusations at him, telling the colonists that he was conspiring against the English, and during the next year, he was summoned to Boston.

None of the charges could be confirmed, and the situation deepened Ninigret's anger at the whites. He was also involved in intertribal problems, attacking the Long Islands Indians, which resulted in the death of his nephew. He intended to declare all out war, but the English got wind of it and gathered some 300 men led by Major Willard. Ninigret tried hard, abandoning his village, and hiding in a nearby swamp, but eventually he was again forced to swallow his pride and agree to a peace treaty in which it was required of him to pay more wampum. Both the Niantic and Narragansett Tribes continued to do battle with the Long Island Indians and Uncas continued to accuse Ninigret and others of various infractions, when it would suit his purpose.

After a colonist's home was set on fire by an unknown tribal member, Ninigret, along with other chiefs were ordered to deliver the perpetrators to Boston for punishment, otherwise they would have to pay more wampum fines. In addition, Ninigret was presented with a bill for his outstanding fines from before, and was issued a threat that if it were not paid, his people would be sold into slavery in the Barbados Islands. It is doubtful that the British were ever paid their wampum, as authorities later accepted a mortgage on Niantic land. After a time, Ninigret backed off from the fray and began to live out the rest of his years quietly, avoiding too much involvement in King Philip's War of 1675-1676. He died at his Wequapaug home. He had his admirers, including Roger Williams, who described him as "proud and fierce".

NIPMUC

The Nipmuc (from *nipamaug* "freshwater fishing place") are one of the inland tribes of central Massachusetts that originally lived chiefly in the south part of Worcester County, extending into Connecticut and Rhode Island. Their chief seats were on the headwaters of the Blackstone and Quinebaug rivers, and around the ponds of Brookfield. Hassanamesit seems to have been their principal village in 1674, but their villages had no apparent political connection, and the different parts of their territory were subject to their more powerful neighbors, the Massachusetts, Wampanoag, Narragansett, and Mohegan, and even the Mohawk.

The Nashua, dwelling farther north, are sometimes classed with the Nipmuc, but were rather a distinct body. The New England missionaries had seven villages of Christian Indians among them in 1674; but at the outbreak of King Philip's War in the next year, almost all of them joined the hostile tribes. At its close, they fled to Canada or westward to the Mahican and other tribes on the Hudson. During the early 20th century, social activities and public education were begun, and the Council of New England Indians was founded, with a Nipmuc chapter formed later. In the 1970s, the Massachusetts Commission on Indian Affairs was created, and this reaffirmed stewardship by the state.

The tribe petitioned for federal acknowledgment in the 1980s. Although the Nipmuc has no land, two parcels are held privately for their use, the Chaubunagungamaug Reservation in Thompson, Connecticut, and the Hassanamesit in Webster, Massachusetts. The group today has organized the Nipmuc Tribal Acknowledgment Project in Worcester, which is funded by grants and private support.

Economic and social development programs have been planned, and the project will also aid in publishing information on Nipmuc history and culture. A government was created in 1991, and its organization is being formed and initiated. Distinct social groups continue to be maintained, and a number of powwows, festivals, and ceremonial events are held. Crafts, language, and traditional philosophy are maintained through the Algonquian School in Providence, Rhode Island.

ONASAKENRAT, JOSEPH

Joseph Onasakenrat (Mohawk, September 4, 1845 - February 8, 1881), also known as White Feather, was a chief who was noted for his translations of religious works into his native language. Born on his father's farm, near Oka, Canada. At fourteen years of age, he was sent to Montreal College to be educated for the priesthood, remainin about four years. He was afterward converted to Protestantism and became an evangelical preacher.

On June 15, 1877, the Catholic Church of Oka was burned, and Chief Joseph was tried for the offense, but was not convicted. Among his translations into the Mohawk dialect are the Gospels (1880) and a volume of hymns. He died suddenly, February 8, 1881, at Caughnawaga. At the time of his death, he was engaged in translating the remainder of the Bible, having reached the Epistles to the Hebrews.

ONEIDA

(SEE 5 NATIONS IROQUOIS) Oneida is an Anglicized compressed form of the common Iroquois term *tiionen'iote*, "there it is - rock has - set up (continuative)," i.e. "a rock that something set up and is still standing", referring to a large boulder near the site of one of their ancient villages. A tribe of the Five Nations Iroquois Confederacy, the Oneida formerly occupied the country south of Oneida Lake, Oneida County, New York, and including the upper waters of the Susquehanna. According to authentic tradition, the Oneida was the second tribe to accept the proposition of Dekanawida and Hiawatha to form a defensive and offensive league of all the tribes of men for the promotion of mutual welfare and security. In the federal council and in other federal assemblies, they had the right to representation by nine federal chieftains of the highest rank.

Like the Mohawk, the Oneida had only three clans: The Turtle, the Wolf, and the Bear, each clan being represented by three of the nine federal representatives of this tribe. Insofar as eldership, a member of a clan phratry can give precedence in roll-call and the right to discuss first in order all matters coming before its side of the council fire. The Oneida were the dominant tribe within the tribal phratry, called the Four (originally Two) Brothers and "Offspring," to which they belonged. In tribal assemblies, the Turtle and the Wolf constituted a clan phratry, and the Bear another. The Oneida were usually conservative in dealing with others.

In 1635 they, with the Onondaga, Cayuga, and Mohawk, sought to become parties to the peace concluded in the preceding year between the Seneca and the Hurons. At this period they were called sedentary and quite populous, but only from Indian reports. The *Jesuit Relation* for 1646 said that with the exception of the Mohawk, there was no treaty, properly speaking, then in existence between the Iroquois tribes inclusive of the Oneida and the French.

From the same book, it was learned that "Onnicoute" (*Oneniote*), the principal Oneida village of that time, having lost the greater portion of its men in a war with the "upper Algonquin," was compelled to request the Mohawk to lend aid in repeopling the village by granting thereto a colony of men, and that it was for this reason that the Mohawk ceremonially and publicly call the Oneida their daughters or sons.

This story was probably due to a misconception of the fictitious political kinships and relationships established between the several tribes at the time of the institution and organization of the League. The Cayuga and the Tuscarora were likewise called "Offspring," but not for the same reason. The *Jesuit Relation* for 1648) first definitely located the Oneida.

From the *Relation* for 1641, it is gathered that the Jesuit fathers had learned that the Oneida had a peculiar form of government in which the rulership alternated between the two sexes. This statement was likewise apparently due to a misconception of the fact that among Iroquois tribes, the titles to the chieftanships belonged to the women of certain clans in the tribe and not to the men, although men were chosen by the women to exercise the rights and privileges and to perform the duties pertaining to these chieftanships.

There were, and still are, a number of women filling federal chief-tanships bearing the name of the highest class. These women chief-tains had approximately the same rights, privileges, and immunities as the men chiefs, but exercised them fully only in emergencies. They also maintained the institutions of society and government among women. The *Jesuit Relation* for 1667 declared that the Oneida were, at that time, the least tractable of the Iroquois tribes. It was at this period that Father Bruyas was stationed at the mission of Saint Francois Xavier among the Oneida. This same source relates that the Mohegan and the Conestoga menaced the Oneida. While on this mission, Father Bruyas suffered malnutrition a part of the year and was compelled to live on dried frogs.

By the end of 1669, he had baptized 30 people. In 1660, the Oneida with the Mohawk were the least populous of the Iroquois tribes. *The Jesuit Relation* for 1669-70 speaks of the Oneida being present at a "feast of the dead" held at the Mohawk village of Caughnawaga, showing that in a modified form at least, the decennial ceremony of the so-called "Dead Feast" was practiced among the Iroquois when first known. On January 30, 1671, the Oneida prolonged the torture of a captive Conestoga woman through two days and two nights. Some records say that a town that was defended by four lines of palisades closely fastened together, and attacked by Champlain with Huron and Algonquian allies in 1615 was an Oneida village, Other authorities place it elsewhere, on Onondaga territory.

In fact, the wars of the Oneida were those of the League, although like the other tribes, they seem to have put forth most energy against their greatest enemies, the Catawba and Muskhogean tribes, as well as the Susquehanna River Indians, and the Conestoga. After the conquest of the tribes on the Susquehanna and its tributaries, and those on the Potomac, chiefly by the warriors of the Oneida, the Cayuga, and the Seneca, and those tribes which had submitted to Iroquois rule, a question arose as to the propriety of the Mohawk receiving bounty while not having aided in the struggle.

For a time the Mohawk received no enrichment from this source, until the Iroquois tribes became divided and the Mohawk sold the lands in the Wyoming Valley region of Pennsylvania to the Susquehanna Land Company of Connecticut. In 1728, the great federal council of the league at Onondaga sent Shikellamy, an Oneida chief,

181

as a superintendent, to the forks of the Susquehanna to watching over the affairs and the interests of the Six Nations of Iroquois in Pennsylvania. At first, Shikellamy supervised only the Shawnee and the Delawares, who thereafter had to consult him in all matters concerning the proprietary government. He performed his duty so well that in 1745, Shikellamy was made full superintendent over all the dependent tribes on the Susquehanna, with his residence at Shamokin. He showed great astuteness, seeking at all times to promote the interests of his people.

Such was the influence that the Oneida exercised on the Susquehanna. In 1687 the Oneida were included in the warrant of the King of Great Britain to Governor Dongan of New York authorizing him to protect the Five Nations as subjects of Great Britain. In 1696, Count Frontenac burned the Oneida castle, destroyed all their corn, and made prisoners of 30 men, women, and children. In 1645-46, the Oneida were at war with the Nipissing, and one band of 17 warriors from "Ononiiote" defeated an Algonquin party under Teswshat, their one-eyed chief, killing his son and taking two women prisoners. This Iroquois party was afterward defeated by 30 Hurons, and the two women were recaptured.

In the *Jesuit Relation* for 1666-68, Father Bruyas wrote that the Oneida were reputed to be the most cruel of all the Iroquois tribes, that they always made war on the Algonquin and the Hurons, and that two-thirds of their villages were composed of the people of these two tribes who had become Iroquois in temper and inclination. This missionary added that the nature of the Oneida was then altogether barbarous, cruel, sly, cunning, and prone to bloodshed and carnage. In 1655, a party of 60 Oneida warriors was sent against the Amikwa, or Beaver Indians.

This war was still in progress in 1661, for in that year, two bands, one of 24 and the other of 30 warriors, were encountered on their way to fight the Amikwa. Chauchetiere, in a letter in (Jesuit Relations, Thwaites ed., LXII, 185,) 1900 said that "war is blazing in the country of the Outaouaks," and that the Iroquois, especially the Oneida, continued their hatred of the Outagami (Foxes) and the Illinois, and so had slain and captured many Illinois. In 1681, they killed or captured about 1,000 of these unfortunate people. In 1711, about half of the Tuscarora tribe then dwelling in North Carolina, seems to have conspired with several alien neighboring tribes and bands to destroy the Carolina settlers.

The colonists, however, recollecting the ancient feud between the Southern and the Northern Indians, allied themselves with the Catawba and some Muskhogean tribes. The Tuscarora, sustaining several severe defeats, were finally driven from their homes and hunting grounds. This act of the Southern Indians made the hatred of the Iroquois against the Catawba more bitter and merciless. The Oneida were at times friendly to the French and to the Jesuit missionaries, while the other Iroquois were their determined enemies. A great part of the Oneida and the Tuscarora, through the influence of Reverend Samuel Kirkland, remained neutral in the American Revolution, while the majority of the confederation of the Iroquois were divided and did not act as a unit in this manner.

Early in that struggle, the hostile Iroquois tribes attacked the Oneida and burned one of their villages, forcing them to take refuge near the Americans in the vicinity of Schenectady, where they remained until the close of the war. Shortly after, the main body of the tribe returned to their former homes. At a later period, many imigrated to Canada and settled on Grand River and Thames River, Ontario. Another small band, called Oriskas, formed a new settlement at Ganowarohare, a few miles from the main body in Oneida County, New York.

At different earlier periods, the Oneida adopted and gave lands to the Tuscarora, the Stockbridges, and the Brothertons. The Tuscarora moved afterward to land granted by the Seneca in western New York. In 1846, having sold most of their lands in New York, the greater part of the Oneida, together with their last two adopted tribes, moved to a tract on Green Bay, Wisconsin.

Among those living in New York when moved were two parties known respectively as the First Christian and the Second Christian or Orchard party. The Oneida entered into treaties with the United States at Fort Stanwix, New York on October 22, 1784; at Fort Harmar on January 9, 1789; at Canandaigua, New York on November 11, 1794; Oneida, New York on December 2, 1794; at Buffalo Creek, New York on January 15, 1838; and at Washington, D.C. on February 3, 1838.

They also held no fewer than 30 treaties with the State of New York between the years 1788 and 1842. Oneida towns, so far as known, were: Awegen, Brothertown, Cahunghage, Canowdowsa, Cowassalon,

Chittenango, Ganadoga, Hostayuntwa, Oneida, Opolopong, Oriska, Ossewingo, Ostogeron, Schoherage, Sevege, Solocka, Stockbridge, Tegasoke, Teseroken, Teiosweken, and Tkanetota. In 1792, about 630 Oneida were left in New York. About this time, they began selling their lands and looking for homes farther west, free from encroachment from whites. Most other Oneida, who were loyal to the British, had moved to Canada.

The Oneida purchased land in the early 1800s from the Memominees in Wisconsin. Most of this land was later lost through legal battles, treaties, and fraud. In more recent times, about 2,000 tribally owned acres remained, along with nearly 500 acres of allotted lands.

About 3,000 Oneida were living in the Wisconsin area, and another 2,000 were living either in New York or along the Thames River in Ontario, Canada.

Today, there are three separate Oneida communities, each with its own political system. They include the Wisconsin, the Ontario, and the New York Oneidas. The Wisconsin community is located in the Green Bay area. Many members of the Wisconsin tribe belong to the Episcopal and Methodist churches. Some also practice the Longhouse Religion of Handsome Lake.

Few members still speak the native language. However, the tribal school holds language classes. Arts and crafts have continued, including beadwork, silverwork, and carving. An annual powwow is held by the tribe. In a recent count, the community has 11,000 tribal members. The New York tribe lives near Oneida, New York.

A traditional system functions, although there has been much conflict between factions within the tribe. There were recently 700 tribal members, and many Christian denominations have followers among them. Many individuals also practice the Longhouse Religion. The Ontario Oneidas are ruled by an elective system consisting of 12 members and one chief. Conflicts have arisen between those who practice traditional religious beliefs and those who belong to other religions.

About 3,000 tribal members were counted recently in Ontario, Canada. Through the twentieth century, each of the tribes retained its identity. The two tribes located in the United States have facilities for gambling. All three tribes have filed a land claim against New York State asking for the return of, or payment for, land taken from them in the 18th and 19th centuries. Although they have won twice in the

United States Supreme Court, resolution of the case has been ongoing for more than twenty years.

ONONDAGA

An important tribe of the Five Nations Iroquois Confederation, The Onondaga formerly lived on the mountain, lake, and creek bearing their name, in the present Onondaga County, New York, and extending northward to Lake Ontario and southward perhaps to the Susquehanna River. In Iroquois councils they are known as *Hodisennageta*, "they (are) the name bearers." their principal village, also the capital of the confederation, was called Onondaga, later Onondaga Castle; it was situated from before 1654 to 1681 on Indian hill, in the present town of Pompey.

In 1677, it contained 140 cabins. It was removed to Butternut Creek, where the fort was burned in 1696. In 1720 it was again removed to Onondaga Creek, and their later reserve was in that valley, a few miles south of the lake. The Onondaga of Grand River Reservation, Canada, have 9 clans, namely: Wolf, Tortoise, Bear, Deer, Eel, Beaver, Ball, Plover, and Pigeonhawk. The Wolf, Bear, Plover, Ball, and Pigeonhawk clans have each only one federal chiefship; the Beaver, Tortoise, and Eel clans have each two federal chiefships, while the Deer clan has three. The reason for this marked difference in the quotas of chiefships for the several clans is not definitely known, but it may be due to the adoption of groups of persons who already possessed chieftanship titles.

In federal ceremonial and social assemblies, the Onondaga by right of membership therein, take their places with the tribal phratry of the "Three Brothers," of which the Mohawk and the Seneca are the other two members. In federal councils of all the five (latterly six) Iroquois tribes, the Onondaga tribe itself constitutes a tribal phratry; while the Mohawk and the Seneca together form a second; and the Oneida and the Cayuga originally, and later the Tuscarora, form a third tribal phratry.

The federal council is organized on the basis of these three tribal phratries. The functions of the Onondaga phratry are in many respects similar to those of a judge holding court with a jury. The question before the council is discussed respectively by the Mohawk and Seneca tribes on the one side, and then by the Oneida, the Cayuga, and, later, the Tuscarora tribes on the other, within their own phratries. When these two phratries have independently reached the same or a differing opinion, it is then submitted to the Onondaga phratry for confirmation or rejection.

Confirmation of a common opinion or of one of the two differing opinions makes it the decree of the council. In refusing to confirm an opinion, the Onondaga must show that it is in conflict with established custom or with public policy; when two differing opinions are rejected, the Onondaga may suggest to the two phratries a course by which they may be able to reach a common opinion; but the Onondaga may confirm one of two differing opinions submitted to it. Each chieftain has the right to discuss and argue the question before the council either for or against its adoption by the council, in a speech or speeches addressed to the entire body of councilors and to the public.

Champlain related that in 1622, the Montagnais, the Etchemin, and the Hurons had for a long time sought peace between themselves and the Iroquois, but that up to that time there was always some serious obstacle to the consummation of an agreement on account of the fixed distrust which each side had for the other. Many times they asked Champlain himself to help make a firm and durable peace.

They informed him that they understood by making a treaty that the interview of the ambassadors must be amicable, the one side accepting the words of faith of the other not to harm or prevent them from hunting throughout the country, and they on their side agreeing to act in like manner toward their enemies, in this case the Iroquois, and that they had no other agreements or compacts precedent to the making of a firm peace.

They importuned Champlain many times to give them his advice in this matter, which they promised faithfully to follow. They assured him that they were then exhausted and weary of the wars which they had waged against each other for more than fifty years, and that, on account of their burning desire for revenge for the murder of their kin and friends, their ancestors had never before thought of peace. In this last statement is probably found approximately the epoch of that historic feud mentioned in the *Jesuit Relation* for 1660 and by Nicholas Perrot, which made the Iroquois tribes, on the one hand, and the Algonquin on the Ottawa and Saint Lawrence Rivers, on the other, inveterate enemies, although this may have been but a renewal and widening of a still earlier quarrel.

In 1535, Cartier learned from the Iroquoian tribes on the Saint Lawrence River that they were continually tormented by enemies to the southward, called Toudamani (probably identical with Tsonnontouan, or Seneca, a name then meaning 'Upper Iroquois'), who continually waged war on them. In September 1655, the Onondaga sent a delegation of 18 persons to Quebec to confer with Governor de Lauson and with the Algonkin and Hurons. The Onondaga spokesman used 24 wampum belts in his address; the first 8 were presents to the Hurons and the Algonquin, whose leading chiefs were there.

Each present had their name. The Onondaga professed to speak for the "four upper Iroquois Nations," namely, the Seneca, Cayuga, Oneida, and Onondaga, thus leaving only the Mohawk, the "lower Iroquois," from this peace conference, but the Onondaga speaker promised to persuade the Mohawk to change their minds and to make peace.

The Onondaga asked for priests to live among them and for French soldiers to aid them in their war against the Erie. In May 1657, 10 years after the dispersal of the Hurons from their motherland, the Onondaga sought, by the giving of numerous presents and by covert threats of war, to persuade the Hurons who had fled to the vicinity of Quebec to return to their country and to form with them a single people.

The Mohawk and the Seneca also were engaged in this business. Finally, the Hurons were forced to submit to the persistent demands of the Iroquois tribes. In 1686, the Onondaga were at war against the Cherermons. They were divided into two bands, one of 50 and another of 250, 50 of the latter being from other tribes. But in 1688, the Onondaga were considerably under French influence and were regarded as chief among the Iroquois tribes. In 1682, at Albany, the Onondaga, with the Mohawk, the Oneida, the Cayuga, and the Seneca, entered into a treaty of peace with the commissioners from the colony of Maryland, who contracted not only for the white settlers, but also for the Piscataway Indians.

With the exception of a part of the Seneca, the Onondaga were the last of the five tribes originally forming the League of the Iroquois to accept fully the principles of the universal peace proposed by

Dekanawida and Hiawatha. Early in 1647, a band of Onondaga approaching the Huron country was defeated by a troop of Huron warriors, the Onondaga chief being killed and a number were taken prisoners. Among the latter was Annenraes, a man of character and authority among the Onondaga. In the following spring, he learned that some of the Hurons who had been bitterly disappointed because his life had been spared intended to kill him.

To some of his Huron friends, he related what he had heard, and that he intended to escape. His resolution, and the reason for making it, was reported to the leading Huron chiefs of the council, and they concluded to aid him, trusting that he would render service in return. Giving presents and provisions, they sent him off secretly at night. Crossing Lake Ontario, he unexpectedly encountered 300 Onondaga making canoes to cross the lake for the purpose of avenging his death (believing he had been killed by the Hurons), and awaiting the arrival of 800 Seneca and Cayuga reinforcements.

His countrymen regarded Annenraes as one risen from the dead. He persuaded the 300 Onondaga to give up all thought of war, whereupon the band, without waiting for the expected reinforcements, returned to Onondaga.

A tribal council resolved to send an embassy with presents to the Hurons to negotiate peace. The chief of this embassy was by birth a Huron named Soiones, so naturalized in the country of his adoption that it was said of him that "no Iroquois had done more massacres in these countries, nor blows more wicked than he." He was accompanied by three other Hurons, which had not long been captives at Onondaga. The embassy arrived at Saint Ignace July 9, 1647, and found the Hurons divided as to the expediency of agreeing to the Onondaga proposals; the Bear Tribe of the Hurons justly feared duplicity, though the enemy bore presents.

However, the Rock Tribe and many villages desired peace, hoping for the return of their kin, captured by the Onondaga. After many councils and conferences, an embassy was sent to Onondaga to better to fathom this matter. For presents, the Hurons took valuable furs, while the Iroquois Onondaga used belts of wampum. The Huron embassy was well received at Onondaga, where a month was spent in holding councils. Finally the Onondaga resolved to send back a second embassy, headed by Skanawati (Scandaouati), a federal chieftain,

60 years of age, who was to be accompanied by two other Onondaga and by 15 Huron captives. One of the Huron embassy remained as a hostage.

This embassy was 30 days on the way, although it was in fact only 10 days' journey. Jean Baptiste, the returning Huron delegate, brought back 7 wampum belts of the largest kind, each composed of 3,000 or 4,000 beads. By these belts the Onondaga sought to confirm the peace, assuring the Hurons that they could hope for the deliverance of at least 100 more of their captive kin.

The Onondaga desired this peace not only because the life of Annenraes had been spared, but also because they were jealous that the Mohawk, who had become insolent from their victories and were overbearing even to their allies, might become more so if the Hurons failed to unite all their forces against them, and further because of fear of the power of the Conestoga.

In this Onondaga project of peace, the Cayuga and Oneida showed favorable interest, but the Seneca would not listen to it. The Mohawk were still more averse to it as they were jealous of what had been done by the Onondaga. Hence these last two tribes sent forces to attack the village of Saint Ignace at the end of the winter of 1647-48. Early in January 1648 the Hurons sent another embassy to Onondaga. They sent six men, accompanied by one of the three Onondaga ambassadors then in their country, the other two, including Skanawati, the head of the Onondaga embassy, remaining as hostages.

Unfortunately the new Huron embassy was captured and killed by a force of 100 Mohawk and Seneca who had come to the borders of the Huron country. The Onondaga accompanying this embassy was spared, and two Hurons escaped. Early in April, when the distressing news reached the ears of Skanawati, the proud Onondaga ambassador remaining with the Hurons as a hostage, he suddenly disappeared.

The Hurons believed that he had stolen away, but, a few days after his disappearance, his corpse was found in the forest lying on a bed of fir branches, where he had taken his own life by cutting his throat.

His companion, who was notified in order to exonerate the Hurons, said that the cause of his despair was the shame he felt at the contempt shown for the sacredness of his person by the Seneca and the Mohawk, by their going to the Huron country and massacring the Huron people, while his life was pledged for the keeping of the faith of his people.

Of such men was the great federal council of the Iroquois composed. The Onondaga had good reason for fearing the Conestoga, for the *Jesuit Relation* for 1647-48 states that in a single village there were 1,300 men capable war, indicating for this village alone a population of more than 4,500.

At this time the Conestoga chiefs, through two messengers, informed the Hurons that if they felt too weak to defend themselves, they should send the Conestoga word by an embassy. The Hurons eagerly seized this opportunity by sending on this mission four Christian Indians and four "infidels," headed by one Charles Ondaaiondiont. They arrived at Conestoga early in June 1647.

The Huron deputies informed their Conestoga friends that they had come from a land of souls, where war and the fear of their enemies had spread desolation everywhere, where the fields were covered with blood and the lodges were filled with corpses, and they themselves had only life enough left to enable them to come to ask their friends to save their country, which was drawing rapidly toward its end. This spirited but laconic address moved the Conestoga to send an embassy into the Iroquois country to urge upon the Iroquois the advantage of making a lasting peace with their Huron adversaries.

Jean Baptiste, a Huron ambassador mentioned before, being at Onondaga at the end of summer, learned that this embassy of the Conestoga had reached the Iroquois country, as he even saw some of the Conestoga presents. It was the purpose of the Conestoga to bring about firm peace with the Hurons and the Onondaga, the Oneida and the Cayuga, and, if possible, the Seneca, and to renew the war against the Mohawk, should they then refuse to become parties to it.

The Conestoga did not fear the Mohawk. The *Jesuit Relation* for 1660 states that about the year 1600, the Mohawk had been greatly humbled by the Algonquin, and that after they had regained somewhat their former standing, the Conestoga, in a war lasting 10 years, had nearly exterminated the Mohawk, who since, however, had partially recovered from the defeat. Many of the Onondaga joined the Catholic Iroquois colonies on the Saint Lawrence River, and in 1751 about half the tribe was said to be living in Canada.

On the breaking out of the American Revolution in 1775, nearly all the Onondaga, together with the majority of the other Iroquois tribes, joined the British, and at the close of the war, the British government granted them a tract on Grand River, Ontario, where a portion of them still reside. The rest are still in New York, the greater number being on the Onondaga Reservation, and the others with the Seneca and Tuscarora on their several reservations.

The Onondaga made or joined in treaties with the state of New York at Fort Schuyler (formerly Fort Stanwix), September 12, 1788; Onondaga, November 18, 1793; Cayuga Ferry, July 28, 1795; Albany, February 25, 1817, February 11, 1822, and February 28, 1829. They also joined in treaties between the Six Nations and the United States at Fort Stanwix, New York, October 22, 1784; Fort Harmar, Ohio, January 9, 1789; Canandaigua, New York, November 11, 1794, and Buffalo Creek, New York, January 15, 1838.

The Jesuits estimated the Onondaga at about 1,500 persons, while Greenhalgh in 1677 placed them at 1,750, probably their greatest strength. Later authorities give the numbers as 1,250 (1721), 1,000 (1736), 1,300 (1765), and 1,150 (1778), but these figures do not include those on the Saint Lawrence. In 1851 Morgan estimated their total number at about 900, including 400 on Grand River. In 1906 those in New York numbered 553, the rest of the tribe being with the Six Nations in Canada.

Today, most of the Onondaga live on reservation lands of 6,100 acres south of Syracuse, New York. The New York tribe, in a recent count had some 1,600 members. The Six Nations Reserves in Ontario had about 500 members. In the 1960s and 1970s, the Onondaga led a unity movement and assumed political leadership among the Iroquois tribes, especially those allied with the Confederacy.

In the next two decades, political activism resulted in return of many wampum belts that had been held by the New York State Museum. In the early 1970s, a school boycott called attention to education concerns of the tribe, and negotiations with the State Education Department began.

The reservation continues to operate a grade school. The tribe also fought against the state taking their land to widen Interstate 81, and then Governor Rockefeller met with tribal members to settle the dispute. The tribe then began plans to file land claims against the state.

The Onondaga are governed by a Council of hereditary chiefs selected by clan mothers; both religious and secular affairs are handled by the council. All chiefs must be followers of teachings of Handsome Lake, and this links them to Longhouses on the other Iroquois reservations. Chiefs also represent the tribe at Confederacy councils, and continue to affirm traditional Iroquois ideology and culture.

A number of renowned artists and athletes are Onondagas, and the community is a well-known training ground for world-class lacrosse players. Some tribal members hold jobs in nearby Syracuse as tradespeople, construction workers (especially high steel), railroad workers, and service workers, and others are professionals in administration and teaching. However, unemployment remains high.

ORATAMIN

Oratamin (Hackensack, 17th Century), also known as Oratam, Oratan, Oraton, or Oritany (Oratamy), was a 17th century Hackensack chief (D.C. 1667) in what is now New Jersey, who exercised prominent roles in treaty relations between the Dutch and neighboring Indian tribes, especially the Esopus. A period of border warfare between the Dutch and 10 or 11 area tribes was caused by the slaughter of 80 to 120 Indians at Pavonia and Corlaer's Hook (February 25, 1643).

Oratamin represented the Hackensack, Tappan, Manhattan, Kitchawank, and Sitsink in a treaty of conciliation signed April 22, 1643. Although new hostilities led by younger warriors erupted immediately, a new treaty drawn at Fort Amsterdam, New Netherland, August 30, 1645, through Oratamin's efforts led to a general peace among all the Indians.

Through 1660 Oratamin participated in and often initiated discussions that established the principle of negotiation to settle all intertribal and tribal-settler disputes, and that brought about peace treaties between the Dutch and the Wappinger on May 18, 1660, and finally Esopus on July 15, 1660, who had been the constant enemy of the settlers and a disgrace to the surrounding Indian nations.

The treaties of 1660 did not survive. Within months the Wappinger aided the Esopus in hostility against the Dutch. Wishing to contain the war, Oratamin served as in intermediary and "intelligence officer" for Peter Stuyvescant, governor of New Netherlands. Oratamin, with the Nyack chief Matteno, were called upon to establish negotiations between the two sides. By November 1663, after the Wappinger and Esopus were informed that the British would not assist them, an armistice was called. With the return of Dutch captives held by the Indians, three Esopus chiefs presented themselves at Fort Amsterdam and formalized a peace treaty on May 16, 1664, which was ratified by most of the surrounding Indian nations and for which Oratamin and Matteno offered themselves as security.

PARKER, ELY SAMUEL

Ely Samuel Parker (Seneca, 1828 - August 31,1895), also known as Hasanoanda, "The Reader," and Donehogawa, "He Holds the Door Open," was a sachem of the Seneca Tribe who was the military secretary to General Ulysses S. Grant during the Civil War. Born at Indian Falls at Pembroke near New York, he attended a mission school and various local academies.

Although he studied law, he was not allowed to become a member of the bar because as an Indian, he was not considered to be a citizen. However, it was only a small setback for Parker, who traveled to Washington, D.C. as his tribe's representative in order to prosecute land claims on their behalf.

While there, he impressed a number of prominent people, and was even invited to dine with President Polk. In 1951, Parker and ethnologist Lewis H. Morgan published the first scientific study of a North American Indian tribe entitled, League of the Iroquois. A year later he was named as a Seneca chief.

PENNACOOK

The Pennacook were among the Western Abenaki-speaking groups whose ancestors lived along the upper Merrimack River, especially in the neighborhood of present Concord, New Hampshire, and between the Merrimack and Connecticut Rivers. Western Abenaki was still spoken in 1973 in Odanak. *Pennacook* is derived from the Massachusetts Algonquian words for "crooked river" or "the place where the river bends." *Abenaki* (sometimes *Abnaki*) means "eastern" or "dawn" people.

The Pennacook lived in a northern environment of mixed forest suitable for light farming. Deer, moose, bear, small mammals, fish from fresh water rivers and lakes, migratory birds, salt water fish, and shellfish contributed most of the diet in season. Although the area is rather north for agriculture, maize and probably beans were raised. Fish caught were sturgeon, shad, and alewives; turtles and clams were harvested. Wild plant foods were grapes, berries, and maple syrup and sugar.

Any one family or village-group occupied more than one residence. In deep winter, groups lived together far inland where hunting was best. In spring and summer, they camped near saltwater shores where shellfishing was most easily done; in summer, they lived along river valleys where planted food seeds could grow best. They are therefore best described as riverine people. Fifty to 300 persons formed a village, often pallisaded.

Transportation was by dugout canoes and backpacking. Varied traps, nets, hooks, spears, and weirs were used to gather seafoods, and for animals later used for food or clothing. More permanent villages were located at Pawtucket Falls and Wamesit Falls and present Concord, New Hampshire. Implements were made of stone, bone, turtle shell, grasses, and reeds. They took the form of stone projectile points, gorgets, and "banner stones" which probably helped project darts and spears before the advent of the bow in about A.D. 1100. Pottery with incised decoration and clay pipes was made.

Art took the form of geometrical incision of pottery, animal forms on pipes, and mostly geometric or symbolic designs on woven baskets and mats. Houses were bark-covered, either conical one-family homes, or rectangular, tunnel-shaped, multifamily buildings, all built on pole frames. The political life of a village has been described as "despotic" or "paternal."

These descriptions can be interpreted to mean that the chief of a village behaved in a paternalistic way, was autocratic on occasion, but could not hold individuals, including "minor chiefs," to fight with and for him, and anyone could expatriate himself at will. The position of chief was hereditary and seems to have been at least partly in the male line.

However, the intermarriage between ruling families within an area makes it difficult to determine rules of chiefdom inheritance. Social life was focused in the extended family. There were rather rigid sex dichotomies as to work. Polygamy was accepted, and divorce could be initiated by either sex.

Lineage was matrilineal except, possibly, in chieftan families. Next to the chief in communal importance was the medicine man, or shaman. He (sometimes she), was primarily a healer using herbs as supernatural means to effect cures. There was also an undescribed water cure. The shamans were also influential in secular affairs, advising the chiefs, and sometimes becoming chiefs themselves. This position may have been due to their status in the genealogy of chieftan families. An example is Chief Passaconaway, reputed to make trees dance, boulders march, snow burn, flowers grow through ice, and trees to grow leaves in midwinter. The religion also included veneration of the sun, moon, and a few star constellations. The changes of the seasons were considered to have supernatural power. Humans and animals were believed to have immortal souls that went to the far southwest.

Two interesting archaeological finds revealed something of religious practices. One was the skeleton of a man buried in a sitting position facing east; his skull had been fractured. Near him, the skeleton of a woman was found. Another find was a dugout canoe found at the bottom of a lake. The canoe had been filled with stones, thus purposefully sunk. Besides obviously religious rituals, the Indians played Lacrosse, gambled, and did mimetic dances, some of which had religious significance.

Concerning intertribal ritual, the Algonquian-speaking Indians seem to have had a mostly peaceful relationship among them selves, but at the beginning of recorded history, the Mohawks were encroaching into their territory. In 1670, the Mohawks invaded Pennacook area and defeated and killed most of the local groups that resisted them. In 1614, Captain John Smith was the first European to record a visit to the Merrimack River. A few years after his exploration, trading with the Indians began.

The Indians exchanged food, furs, and baskets, mostly for English manufactured goods. Between 1614 and 1620, the mysterious two-year pestilence that ravaged coastal New England, from southern Maine to Narragansett Bay, caused disastrous decimation of Indian population and affected the Indians of the Merrimack River as well. English domination over the Indians of the Pennacook area started in the late 1620s. Chief Passaconaway, first mentioned in 1623, deeded a large tract of land to an individual Englishman. Chief Passaconaway's compliance with, and submissiveness to, the English was practically absolute.

For example, he sent to Boston for punishment, probably hanging, one of his tribe who had killed an English trader. Also, after an outrage to his son and daughter-in-law, he apologized and gave the English all his guns. In 1644, he was the first chief of the area to submit to a redivision of his lands. In 1660, upon abdication, he warned the Indians not to fight the English because of reprisals too great to withstand. Conversion began in or shortly before 1653, when John Eliot obtained an act from the General Court to reserve an undocumented tract of land for exclusive Indian use.

Within this tract, the village Wamesit was overseen by Daniel Gookin and taught Christianity by John Eliot. In 1675, King Philips' War began in southern New England and from then on, the English performed acts of arrogance and wanton destruction against the Indians of the Merrimack River area.

After the English victory over the southern New England tribes, and the killing of King Philip in 1676, the fighting continued in the northern part of Massachusetts Colony. By then the Indians had lost population and reserve food. During this time, sachem Wanalancet not only maintained neutrality, but also signed a treaty not to harm any English. To ensure this, he and most of his tribe retreated north into the forest.

Through a ruse, 200 Indians of the Neutral area were taken to Boston, where some were hanged and some were "sold into slavery in foreign parts," mostly the West Indies and Bermuda. Eventually, in 1677, a group of Indians from the Pennacook area went to the Saint Francis Mission on the Saint Lawrence River in Quebec, where some identity has been maintained through their language. Throughout the 18th century, Pennacooks and other Western Abenakis were confusedly drawn into other colonial wars and the American Revolution.

In the 20th century, some tribal members have returned to ancestral lands to hunt, fish, and guide non-Indian sportsmen. Industry around Concord also attracted some back. In a recent census, there were over 360 Indian residents in New Hampshire with no listed tribal identity.

PEQUOT

Before the arrival of Europeans, the old settled Algonquian tribes that occupied the Connecticut River Valley, were harassed by fierce invaders from New York whom they called *Pequots* ("destroyers"). The settled tribes were the Podunk, Poquenock, Nipmuck, Niantic,

Quinnipiac, Saukiog, Wangnuk, Hammonasset, Montowese, Menunktuck, Paugusset, Swianog, and Tunxis.

The invaders were Mohegans, who conquered and exacted tribute from the native tribes. In 1633 the Pequot-Mohegans sold land to the Dutch, who established a short-lived trading post, Fort Good Hope, at what is now Hartford. Hoping to balance this power combine, the Connecticut tribes sold land to English settlers from the Massachusetts Bay Colony.

The Dutch soon became exasperated with the Pequots and killed their sachem, Wopigwooit, who was succeeded by his son Sassacus.

Sassacus intermittently warred against the Dutch to avenge his father's death. In addition, the Pequots were held responsible for the death of two English traders, and consequently the English, under John Endicott, led a punitive expedition against them, burning their villages.

Sassacus retaliated by burning the English settlement at Saybrook, and attacking Wethersfield, killing eight settlers and taking two girls captive. This called for a full-scale war, launched by the English under Captain John Mason in 1637.

He was aided by the Sagamore, Uncas, a rival of Sassacus for tribal leadership, who withdrew from the Pequots with a number of followers, the Mohegans, and joined the English. The Narragansett Indians and some of the conquered tribes were also allies. In a surprise attack, the English stormed and burned the Pequot's palisaded stronghold near the Mystic River, killing 400 inhabitants and taking seven captives.

Another colony of Pequots, who were trapped in a swamp while fleeing the English, was taken captive and sold into slavery. Sassacus escaped, but was put to death by the Mohawks from whom he sought asylum. The power of the Pequots was decisively crushed, but the Mohegans, protected by the English, were able to harass the peaceful tribes until the death of their leader, Uncas, in 1683.

In the last half of the seventeenth century, two separate Pequot Indian tribes were granted land in Connecticut: the federally recognized Mashantucket or Western Pequot of Ledyard, and the state-recognized Paucatuck or Eastern Pequots. The latter occupy the Lantern Hill Reservation in North Stonington. For both groups, the 20th century became a period of decline for many decades. For the Eastern Pequots, efforts were begun in the 1970s to gain federal recognition, and the issue remains to be settled. Today there are about 18 homes on the reservation of 226 acres. A principal conflict remains between the State of Connecticut and the tribe relating to land claims.

Factionalism within the tribe had made resolution of the issue a difficult task. However, efforts to provide leadership during the conflicts continue. The Mashantucket Pequots reorganized their tribal government in 1974, and a constitution was drafted. A chairman now heads the Mashantucket Pequot Tribal Council. In 1976, efforts were begun for filing suit over lands taken from the tribe. After years of negotiation, the land claim was settled in 1983 and the group was provided federal recognition. Changes since federal recognition have been dramatic for the Mashantucket Pequots. The land base was increased from 214 acres in 1983 to 1,795 acres in 1991.

A number of economic development initiatives have been implemented, and employment has increased on the reservation. A high-stakes bingo operation was developed, and a gambling casino was opened in 1992. A recent census showed about 282 enrolled tribal members of the Mashantucket Pequot.

PHILIP

Philip (Wampanoag, 1638 - August 12, 1676), also known as Metacomet of Pokanoket, was one of the first Indians to comprehend the threat posed by European settlement in the New World, and he formed a short-lived confederacy in an abortive attempt to drive the English from the land. Second son of Massassoit, who had lived on peaceful terms with the whites from the founding of Plymouth colony in 1620 to his death in 1661, Philip was a marked contrast to his father in terms of both temperament and objectives. Massasoit had sold substantial amounts of Indian land in order to enhance his own power and prestige through an alliance with the English.

By the time Philip became sachem in 1662, the white settlements had penetrated deep into the wilderness of southeastern Massachusetts. Philip saw clearly that if white encroachments were not stopped quickly, tribal lands would be overwhelmed. From the day he donned the wampum mark of chieftainship at Mount Hope in Rhode Island until his death there in 1676, Philip plotted and nearly executed the extermination of every settler in New England. From 1662 to 1675, Philip kept the colonists wondering. Unlike his father, Philip could not be bribed into submission, a state of affairs that profoundly distressed the Puritan community.

They never knew whether Philip would soon again be on the warpath. Actually, Philip was a realist, and he knew that the Wampanoags by themselves were too few to destroy the enemy. He recognized that the road to salvation led to a confederation of all the regional tribes, despite past rivalries and hostilities. Therefore, he devoted himself to forging alliances based strictly upon race; it was to a confederation of Indians, regardless of tribe, against the invaders. For thirteen years, he "traveled throughout the area, frying to enlist support, but when the inevitable war began, Philip still was not ready. He was able to ally the Nipmucks and the Narragansets, but the active opposition of other tribes against Philip's forces is probably what turned the tide in the Puritans' favor during "King Philip's War".

The shooting started shortly after three of Philip's warriors were hanged, following their conviction for the murder of an Indian informer named John Sassamon. Sassamon had told the settlers of Philip's plotting, but Philip claimed that the entire incident fell outside of Plymouth colony's jurisdiction. Several Wampaneags went on the warpath (June 20, 1675) in retaliation for the hangings, and Philip followed with strikes against outlying white settlements.

As the Puritans responded in panic, Philip divided his time between strengthening his confederation and scalping as many whites as possible. Hostilities quieted during the winter, but flared again in February 1676. Wampanoag, Nipmuck, and Narraganset warriors attacked 52 out of the 90 white settlements in New England, totally destroying twelve of them. Philip even led a strike inside the town of Plymouth itself. Just at the moment that victory seemed possible, however, Philip's confederation began to collapse. Combinations of pro-white natives and colonists began to track down the marauding bands, inflicting so many casualties that Philip's forces disintegrated.

With the losses, more braves allied to Philip went over to the colony, and the defections snowballed. Those loyal to the Wampanoag chief faced starvation as summer approached and they were deprived of their hunting and planting grounds. Realizing that defeat was inevitable but unwilling to surrender, Philip led a small band of his followers back to Mount Hope; he wished to die on the lands of his ancestors. The victim of constant betrayals during his lifetime, Philip was to be so victimized one more time. One of his warriors went to the colonists and offered to lead them to Philip's hideout.

On August 12, 1676, the combined native and English force killed Philip, quartered his body, and carried his head back to Plymouth. It remained on public display for 25 year, a reminder of the fate in store for any Indian who dared to resist the march of civilization.

POCOMTUC

The Pocomtuc tribe formerly lived on the Deerfield and Connecticut Rivers in Franklin County, Massachusetts. Their principal village, of the same name, was near the present Deerfield Indians. They had a fort on Fort Hill in the same vicinity, which was destroyed by the Mohawks after a hard battle in 1666. They were an important tribe, and seem to have ruled over the other Indians of the Connecticut Valley within the limits of Massachusetts, including those at Agawam, Nonetue, and Squawkeag. They combined with the Narragansett and Tunnis in attacks on Uncas, the Mohegan chief. All these tribes joined the hostile Indians under King Philip in 1675.

QUINNEY, JOHN W.

John W. Quinney (Stockbridge, 1797 - July 21, 1855), was a highly educated leader and elected chief in 1852 of the Stockbridge, New York Iroquois, whose relations with the United States government displayed his brilliance as a negotiator and gained him the complete trust of his tribe. In 1822 he assisted in the negotiations with the Menominee in purchasing land in the area of Green Bay, Wisconsin, for the relocation of the tribe. Three years later he was largely was responsible for the New York legislature paying the Stockbridge the market value of their New York lands, enabling them to move to Wisconsin. Under the Treaty of Butte des Morts (1827), the Menominee ceded the land around the southern end of Green Bay to the Stockbridge.

In 1828 Quinney approached the United States Congress to establish the tribe's legal rights to the land, but by 1830 the Winnebago Indians and Green Bay whites were urging the Menominee to disavow the treaty. The matter was referred to the federal government. Although the tribe eventually lost this land, after protracted work within the Congress, Quinney secured $25,000 for improvements made and the grants to two townships on the eastern side of Lake Winnebago. By 1843 the United States demanded the relocation of the Stockbridge.

Quinney concluded a treaty in which assistance in finding an acceptable new home west of the Mississippi River, and in relocating the tribe was promised. United States citizenship previously granted to the tribe was revoked through his efforts, thereby maintaining tribal self-government under a constitution he framed in 1833, which protected tribal customs. The tribe met with no success in finding land for relocation. Quinney returned to Washington with a uniquely bold proposal. A new treaty was signed, and in 1854 Congress passed a law giving the tribe title to 460 acres in Stockbridge, New York.

John Quinney died with the distinction not only of successfully having steered his tribe away from the horrors of Indian relocation, but also of eventually having won the encounter.

RED JACKET

Red Jacket (Seneca, 1758 - January 20, 1830), also known as Otetiani, assumed the name Sagoyewatha upon his election to the Seneca chieftainship. Although accused of cowardice in battle, he used his gift for oratory to remain Chief. Red Jacket, of course, was his English name, bestowed upon him as a result of the succession of red coats he wore while on the British side during the American Revolution. Red Jacket, along with some Seneca warriors, though, retreated precipitously at the approach of General Sullivan's troops in 1779.

He even attempted to conclude a separate peace with the Americans, but the plan was frustrated by Chief Joseph Brant, of the Mohawk Tribe. For all these actions, Red Jacket was considered a coward by many of his own people. When many of the braver chiefs and warriors were killed, moreover, Red Jacket seized the opportunity to consolidate his power. In 1786, at an Indian council along the Detroit River, Red Jacket used his splendid oratory to protest the inevitable peacemaking with the United States. Most likely, the hostile position he assumed was political trickery aimed primarily at currying favor with those who had thought their chief cowardly in combat.

Red Jacket constantly sought to portray himself as a bitter enemy of the whites and protector of his people, but to a great extent his oratory was a facade, masking his naked ambition for all forms of self-aggrandizement. For example, in 1787, 1788, and 1790, he publicly opposed land sales in order to maintain his popularity with the Seneca, but he secretly signed the property cessions in order to protect his prestige with the Americans. As he strengthened his leadership position, however, he seems to have become more sincere in his protestations against white influence upon the customs, religion, and language of his tribe. He vehemently opposed missionaries living on Indian lands. Following the New York legislature's decree in 1821 forbidding white residence on Indian Territory, Red Jacket led a contingent of the tribe in ousting the local missionary.

He also vainly attempted to preserve Indian jurisdiction over criminal acts committed on Indian property. In the Tommy Jemmy case (1821), Red Jacket stated that the Seneca council, which had tried a squaw for witchcraft, and the warrior who had executed her were outside the jursidiction of the United States. During the 1820s, Red Jacket began to lose prestige as his drinking and general dissipation grew more observable. In 1827 his wife joined the church, and Red Jacket fulfilled his threat to leave her, an action which prompted his further denigration. Although he returned to his wife a few months later, he was deposed as chief by a council of 26 tribal leaders, only to be reinstated through a personal effort at reform and the help of the United States Office of Indian Affairs.

The reinstated chief quickly fell back into his old ways, however. By the time of his death in 1830, Red Jacket's antiwhite and anti-Christian policies were long out of date, and he was surrounded by a largely Christianized tribe in which he was an alien presence. In fact, though his wishes were to the contrary, Red Jacket was given a Christian funeral and was buried in the cemetery of his reservation's Christian mission.

SASSACUS

Saccassus (Pequot, 1560 - 1637), perhaps the same as Massachusetts *Sassakusu,* "he is wild", was the noted and last important chief of the Pequot tribe. He was the son and successor of Wopigwooit, the first chief of the tribe contacted by whites. He was killed by the Dutch, about 1632, at or near the site of Hartford, Connecticut, then the principal Pequot settlement. Soon after becoming Chief in October, 1634, Sassacus sent an emissary to the governor of the Massachusetts Bay colony to ask for a treaty of friendship, offering as an inducement, to surrender all rights of the Pequot to the lands they had conquered, provided the colonists would settle a plantation among his people.

It was an offer that he must have known he could not carry out, and perhaps had no intention of trying to fulfill, as he bitterly hated whites. This proposal had the effect of turning Uncus, the Mohegan chief, against him. Pequot territory during Sassacus's leadership extended from Narragansett Bay to the Hudson River, and included the larger part of Long Island.

It is said that at the height of his prosperity no fewer than 26 sachems were subordinate to him. Because of his depredations especially on the neighboring tribes, the colonists decided in 1636 to make war on the Pequot. The name of Sassacus had inspired such terror among the surrounding tribes that the Indian allies of the whites could not believe the latter would dare to make a direct attack on the stronghold of this wily chief. The war was soon ended, and Sassacus, having suffered defeat and the loss of most of his people, fled with 20 or 30 of his warriors to the Mohawk country.

He found no safety, and in late 1637 his scalp and those of his brother and five other Pequot chiefs were sent to the Governor of Massachusetts by the Mohawk. As Sassacus had taken much wampum on his flight, Mohawk desire for this treasure of strung beads may have led to the murders.

SCAROUADY (HALF KING)

Scarouady (Oneida, 18th century), also known as Half King, was chief of the Oneida Indians in western Pennsylvania. He allied himself and his tribe firmly with English colonists during the British-French imperial conflicts of the 1750s. Scarouady hated the French, and to escape their influence he moved from Logstown to Aughwick, Pennsylvania in 1754.

There he assumed command over the western Pennsylvania Oneida, succeeding Half-King Scruniyatha. A great orator, frequently the leading speaker at intertribal conferences, Scarouady summoned all his considerable talent in 1754 to urge the Indians of Fort Cumberland to accompany the British expedition under General Braddock on its ill-fated march against the alliance of French and Indians along the western frontier.

By 1756, however, the Oneida chief was making speeches advocating peace. One such speech occurred on July 1, 1756 before Sir William Johnson, British representative to the North American tribes, at a conference of the Six Nations.

SENECA

(Also see FIVE NATIONS IROQUOIS). Seneca, the name of the tribe means "place of the stone"; it is the Anglicized form of the Dutch enunciation of the Mohegan rendering of the Iroquoian ethnic appellative *Oneida*, with a different ethnic suffix, meaning "people of the standing or projecting rock or stone." They are a prominent and influential tribe of the Iroquois. When first known, they occupied the part of western New York between Seneca Lake and Geneva River, having their council fire at Tsonontowan, near Naples, in Ontario County.

After the political destruction of the Erie and Neutrals, about the middle of the seventeenth century, the Seneca and other Iroquois people migrate to Lake Erie and southward along the Allegheny River, into Pennsylvania.

They also accepted into their tribe some of the conquered Indians, becoming the largest tribe of the confederation and one of the most important. The Seneca are now chiefly settled on the Allegany, Cattaraugus, and Tonawanda reservations in New York.

A portion of them remained under British jurisdiction after the declaration of peace, and lived on the Grand River Reservation, Ontario. Various local bands have been known as Buffalo, Tonawanda, and Cornplanter Indians; and the Mingo, formerly in Ohio, have become officially known as Seneca from the large number of that tribe among them. No considerable number of the Seneca ever joined the Catholic Iroquois colonies. In the third quarter of the 16th century, the Senecas were the last, save one, of the Iroquois tribes to vote in favor of the abolition of murder and war, the suppression of cannibalism, and the establishment of the principles upon which the League of the Iroquois was founded.

However, a large division of the tribe did not initially adopt the course of the main body, but, on obtaining coveted privileges and prerogatives, the recalcitrant body was admitted as a constituent member in the structure of the League. The two chiefships last added to the quota of the Seneca were admitted on condition of their exercising functions belonging to a sergeant-at-arms of a modern legislative body, as well as those belonging to a modern secretary of state for foreign affairs, in addition to their duties as federal chieftains.

Indeed, they became the warders of the famous "Great Black Doorway" of the League of the Iroquois, called *Ka'nho'hwadji'go'na* by the Onondaga. In historical times, the Seneca have been by far the most populous of the five tribes originally composing the League of the Iroquois. The Seneca belong in the federal organization to the tribal clan known by the political name *hondonnus*, meaning, "they are clansmen of the fathers." The Mohawk are the other members, when the tribes are organized as a federal council; but when ceremonially organized, the Onondaga also belong to this clan.

In the federal council, the Seneca are represented by eight federal chiefs, but two of these were added to the original six present at the first federal council, to give representation to that part of the tribe which had at first refused to join the League. Since the organization of the League of the Iroquois, approximately in the third quarter of the 16th century, the number of Seneca clans, which were organized into two phratries for the performance of both ceremonial and civil functions, have varied.

In a list of clan names made in 1838 by General Dearborn from information given him by Mister Cone, an interpreter of the Tonawanda band, the Heron clan is called the Swan clan with the native name given above. Of these clans, only five had an unequal representation in the federal council of the League: namely, the Sandpiper, three; the Turtle, two; the Hawk, one; the Wolf, one; and the Bear, one.

One of the earliest known references to the ethnic name Seneca is that on the Original Carte Figurative, annexed to the Memorial presented to the States General of the Netherlands, August 18, 1616, on which it appears with the Dutch plural as *Sennecas*. This map is remarkable also for the first known mention of the ancient Erie, sometimes called Gahkwas or Kahkwah. The name did not originally belong to the Seneca, but to the Oneida.

In the early part of December 1634, Arent Van Curler (or Corlaer), the commissary or factor of the Manor of Rensselaerwyck (his uncle's estate), set out from Fort Orange, now Albany, New York, in the interest of the fur trade, to visit the Mohawk and the Sinnekens. Strictly speaking, the latter name designated the Oneida, but at this time it was a general name, usually comprising the Onondaga, the Cayuga, and the Seneca, in addition. At that period, the Dutch and the French commonly divided the Five Iroquois tribes into two identical groups; to the first, the Dutch gave the name Maquas (Mohawk), and to the latter, Sinnekens (Seneca, the final-ens being the Dutch genitive plural), with the connotation of the four tribes mentioned above.

The French gave to the latter group the general name "les Iroquois Superieurs," i.e., the Upper Iroquois "les Hiroquois des pays plus hauts, nommes Sontouaheronnons," (literally, 'the Iroquois of the upper country, called Sontouaheronnons'), the latter being only another form of *les Tsonnontouans* (the Seneca); and to the first group the designations "les Iroquois inferieurs" (the Lower Iroquois), and "les Hiroquois d'en teas, nommes Agnechronnons" (the Mohawk; literally, 'the Iroquois from below, named Agnechronnons').

This geographical, rather than political division of the Iroquois tribes, first made by Champlain and the early Dutch at Fort Orange, prevailed until about the third quarter of the 17th century. Indeed, Governor Andros, two years after Greenhalgh's visit to the several tribes of the Iroquois in 1677, still wrote, "Ye Oneidas deemed ye first nation of sineques."

The journal of Van Curler records the interesting fact that during his visit to the tribes, he celebrated the New Year of 1635 at a place called Enneyattehage or Sinnekens. The first of these names was the Iroquois, and the second, the Mohegan name for the place, or, preferably, the Mohegan translation of the Iroquois name. The Dutch received their first knowledge of the Iroquois tribes through the Mohegan. At that date, this was the chief town of the Oneida.

Van Curler's journal identifies the name Sinnekens with this town, which is presumptive evidence that it is the Mohegan rendering of the Iroquois local name Onen'iute', 'it is a standing or projecting stone', employed as an ethnic appellative. The derivation of *Sinnekens* from Mohegan appears to be as follows: *a'sinni*, 'a stone, or rock', *-ika* or *-iga*, denotive of 'place of', or 'abundance of', and the final *-ens* supplied by the Dutch genitive plural ending, the whole Mohegan synthesis meaning 'place of the standing stone'; and with a suitable pronominal affix, like *oor wa-*, which was not recorded by the Dutch writers, the translation signifies, 'they are of the place of the standing store.'

206

This derivation is confirmed by the Delaware name, W'tassone, for the Oneida, which has a similar derivation. The initial "w" represents approximately an "o" sound, and is the affix of verbs and nouns denotive of the third person; it is evident that assone is only another form of *a'sinni*, 'stone', cited above. Therefore it appears that the Mohegan and Delaware names for the Oneida are cognate in derivation and identical in significance.

Heckewelder erroneously translated *W'tassone* as "stone pipe makers". Previous to the defeat and dissipation of the Neutrals in 1651 and the Erie in 1656, the Seneca occupied the territory drained by the Genesee River, eastward to the lands of the Cayuga along the line of the watershed between Seneca and Cayuga lakes.

The political history of the Seneca is largely that of the League of the Iroquois, although owing to petty jealousies among the various tribes, the Seneca, like the others, sometimes acted independently in their dealings with aliens. However, their independent action appears never to have been a serious and deliberate rupture of the bonds uniting them with the federal government of the League, thus vindicating the wisdom and foresight of its founders in permitting every tribe to retain and exercise a large measure of autonomy in the structure of that government. It was sometimes apparently imperative that one of the tribes should enter into a treaty or other compact with its enemies, while the others might still maintain a hostile attitude toward the aliens.

During 1622, the Montagnais, the Algonquin, and the Hurons sought to conclude peace with the Iroquois (Iroquois Mohawk Division?), because "they were weary and fatigued with the wars which they had had for more than 50 years." The armistice was concluded in 1624, but was broken by the continued guerrilla warfare of the Algon quin warriors; for this reason, the Seneca killed in the "village of the Yrocois" those in the embassy, a Frenchman, Pierre Magnan, and three Algonquin ambassadors. This resulted in the renewal of the war.

So in September 1627, the Iroquois, including the Seneca, declared war against the Indians and the French on the Saint Lawrence and its northern effluents by sending various parties of warriors against them. From the *Jesuit Relation* for 1635, it was learned that the Seneca, after defeating the Hurons in the spring of 1634, made peace with them. The Hurons in the following year sent an embassy to Sonontouan, the chief town of the Seneca, to ratify the peace, and while there, learned that the Onondaga, the Oneida, the Cayuga, and the Mohawk wished to become parties to the treaty.

In 1639, the war was renewed by the Hurons, which in May, captured 12 prisoners from the Seneca, then regarded as a powerful people. The war continued with varying success. The *Jesuit Relation* for 1641 said that the Seneca were the most feared of the enemies of the Hurons, and that they were only one day's journey from Ongniaahra (Niagara), the most easterly town of the Neutrals.

The *Jesuit Relation* for 1643 said that the Seneca, including the Cayuga, the Oneida, and the Onondaga, equaled, if not exceeded, in number and power, the Hurons, who previously had had this advantage; and that the Mohawk at this time had three villages with 700 or 800 men of arms who possessed 300 arquebuses (matchlock guns fired from a support) that they had obtained from the Dutch and which they used with skill and boldness.

According to the *Jesuit Relation* for 1648, 300 Seneca attacked the village of the Aondironnons, and killed or captured as many of its inhabitants as possible, although these people were a dependency of the Neutrals who were at peace with the Seneca at this time. This affront nearly precipitated war between the Iroquois and the Neutrals.

Seneca warriors composed the larger part of the Iroquois warriors who in 1648-49, assailed, destroyed, and dispersed the Huron tribes; it was likewise they who, in 1649, sacked the chief towns of the Tionontati, or Tobacco tribe; and the Seneca also took a leading part in the defeat and subjugation of the Neutrals in 1651, and of the Erie in 1656. From the *Journal des PP. Jesuites for 1651-52,* it was learned that in 1651, the Seneca, in waging war against the Neutrals, had been so soundly defeated that their women and children were compelled to flee from Sonontowan, their capital, to seek refuge among the neighboring Cayuga.

In 1652, the Seneca were plotting with the Mohawk to destroy and ruin the French settlements on the Saint Lawrence River. Two years later, the Seneca sent an embassy to the French for the purpose of making peace with them, a movement which was probably brought about by their rupture with the Erie. But the Mohawk, not desiring peace at that time with the French, perhaps on account of their desire to attack the Hurons on Orleans Island, murdered two of the three Seneca ambassadors, the other having remained as a hostage with the French.

This act almost resulted in war between the two hostile tribes. Foreign affairs, however, were in such condition as to prevent hostility. On September 19, 1655, Fathers Chaumonot and Dablon, after pressing invitations to do so, started from Quebec to visit and view the Seneca country, and to establish there a French habitation, and to teach the Seneca their religion. In 1657 the Seneca, in carrying out the policy of the League to adopt conquered tribes upon submission, and the expression of a desire to live under the form of government established by the League, had thus incorporated eleven different tribes. In 1652, Maryland bought from the Minqua, or Susquehanna Indians, i.e. the Conestoga, all their land claims on both sides of Chesapeake Bay up to the mouth of the Susquehanna River.

In 1663, 800 Seneca and Cayuga warriors from the Confederation of the Five Nations were defeated by the Minqua, aided by the Marylanders. The Iroquois did not terminate their hostilities until famine had so reduced the Conestoga that in 1675, when the Marylanders disagreed with them and withdrew their alliance, the Conestoga were completely subdued by the Five Nations. The Five Nations thereafter claimed a right to the Minqua lands up to the head of the Chesapeake Bay.

In 1744, the influence of the French was rapidly gaining ground among the Seneca; meanwhile, the astute and persuasive Colonel Johnson was gradually winning the Mohawk as close allies of the British, while the Onondaga, Cayuga, and Oneida, under strong pressure from Pennsylvania and Virginia, sought to be neutral.

In 1686, 200 Seneca warriors went west against the Miami. The Illinois, in the meantime, had been overcome by the Iroquois in a war lasting about five years. In 1687, the Marquis Denonville assembled a great horde of Indians from the region of the upper lakes and from the Saint Lawrence River: Hurons, Ottawa, Chippewa, Missisauga, Miami, Illinois, Montagnais, Amikwa, and others under Durantaye, Du-Luth, and Tonti, to serve as an auxiliary force to about 1,200 French and colonial levies. They were used to attack and destroy the Seneca.

After reaching Irondequoit, the Seneca landing place on Lake Ontario. Denonville built a stockade there in which he left a garrison of 440 men. While advancing to attack the Seneca villages, he was am-

bushed by 600 to 800 Seneca, who charged and drove back the colonials and their Indian allies, and threw the veteran regiments into disor-
der. Only by the overwhelming numbers was the traitorous Denonville
saved from disastrous defeat. In 1763, at Bloody Run and the Devil's
Hole, situated on Niagara River about 4 miles below the falls, the Seneca ambushed a British supply train on the portage road from Fort
Schlosser to Fort Niagara, with only three escaping from a force of
nearly 100. At a short distance, the same Seneca ambushed a British
force of two companies hastening to aid the supply train.

Only eight escaped massacre. These bloody and harsh measures
were the direct result of the general unrest of the Six Nations and the
western tribes, arising from the manner of the British, after the surrender of Canada by the French on September 8, 1760. They contrasted the sympathetic and bountiful paternalism of the French regime
with the neglect that characterized British rule.

On July 29, 1761, Sir William Johnson wrote to General Amherst:
"I see plainly that there appears to be an universal jealousy amongst
every nation, on account of the hasty steps they look upon we are taking towards getting possession of this country, which measures, I am
certain, will never subside whilst we encroach within the limits which
you may recollect have been put under the protection of the King in
the year 1726, and confirmed to them by him and his successors ever
since and by the orders sent to the governors not to allow anyone of his
subjects settling thereon ... but that it should remain their absolute
property."

However, by the beginning of the American Revolution, so well had
the British agents reconciled them to the rule of Great Britain that the
Seneca, together with a large majority of the people of the Six Nations,
notwithstanding their pledges to the contrary, reluctantly espoused the
cause of the British against the colonies. Consequently, they suffered
retribution for their folly when General Sullivan, in 1779, after defeating their warriors, burned their villages and destroyed their crops.
There is no historical evidence that the Seneca on the Ohio and the
southern shore of Lake Erie in the 18th and 19th centuries were
chiefly an outlying colony from the Iroquois tribe of that name living
in New York.

In fact, in historical times their affiliations were never with the Iroquois, but rather with tribes usually hostile to them. This is explained

210

by the presumption that they were rather some remnant of a subjugated tribe dependent on the Seneca and living on lands under the jurisdiction of their conquerors. It is a fair inference that they were largely subjugated Erie and Conestoga. Regarding the identity of these Indians, the following citation from Howe is pertinent: "The so-called Senecas of Sandusky owned and occupied 40,000 acres of choice land on the east side of Sandusky River, being mostly in this (Seneca) and partly in Sandusky County.

Thirty thousand acres of this land was granted to them on the 29th of September, 1817, at the treaty ... of Maumee Rapids ... The remaining 10,000 acres, lying south of the other, was granted by the treaty at Saint Mary's ... 17th of September, 1818." By the treaty concluded at Washington on February 28,1831, these Seneca ceded their lands in Ohio to the United States and agreed to emigrate southwest of Missouri, on Neosho River.

The same writer stated that in 1831 "their principal chiefs were Coonstick, Small Cloud Spicer, Seneca Steel, Hard Hickory, Tall Chief, and Good Hunter, the last two of whom were their principal orators. The old chief Good Hunter told Henry C. Brish, their subagent, that this band (which numbered 390 in 1908) were in fact the remnant of Logan's tribe, and says Mister Brish in a communication: "I cannot to this day surmise why they were called Senecas.

"I never found a Seneca among them. They were Cayugas, who were Mingoes, among whom were a few Oneidas, Mohawks, Onondagas, Tuscarawas, and Wyandots." The majority of them were certainly not Cayuga, as Logan was Conestoga or Mingo on his maternal side. In 1677, the Seneca had but four villages, but a century later, the number had increased to about 30.

The following are the better known Seneca towns, which were not at all contemporary: Canadasaga, Canandaigua, Caneadea, Catherine's Town, Cattaraugus, Chemung, New Chemung, Old Chemung, Chenango, Cheronderoga, Chinoshageh, Condawhaw, Connewango, Dayoitgao Deonundagae, Deyodeshot, Deyohnegano, Deyonongdadagana, Dyosyowan, Gaandowanang, Gadaho, Gahato, Ganos, Gaousge, Geneseo, Kannassarago, Newtown, Onnahee, Onondarka, Sheshequin, Sonojowauga, Tonawanda, Tsonontowanen, Yoroonwago.

The earliest estimates of the numbers of the Seneca, in 1660 and 1677, gave them about 5,000 members. Later estimates of the population were: 3,500 (1721); 1,750 (1736); 5,000 (1765); 3,250 (1778); 2,000 (1783); 3,000 (1783), and 1,780 (1796). In 1825, those in New York were reported at 2,325. In 1850, according to Morgan, those in New York numbered 2,712, while about 210 more were on Grand River Reservation in Canada. In 1909, those in New York numbered 2,749 on the three reservations, which, with those on Grand River, Ontario, would have given them a total of 2,962.

Today, the Seneca live in four main political and community groups in the United States and Canada. They include the Seneca Nation of Indians, located on three reservations in Cattaraugus and Allegany counties in New York; the Tonawanda Band of Seneca near Akron, New York; the Six Nations Reserve near Brantford, Ontario; and the Seneca-Cayuga Tribe, located in northeastern Oklahoma.

During the twentieth century, the Seneca Nation of Indians and the Tonawanda Band of Senecas fought against government intrusions. Both tribal governments rejected the Indian Reorganization Act of 1934. After Congress unilaterally transferred criminal and civil jurisdiction over American Indian affairs to New York state, the two tribes contested, but lost their battles with the courts.

The Seneca Nation faced a major crisis when the federal government constructed the Kinzua Dam in the 1960s. The dam flooded more than 9,000 acres of the Cornplanter tract and Allegany Reservation, and traditional Seneca life was disrupted. More recently, the Seneca Nation has attempted to settle the problem of 3,000 ninety-nine year leases on their lands in and around Salamanca, New York.

In 1990, they received a $35 million settlement award from the federal government for its failure to protect Indian rights in the matter. In 1992, they received $25 million from New York State for further compensations. The leases have been renewed under new terms with the city of Salamanca.

Both main groups have sought economic self-determination in their opposition to the states' taxing of reservation sales of petroleum and tobacco to non-Indians. Many Seneca have jobs in Rochester and Buffalo, and the Seneca Nations have convenience stores in several locations. Bingo operations are held on the Allegany and Cattaraugus reservations.

Tribal government is also a major employer, and casino gambling has been proposed, although opposing factions within the tribe have not reached any agreement. Seneca arts and crafts have been stimulated by such projects as the WPA Indian Arts Project and the World's Fair of 1939. The Tonawanda Indian Community House, another WPA project, was built by Indian labor in the 1930s. The community house was the first of its kind in New York, and still aids the tribe's social service, education, and health needs. Recent achievements of the Senecas include the Seneca Nation health department, created to deliver services to the Cattaraugus and Allegany reservations and the urban Seneca population; direct clinic services are a function of the department.

The Seneca maintain their matrilineal kinship system. Clan affiliation and traditional religion also continue to be important to the group. Today, there are 6,241 members of the Seneca Nation; 600 members of the Cornplanter Grant; 1,050 members of the Tonawanda Band; 539 Canadian Senecas; and 2,460 members of the Seneca-Cayuga.

SHAWNEE

The Shawnee were formerly a leading tribe of South Carolina, Tennessee, Pennsylvania, and Ohio. The indefinite character of their name, their wandering habits, their connection with other tribes, and their interior position away from the traveled routes of early days made the Shawnee a stumbling block to investigators. Attempts have been made to identify them with the Massawomec of Smith, the Erie of the early Jesuits, and the Andaste of a somewhat later period, while it has also been claimed that they originally formed one tribe with the Sac and Fox. None of these theories, however, rests upon sound evidence, and all have been abandoned.

Linguistically, the Shawnee belongs to the group of Central Algonquian dialects, and is very closely related to Sac-Fox. The name "*Sa vanoos*," applied by the early Dutch writers to the Indians living upon the east bank of the Delaware River in New Jersey, did not refer to the Shawnee, and was evidently not a proper tribal designation, but merely the collective term; just as "southerners" was the collective term for those tribes southward from Manhattan Island, such as *Wappanoos*, "easterners" was the collective term for those living toward the East. Evelin, writing in 1646, gave the names of the different small bands in the southern part of New Jersey, while Ruttenber named those in the North, but neither mentioned the Shawnee.

The tradition of the Delaware, as embodied in the *Walum Olum*, made themselves, the Shawnee, and the Nanticoke originally one people; the separation took place after the traditional expulsion of the Talligewi from the North, it being stated that the Shawnee went south.

Beyond this, it is useless to theorize on the origin of the Shawnee or to strive to assign them any earlier location than that in which they were first known, and where their oldest traditions place them, the Cumberland Basin in Tennessee, with an outlying colony on the middle Savannah in South Carolina.

In this position, as their name may imply, they were the southern advance guard of the Algonquian stock. Their real history begins in 1669-70. They were then living in two bodies at a considerable distance apart, and these two divisions were not fully united until nearly a century later, when the tribe settled in Ohio. The attempt to reconcile conflicting statements without knowledge of this fact has occasioned much of the confusion in regard to the Shawnee. The apparent anomaly of a tribe living in two divisions at such a distance from each other is explained when it is remembered that the intervening territory was occupied by the Cherokee, who were friends of the Shawnee at that time.

The evidence afforded by mounds shows that the two tribes lived together for a considerable period, both in South Carolina and in Tennessee. It is a matter of history that the Cherokee claimed the country vacated by the Shawnee in both states after their move to the North. It is quite possible that the Cherokee invited the Shawnee to settle upon their eastern frontier in order to serve as a barrier against the attacks of the Catawba and other enemies in that direction. No such necessity existed for protection on their northwestern frontier.

The earliest notices of the Carolina Shawnee represent them as a warlike tribe, the enemies of the Catawba and others, who were also the enemies of the Cherokee. In Ramsey's Annals of *Tennessee* is the statement made by a Cherokee chief in 1772, that 100 years previously, the Shawnee (by permission of the Cherokee) moved from the Savannah River to the Cumberland, but were afterward driven out by the Cherokee, aided by the Chickasaw, caused by a quarrel with the Cherokee.

While this tradition does not agree with the chronological order of Shawnee occupancy of the two regions, as borne out by historical evi-

214

dence, it furnishes additional proof that the Shawnee occupied territory on both rivers, as permitted by the Cherokee. De I'sle's map of 1700 places the "Ontouaganaha," which here means the Shawnee, on the headwaters of the Santee and Pedee Rivers in South Carolina, while the "Chiouonons" are located on the lower Tennessee River. Senex's map of 1710 located a part of the Chaouenons on the headwaters of a stream in South Carolina, but seems to place the main body on the Tennessee. Moll's map of 1720 has "Savannah Old Settlement" at the mouth of the Cumberland, showing that the term Savannah was sometimes applied to the western as well as to the eastern band.

The Shawnee of South Carolina, who included the Piqua and Hathawokela divisions of the tribe, were known to the early settlers of that state as Savannahs, it being nearly the form of the name in use among the neighboring Muskhogean tribes. A good deal of confusion has arisen from the fact that the Yuchi and Yamasee, in the same neighborhood, were sometimes also spoken of as Savannah Indians. Bartram and Gallatin particularly were confused upon this point, although it is hardly necessary to state that the tribes are entirely distinct.

Their principal village, known as Savannah Town, was on Savannah River, nearly opposite the present Augusta, Georgia. According to a writer of 1740, it was at New Windsor, on the north bank of the Savannah River, 7 miles below Augusta. It was an important trading point, and Fort Moore was afterward built upon the site. The Savannah River takes its name from this tribe, as appears from the statement of Adair, who mentioned the "Savannah River, so termed on account of the Shawano Indians having formerly lived there," plainly showing that the two names are synonyms for the same tribe.

Gallatin said that the name of the river is of Spanish origin, by which he probably meant that it referred to savanas or prairies, but as almost all the large rivers of the Atlantic slope bore the Indian names of the tribes upon their banks, it is not likely that this river is an exception, or that a Spanish name would have been retained in an English colony.

In 1670, when South Carolina was first settled, the Savannah were one of the principal tribes south of Ashley River. About 10 years later, they drove back the Westo, identified by Swanton as the Yuchi, who had just previously nearly destroyed the infant settlements in a short but bloody war.

The Savannah seemed to have remained at peace with the whites, and in 1695, according to Governor Archdale, were "good friends and useful neighbors of the English." By a comparison of Gallatin's paragraph with Lawson's statements, from which he quotes, it is seen that he misinterpreted the earlier author, as well as misquoted the tribal forms.

Lawson traveled through Carolina in 1701, and in 1709 published his account, which has passed through several reprints, the last being in 1860. He mentions the "Savannas" twice, and it is to be noted that in each place he called them by the same name that, however, is not the same as any one of the three forms used by Gallatin in referring to the same passages.

Lawson first mentioned them in connection with the Congaree as the "Savannas, a famous, warlike, friendly nation of Indians, living to the south end of Ashley River." In another place, he spoke of "the Savanna Indians, who formerly lived on the banks of the Messiasippi, and removed thence to the head of one of the rivers of South Carolina, since which, for some dislike, most of them are removed to live in the quarters of the Iroquois or Sinnagars (Seneca), which are on the heads of the rivers that disgorge themselves into the bay of Chesapeak." This is a definite statement, plainly referring to one and the same tribe, and agrees with what is known of the Shawnee.

On De I'Isle's map was also found the Savannah River, called "R. des Chouanons," with the "Chaouanons" located upon both banks in its middle course. Gallatin's statement is that the name of the Savannahs was dropped after Lawson's mention in 1701; this was noted in numerous references from old records in Logan's *Upper South Carolina*, published after Gallatin's time. All through the period of the French and Indian War, 50 years after Lawson wrote, the "Savannahs" were constantly making inroads on the Carolina frontier, even to the vicinity of Charleston. They were described as "northern savages" and friends of the Cherokee, and were undoubtedly the Shawnee.

In 1749 Adair, while crossing the middle of Georgia, fell in with a strong party of "the French Shawano," who were on their way, under Cherokee guidance, to attack the English traders near Augusta. After committing some depredations, they escaped to the Cherokee. In an-

216

other place, he spoke of a party of "Shawano Indians," who, at the instigation of the French, had attacked a frontier settlement of Carolina, but had been taken and imprisoned. Through a reference by Logan, it was found that these prisoners were called Savannahs in the records of that period. In 1791, Swan mentioned the "Savannas" town among the Creeks, occupied by "Shawanese refugees."

Having shown that the Savannah and the Shawnee are the same tribe, it remains to be seen why and when they migrated north from South Carolina. The move was probably due to dissatisfaction with the English settlers, who seemed to favor the Catawba at the expense of the Shawnee. Adair, speaking of the latter tribe, said they had formerly lived on the Savannah River, "till by our foolish measures they were forced to withdraw northward in defence of their freedom." In another place, he said: "... by our own misconduct we twice lost the Shawano Indians, who have since proved very hurtful to our colonies in general." The first loss referred to is probably the withdrawal of the Shawnee to the north, and the second is evidently their alliance with the French in consequence of the encroachments of the English in Pennsylvania.

Their removal from South Carolina was gradual, beginning about 1677 and continuing at intervals through a period of more than 30 years. The ancient Shawnee villages formerly on the sites of Winchester, Virginia, and Oldtown, near Cumberland, Maryland, were built and occupied probably during this migration. It was due mainly to their losses at the hands of the Catawba, the allies of the English, that they were forced to abandon their country on the Savannah; but after the reunion of the tribe in the North, they pursued their old enemies with unrelenting vengeance until the Catawba were almost exterminated.

The hatred cherished by the Shawnee toward the English is shown by their boast in the American Revolution that they had killed more of that nation than had any other tribe.

The first Shawnee seem to have moved from South Carolina in 1677 or 1678, when, according to Drake, about 70 families established theirselves on the Susquehanna River, adjoining the Conestoga River in Lancaster County, Pennsylvania, at the mouth of Pequea Creek. Their village was called Pequea, a form of Piqua. The Assiwikales (Hathawekela) were a part of the later migration. This, together with the absence of the Shawnee names Chillicothe and Mequachake, east of the Alleghenies, would seem to show that the Carolina portion of the tribe belonged to the first named divisions.

Wapatha, or Opessah, the chief of Pequea, made a treaty with Penn at Philadelphia in 1701, and more than 50 years afterward, the Shawnee, then in Ohio, still preserved a copy of this treaty. There is no proof that they had a part in Penn's first treaty in 1682. In 1694, by invitation of the Delawares and their allies, another large party came from the South, probably from Carolina, and settled with the Munsee on the Delaware, the main body fixing themselves at the mouth of the Lehigh River, near the present Easton, Pennsylvania, while some went as far down as the Schuylkill. This party is said to have numbered about 700, and they were several months on the journey.

Permission to settle on the Delaware was granted by the Colonial government, on the condition of their making peace with the Iroquois, who then received them as "brothers," while the Delawares acknowledged them as their "second sons," i.e., grandsons. The Shawnee today refer to the Delawares as their grandfathers. From this, it is evident that the Shawnee were never conquered by the Iroquois; in fact, the western band, a few years previously, had assisted the Miami against the latter.

However, as the Iroquois had conquered the lands of the Conestoga and Delaware on which the Shawnee settled, the former still claimed the prior right of domain. Another large part of the Shawnee probably left South Carolina about 1707, as appears from a statement made by Evans in that year, which shows that they were then hard pressed in the South.

He said: "During our abode at Pequehan (Pequea), several of the Shaonois Indians from ye southward came to settle here, and were admitted so to do by Opessah, with the governor's consent, at the same time an Indian, from a Shaonois town near Carolina came in and gave an account that four hundred and fifty of the flat-headed Indians (Catawba) had besieged them, and that in all probability, the same was taken.

"Bezallion informed the governor that the Shaonois of Carolina, he was told, had killed several Christians; whereupon the government of that province raised the said flat-headed Indians, and joined some Christians to them, besieged and have taken, as it is thought, the said

Shaonois town." Those who escaped probably fled to the north and joined their relatives in Pennsylvania.

In 1708, Governor Johnson of South Carolina reported the "Savannahs" on Savannah River as occupying three villages and numbering about 150 men. In 1715, the "Savanos" still in Carolina, were reported to live 150 miles northwest of Charleston, and still to occupy three villages, but with only 233 inhabitants in all. The Yuchi and Yamasee were also then in the same neighborhood.

A part of those who had come from the South in 1694 had joined the Mahican and become a part of that tribe. Those who had settled on the Delaware, after remaining there some years, removed to the Wyoming Valley on the Susquehanna River and established themselves in a village on the west bank near the present Wyoming, Pennsylvania. It is probable that they were joined there by that part of the tribe that had settled at Pequea, which was abandoned about 1730.

When the Delawares and Munsee were forced to leave the Delaware River in 1742, they also moved over to the Wyoming Valley, then in possession of the Shawnee, and built a village on the east bank of the river, opposite the Shawnee.

In 1740, the Quakers began work among the Shawnee at Wyoming; they were followed two years later by the Moravian Zinzendorf. As a result, the Shawnee on the Susquehanna remained neutral for some time during the French and Indian War, which began in 1754, while their brethren on the Ohio were active allies of the French.

About the year 1755 or 1756, a quarrel with the Delaware, said to have been caused by a childish dispute over a grasshopper, resulted in the Shawnee abandoning the Susquehanna and joining the rest of their tribe on the upper waters of the Ohio, where they soon became allies of the French.

Some of the eastern Shawnee had already joined those on the Ohio River, probably in small parties and at different times, for in the report of the Albany Congress of 1754, it was found that some of that tribe had removed from Pennsylvania to the Ohio about 30 years previously, and in 1735, a Shawnee band known as Shaweygria (Hathawekela), consisting of about 40 families, described as living with the other Shawnee on the Allegheny River, refused to return to the Susquehanna at the solicitation of the Delawares and Iroquois.

219

The only clue in regard to the number of these eastern Shawnee is Drake's statement that in 1732, there were 700 Indian warriors in Pennsylvania, of whom half were Shawnee from the south. This would give them a total population of about 1,200, which is probably too high, unless those on the Ohio are included in the estimate.

Having shown the identity of the Savannah with the Shawnee, and followed their wanderings from the Savannah River to the Ohio during a period of about 80 years, it remains to trace the history of the other, and apparently more numerous, division upon the Cumberland, who preceded the Carolina band in the region of the upper Ohio River, and seem never to have crossed the Alleghenies to the east. These western Shawnee may possibly be the people mentioned in the *Jesuit Relations* of 1670, under the name of "Ouchaouanag," in connection with the Mascoutens, who lived in northern Illinois.

In the *Jesuit Relations* of 1670, the Chaouanon were mentioned as having visited the Illinois the preceding year, and they are described as living some distance to the southeast. From this period until their move to the north, they were frequently mentioned by French writers, sometimes under some form of the collective Iroquois name of *Toagenha*, but generally under their Algonquian name of *Chaouanon*.

LaHarpe, about 1715, called them Tongarois, another form of Toagenha. All these writers concur in the statement that they lived upon a large southern branch of the Ohio River, at no great distance east of the Mississippi. This was the Cumberland River of Tennessee and Kentucky, which is called the River of the Shawnee on all the old maps down to about the year 1770.

When the French traders first came into the region, the Shawnee had their principal village on that river near the present Nashville, Tennessee. They seem to also have ranged northeastward to the Kentucky River, and southward to the Tennessee. Therefore, it was assumed that they were not isolated from the great body of the Algonquian tribes, as was frequently assumed to be the case, but simply occupied an interior position, adjoining the related Illinois and Miami, with whom they kept up constant communication. As previously mentioned, the early maps plainly distinguish these Shawnee on the Cumberland from the other division of the tribe on Savannah River.

These western Shawnee are mentioned about the year 1672 as being harassed by the Iroquois, and also as allies and neighbors of the Andaste, or Conestoga, who were their selves at war with the Iroquois. As the Andaste were then incorrectly supposed to live on the upper waters of the Ohio River, the Shawnee would naturally be considered their neighbors.

The two tribes were probably in alliance against the Iroquois, as it was noted that when the first body of Shawnee moved from South Carolina to Pennsylvania around 1678, they settled adjoining the Conestoga, and when another part of the same tribe desired to move to the Delaware in 1694, permission was granted on the condition that they make peace with the Iroquois. Again in 1684, the Iroquois justified their attacks on the Miami by asserting that the latter had invited the Satanas (Shawnee) into their country to make war upon the Iroquois. This is the first historic mention of the Shawnee, evidently the western division, in the country north of the Ohio River.

The Cumberland region was out of the usual course of exploration and settlement, but few notices of the western Shawnee are found until 1714, when the French trader, Charleville, established himself among them near present Nashville. They were then gradually leaving the country in small groups, a consequence of a war with the Cherokee, their former allies, who were assisted by the Chickasaw.

From the statement of Iberville in 1702, it seems that this was due to the latter's efforts to bring them more closely under French influence. It is impossible now to learn the cause of the war between the Shawnee and the Cherokee. It probably did not begin until after 1707, the year of the final expulsion of the Shawnee from South Carolina by the Catawba, as there is no evidence to show that the Cherokee took part in that struggle.

From Shawnee tradition, the quarrel with the Chickasaw would seem to be from a previous time. After the reunion of the Shawnee in the north, they secured the alliance of the Delawares, and the two tribes turned against the Cherokee until the latter were compelled to ask for peace, and the old friendship was renewed.

Soon after the coming of Charleville in 1714, the Shawnee finally abandoned the Cumberland Valley, being pursued to the last moment by the Chickasaw. In a council held at Philadelphia in 1715 with the Shawnee and Delaware, the former, who lived at a great distance, asked the friendship of the Pennsylvania government. These are evidently the same who, about this time, were driven from their home on

Cumberland River. On Moll's map of 1720, this region was marked as occupied by the Cherokee, while "Savannah Old Settlement" is placed at the mouth of the Cumberland, indicating that the removal of the Shawnee had then been completed.

They stopped for some time at various points in Kentucky, and perhaps also at Shawneetown, Illinois, but finally, about the year 1730, collected along the north bank of the Ohio River in Ohio and Pennsylvania, extending from the Allegheny down to the Scioto. Sawcunk, Logstown, and Lowertown were probably built about this time.

The land thus occupied was claimed by the Wyandotte, which granted permission to the Shawnee to settle upon it, and many years afterward, threatened to dispossess them if they continued hostilities against the United States.

They probably wandered for some time in Kentucky, which was practically a part of their own territory and not occupied by any other tribe. Blackhoof (Catahecassa), one of their most celebrated chiefs, was born during this stay in a village near present Winchester, Kentucky. Down to the Treaty of Greenville, in 1795, Kentucky was the favorite hunting ground of the tribe.

In 1748, the Shawnee on the Ohio were estimated to number 162 warriors or about 600 souls. A few years later they were joined by Susquehanna relatives, and the two bands were united for the first time in history. There is no evidence that the western band, as a body, ever crossed to the east of the mountains. The nature of the country and the fear of the Catawba would seem to have forbidden such a movement, aside from the fact that their eastern brothers were already beginning to feel the pressure of advancing civilization.

The most natural line of migration was the direct route to the upper Ohio River, where they had the protection of the Wyandotte and Miami, and were within easy reach of the French.

For a long time, an intimate connection existed between the Creeks and the Shawnee, and a body of the latter, under the name of Sawanogi, was permanently incorporated with the Creeks. These may have been the ones mentioned by Penicaut as living in the vicinity of Mobile about 1720. Bartram, in 1773, mentioned this band among the Creeks and spoke of the resemblance of their language to that of the Shawnee, without knowing that they were a part of the same tribe.

The war in the Northwest, after the close of the American Revolution, drove still more of the Shawnee to take refuge with the Creeks. In 1791, they had four villages in the Creek country, near the site of Montgomery, Alabama, the principal being Sawanogi. Many also joined the hostile Cherokee about the same time. As these villages are not named in the list of Creek towns in 1832, it is possible that their inhabitants may have joined the rest of their tribe in the West before that period.

There is no good evidence for the assertion by some writers that the Suwanee in Florida took its name from a band of Shawnee once settled upon its banks.

The history of the Shawnee after their reunion on the Ohio is well known as a part of the history of the Northwest Territory, and may be dismissed with brief notice. For a period of 40 years, from the beginning of the French and Indian War to the Treaty of Greenville in 1795, they were almost constantly at war with the English or the Americans, and distinguished themselves as the most hostile tribe in that region.

Most of the expeditions sent across the Ohio during the Revolutionary period were directed against the Shawnee, and most of the destruction on the Kentucky frontier was the work of the same tribe. When driven back from the Scioto, they retreated to the head of the Miami River, from which the Miami had withdrawn some years before.

After the Revolution, finding themselves left without the assistance of the British, large numbers joined the hostile Cherokee and Creeks in the South, while a considerable body accepted the invitation of the Spanish government in 1793 and settled, together with some Delawares, on a tract near Cape Girardeau, Missouri, between the Mississippi and the Whitewater Rivers, in what was then Spanish territory.

Wayne's victory, followed by the Treaty of Greenville in 1795, put an end to the long war in the Ohio Valley. The Shawnee were obliged to give up their territory on the Miami in Ohio, and retired to the headwaters of the Auglaize. The more hostile part of the tribe crossed the Mississippi and joined those living at Cape Girardeau. In 1798, a part of those in Ohio settled on the White River in Indiana, by invitation of the Delawares.

A few years later, a Shawnee medicine man, Tenskwatawa, known as The Prophet, the brother of the celebrated Tecumseh, began to

223

preach a new doctrine among the various tribes of that region. His followers rapidly increased and established themselves in a village at the mouth of the Tippecanoe River in Indiana. It soon became evident that his intentions were hostile, and a force was sent against him under General Harrison in 1811, resulting in the destruction of the village and the total defeat of the Indians in the decisive battle of Tippecanoe.

Tecumseh was among the Creeks at the time, endeavoring to secure their aid against the United States, and returned in time to take command of the northwest tribes in the British interest in the War of 1812.

The Shawnee in Missouri were forced by the Government to sell their lands in 1825 and were moved to a reservation in Kansas. A large part of them had previously gone to Texas, where they settled on the headwaters of the Sabine River, and remained there until driven out by encroaching white settlers about 1839. The Shawnee of Ohio had to sell their remaining lands at Wapakoneta and Hog Creek in 1831, and joined those in Kansas. The mixed band of Seneca and Shawnee at Lewistown, Ohio, also forced to relocate to Kansas about the same time.

A large part of the tribe had to leave Kansas about 1845 and settled on the Canadian River, Indian Territory, (now Oklahoma), where they became known as Absentee Shawnee. In 1867, the Shawnee living with the Seneca also were moved from Kansas to the Territory and became known as Eastern Shawnee. In 1869, by intertribal agreement, the main body became incorporated with the Cherokee Nation in the present Oklahoma, where they are now residing. Those that were known as Black Bob's band refused to be removed from Kansas with the others, but later joined them.

The Shawnee have five divisions, which may be regarded as clans, or perhaps as originally distinct tribes, and the members of these divisions occupied different sides of the council house in their public assemblies. Their names are Chilabcahtha (Chillicothe), Kispokotha (Kispogogi), Spitotha (Mequachake?), Bicowetha (Pique), and Assiwikale (Hathawekela). The villages of the tribe have generally taken their names from these divisions. The Woketamosi division mentioned by Heckewelder is probably one of these, but is not the Piqua.

Today there are three distinct political groups in Oklahoma: the Absentee Shawnee, the Eastern Shawnee, and the Loyal Shawnee. Another group consisting of descendants of scattered families who escaped removals in the nineteenth century has achieved state recognition from Ohio; these are the Shawnee Nation United Remnant Band.

ABSENTEE SHAWNEE: This group was organized under the Oklahoma Indian Welfare Act of 1936 as the Absentee Shawnee Tribe of Indians of Oklahoma. They are under federal jurisdiction of the Shawnee Indian Agency, a part of the Bureau of Indian Affairs Anadarko Area Office. A constitution has been adopted, and an Executive Commuttee is presided over by a governor. They maintain a tribal court of law and police force, and most of their health services are provided by the tribal complex just outside of Shawnee. In 1981, population of the group was 1,384, and more recent estimates place numbers at over 2,000. Income is derived from farming, livestock, oil and gas taxes, bingo, and tax-free sales. Religious practices include Baptist and Friends denominations, and dances such as the Green Corn Dance are celebrated in Spring and Fall. A ceremonial War Dance is held in August near Little Axe. The group speaks Algonquian and comprise the largest Oklahoma group of such speakers.

EASTERN SHAWNEE: This group resides in Ottawa County in the northeastern part of the state. They belong to the Indian Agency branch of the Bureau of Indian Affairs Muskogee Area Office. They were historically linked with the Seneca tribe, and were known collectively as the United Nation or Mixed Band of Seneca and Shawnee in 1832. In 1937, they organized as the Eastern Shawnee Tribe of Oklahoma under the Oklahoma Indian Welfare Act, and were officially separated from the Seneca. A constitution was adopted, and the Eastern Shawnee Business Committee was established. A Tribal Charter was issued by the Secretary of the Interior in 1940.

The tribe's 813 members shared a claim award of 110,000 dollars for depredations suffered during the Civil War. Current population is 1,550 members. The tribal complex, located in West Seneca, Oklahoma, has an administration building, a community building, a bingo hall with seating for 750, a one-quarter acre recreational park, and an eye clinic. Much of their health care is provided by the group, and a nutrition program operates to feed the elderly. Few speak the Native language.

LOYAL SHAWNEE: They are primarily located in northeast Oklahoma in the town of Whiteoak, and some members are scattered throughout the United States. They are not officially recognized, and for most federal purposes, they are enrolled as Cherokee citizens. They have a political structure consisting of a chairman, vice chairman, secretary-treasurer, historian, and four elected members serving two-year terms. A grievance committee investigates misconduct complaints and actions of the Business Committee.

The group maintains a Loyal Shawnee Cultural Center. Each year, dances are held in spring and fall, including the Green Corn Dance. Few still speak the language. Population of the group today is about 8,000 members.

SHIKELLAMY

Shikellamy (Oneida, ? - 1748), an Oneida chieftain, was the exponent of the colonial policy of the great federal Iroquois council at Onondaga, and was sent by it to the forks of the Susquehanna in 1728 to conserve the interests of the Six Nations and to keep watch over the Shawnee and Delaware Indians. A man of great dignity, he always showed marked kindness, especially to the missionaries. In the execution of his trust, Shikellamy conducted many important embassies between the government of Pennsylvania and the Iroquois council at Onondaga, and he also attended many if not most of the councils held at Philadelphia, Conestoga, and elsewhere.

His importance is evident in that the valley of the Susquehanna, after the Conestoga were subjugated in 1676 by the Iroquois, was assigned by the Five Nations of Iroquois as a hunting ground to the Shawnee, Delawares, Conoy, Nanticoke, Munsee, Tutelo, Saponi, and Conestoga tribes.

When the Mohawk sold the Wyoming region in Pennsylvania to the Susquehanna Land Company, although his tribe had never aided in conquests in this valley, the council at Onondaga began to realize that this section, with its valuable land and many dependent tribes, was worthy of careful attention; hence these tribes were made to understand that in the future they must transact all business with the proprietary government solely through their deputy.

With his residence fixed at Shamokin (now Sunbury), Pennsylvania, Shikellamy was promoted in 1745 to full Vice-General over the tributary tribes in the Susquehanna valley, and intricate and important interests committed to him received the care of an astute statesman and diplomat. The effects of the liquor traffic on the Indians led to prohibitory decrees on the part of the government of Pennsylvania, and later, evidently through the influence of traders, when these prohibitive measures became lax, Shikellamy in 1731 delivered an ultimatum to the Pennsylvania government that unless the liquor trade was better regulated, friendly relations between the proprietary government and the Six Nations would cease.

As the difficulties arising from the sale of liquor had forced a large number of Shawnee to migrate from the Susquehanna to the Ohio River in 1730, and as French emissaries were taking advantage of this condition to alienate the Shawnee from the English interest, a governor decided in 1731 to send Shikellamy, "a trusty, good man, and a great lover of the English," to Onondaga to invite the Six Nations to Philadelphia. In 1736 Shikellamy's influence was enlisted to bring about a conference at which the entire confederation of the Six Nations would be represented, and in less than two months' time Conrad Weiser informed the Governor of Pennsylvania that more than a hundred chiefs of the Iroquois, with their retinues, were on their way to Philadelphia.

By this treaty of 1736 the Six Nations deeded all their Susquehanna lands south and east of the Blue Mountains. Some weeks later, when nearly all the leading Indians had departed, another deed was prepared and signed by the remaining Indians, which purported to include the lands ostensibly claimed by the Six Nations within the drainage of Delaware River south of the Blue Mountains, a treaty that, "established a precedent for an Iroquois claim to lands owned by the Delaware Indians," a claim that had never been advanced before. Weiser helped Shikellamy sow the seed that drenched Pennsylvania in blood from 1755 to 1764.

In a war with the Delaware, Weiser had many good reasons for regarding Shikellamy as the key to the secret policies of the council of the Iroquois at Onondaga. In 1745 Shikellamy was requested by Governor Thomas to visit the Six Nations and gain peace with the Catawba. The acquisition of firearms became a necessity to the Indian hunters and warriors. Shikellamy persuaded the colonial government to establish a forge at Shamokin. This was granted on condition that the Indians would permit the Moravians to begin a mission at the place, which the missionaries regarded as the greatest stronghold of paganism. To this proposal Shikellamy readily consented, and in

April 1747, a blacksmith shop and a mission house were erected there. A year later, Zeisberger, who had become proficient in the Mohawk tongue, became an assistant missionary at Shamokin, and while there began the preparation of an Onondaga dictionary under the interested instruction of Shikellamy.

During 1748 Shikellamy received from Count Zinzendorf a silver knife, fork, and spoon, and an ivory drinking cup richly mounted in silver, accompanied with a message entreating him to hold fast to the gospel which he had heard from the count's own lips. This resulted in the conversion of Shilkellamy at Bethlehem shortly afterward. He was not baptized by the Moravians because he had been baptized many years before by a Jesuit priest in Canada. On his way to Shamokin he fell ill at Tulpehocking. Zeisberger, who had returned to his post, ministered to the stricken chieftain until his death. The colonial government sent a message of condolence, and requested the eldest son of Shikellamy, John or Thachnechtoris (Tagheghdoarus) to serve as the Iroquois deputy governor until the council at Onondaga could make a permanent appointment.

SHINNECOCK

The Shinnecock were an Algonquian tribe or band on Long Island, New York, formerly occupying the southern coast from Shinnecock Bay to Montauk Point. Many of them joined the Brotherton Indians in New York. About 150 still remained on a reservation of 750 acres, three miles west of Southampton, having intermarried with blacks until their aboriginal character was almost obliterated. Nowedonah, brother of the noted Wyandanch, was once their chief, and upon his death, his sister, wife of Cockenoe, became his successor.

In December of 1876, 28 Shinnecock men died in an attempt to save a ship stranded off Easthampton, after which a number of members, especially the younger people, left the reservation and became scattered. They had a Presbyterian and an Adventist church. The men gained a livelihood by employment as farmhands, baymen, berry pickers, etc., and the women as laundresses. A few families made and sold baskets and a sort of brush made of oak splints. There was almost no agriculture. In recent times, the population of the mixed-blood tribal members numbered approximately 200.

By the beginning of the 20th century, almost all of the Shinnecock culture, including their Algonquian language, had disappeared. The remaining members honored their heritage by staging an annual Labor Day Powwow. Today, there are about 400 descendants of the tribe and those of other Long Island Tribes, including the Montauk, Corchaug, Shinnecock, Manhasset, Rockaway and Patchogue. They live in small area communities, including the Shinnecock Indian Reservation, which is located on the south fork of eastern Long Island in the town of Southampton in New York, plus on the Poosepatuck Reservation and in the Montauk Indian Village. Many return regularly to participate in tribal events and family gatherings. The group maintains houses, a cemetery, powwow grounds, tribal programs, beaches, and offices on land surrounded by the Shinnecock Bay.

SIWANOY

From having lived on the seacoast, the tribal name Siwanoy may be a corruption of "*Siwanak*", "salt people", a dialectic form of "*Suwanak*", a name given by the Delawares to the English, according to Gerard. The Siwanoy were a principal tribe of the Mahican Wappinger confederacy, formerly living along the north shore of Long Island Sound, from New York to Norwalk, Connecticut, and inland as far as White Plains.

They were one of the seven tribes of the seacoast and had a number of villages, the principal one in the 1600s being Poningo. *Siwanoy* has traditionally been used to refer to a number of poorly known Munsee-Delaware-speaking groups. Johan de Laet specifically located them in 1625 as dwelling "along the coast for 8 leagues (24 miles) to the neighborhood of Hellegate" at the confluence of the East and Harlem rivers by Bronx, Manhattan, and Queens Counties, New York City. Last mentioned as the Siwanoys in the 1656 van der Donck map, these groups thickly inhabited the coastline and adjacent interior from Bronx County, New York to Norwalk, Connecticut.

The first Dutch voyages of exploration between 1614 and 1616 discovered a substantial number of populous settlements located at the mouths of the many rivers that flowed into Long Island Sound. These were later known as Snakapins, on Clasons Point, Bronx County, Poningo, at Rye, New York, the settlements of Assamuck, Patomuck, Petucquapoch, Sachus, Shippan, and Toquams between Greenwich and Stamford, Connecticut, and the towns of Makentouh and Norwalk at Norwalk, Connecticut. Two other groups, the Pachami and the Tankiteke lived in an as yet undetermined area in the interior between Long Island Sound and the Hudson River beyond the headwaters of the coastal rivers.

All of the above mentioned groups had intimate connections with the Wiechquaesgeck, Kichtawanck, and other groups along the eastern banks of the lower Hudson River. The Long Island Sound peoples were blessed with a moderate climate and ample rainfall. Their settlements were shielded by the mass of Long Island from the violent storms blowing in from the Atlantic Ocean. Major towns were on lagoons and islands at the mouths of estuaries. Each group controlled a river drainage, with settlements at the fall-line between fresh and salt water, and along the upper reaches of the river valley.

Their settlement pattern followed the flow of the seasons. During winter they lived in scattered hunting camps in the sheltered interior valleys. In springtime they gathered at the fall line to harvest runs of salmon, herring, shad, and other anadromous fish that ascended the rivers in the millions. As the weather moderated, they moved to large coastal villages for rich saltwater fish and shellfish. The well-drained sandy soils of the coast further supported fine crops of corn, beans, squash, melons, tobacco, and other cultivated plants. Huge flocks of passenger pigeons, ducks, geese, and other migratory birds darkened the late spring and early autumn skies.

The peoples of the Long Island Sound coast lived in large villages made up of two or more longhouses or roundhouses. Constructed of bent timbers and covered with a combination of grass mats and sheets of bark, each structure housed a matriclan consisting of a number of related women, their children, and their husbands. These clustered together in fortified settlements surrounded by log stockades in the interior swamps and remote valleys during times of war. The fall-line fishing villages also served as festival sites for the observance of the many major religious ceremonies. The Siwanoy were among the first Native groups in New Netherland to experience direct and overwhelming European contact.

The Dutch took an early interest in their lands, and a number of land sales were finalized during the 1630s. The Siwanoy fell victim to the massive measles, plague, and smallpox epidemics that swept the coastal villages during the first half of the seventeenth century. These diseases killed uncounted thousands of coastal Long Island people. Put under tribute by the powerful Pequot group of eastern Connecticut, they were compelled to give a sizable portion of their yearly produce to them.

The Siwanoy were further victimized by the unfair trading practices of the Dutch. Fascinated by alcohol, they were continually made drunk by Dutch traders and defrauded of their trade goods and possessions. Tensions were reaching the breaking point when the Dutch called upon the Long Island Sound people to join them in their war against the Raritan and their allies in central New Jersey in 1641.

Siwanoy war parties were soon at the gates of Fort Amsterdam on the southern tip of Manhattan Island with trophies from slain Raritan warriors. The tables were turned when a number of Siwanoy were counted among the lower Hudson River people killed by the Dutch in their surprise attack upon the refugee camps near Fort Amsterdam and at Pavonia, now Jersey City, New Jersey during the night of February 25, 1643. The Siwanoy did not immediately retaliate, but chose to await a more favorable opportunity to strike back. Their warriors finally fell upon the English and Huguenot settlements in their territories during the autumn of 1643.

Among their victims was Anne Hutchinson, the Puritan freethinker who squatted upon unpurchased Siwanoy land in Pelham, New York after she was banished from the Massachusetts Bay Colony. The Long Island Sound peoples were swiftly subjected to several Dutch assaults. A mixed force of Dutch and English under the command of John Underhill, who had participated in the 1637 destruction of the Pequot, located a large village of Wiechquaesgeck, Siwanoy, and Wappingers deep in the interior of Westchester County in today's Ward Pound Ridge Reservation during the winter of 1643-1644

They destroyed the village and killed some five hundred Indians. This catastrophe effectively removed the Long Island Sound peoples from the struggle, and the Mahican chief Aepjen signed the treaty ending the conflict, known as the Governor Keift War, on their behalf on August 30, 1645. The Dutch increased the tempo of their land seizing along the north shore of Long Island Sound following the end of the war. Increased friction led the natives to join allies against the Dutch during the Peach War, 1655-1657. Participation in this desultory struggle did not, however, discourage Dutch efforts to possess the Long Island Sound coast, and most of it was in Dutch hands when the English conquered New Netherland on September 6, 1664.

The English corrected many of the abuses of the Dutch regime and permitted the natives to live at their old settlements along the shore during the warmer months. The land sales had forced those Native people who elected to remain in their homeland deep into the highland interior river valleys. Many clustered in small settlements under the sachem Katonah in the uplands above Bedford, New York around the modern villages of Cross River and Katonah. Those living further east congregated in settlements along the Byram and Rippowam rivers in Fairfield County, Connecticut. These became collectively known as the Stamford Indians.

The English attempted to intern both groups at the Hellgate during the King Phillip's War, 1675 to 1676. The natives convinced the English of their peaceful intentions, and were permitted to remain on their lands after surrendering their firearms until the war ended. A substantial number of Long Island Sound people moved northward among the Mahican groups of the upper Housatonic and northern Hudson River valleys following the death of Katonah and a number of influential Stamford Indian chiefs during the opening decades of the eighteenth century.

Most, however, remained in a number of tiny family hamlets scattered through the interior of Fairfield County. These people made their living by traveling widely through the region laboring on white-owned farms, curing the sick, dispensing herbs, and selling homemade baskets, brooms, and other handicrafts. In 1761, it was reported that Kockopotananh, "sachem of the Derby, Milford, and Stratford Indians" had sixty men under him when he died in 1731.

Large numbers of his followers and other Long Island Sound people became involved in the first mission settlement on the upper Housatonic. Established by the Reverend John Sergeant in 1735, it became known as Stockbridge.

In time, Stockbridge became the major mission community in the region and attracted large numbers of upper Hudson River Delaware-ans, Mahicans, and several Connecticut groups. Other Long Island Sound people joined the Moravian mission villages at Shekomeko and Pleasant Plains, Dutchess County, New York, following their establishment in 1744. Most moved with the settlements to the Bethlehem, Pennsylvania area following their eviction by white authorities in 1746. At least sixty-one Native people were reported living in Fairfield County on January 1, 1774. Many of these joined with the Stockbridge on the Continental side against the English in the War of Independence.

These volunteers suffered dreadful losses during the conflict, and many families were forced to join their brethren at Schagiticoke, New York and in villages in Pennsylvania and Ohio. Most of the Stockbridge moved among the Oneida in New York following the end of the war. Their descendants today reside on the Stockbridge-Munsee Reservation in Wisconsin. A small number of their relatives refused to leave the valleys of their ancestors. The state of Connecticut created a small reservation for them at Schagiticoke, near Kent, along the upper reaches of the Housatonic River. Many Native people moved to the reserve, but most also maintained dwellings off the reservation. The land remains today, but the people continue to live off the reservation.

SKENANDOA

Skenandoa (Oneida, 1704 - March 11, 1816), also known as Schenandoah, Shenondoa, Scanondo, and Skennondon, was a principal Oneida chief in New York, and a friend of white colonists. During the American Revolution he championed Iroquois confederacy neutrality but often gave assistance to the United States. He aided the Boston colonists at the outbreak of hostilities, helped prevent invasions from Canada, preventing the destruction of the German Flats, New York settlements, and provided scouts and spies to the colonists.

In May 1775, he led 11 other Oneida chiefs in officially declaring neutrality. In September 1776 he refused to participate in the Niagara council ending Iroquois neutrality, and was joined by a number of Tuscarora chiefs. The Oneida and Tuscarora were considered "dissenting bodies" by the other Iroquois nations, and toward the end of the Revolution Skenandoa had to take refuge at Schenectady from the British and pro-British Indians who, under General John Burgoyne, attacked the main Oneida village. In 1794 Skenandoa pledged continued neutrality during the Iroquois uprisings. He protested but permitted recruiting of Indian volunteers during the War of 1812.

233

To him the conflict was the confrontation between Tecumseh's teachings and Christianity. When first introduced to the Iroquois nations, alcohol was taken usually only during celebrations, but like many chiefs of his day Skenandoa became a chronic alcoholic. While in Albany in 1775 he became so drunk that his badge of chieftainship was stolen from him. He pledged never to drink again, and through the Reverend Samuel Kirkland, Missionary to the Oneida, became a devout Christian. After the Revolution the economic and social situation of the Indians declined rapidly. By 1812 Skenandoa resumed drinking. He died at Oneida Castle, New York.

STOCKBRIDGE

The Stockbridge-Munsee Reservation community in Wisconsin is the last in a series of missionary-sponsored experimental communities bearing this name. Its population consists of the sole surviving group of the Old Mahican Confederacy that, until the middle 1600s, dominated the upper Hudson River Valley and the Housitanic River Valley from Duchess County, New York, north to Lake Champlain. As speakers of an eastern Algonquian language, the Mahican regularly incorporated a variety of remnants of other New England Algonquian tribes, and this process continued through the mid- nineteenth century. However, the core of this heterogeneous group remained Mahican speaking, and this language was used to transact business until it disappeared.

Their own traditional name is derived from *Muhheakunnak,* a place name alluding to the tidal ebb and flow of the Hudson River. They acquired their better known name from an English variation of the Delaware pronunciation. The English also called them the River Indians and the Wolves, from whence comes the French Loups. Although the modern Stockbridge community represents the last of the Mahicans, it should not be confused with the Mohegans, a different, neighboring eastern Algonquian tribe. Like other neighboring Algonquian and Iroquoian societies in the East, the Mahican were a matrilineal people who built small palisaded villages on hilltops; planted their gardens in nearby burned-over fields; took large quantities of shad and herring from the rivers in season; engaged in collective deer hunting in the fall; and scattered to small hunting camps in winter.

The chief sachem retained his hereditary position and power, but much of the governing authority was taken over by town councils. The first Stockbridge community, therefore, was mixed Mahican, Housatonic, and English in population and culture, but Mahicans remained the core of the groups, and the Mahican language predominated. By 1740, the population consisted of only 120 persons, and that year the last traditional chief sachem died, whereupon Stockbridge became the symbolic center of the remnants of the Mahican tribe scattered through the area.

By the late 1700s, in addition to accepting dependency on manufactured European goods, the Stockbridge people had developed new technological skills of economic value. These amounted to a kind of cottage industry, with women plaiting splint baskets and making moccasins and wooden bowls for the colonial market, and the men working seasonally as farm laborers. Essentially, the missionaries were encouraging the Stockbridge to take on the role of the landless rural English poor, but the men continued to prefer hunting and military service to farm work.

As the traditional subsistence economy failed, Stockbridge warriors increasingly served English authorities in colonial wars against the French and the Pontiac.

Later, more than half the Stockbridge died fighting on the American side during the American Revolution.

SUSQUEHANNOCK

Now extinct, the Susquehannock were a group of one of the least-known tribes of the northeast. They appeared along the Susquehanna watershed at the beginning of white colonization, fought bitterly with both the Delaware and the Five Nations, and then faded into obscurity. Although of Iroquoian stock, they reorganized no allegiance to the Massomacks, the Iroquois name for the confederacy. Several explanations are suggested for the derivation of their name, one being that it comes from the Algonquian *Sas-k-we-an-og,* meaning "The river that rubs upon the shore."

All the Susquehanna Iroquoian groups, however, were called Carantouan by the Five Nations. The most important were the Susquehannock on the lower reaches of the river. Those along the upper river were known as the Andaste. They were first visited by a white man in 1616, when Etienne Brule, Champlain's interpreter, came down from Canada to enlist their aid in a French attack against the Five Nations stronghold in New York. It was this alliance of the Carantouan and Huron with the French that later led to the destruction of these tribes by the Iroquois. The early Swedes in Pennsylvania called the Susquehannock "Black Minquas."

This term probably came from the Lenape, who used the Algonquian mingee or mengwe ("treacherous") as a classification for all detached bands of Iroquois. Corrupted to "Mingo," the term was widely and loosely applied by Indian and white settlers alike from early Colonial days until long after the American Revolution. In some parts of the State, entire tribes or their remnants became known as Mingo, while further confusion in classification of tribal units resulted from amalgamation, adoption, and intermarriage.

The Susquehannock were tall, aggressive, and keen-minded. They had dispersed the Raritan and Piscataway in the Chesapeake Bay area and were in control of that territory when Captain John Smith encountered them in 1608. Excavations of their early burials indicate that some used platforms on which to place their dead until the flesh disappeared.

Skeletal remains were then buried at a depth of three feet, with the skull surmounting the pile. The power of the Susquehannock in Maryland and Virginia was broken by conflict with the whites early in the seventeenth century. In Pennsylvania, however, their war activities were centered chiefly against the Five Nations, for whom they had an undying hatred. The seat of their power in Pennsylvania was a stronghold near what is now Washington Borough. In 1663 they repulsed an attack of Seneca and Cayuga warriors, and sent the defeated Iroquois back to their longhouse bearing messages of derision. By 1667, however, the Susquehannock had begun to feel the effects of continued warfare and sickness, and in 1670 they sent emissaries to the Five Nations in an attempt to make peace.

The enraged Iroquois refused to bury the tomahawk, and hostilities continued until most of the Susquehannock were captured or slain. The main body of the survivors fled to Maryland. Others found refuge along the Susquehanna's west branch, and those remaining were absorbed by tribes of the confederacy. Many years later a group of exiled

Susquehannock returned to their former home in Lancaster County and became known as the Conestoga.

Crowded on all sides by white settlers and by tribes they once held in contempt, the Conestoga diminished until in 1763, only a few remained. In that year, a band of white rioters, known as the "Paxton Boys," inflamed by accounts of Indian depredations along the frontiers, broke into the Lancaster jail where the Conestoga had taken refuge, and murdered all of them.

With this massacre, the last known group of Susquehannock passed out of existence. (See CONESTOGA)

TAMAQUE

Tamaque (Delaware, 1725 - 1770), also known as The Beaver, and King Beaver, was alternately friendly and hostile to 18th century English settlers along the frontier. Brother of Shingas, a merciless and treacherous enemy of colonial pioneers in western Pennsylvania, Tamaque, like his brother, became an important Delaware chieftain.

Moving to Fort Ohio following the British occupation of Fort Duquesne, he settled near the junction of the Tuscarawas and Big Sandy at a village called The Beaver's Town.

There he carried on friendly relations with the English until 1755, but following British General Braddock's defeat at the hands of a combined French and Indian force, Tamaque switched his alliance from the English to the French. By 1758 the chief was expressing his desire to resume good relations with the English, and he attended a council at Fort Pitt in 1759 and another in 1760 to further this desire.

In 1762 Tamaque promised the colonial governor of Pennsylvania that the Delaware under his command would return all captured whites held as prisoners, but then he joined enthusiastically in Pontiac's conspiracy, leading several Indian raids against frontier settlements. When Pontiac's plans to drive the English out of the Great Lakes region met defeat, however, the fickle Tamaque again agreed to keep the peace.

His years of war-making done, the Delaware chief permitted himself to be converted to Christianity by Moravian missionaries and spent his final years as a zealous advocate of his new faith.

237

TARHE (CRANE)

Tarhe (Wyandotte, 1742 - November, 1818), also known as The Crane, born in Detroit, was a Wyandotte chief and head priest of the Porcupine branch, and was a strong opponent of Tecumseh. In 1774 he fought under the Shawnee chief Cornstalk at the battle of Point Pleasant in present West Virginia. He served under Blue Jacket at the Battle of Fallen Timbers, Ohio, August 2O, 1794, and, although seriously wounded, was the only chief to escape. In 1795, resisting tribal opposition, he was a leader in the negotiations that resulted in the August 3, Treaty of Greenville, Ohio signed by 12 Indian tribes, opening the territory to white settlers. As a result of this treaty Tarhe became a United States pensioner. Tarhe was a leader in the opposition to Tecumseh's plans.

Although he too was aware of the continued encroachments by whites upon Indian lands, he refused to join Tecumseh. Acting for the United States government, Tarhe called a meeting of Northwest Indian chiefs loyal to the United States at Brownstown on the Detroit River to plead for their continued neutrality. At the same time Tecumseh, in response to Tarhe's actions called a meeting of anti-United States chiefs at Amhertsburg, Ontario, Canada, across the Detroit River from Brownstown, Although Tecumseh soon invaded the Brownstown encampment and pressed many of the chiefs into joining him, Tarhe fled upon learning of the imminent attack and avoided facing Tecumseh.

During the War of 1812 Tarhe led his warriors in the service of General William H. Harrison in his campaign into Canada, and helped defeat Tecumseh at the October 5, 1813 Battle of the Thames River. After the War, Tarhe returned to central Ohio where he became well known to white settlers. His friendship was held highly by everyone, especially Harrison. Tarhe died at Cranetown near Upper Sandusky, Ohio.

TEEDYUSCUNG

Teedyuscung (Delaware, 1700 - 1763), was an leader in colonial Pennsylvania during the period of the land cessions and frontier wars which forced these Indians westward toward the Ohio country. He advocated resistance to white pressures and became a notable Delaware spokesman at numerous treaties and councils. Teedyuscung was born about 1700 in New Jersey, near present-day Trenton, and lived in the remnant Indian community until about 1830, when the family moved across the Delaware River and settled along the Lehigh Valley.

The Indians were ousted from there in 1737 by the so-called Walking Purchase. The purchase allegedly covering these lands actually had been made years before but it was not until 1737 that, according to the provisions of a later agreement, two well-supplied white men walked off its extent in a day-and-a-half. The Indians protested, charging that the intent had been to alienate far less land, and that the government of Pennsylvania was perpetrating a fraud. Resentment over the Walking Purchase was in large part responsible for Teedyuscung's and other Delaware Indian's demands at later treaties and eventually for the defection of Teedyuscung's band to the French side during the French and Indian War.

At first, however, Teedyuscung attempted to remain on the lands. However, white settlers began to enter the Forks of the Delaware, and the Iroquois, who claimed an authority of sorts over the Delaware, in 1742 ordered the Delaware of the Forks to vacate their lands, and in 1749 the Iroquois purported to sell these and other lands to the Penns. Many of the Indians now left for new homes on the Susquehanna. Teedyuscung remained, converting to the Moravian faith and living in the communal settlement of some 500 Christian Indians at Gnadenhutten, north of the Moravian headquarters at Bethlehem.

He remained there until 1754, when along with most of the others, under Iroquois insistence, he moved to Wyoming, on the Susquehanna (where Wilkes-Barre now stands). His political career dates from that move. Before 1754 and his death in 1763, Teedyuscung was active as a council speaker for the Delaware Indians of Wyoming. During the hostilities on Pennsylvania's frontier, he was a warrior and leader of the Wyoming Delaware.

The faction used the military crisis to extort concessions from the province of Pennsylvania, threatening (and occasionally carrying out) reprisal raids if redress was not offered for land grievances and if Pennsylvania did not cease to endorse, or even promote, the Iroquois claims to sovereignty over the Delaware.

At a series of council meetings with whites from 1756 to 1760, he articulated the Delaware position in eloquent speeches. These speeches were set down, in English translation, and published in the minutes of Indian treaties printed by Benjamin Franklin. He thus came to be widely known as a persuasive Indian spokesman. Teedyus-cung was given political support by the Quakers of the province who wanted to embarrass their opponents, the Proprietary party, by publi-cizing the Delaware charges of misconduct in Indian affairs.

This did not endear him to the government of Pennsylvania, or to Sir William Johnson, the Crown's Superintendent of Indian Affairs, and they did much to discredit him. He died at Wyoming, however, re-sisting an invasion by Connecticut settlers. He was allegedly was murdered. Teedyuscung's diplomacy was unable to prevent the rapid erosion of the Indian position in the east. Whether or not his specific charges were valid, he was a widely cited symbol of Indian resistance to white rapacity, because of the publicity given to his cause by the Quakers and the printing of the Indian treaties.

He, and other Indian spokesmen like him, was able to insist on an policy less destructive to Indians than that desired by many frontiers-men and land speculators.

TIONONTATI

In the second half of the Seventeenth Century the Wyandottes were often known to both the French and the English by variants of the name of their largest constituent group, the Tionontati (Petun). The English continued this usage into the mid-1700s. Examples from French sources are; Tionnontatehronnons, 1654; Tionnontate, 1672; Tionontates, 1682; Donondates; and Tynondady, 1757. Equivalent to this is the Onondaga name *tyonontate-ka*, according to Hewitt.

UNCAS

Uncas (Mohegan; ? - 1682), also known as Fox, (literally the cir-cler), was chief of the Mohegan, played an important role in the Indian history of colonial southern New England. As a subchief under Pequot Chief Sachem Sassacus, Uncas rebelled and with a band of followers settled on the west bank of the Pequot (Thames) River about three miles south of the present Norwich, Connecticut.

This group known as Mohegan is mentioned as a tribe in early rec-ords beginning about 1636. Uncas and the Mohegan supported the English in the Pequot War (1636), King Philip's war (1675), and through the Revolutionary Period. Uncas was noted for his strategy and cunning in warfare; for being a faithful friend; and for being relentless toward his enemies.

Uncas, wiley strategist that he was, saw that it was to his advantage to support the English and adopt their ways as a means of survival for his people. For this stand he was condemned by many and lauded by others. Uncas was the older of two sons of Oweneco and Meeken-ump. His brother was named Waweequa. References to the early life of Uncas are lacking. As for tribal affiliations it appears that the Mohegan (Mohican Wolf people) migrated from the upper Hudson River valley in the early 1600s to the present Connecticut and parts of eastern New York and western Massachusetts.

Local tribes called them pequataug meaning destroyers or invaders hence the name Mohegan Pequot. The Moihican (Mohegan, Mahikan) were related to the northern or "Wolf" division of the Delawares or Lenni-Lenape. According to Delaware tradition, "Some of the Wolves went east", and the Connecticut Mohegan always maintained that, "Our people came from the northwest", indicating the area in eastern New York state and northwestern Massachusetts.

The group finally settled near the towns of New London and Groton, Connecticut, and were generally known as Pequot. In 1626, Uncas married the daughter of Sassacus, Grand Sachem of the Pequot. Claiming to be a distant cousin of Sassacus this union made him more closely connected with the Royal Family, and he felt that he should be granted more authority within the band of followers withdrawing and settling on the west bank of the Pequot (Thames) River. This group, known as Mohegan, is mentioned in Colonial records beginning about 1636.

Uncas and the Mohegan were friendly toward the Colonists, much to the displeasure of the Pequot and other local Indian leaders in the area. Uncas realized that having a small band of less than a hundred, they would soon be dominated by white men, as would be the other small tribes in the area, so it was to his advantage to adopt the ways of the colonists.

Trouble was brewing within the Pequot and English villages and following hostilities against the English, the Pequot became involved in a war with the colonists in 1637. Uncas assisted Roger Williams in securing the aid of Indian allies in joining an attack on the Pequot Fort at Mystic that annihilated most within the fort. An estimated 700 men, women and children were believed to have been within the village and only a few escaped. English losses were light, with only some twenty wounded and two killed. Survivors sought refuge with other Indians. Sassacus fled to the Mohawk where he was slain.

With the death of Sassacus, the Pequot no longer had an existing power in Indian affairs. Uncas was in control of the remaining Indian tribes throughout Connecticut. There was more trouble ahead for Uncas and the Mohegan when word was received that Chief Miantonomoh and the Narragansett chiefs had existed for a long time and in 1643 the battle was on at the Great Plain in Mohegan territory outside present Norwich, Connecticut.

Mohegan scouts informed Uncas of the approaching Narragansett chief and his warriors. Estimates vary, but It seems likely that the Narragansett numbered around 500 and the Mohegan not more that 200. Uncas sent one of his men to ask Miantonomoh if he would agree to the two chiefs meeting man to man to settle their grievances. The offer was rejected. Miantonomoh said "My men came to fight and fight they will." Uncas had told the Mohegan men that if his offer was rejected that he would fall on his face as a signal for them to charge the enemy.

Upon receiving the negative reply, Uncas fell on his face and the Mohegan put the Narragansett to flight, many losing their lives as they attempted to leap over the falls of the Yantic River. Miantonomoh was pursued by a Mohegan, Tantaquiesen (Tantaquidgeon) an aide to Uncas who was "the first to lay hands on the enemy chief.

"This enabled Chief Uncas to have the honor of capturing Miantonomoh. Traditionally "A Chief must take a Chief" thus Tantaquidgeon being of lesser rank could not have the honor. This has been referred to as the most purely Indian battle in the annals of New England." Only bows and arrows and clubs were used and the English were not directly concerned. Miantonomoh was taken to the Fort of Uncas and a meeting was arranged with the Commissioners at Hartford, Connecticut, to discuss his fate. Uncas was told that he could use his judgment in disposing of his captive but it must be carried out beyond the boundaries of Hartford, in other words, in Mohegan territory.

Miantonomoh was slain by Uncas' brother, Waweequa. Angered by the capture and death of their chief at the hands of Uncas, the Narragansett besieged the Mohegan village at Fort Shantok in 1645. Food supplies were low and Uncas sent a scout to Saybrook, the nearest English settlement, to tell them of the plight of the Mohegan. In response to Uncas' plea for aid, beef, beans, and corn were brought by boat up the Pequot (Thames) river and smuggled into the Fort under cover of darkness. At daybreak, the Mohegan hoisted a piece of beef on a pole outside the Fort. Seeing the beef and some Englishmen in the area, the Narragansett left the scene.

In 1765, Uncas and a few Mohegan men joined the English in the struggle known as King Philip's War, which lasted most of the year. None of the battles were fought on Connecticut soil but Connecticut tribes were involved, in some conflicts with Indians; others with the English.

This proved to have been the last open warfare between the Indian tribes of southern New England and the colonists. Through the years, Uncas and his sons, Oweneco and Attawanhood (Joshua) had deeded many acres of Mohegan land to their English friends for favors accorded them during times of warfare.

Uncas and his remaining tribal members survived on surviving tribal grounds with more and more non-Indians taking up residence among them. Uncas finally retired to his wigwam at a place called Uncas Hill in Mohegan, Montville Township, Connecticut.

There he died at a great age in 1682 or 1683. At the top of Mohegan Hill, on Connecticut Route 32, is a marker erected by the State, which reads, "Mohegan: Seat of Uncas-Friend of the English." Here live 35 of the known 200 descendants of the Mohegan, on land that is individually owned.

The reservation system was terminated in 1860 at the request of Mohegan leaders. Nearby, is a small Indian museum owned and operated by Chief Harold Tantaquidgeon X and his sister, Gladys Tantaquidgeon, tenth generation descendants of Chief Uncas. The museum is dedicated to the history and traditions of the Mohegan and other New England Indians.

WABAN

Waban (Nipmuc, ? - 1677), was a 17th century Nipmuc Indian, a friend of missionary John Eliot, and a leader of the Christian converts among the Indians. Waban was probably born at Musketaquid, which is now Concord, Massachusetts. He was living at Nonantum (now

243

Newton) in 1646, when he welcomed John Eliot as a Chief Minister of Justice at the time. Eliot conducted his first service in the Algonquin language at Nonantum and returned there regularly to preach. Waban requested of Eliot land on which to build a town, and this Eliot obtained from the General Court of Massachusetts.

When the new town was established at Natick in 1651, Waban was its town clerk. At Eliot's recommendation, the government of the town followed the Biblical pattern of a hierarchy of one ruler of one hundred, two rulers of 50, and ten rulers of ten. Waban was chosen as a ruler of fifty.

He was later the Justice of the Peace, and in 1670 was said to be the chief ruler of this community of Christian Indians (which four years later numbered 29 families, or about 145 persons). Shortly before the outbreak of King Philip's War in 1675, Waban learned of the impending Indian attack and warned the English. However, the whites suspected the Christian Indians of duplicity, and Waban was among many sent as prisoners to Deer Island later that year. He was among the sick who were returned in 1676.

He probably died about 1677. Waban encouraged many other Indians to accept Christianity. Daniel Gookin described him as "a person of great prudence and piety." Eliot stated that Waban's gift lay in "ruling, judging of cases, wherein he is patient, constant, and prudent, insomuch that he is respected among them, for they have chosen him a ruler of fifty, and he ruleth well according to his measure."

WAMPANOAG

The Wampanoag are one of the tribes associated with the original group of Pilgrims who came to North America on the Mayflower. One tribal member was an Indian the Pilgrims would soon rank as "a special instrument sent of God; for their good beyond their expectation." This Indian was Squanto, Tisquantum being his Indian name, the last of the Patuxet. He had been carried off to slavery in Spain, been owned for a while by some local friars, and had finally escaped to England, where he had lived some years with a wealthy merchant in Cornhill, London, before he finally made his way back to America. He had arrived at Patuxet six months before the arrival of the Mayflower, and finding not one of his tribe alive, he went back to Sowams, Massasoit's village.

A man named Samoset brought Squanto back because his English was much better, and without Squanto and his native skill and knowledge of the country, the Pilgrims would have perished. Starvation haunted them, and they barely managed to pull through. Almost an hour after Squanto's appearance, Massasoit arrived with sixty warriors behind him. If he had come to fight, he could have swept Plymouth out of existence, but he came in peace, and with Samoset and Squanto as interpreters, Massasoit and Governor Carter of Plymouth signed the Treaty of Plymouth, a non-aggression pact.

Provisions stated that if an Indian botke the peace, he would be sent to Plymouth for punishment; if broken by a Pilgrim, he would be sent to Sowams for punishment. Indians coming to visit Plymouth were to leave their arms behind, and the Pilgrims were to do the same on their visits. If anyone "unjustly" attacked either party to the Treaty, the other was to come immediately to his assistance. The pact was to apply to all tribes under the dominion of the Wampanoag, and Massasoit undertook "to certisfie them of this."

This non-aggression pact was repeatedly renewed during the 40 years of Massasoit's life, but after his death the old alliance between Pilgrim and Indian began to give way to constant suspicion. Massasoit's sons, Wansutta, Alexander to the English, now sachem, and Metacom, Philip to the English, came to Plymouth to sign the old nonaggression pact, but it was not long before rumors from Boston reported that Alexander was plotting against the Pilgrims.

When he failed to appear at the General Court to explain, Major Winslow and ten armed men seized Alexander at a hunting lodge, treating him as a felon, with a pistol at his back, instead of as a sovereign ally.

Questioned by Governor Prence, Alexander was released, desperately sick of fever, and died within two or three days at Plymouth. His warriors carried him on their shoulders to Sowams for burial among his people, but his brother Philip always believed he was poisoned. The fundamental cause of conflict lay in the opposed land systems of the whites and the Indians, and the irritation became acute when the Wampanoags began complaining that the Pilgrims were encroaching on their hunting grounds. Other things annoyed the Indians. By 1643, no "stray" Indian was to be allowed in Plymouth. And if an Indian was guilty of theft, he was to make fourfold restitution; if he was unable to do so, he was to work it off at 12 pence a day or "be sold for his theft."

By 1656, Plymouth decreed that no boats, or sails or riggings, and no horse, mare, colt, or foal could be sold to an Indian. No colony would legally sell liquor or firearms to any Indian, but the Pilgrims were increasingly distressed by the alleged traffic, especially in firearms. Probably what most infuriated the Pilgrims was that, like his father Massasoit, Philip refused to let anyone try proselytizing his tribe.

When John Eliot tried to convert Philip, the Indian snapped the missionary's jacket button and said, "I care no more for your gospel than that." Things continued to go from bad to worse, and by 1675, war was inevitable, the beginning of one of the great Indian wars. By the most brilliant diplomatic skill, Philip had managed to break down age-old jealousies and had rallied practically every New England tribe to his side. In the spring of 1676, however, the tide began to turn against Philip. The Indians had no food, and diseased, hungry, and weak, they began to desert.

Philip had gone back to the land of his ancestors, to Mount Hope, and a traitor to his cause offered to show the Pilgrims his hiding place. Then a "Praying Indian" managed to shoot him, and his severed head was placed on a pike in the watchtower at Plymouth for more than 20 years. When the war ended, 900 Indians were dead, 800 white men killed, 25 white towns burned to the ground, and more than 127,000 ($1,350,000) was the Colonies' war debt. As Indian captives, men, women, and children poured into Plymouth, all were sold into slavery, some to local planters, but most in the West Indies.

"To sell souls for money seemeth to me a dangerous merchandise," said John Eliot in protest, and Captain David Gookin, superintendent of the Praying Indians, gave his own opinions so vigorously that he began to be "afraid to go about the streets." In Massachusetts, where 200 Praying Indians deserted to Philip, there had been panic, and even on Cape Cod, drastic measures had to be taken. Indian women were seized as hostages, and no Indian was allowed to approach nearer to Plymouth than Sandwich, on pain of instant death.

In spite of all this, the Cape tribes technically under Philip, remained useful allies to the English, serving particularly as scouts. Today, the Wampanoag are divided into five regional, autonomous groups, including Gay Head on Martha's Vineyard, Mashpee on Cape Cod, Assonet from New Bedford to Rehoboth, Herring Pond from Wareham to Middleboro, and Nemasket in the Middleboro area. Tribal councils manage the political affairs of the bands, and represent them at state and federal levels. They have continued to petition the federal government for federal recognition. There were 2,600 to 2,800 Wampanoag members in a recent count. The Gay Head group on Martha's Vineyard does not have a reservation, but the tribe owns lands in trust.

Tourism has become an economic development here, and many tribal members operate snack bars and shops of the island. In 1987, the Gay Head group won federal recognition, and a number of educational, social, and housing services have been provided. The group maintains many of their traditional celebrations. Population recently totaled 260 members. The Mashpee living in Mashpee filed a claim with the federal government in 1976 to recover the town of Mashpee. They claimed the state had violated the Federal Nonintercourse Act of 1799 by splitting up tribal territory among individual Indians and allowing non-Indians to buy the land without Congressional approval.

When the case came to trial in January 1977, a Federal jury ruled against the Wampanoags on the theory that they were not a tribe when the first of the Nonintercourse Acts passed, and that while they might have been after that date, they had not been one for more than a century. After that ruling, the tribe took their case to the United States Supreme Court, which refused to hear the case. The Wampanoag case was financed by the Native American Rights Fund. Although the group has felt overwhelmed by land purchases by whites in the area, and a 1988 shooting of a tribal member by a policeman threatened to further deteriorate an already difficult relationship between whites and Indians, recently the two opposing groups have begun a dialogue to resolve the issue and other concerns that threaten the well-being of all community members.

The Mashpee Tribal Council, the political arm of the tribe, is primarily responsible for the continuing land suit as well as other issues. The group maintains traditional ceremonies, bringing together local members and those from around the country. Recently there were 1,060 members of the Mashpee group, with about 600 living in Mashpee.

WAPPINGER

The Wappinger were a Mahican Algonquian-speaking group that inhabited the eastern banks of the mid-Hudson River Valley of New York, above the Hudson Highlands. First identified as the Wappenox in 1626, they were described as active participants in the riverside fur trade with Dutch peddlers. The "Wappenos" reportedly drove a number of lower Hudson River Delawarean-speaking groups from their homes sometime prior to 1628. Long-standing allies of the Dutch colony of New Netherland, Wappinger warriors participated in a number of raids against the Raritan during 1641 and 1642. The Dutch massacre of over 120 lower Hudson River refugees from a Mahican attack on the night of February 25-26, 1643 dramatically reversed Wappinger allegiance.

Their war parties attacked Dutch shipping on the Hudson River during the spring of 1643, effectively cutting communication between Fort Amsterdam at the mouth of the Hudson River and Fort Orange near Albany, New York. Some 25 Wappingers were killed in the Dutch assault upon the large Wiechqusesgeck village in the Pound Ridge area of Westchester County, New York, during the winter of 1643-44. This disaster led the Wappinger to sue for peace along with the Kichtawanck, Wiechquaesgeck, Sintsing, and Nochpemm on April 6, 1644.

The Mahican sachem Aepjen represented these groups in the final peace treaty ending the conflict, known as the Governor Kieft War (1640-1645), on August 30, 1645. The Wappinger next went to war against the Dutch during the Peach War (1655-1657). Still belligerent following the end of that conflict, the Wappinger managed to avoid direct involvement in the first years of the Esopus War (1659-1664).

Wappinger diplomats alternately served as intermediaries between the Dutch and Esopus and covert allies of the Esopus troupe. They participated in the July 15, 1660 treaty that ended the first phase of the fighting, and a number of Wappinger warriors fought with the Esopus when fighting broke out again during the summer of 1663. On July 8, 1663, nine Wappinger and thirty Minisink men were included among the 200 Esopus warriors. Other Wappinger families held a number of Dutch captives and sheltered the relatives of Esopus warriors.

On May 15, 1664 "t'Sees-Sagh- Gauw, chief of the Wappinghs" signed the peace treaty ending the Esopus War. The Dutch colony of New Netherland fell to the English on September 6, 1664. On September 24, 1664 the "Wampings and Espachomy (Esopus)" submitted themselves to English protection. This protection was not immediately forthcoming, however, and the Wappinger were attacked by the Mohawks in 1669.

On December 29, 1669, the Highland Indians often mentioned in the English records were identified as the "Wappingoes and Wickershick (Wiechquaesgeck)." Increasing number of Wiechquaegeck, Kichtawanck, and Siwanoy moved north among the Wappinger during the last decades of the seventeenth century.

Many Wappinger, disenchanted with the English and resentful of their continued demands for lands and labor, moved further north to the French settlements along the Saint Lawrence River below Montreal, Canada. The Wappinger and their neighbors came to be known collectively as River Indians during the late 17th century. Many of these people extended hunting and trapping grounds far west into the Ohio River Valley during the 1680s. A large number of River Indian men served with the English against the French during the King William's War (1689 and 1697).

This war was an unqualified disaster for the River Indians; on April 19, 1698, it was reported that only 90 River Indian men out of 250 had survived. By 1700, many of these moved to the village of Schagticoke above Albany, New York. On July 20, 1702 it was noted that 110 River Indians were "at Skachcock and 87 below ye towne" in their traditional territories. The Schagticoke village served as an outpost that protected the northern New York frontier from surprise attacks by the French and their Native allies. The River Indians became increasingly associated with their Mahican neighbors during the opening decades of the 1700s. The Wappingers greatly increased their settlement area at that time, and they came to inhabit small hamlets located in western Connecticut, the Hudson River drainage, and along the upper Delaware River valley between New York and Pennsylvania.

They followed a wide-ranging seasonal round of activities that carried them through this region at various times of the year. Many Wappinger were undoubtedly among the numerous River Indian parties reported to be as far west as the Mississippi River country during the early eighteenth century. Some 98 River Indians, including "19 lowermost River Indians and 21 highland Indians," joined the English in an expedition against French Canada on August 24, 1711, during the Queen Anne's War (1702-1713). An increasing number of River Indians moved to Canada following the war to escape the liquor trade that pauperized them and put them in debt to English traders.

In 1735, a large number of River Indians moved to the Stockbridge mission settlement on the upper Housatonic River in Connecticut. Others, including a large number of Wappinger, went to the Moravian missions at Shekomeko and Pleasant Plains in 1744. Most of these Wappinger then removed to the Moravian settlements at the Forks of the Delaware River near Easton, Pennsylvania, following their eviction from Dutchess County in 1746.

The pagan Wappinger continued to inhabit their substantial range in the region. Their main settlements were at Wikopy, in Dutchess County, New York; Pompton, in north Central New Jersey; and Cochecton, a large village on the upper Delaware River. On January 3, 1745, a party of 12 "Cashington Indians" came to Goshen, New York to enter into a "friendship" agreement with the New York government.

This was agreed to on January 17, 1746, and the mixed Wappinger, Esopus, Minisink, and Wappinger community at Cochecton both hunted and patrolled the western frontier of the province of New York for a decade. War between the English and the Delaware, Minisink, and the "Opings or Pomptowns" broke out in 1755 as part of the widening struggle known as the Seven Year's War (1735 and 1762).

Their sachem, Nimham, led the Wappinger warriors in a series of devastating raids upon the English settlements in eastern Pennsylvania and western New Jersey during the first years of the conflict. He signed over Wappinger land claims in northern New Jersey and concluded a peace with the English on October 23, 1758. Most of his followers moved with the Minisink and their Mahican brothers to the Wyoming Valley in the upper Susquehanna drainage.

By August 26, 1761, it was reported that "the chief of the Mohickons Opies have settled with Six Nations, at a place called Chenango" above Binghamton, New York. Dissatisfied with living as exiles in Pennsylvania, and unwilling to move further west as English pressure increased, Nimham led his people back to their Dutchess County homeland during the early 1760s. In 1765, he litigated for the right to retain title to land in Dutchess and Columbia counties. Though he failed to legally regain title to the Wappinger lands there, his people were permitted to live in small settlements scattered through the back-country of both counties. These Wappinger became increasingly involved with the Stockbridge Indian community, which by then had moved to near Albany, New York. About 300 fighting men were listed among the River Indians on June 11, 1774.

These included the "Montocks and others of Long Island, Wappingers of Dutchess County, Esopus, Papagonck & Co. in Ulster County, and a few Skachticokes." The Wappinger and other River Indians elected to join the rebels during the American Revolution (1775-1781). A force of some 60 Wappinger warriors set out to join Washington's forces during the summer of 1778. The British surprised this force at Yonkers, New York, and nearly 40 of them were either killed or wounded on July 30, 1778, in the battle of Cortland's Ridge.

Nimham was killed during the struggle, and the survivors returned to their homes at Stockbridge for the remainder of the war. The Wappinger chose to remain at the Stockbridge settlement after the war. This mixed Wappinger, Mahican, and Housatonic community moved to the settlement of New Stockbridge among the Oneida in 1785. There they became involved with the Brotherton of southern New Jersey and New England, as well as with their Oneida hosts.

This community, heavily influenced by its Christian missionaries and highly skilled in white customs, remained in New York until the 1820s.

White land sales resulted in the virtual extinction of Native title to lands in New York during the first decades of the nineteenth century. Speculators and settlers exerted pressure to induce the Stockbridge and their Oneida hosts to migrate westward. In 1821 the Stockbridge bought some land in Wisconsin from the Menominee and Winnebago. The New Stockbridge people began moving to the new reservation shortly thereafter, and the mission officially reopened there in 1835.

This reservation, known as the Stockbridge-Munsee Reservation, persists to the present day, and the modern descendants of the Wappinger reside there as relatively affluent middle class Christians. Well-educated, economically prosperous, and blessed with a growing population, the Stockbridge-Munsee community is among the most successful reservation groups in the country.

A recent count showed some 1500 Indians on the Stockbridge-Munsee Reservation, which sits in a rural, woodland area in Shawano County, In North Central Wisconsin, near the village of Bowler. Reservation boundaries hold two townships, Bartelme, and Red Springs, with a total of some 46,000 acres. About 16,00 acres of this land is held in trust for the tribe, which has resisted breaking the reservation into allotments.

WHITE EYES

White Eyes (Delaware, 1730 - November 1778), also known as Co-quetakeghton "that which is put near the head" because of his light-colored eyes, the Delaware war captain Koquethagetchan, was called White Eyes, sometimes Grey Eyes. Possibly there was white ancestry in his background.

The date and place of his birth are unknown, but in 1762 he was living at a Delaware Indian town at the mouth of Beaver Creek, a tributary of the Ohio River, south of Pittsburgh, Pennsylvania. With other migrant Delawares, whose original homes were in the Delaware River area, he moved to the Muskingum valley in Tuscarawas County, Ohio prior to the American Revolution.

Colonel George Morgan, Indian agent for the Continental Congress, became a good friend of White Eyes, and persuaded him to use his influence to consolidate the Delawares at a new location at present Coshocton, Ohio. There a new council fire was kindled. Small but resolute, brave, and highly intelligent, White Eyes was selected in 1776 by the Delaware Great Council to replace the aging and infirm principal chief, Netawatwees. He appeared before the Congress in Philadelphia where he was officially thanked for promoting peace between the Delawares and the whites.

Congress gave him 300 dollars and two fine horses with saddles and bridles. White Eyes agreed that in the event of war with the British, the Delawares would aid the Americans, and he proposed that the Delaware tribe should constitute a fourteenth state in the American union. These points were incorporated in a treaty at Pittsburgh, September 17, 1778, of which he, along with John Killbuck, Junior, and Captain Pipe, were signatories. He was commissioned a Lieutenant Colonel, and while serving as a guide for troops under command of

General Lachlan McIntosh, was murdered in November 1778 by an unknown assailant.

Following his death, a pro-British faction seized control of the tribe and persuaded the majority of the Delaware warriors to war against the Americans. The hostility broke the treaty of 1778, and alienated Americans from the Delawares. George White Eyes and Joseph White Eyes were two of the chief's sons, but the names of his wife and other children are not known.

WYANDOTTE

The people who became known as Wyandottes to the English and Americans represent an emergent tribal society that developed out of the surviving remnants of three great Ontario Iroquoian confederacies, the Huron, Petun, and Neutrals. Wyandotte, the name that this group selected for themselves in the 1740s, is a corruption of the old self-name of the Huron Confederacy, Wendat. Earlier, these refugees had been known to the French as the Hurons of the West, or the Petun (Tobacco) Hurons, and to the English as the Dionondade.

Because those who finally settled in Ohio and Pennsylvania insisted on being identified as Wendat, a name the English authorities finally accepted, they produced one of the rare instances in Indian history where an Indian society reasserted its traditional identity after decades of being called names derived by Europeans. After the defeat and dispersal of the Ontario Iroquoian confederacies by the New York Iroquois in 1651, some of the survivors fled to the Upper Great Lakes country with their traditional partners, the Ottawa.

There followed a complicated series of migrations into Wisconsin, Minnesota, Michigan, and Iowa, as these refugees sought to establish themselves in a productive new habitat where they might forge a new tribal organization. Driven by the Sioux from their Chequamegon Bay base in 1670, they moved next to Michillimackinac, where they lived until 1704, when they again resettled near Detroit under French auspices. It was from this Detroit village that dissident members of the Turtle clans, anti-French and anti-Catholic, began moving into long-vacant Ohio country along the richly fertile Sandusky River valley and plain.

During their years as refugees in the west (1650-1703) the Wyandottes worked to maintain their old position as a favored middleman in the fur trade with the French. However, they were too few to dominate their Algonquian neighbors and allies, mainly the Ottawa, Chippewa, and Potawatomi, or to overawe and conquer their enemies such as the Sioux, for their population did not exceed 1500 in the years 1651-1703. Hence they were constantly involved in political intrigue, playing one ally against another.

Eventually they developed a reputation for such untrustworthiness that their old allies threatened war with them. However, once settled in Ohio, they emerged as the symbolic leaders of the loose intertribal coalition composed of Michigan, Indiana, and Ohio tribes. Thus for many years, their villages near Detroit and Sandusky were used as the sites for important councils, as well as the depository for the valuable wampum belts which were the diplomatic records and documents of such negotiations. The Wyandottes, who were mainly Petun (Tionontate) and Huron (Wendat) in origin, spoke a northern language.

Their culture history after 1650 is one of near constant migration and readjustment to the unsettled conditions of the frontier in the Old Northwest Territory, and they also maintained several small villages in Ontario at modern Windsor and Amherstburg. Those who lived in British territory continued to be called Hurons of Lorette on the Saint Lawrence River, who were a different group of refugees.

Before the diaspora of the 1650s, these Iroquoians had been the target of major French missionary effort, and this acculturative influence continued strong in the west, particularly so at Michillimackinac and Detroit. But it also produced the reaction of an anti-French factional split in the 1730s. The anti-French faction, mainly representing the Turtle clans led by Nicholas Orontony, broke away, settling in Ohio, and developed relationships with English colonists, while the Deer and Wolf clans remained attached to the French.

After Orontony led an abortive attempt to destroy the French fort at Detroit, most of the Wyandotte settled in Ohio, where they nurtured their influence, ultimately inviting the Delaware and Shawnee to join them there in an alliance with the English. After the British defeated the French in 1760, the Wyandotte became extremely reluctant supporters of Pontiac, and it was the Wyandotte who welcomed Sir William Johnson to Detroit after the Ottawa leader's defeat. But by that year, 1764, the Wyandotte control of the Ohio heartland had only a half century to run, for by moving eastward they occupied valuable ground squarely in the path of American expansion.

Therefore, after the Revolutionary War, in which the Wyandottes joined the English and the Great Lakes tribes in opposing the Americans, they came under heavy pressure to cede their lands. The Wyandottes had already participated in three treaties with Americans when they met with General Anthony Wayne, the victor of Fallen Timbers, at Fort Greenville in 1795. In the treaty negotiations that year, their chief Tarhe (The Crane) stood out as the main speaker for all the tribes participating. Tarhe made it plain that the Wyandotte fully recognized that a new era had dawned, acknowledging American sovereignty over the Great Lakes- Ohio Valley area.

Through the 1830s, while the Wyandottes were ceding most of their lands to the Americans, their kinsmen, the Hurons of Anderdon, were similarly negotiating with British authorities. Although under very heavy pressure to sell their last reservation in Ohio and Michigan, and to move west of the Mississippi, the Wyandottes resisted until 1843. Finally selling their last lands, that year they boarded steamboats and traveled west to take possession of a 36-section tract where modern Kansas City, Kansas now stands.

The 1842 treaty was supported by the Wyandotte Pagan faction and opposed by the Citizen party. The former, consisting of most of the traditional Wyandotte, saw the West as a place to escape problems of living in dense American agricultural settlements in Ohio. The Citizen faction was led by the well-educated sons of British and American agents and traders, which had married into the tribe.

On their Ohio Reservation, the Wyandottes had governed themselves under a written constitution, with their own legislative, judicial, and police systems. This practice, Protestant missionary developed, continued in Kansas, but the community there was short lived, for once again they had selected as their home, lands coveted by American speculators and settlers. Most of the Wyandotte by that time had converted to the Methodist Episcopal Church; and in Kansas, during the disturbed years before the Civil War, they became embroiled in the anti-slavery controversy.

Since the Wyandotte tribe had assimilated as full citizens a number of freed Blacks and escaped slaves, they were opposed to slavery. In these same years, some Wyandottes were caught up by the Gold Rush

255

and resettled in California, while several leaders worked at organizing Nebraska Territory. Indeed, one leader was elected the first provisional governor of that territory, but lost his position because of the anti-slavery stance. In 1855 the Wyandotte tribe, under a new treaty, was disbanded and their lands divided into individual holding.

By 1857 several hundred had migrated to Oklahoma to settle on the Seneca Reservation there. Meanwhile, their lands in Kansas were entirely lost through sale or tax foreclosure. By 1872 most identifiable Wyandottes had moved to Oklahoma, where 220 of them lived that year. At that point, all were American citizens and farmers, and acculturation pressure continued strong, so much so that by the 1960s, only two elderly people could still use the language, while by then the traditional culture and social institutions had disappeared.

During their years of migration, the Wyandottes were known by various names to their French, British, American, and Indian neighbors. The names mainly reflected the largest parts of this composite refugee population, such as Tionontati (Petun) and Huron (Wendat).

English colonial authorities came to know them, through New York Iroquois intermediaries, as Dionondades or Jenondades. After England took possession of French North America, they continued to call the community at Anderdon (Amherstburg), Ontario Hurons, but by then New York and Pennsylvania colonial authorities had adopted Wyandotte for those south of the Great Lakes. Sometimes parts of the whole tribe were known after the names of their most influential clans, particularly of the Deer phratry, or by the name of the Deer phratry chief, Sastaretsy.

The Central Algonquians of the Great Lakes area, on the other hand, called the Wyandotte Nadowe (Timber Rattlesnakes), as they did all the Northern Iroquoians. Today, the Wyandotte live on the Oklahoma reservation. In 1956, they were singled out for "extermination" as a tribal entity, but after 20 years of protest, they succeeded in regaining federal recognition in 1978. Many new developments have resulted from recognition, including scholarships, daily meals for elders, new homes, a health center, a tribal center and meeting hall, and a preschool facility.

They purchased 10 acres of land in Park City, Kansas to build a gaming enterprise, and have received a grant to fund the Wyandotte Museum and Cultural Center. Additional funds have aided in the location, purchase, and catalogue of the material culture. The Wyandotte tribe seeks to maintain its heritage and the remnants of its language. A library and archives are part of the potential new developments. In a recent count there were over 3,600 enrolled members of the tribe in Oklahoma.

TREATY COMMITMENTS
--a History of Broken Promises

The classic book, *A Century of Dishonor*, by Helen Jackson, was published in 1880. Subtitled "A Sketch of the United States Government's Dealings With Some of The Indian Tribes," it remains a vivid and compelling narrative of the incredibly unjust treatment of America's natives, focusing mainly on the hundred years ending in the late 1870s, the first century of the United States as a nation.

It is highly recommended in its entirety, and with apologies this brief outline of her work is included, using Helen Jackson's words as much as possible. This is the essence of her work, minus many vivid and fascinating details.

The question of whether the United States dealt honorably with the Indians turns on a much disputed and little understood point. Some sentimentalists say that the Indians were the real owners of the land, while some politicians hold that they had no right of ownership whatever. Between these views lay innumerable grades and confusions of opinion.

The Indians "right of occupancy" was recognized by all the great discovering Powers. Did the United States, on taking its place among the Nations, also recognize the Indian "right of occupancy"? On this point there is no doubt.

Stealing is everywhere held to be dishonorable, as is lying, in all its forms. Breaking of promises and betrayals of trust are scorned even among the most ignorant of people. However, when the acts of nations are discussed, there seems to be a less clear conception, a less uniform standard of right and wrong, honor and dishonor.

In charging a government or nation with dishonorable conduct, it should merely be shown that its moral standard ought not differ from the moral standard of an individual. What is cowardly, cruel, and base in a man, is cowardly, cruel, and base in a government or nation.

The right of refusing to submit to injustice, of resisting injustice by force if necessary, is part of the law of nature, and as such is recognized by the law of nations. From this arises the right to a just defense, which belongs to every nation and to every individual. Men pledge justice to each other by promises or contracts, while between nations, treaties are made. National contracts or treaties are even more solemn and sacred than private ones on account of the great interests involved.

It has been said by those defending the Untied States Government's repeated disregard of its treaties with the Indians, that no Congress can be held responsible for the acts of the Congress following it. In other words, each Congress may undo all that has been done by previous Congresses.

This is true of some legislative acts, but is clearly not true of treaties, according to the basic principals of international law. Further, the violation of any one article of a treaty is a violation of the whole treaty.

The robbery, the cruelty which were done under the cloak of this hundred years of treaty-making and treaty-breaking, are greater than can be told. Neither mountains nor deserts stopped them. It took two oceans to set their bounds.

In 1871, Congress, either ashamed of making treaties only to break them, or grudging the time, money and paper it wasted, decided that no Indian tribe would thereafter be considered a foreign nation with whom the United States might contract by treaty. They did add a proviso to the act that it should not be construed as invalidating any treaties already made.

This avowed sense of obligation was short-lived, as they unabashedly negotiated and broke treaty after treaty, calling them "conventions", or "agreements". The difference was in name only. From unquestioned tenets of international law, nations may be held to standards of justice and good faith, as are men.

A nation that steals and lies and breaks its promises, will be no more respected or unpunished than a man who steals and lies and breaks his promises. Certain natural punishment sooner or later comes from evildoing.

To prove all this it is only necessary to study the history of any one of the Indian tribes. The following entries are mere outline sketches of the history of a few of them, containing only the details necessary to show the repeated broken faith of the United States Government toward them. It would take many years and many volumes for a full history of the wrongs that the natives of America have suffered at the hands of military and civil authorities, and of the citizens of this country.

THE DELAWARES

When Hendrik Hudson anchored his ship, the Half Moon, off New York Island in 1609, great numbers of Delawares stood on the shore, ready for a visit with the gods. More than a hundred years later, the aged Moravian missionary Heckewelder recorded a Delaware Chief as saying, "I admit that there are good white men, but they bear no proportion to the bad. The bad must be the strongest, for they rule. They do what they please. They enslave those who are not of their color, although created by the same Great Spirit who created them. They would make slaves of us if they could; but as they cannot do it, they kill us. I know the Long-knives. They are not to be trusted".

The original name of the Delawares was Lenni Lenape, or "original people". Their lands stretched from the Hudson River to the Potomac. They were a noble-spirited, gentle people, under the control ot the arrogant and all-powerful Iroquois, who degradingly called the Delawares "women", who were forced to make war or give up land at the pleasure of their masters.

During William Penn's humane administration of Pennsylvania, the Delawares were his most devoted friends. They called him Elder Brother. In the French and Indian War of 1755, many fought with the French against the English, and in the beginning of the Revolutionary War the majority of the Delawares sided with the English. Most of the Indian massacres during this period were the result of either French or English influence. Neither nation was high-minded enough to scorn having native allies do the bloody work which either would not dare risk national reputation by doing themselves.

The United States' first treaty with the Delawares was made in 1778, at Fort Pitt. It was a treaty of friendship that permitted government troops a right of passage through "the Delaware Nation", upon paying for any supplies they might use. It also stated that the Delawares could send a representative to Congress. The provisions were never fully carried out, starting the pattern of future treaties. The Delawares agreed to send all the warriors they could spare to fight for the Americans.

At that time the rest of the Ohio tribes, most of the New York Tribes, and a large part of the Delawares were in arms on the British side. After the Revolutionary War, they were all forced to make peace as best they could with the Americans, and the next treaty, made at Fort McIntosh in 1785, reinstated the Delaware Chiefs and headmen who had made that old alliance with the Americans, thus having lost caste in their tribe for fighting on the side of the United States. The Wyandottes, Chippewas, and Ottawas joined the Delawares in the treaty.

261

The Indians lands comprised within lines partly indicated by the Cuyahoga, Big Miami, and Ohio Rivers and their Branches, and fronting on Lake Erie. The treaty included the provision that, "If any citizen of the United States, or any other person not an Indian, attempted to settle on Delaware or Wyandotte lands, the Indians may punish him as they please". Michigan, Ohio, Indiana, and Pennsylvania are all largely made up of the lands which were given to the Indians by that treaty.

Five years later, by another treaty at Fort Harmar, the boundaries were changed somewhat, and more accurately defined. Hunting privileges for Indians on all lands reserved to the United States was promised, "So long as they behaved themselves peaceably". It was also promised that white men and Indians committing offences would be punished in the same way.

The Indians had been dissatisfied since the first treaty was made, claiming that it had been made by only a few of them, and in 1786 they complained to Congress of white encroachment. Only the year before the United States expressly told these Indians that any white citizens attempting to settle on their lands could be punished as they pleased.

The very next year the President instructed a "careful examination of the real temper of the Indian tribes in the Northwest Ohio Territory. The treaties which have been made must not be departed from, unless a boundary beneficial to the United States can be obtained. You will not neglect any opportunity that may offer of extinguishing the Indians rights to the westward, as far as the Mississippi".

Even the wildest greedy dream at that time did not look beyond that river.

Not seen in any accounts of the Indian hostilities of the Northwestern frontier during this period is any reference to the repeated permissions given by the United States to the Indians, to defend their lands as they saw fit. Most Americans of that day were honestly unaware, and therefor incredulous, that the Indians had either the provocation or right to kill intruders on their lands.

Thus early in our history was the ingenious plan evolved of first maddening the Indians into war, and then falling upon them with exterminating punishment. Under all these conditions, it is no wonder that the frontier was a scene of perpetual devastation and bloodshed; and that year by year, there grew stronger in the minds of whites a terror and hatred of Indians; and in the minds of the Indians a stronger and stronger distrust and hatred of the whites.

The Delawares were friendly through the earlier part of these troubles. However, in 1792 they were mentioned among the hostile tribes to whom the Government sent this deceptive message,"That you believe the United States want to deprive you of your lands, and drive you out of the country, be assured that this is not so. Remember that no additional lands will be required of you or any other tribe, to those that have been ceded by former treaties".

In 1793 a great council was held, attended by the Delaware chiefs and those of twelve other tribes. The purpose was to settle the vexing boundary question. The United States commissioners would not agree to Indian contentions.

The Indians finally said, "Money to us is of no value, and to most of us unknown: and as no consideration whatever can induce us to sell the land on which we get sustenance for our women and children, we hope we may be allowed to point out a method by which your settlers may be easily removed, and peace thereby obtained. Divide this large sum of money which you have offered us among these people; give to each, also, a proportion of what you say you would give to us annually."

"...We desire you to consider, brothers, that our only demand is the peaceable possession of a small part of our once great country. Look back and review the lands from whence we have been driven to this spot. We can retreat no further, and we have therefore resolved to leave our bones in this small space to which we are confined."

General Anthony Wayne led what would have been a bloody surprise raid on a major Delaware settlement. The natives were able to flee in advance due to a deserter's warning. The General consoled himself that he didn't get to slaughter the large community, reporting that he had "gained possession of the grand emporium of the hostile Indians of the West without loss of blood."

He then burned and destroyed all the well tended villages and fields, finally catching up with the fleeing Indians and killed many in a sharp fight.

After a winter of suffering and hunger, the Indians yielded to the inevitable, and in the summer of 1795 they once more had to make a treaty, and were told again the , "the heart of General Washington, the Great Chief of America, wishes for nothing so much as peace and brotherly love".

By this treaty nearly two-thirds of the present state of Ohio was ceded to the United States, except for, "all other Indian lands northward of the River Ohio, eastward of the Mississippi, and westward and southward of the Great Lakes and the waters uniting them in the year 1783," with the exception of four tracts of land, "to connect the settlements of the people of the United States".

The treaty again explicitly stated that the Indian tribes were to quietly enjoy their lands so long as they pleased, without molestation from the United States. The same old worthless pledge was included, that the Indians could drive off or otherwise punish whites attempting to settle on their land, "in such manner as they shall think fit". With promised (but never fully delivered) immediate payment of goods and annual allotments of more, peace was declared to be "perpetual".

In less than a year, the Delawares were forced into yet another treaty, ceding a tract of land between the Ohio and Wash Rivers, for which they were to receive a three hundred dollar annual pittance. In one more year there was yet another treaty, in which a still further cession of land was made for a "permanent" annuity of one thousand dollars. A General Harrison noted that the Indians were beginning to learn the value of land, but they must not have reached a true estimate of values, as the General said, "the tract now ceded contains at least two million acres, and embraces some of the finest lands in the western country".

The sale was unbelievably cheap at one thousand dollars, even with a black slave thrown in for the Turtle, the Delaware Chief.

Four years later, in 1809, by the Treaty of Fort Wayne, a few more dollars were promised, and a great deal of land taken. In 1817 a new treaty ceded nearly all the Indian land in Ohio, and parts of Indiana and Michigan. At least the Secretary of War had the honesty to admit that the only objection anyone could have to the amount of money paid, was that it, "was not an adequate one". The Indians had lost almost the last of their hunting grounds and would soon be driven to depend wholly upon farming.

In 1818 the Delawares had to cede all of their lands in Indians, and the United States promised to provide them "a country to reside in on the west side of the Mississippi," and to "guarantee to them peaceable possession" of it. The federal government showed a trace of compunction and pity in 1829, saying that since the Delaware were willing to move, that the country in the fork of the Kansas and Missouri Rivers, selected for their home, "shall be conveyed and forever secured by the United States to the said Delaware Nation, as their permanent residence".

The Secretary of War congratulated the country in 1834 on the fact that "the country north of the Ohio, east of the Mississippi, including the States of Ohio, Indians, Illinois, and Territory of Michigan as far as the Fox and Wisconsin rivers," had been practically, "cleared of the embarrassments of

Indian relations," as there were not more than five thousand Indians left in the whole region.

For almost ten years after making this last treaty, there was little official mention of the Delawares, except for fiscal reports. In 1838 they were reported as cultivating one thousand five hundred acres in grain and vegetables, and raising great numbers of hogs, cattle, and horses. "They are a brave, enterprising people, at peace with all neighboring Indians". In ten more years it was noted that "almost every family is well supplied with farming stock. ...They dwell in good log cabins, and some have extremely neat houses, well furnished. In 1853 the Delawares are recorded as being "among the most remarkable of our colonized tribes".

The influx of white settlers into Kansas had become so great by 1854, that it became evident that the Indians reservations there could not be kept intact. The Delawares were coerced into ceding back a large portion of their lands to the United States. For this they were to receive ten thousand dollars and 250 dollar annuities for each of their five aging, poor chiefs.

The next year their agent writes of the results of opening this large tract to white settlers: "The Indians have experienced enough to shake their confidence in the laws which govern the white race. The Government is bound in good faith to protect this people, yet white men have wasted their most valuable timber with an unsparing hand. The trust lands have been greatly injured in consequence of the settlements thereon." Yet nothing was done for the Indians.

The next treaty forced on the Delawares was in 1860, in which they were pressured to give the Leavenworth, Pawnee, and Western Railroad Company right of way and certain lands in their reserve. In 1862 two regiments of Delawares and Osages enlisted as soldiers in an expedition to the Indian Territory. Their Commanding Officer said of them, "The Indian soldiers have far exceed expectations. ...They bore the brunt of the fighting, and had they been properly sustained, would have ended the sway of the rebels in the Indian Territory".

Also during 1862 was a terrible condition in Kansas and the Indian Territory. The Indians were largely on the side of the Southern Rebels, because the Government had wholly failed to keep its treaty stipulations with the Delawares by withdrawing all protection for them, leaving them at the mercy of the rebels. However, the Delawares in 1862 enlisted one hundred and seventy men in the Union Army, out of a population of only two hundred males between the ages of eighteen and forty-five. This was probably the greatest ratio of volunteers in the United States.

Already, however, the "interests" of the white settlers in Kansas were beginning to be clearly in opposition to the interests of the Indians. The Commissioner said in 1863, "I can see nothing in the future for them but destruction. I think it is for the interest of the Indians that they be removed to some other locality as soon as possible."

Reluctantly, The Delawares petitioned to send a delegation of chiefs to the Rocky Mountains, to look for a new home. They were not allowed to, and ordered to the Indian Territory. During 1864, the greater part of their personal property being in livestock, The Delawares lost twenty thousand dollars worth to white thieves. The community was understandably depressed, what with most of the men away at war, old men, women, and children working the farms, and having twenty thousand dollars in stock stolen in one year.

Most of those in the Army were mustered out in 1865. They returned home after having distinguished themselves and were immediately prohibited by the Government from carrying revolvers. Their agent properly replied to that edict, "Many of these Indians are intelligent, only using weapons when any well-disposed white person would have done so; and if one class is disarmed, all must be." The Commissioner replied that they could keep certain hunting weapons, but would have to leave them with their agent when visiting other towns or agencies. A forcible statement was made that any man that went unarmed in Kansas was a fool.

The Indian Commissioner reported in 1866 that, "The State of Kansas is fast being filled by an energetic population who appreciate good land; and as the Indian reservations were selected as being the best in the state, but one result could be expected to follow." That July a treaty was made that moved all the Delawares to the Indian Territory, except those who wished to become citizens of Kansas. Thus the way was clear for the Government to make a quick sale of their lands to more white settlers.

With twenty thousand dollars worth of stock and twenty-eight thousand dollars worth of timber having been stolen in two years from the little village of farmers, it was no wonder that they were said to be "sufficiently prepared to move". The perpetual expectation of being made to move, had unsettled the whole community, and made them indifferent to further effort and improvement. The return of their young men from the Civil War also had a demoralizing effect. Drunken frays were common, in which deadly weapons were used, in spite of the Department's regulations disarming all Indians.

In July, 1867, the Delawares were said to be quite impatient to be gone from their reservation, in order to build houses that autumn for winter use, and to be fencing fields for the coming year. Annuities due them had not been paid, delaying their move. Many of their young men were still away, serving as scouts and guides in the Army. During that year and the next, they moved in detachments to the Indian Territory.

It was decreed in 1869 that they were to lose their nationality and become identified with the Cherokees. By 1870 nearly all the Delawares were in Indian Territory, but owing to a carelessly surveyed boundary, some three hundred of them had been settled outside the Cherokee Reservation, on lands which had been assigned to the Osages. The unfortunate three hundred were made to move again, this time to the land of the Peorias, where they asked for permission to settle.

Enlarging this problem was further Government bungling or indifference: As previous arrangements had been made with the Cherokees, all the Delaware funds, such as they were, were transferred to the Cherokee Nation. With no help from the Government, all parties were admonished to "reconcile there unsettled affairs to mutual advantage."

In official reports there are no further distinctive mention of the Delawares by name during the 1870s, except for a few who had for some time been living in the Indian Territory, and were not included in the treaty provisions at the time of their forced removal from Kansas. This little handful, some eighty-one in all, were all that remained to bear the name of that strong and friendly people to whom, a little more than a hundred years before, were promised that they would be brothers with the white man forever, and be entitled to representation in Congress.

On the Wichita Agency, in Indian Territory, that small band of Delawares was associated with six other dwindled remnants of tribes: The Caddos, Ionies, Wichitas, Towaconies, Wacos, Keechies, and Comanches. It was said of the Delawares in 1878 that they were unable to cultivate as much land as they had intended, "on account of loss of stock by horse-thieves". Thus ended the century of greatest dishonor to the Delawares,

THE CHEYENNES

The first treaty with the Cheyennes was made in 1825, at the mouth of the Teton River. It, like most first treaties with Indians, was merely a declaration of amity and friendship, and acknowledgment on the part of the Cheyennes of the "supremacy" of the United States.

Two years before, President Monroe reported the "Chayenes" to be, "a tribe of three thousand two hundred and fifty souls, dwelling and hunting on a river of the same name, a western tributary of the Missouri, a little above the Great Bend."

Ten Years later, George Catlin, the famous painter of Indians, met a "Shienne" chief and squaw among the Sioux and painted their portraits.
He said, "The Shiennes are a small tribe of about three thousand in number, living neighbors to the Sioux on the west of them, between the Black Hills and the Rocky Mountains. There is no finer race of men than these in North America, and none superior in stature, except the Osages: scarcely a man in the tribe full grown who is less than six feet in height."

They are ," the richest in horses of any tribe on the continent; living where the greatest herds of wild horses are grazing on the prairies, which they catch in great numbers, and sell to the Sioux, Mandans, and other tribes, as well as to the fur-traders."

In 1842 a line running north and south, so as to cross the Missouri about the mouth of the Vermilion River, was proposed to designate the limits beyond which civilized men were never likely to settle. The Cheyennes were spoken of then as, "a wandering tribe on the Platte," and in the same year, D. D. Mitchell, Superintendent of Indian Affairs, wrote, " A beneficent Creator seems to have intended this dreary region as an asylum for Indians, when the force of circumstances shall have driven them from the last acre of the fertile soil which they once possessed. Here no inducements are offered to the ever-restless Saxon breed to erect their huts.

This "civilization line", ran just east of Dakota, through the extreme eastern portion Nebraska, a little to the east of the middle of Kansas through the middle of Indian Territory and Texas, to the Gulf of Mexico. Montana, Idaho, Colorado, and New Mexico all lie west of it.

Nevertheless, the Cheyennes and other Indians living on the Platte complained bitterly of the passage of increasing numbers of emigrants through their country. They felt that they ought to be paid for the right of way, and that the emigrants should be restricted by law and the presence of a military force from burning the grass, and from unnecessary destruction of game. The Indians were systematically plundered and demoralized by traders. Whiskey was plentiful; sugar and coffee sold at the outrageous price of a dollar a pound. Ten-cent calico went for a dollar a yard, and corn whiskey at seventy-five cents a gallon and higher, several-fold what it sold for to whites.

In 1848, estimated returns to traders amounted to some $400,000. Among the items were 25,000 buffalo tongues. Since the Indians were relatively prosperous, hostilities against whites lessened, but it was still perilous to cross the Plains, where some forty-six thousand Upper Missouri Indians lived.

It was forcibly brought to the attention of the United States Government in 1849 that a treaty was needed to open a safe highway across the continent. Even in this late, lopsided diplomacy with the Indians, it was still recognized that the tribes had a right to certain control as well as to occupancy of their homeland.

Treaty provisions promised good will and peace, which attracted the Indians more than and goods or monies offered. All the tribes were looking forward to it. The bill providing for the treaty was passed unanimously by the Senate, but "the unhappy difficulties existing on the subject of slavery" delayed it in the House until it was too late to be carried into effect.

By 1849 the buffalo herds were thinning and disappearing due to gross over-hunting by whites, who wanted only the hides for sale to a clamoring public back east. The buffalo had always furnished the Plains Indians with food, clothing, and shelter. With its disappearance, starvation stared at them, and they knew it. All the tribes of the region were anxious for friendly relations with the federal government, and wanted some arrangement for means of future subsistence, and some certainty of enough land to live on.

In the summer of 1851 this much desired treaty was made. Seven of the prairie and mountain tribes gathered in great force at Fort Laramie. By this treaty the Indians formally conceded to the United States the rights to establish roads, military or otherwise, throughout the Indian country, "so far as they claim or exercise ownership over it".

For all the damages which the Indians had suffered up to that time in consequence of the passing whites, they accepted the presents then received as payment in full. An annuity of $50,000 for fifty years was promised as the price of the "right of way".

"Fifty thousand dollars for a limited period of years is a small amount to be distributed among at least fifty thousand Indians, especially when we consider that we have taken away from them all means of support," said one of the makers of the treaty. A dollar a year, even assured to one for fifty years, seems hardly an adequate compensation for the surrender of all other "means of support."

The Secretary of the Interior, in his report for 1851, speaks with satisfaction of the treaties negotiated during the year, saying, "It cannot be denied that most of the depredations committed by the Indians on our frontiers are the offspring of dire necessity. ...All history admonishes us of the difficulty of civilizing a wandering race who live mainly upon game. To tame a savage you must tie him down to the soil."

The Cheyennes, therefore, pledged to peace and goodwill toward their Indian neighbors, and to the white emigrants pouring thorough their country. For this conceded right of way they were to have a dollar each, in "goods and animals", and it was supposed that they would be able to eke out that support by hunting buffalos, which were still not quite extinct.

Comment on the bad faith of this action on the part of Congress is a waste of words, but its impolicy is so glaring that astonishment can not be kept silent; its impolicy and also its incredible cheapness. A dollar apiece a year, "in goods, animals, et cetera", those Indians had been promised that they should have for fifty years.

It must have been obvious to the weakest intellect that this was little to pay each year to any man from whom was being taken "his means of support". However, unluckily for the Indians, there were fifty thousand of them. Some thrifty Congressman multiplied fifty thousand by fifty, and the total terrified everybody.

The sophistry is too transparent; it does not in the least gloss over the fact that within the first year after making a treaty of any moment with these tribes; while the whole fifty thousand of them kept faith with the Government, The United States broke faith with them in the meanest of ways; robbing them of more than two thirds of the piddling sum that had been promised. Congress voted to amend the treaty to offer the dollar a year for fifteen rather than fifty years, not bothering to tell the Indians, who eventually assented to the "minor change".

Some of the Indians began to raise corn, beans, pumpkins and so forth, but still depended chiefly on hunting. The agent sent distribute the yearly dollar per person, reported, " The Cheyennes and the Arapahoes, and many of the Sioux, are actually in a starving state." In spite of such suffering, these Indians committed no depredations, and showed increasing kindness to and confidence in the whites.

The agent concluded his report with, "the systems of removals, and congregating tribes in small parcels of territory, has eventuated injuriously on those who have been subject to it. It is the legalized murder of a whole nation."

In the summer of 1854 the Cheyennes began to show dissatisfaction and impertinence. At a gathering of the northern band at Fort Laramie, one of the chiefs demanded that the travel over the Platte Road be stopped. If the interpreter was to be relied on, which is doubtful, the chief also said that the Government must send them one thousand white women for wives.

Constantly observed by all friendly Indians, were the hostiles, who continually plundered and attacked emigrant wagon trains, making more profit from war than from peace. The friendly tribes kept their peace, but in the summer of 1856, the Cheyennes, by a disastrous accident, were forced into the position of hostiles.

A small war-band went out to attack the Pawnees. They were in camp near the North Platte Road, and as the mail-wagon was passing, to Cheyennes ran toward it to beg for tobacco. The terrified mail carrier fired on them, and the Indians fired back, wounding him. The chiefs rushed out, stopped the firing, explained the matter, and then severely flogged the Indians who had returned the mail-carriers fire. However, the mischief had been done.

The mail-carrier reported having been shot at by a Cheyenne Indian, and the next day, troops from Fort Kearney attacked the Indians, killing six of the war party. The thoroughly exasperated war-party attacked an emigrant train, killed two men and a child, and took one woman captive. The next day they killed her because she could not ride on horseback and keep up with them.

Shortly, two more small war-bands left the band, attacked wagon trains, and killed two men, two women, and a child. The chiefs were able to bring the raiders back under control and asked their agent what they should do. Through that winter the Cheyennes remained in the agency, and strictly observed the conditions of the agent.

In the following August, however, a military force under General Sumner was sent "to demand from the tribe the perpetrators of the outrages on the whites, and for ample security for their good conduct." General Sumner said the Cheyennes would not yield to his demands, and he therefor attacked them, burning their village and destroying their winter supplies, some fifteen to twenty thousand pounds of buffalo meat.

There is little record of how and where they survived the winter. The next year the Cheyennes were quite anxious for a new treaty, which would assign them to a country in which they could live safely. They knew that the prairies would soon be occupied by white villages. They wanted peace, and as the buffalo would soon disappear, they hoped for a home where they might be provided for and protected against the encroachments of the whites, at least until they had learned farming and other arts of civilized life.

One of the chiefs told the agent of the Upper Platte Agency that not many years before he had traveled to the Mississippi, then to the land of the Winnebagoes in Minnesota, and then to the Lake Michigan, and then to the tribes in the Dakotas. Almost nowhere did he see but a few white men. "Now our White Father tells us that the white man will never settle on our lands, and kill our game, but see!", he said, "The whites cover all those lands I have just described, and also the lands of the Poncas, Omahas, and Pawnees."

"On the South Platte the white people are finding gold, and the Cheyennes and Arapahos have no longer any hunting grounds. Our country has become very small, and before our children are grown up we shall have no game."

It was estimated that during the summer of 1859 over sixty thousand emigrants crossed these plains in their central belt. Valuable trains of wagons and cattle were frequent, and post lines and private expresses were in constant motion. A commissioner was sent in 1860 to hold a council and make a treaty with the Cheyennes and Arapahos at Bent's Fort on the upper Arkansas River. The Arapaho's were fully represented, but there were present only two prominent chiefs of the Cheyennes, Black Kettle and White Antelope, who was one of the chiefs brutally murdered five years later in the infamous Chivington massacre in Colorado.

Because the commissioner could not wait for the rest of the Cheyennes to make the long trip to Fort Bent, the two chiefs distinctly stated that they pledged only themselves and their own bands. The treaty was concluded in February, 1861, at Fort Wise. The chiefs of the Cheyennes and Arapahos there "ceded and relinquished" all the lands to which they had any claim, except a certain tract whose boundaries were defined. Relinquished were lands in Kansas and Nebraska, and all of that part of Colorado which is north of the Arkansas River, and east of the Rocky Mountains.

The desire of the Government to make farmers of these Indians was reiterated in this treaty, and evidenced by pledges of purchase of stock, agricultural implements, and so on. There was a clause that read, "their annuities may, at the discretion of the President of the United States, be discontinued entirely should said Indians fail to make reasonable and satisfactory efforts to improve and advance their condition; in which case such other provision shall be made for them as the President and Congress may judge to be suitable or proper." There could not have been a more complete signing away of all the benefits provided by the treaty.

The treaty also stipulated that the President, with the assent of Congress, would have the power to modify, "any of the provisions of former treaties, in such a manner and to whatever extent" he might best judge to be necessary and expedient for their best interests.

Could a community of people be delivered up more completely bound and at the mercy of the Government? Some of the unrepresented Cheyenne bands were extremely dissatisfied with the treaty, as they had great reason to be. As time went on, all the bands disapproved. Two years later, instead of being settled on their farms "in severalty", the land survey had just been completed, and that a contract, "would soon be made for the construction of a ditch for the purpose of irrigating their arable land."

Things grew rapidly worse in Colorado. Those "preparations for their subsistence by agriculture and grazing", which took so much room to describe in the treaty, had not been made. Many Cheyennes and Arapahos took pilfering reprisals from emigrant wagon trains, and in the resulting fights they murdered many whites. All the tribes on the plains were more or less engaged in these outrages, and it was evident, before midsummer of 1864, that the Government must interfere strongly to protect the emigrants and western settlers from the consequences of its own bad faith with the Indians.

The Governor of Colorado received military aid and authority to wage war on the Indians. In June he proclaimed that all friendly Indians come to designated places to be assured of safety and protection. several bands of peaceful Cheyennes and Arapahos came to Fort Lyon. There on the 29th of November, occurred one of the foulest massacres which the World had ever seen. This camp of friendly Indians was surprised at Daybreak, and men, women, and children were butchered. Most of those who escaped fled north, and joining other bands of the tribe, at once took fearful and natural revenge.

A terrible war followed. Some Cheyenne confederated with the Sioux, and waged relentless war on all the emigrant routes across the plains. The bitter hostilities were in proportion to the bitterness of resentment felt by the refugees of what is now known in the annals of treachery as the Sand Creek Massacre.

273

"It will be long before faith in the honor and humanity of the whites can be reestablished in the minds of these barbarians," says an official report, "and the last Indian who escaped the brutal scene at Sand Creek will probably have died before its effects will have disappeared".

In October of the next year some of the bands gathered to hold a council with the United States Commissioners on the Little Arkansas. Black Kettle, the Chief over whose lodge at Sand Creek the American Flag flew, with a white flag tied beneath it at the time of the wholesale slaughter, said, "I once thought that I was the only man that persevered to be the friend of the white man; but since they have come and cleaned out our lodges, horses, and everything else, it is hard for me to believe white men any more." Continuing with such calm and reason, he said, "That fool-band of soldiers cleared out our lodges, and killed our women and children. This is hard on us."

By the terms of the new treaty, a new reservation was to be set apart for the Cheyennes and Arapahos, and of course the hackneyed lie, "No whites shall be allowed on the reservation", was included. A large tract was to be relinquished by the Indians, but they were permitted to live on it and roam at pleasure through the unsettled portions. The Indians felt that at last they had a treaty they could trust. They hoped that in their new home they would have greater safety and peace.

The Cheyennes could not long remain at peace. In the summer the Senate amended the latest treaty to require that their new reservation be, "entirely outside the state of Kansas, and not within any Indian territory, except on consent of the tribes interested. As the recently designated reservation had been partly in Kansas, and partly on Cherokee land, they were left without any home whatever.

Young men of the tribe began to join with other hostile Indians in raids along the great mail-routes on the plains. Again they received summary vengeance by United States troops, and in the summer of 1867 a Cheyenne village of three hundred lodges was burned by soldiers under General Hancock.

A precarious peace was confirmed by yet another treaty, but was almost immediately broken by Government failure to comply with its provisions. In October of that year, Major Wynkoop, a faithful friend of the Cheyennes and Arapahos ever since the days of Sand Creek, published his last protest on their behalf, in a letter to the Commissioner of Indian Affairs. He said that the failure of the government to deliver promised supplies, and the refusal to allow the Indians promised arms and ammunition, left them without any means of securing game; hence the depredations.

All the Indians of the Upper Arkansas River joined the struggle. On October 27th, 1868, Black Kettle and his entire band were killed by General Custer's command at Antelope Hills, on the Wichita River.

In 1869 many Cheyennes and Arapahos made their way to Montana, and were living among the Gros Ventres. Most of those remaining in the south were quiet, but implored to be moved further north where they might hunt buffalo. Some consideration was shown the southern Cheyennes in 1870, and in 1872 both tribes were reported as allied to the Government in maintaining peace on the border. Raiding bands of Kiowas had made strong inducements to the Cheyennes to join them, but they remained loyal and peaceful.

Thirty Northern Cheyenne lodges rejoined the tribe in 1872, but many still roamed among the Northern Sioux. In 1874 there were said to be over three thousand Northern Cheyennes and Arapahos at the Red Cloud Agency. The Government refused to let them stay, and after protests, the Cheyennes consented to go to Indian Territory. The move was delayed, however, due to fresh troubles among the Southern Cheyennes.

White horse-thieves on the reservation brought on a general war against whites in the region and during the next few months the Cheyennes, Kiowas, Osages, and Comanches raided and murdered many whites. Sixty lodges of Cheyennes took refuge under the troops at the agency, and the old problem arose, of how to punish the guilty without harming the innocent. After a vigorous campaign by General Miles' command, the main body of hostiles surrendered in the Spring of 1875.

The defeated Indian bands straggled in, half-starved, half-naked, without lodges and ponies. It was amazing that they had held out so long. Thirty-three of the most desperate hostiles were to be sent to prison in Saint Augustine, Florida, but before the selection could be made, the surrendered braves stampeded, and 400 escaped.

They held their ground from two P.M. until dark, against three cavalry companies and two Gatlin guns. They escaped during the stormy night that followed, leaving only three dead.

The friendly Cheyennes remained loyal, despite not having enough food, and being cut off from hunting. In 1875 their agent wrote, "On last year's flour contract not a single pound was received until the fourteenth day of First Month, 1875, when six months of cold weather and many privations had passed, notwithstanding the many protestations and urgent appeals from the agent."

The Northern Cheyennes on the Red Cloud Agency remained troublesome and restless. In 1877 they were moved to the Cheyenne and Arapaho Agency, in Indian Territory. Reports say they asked to be taken there. In Autumn, the reunited tribe went on a grand buffalo hunt, accompanied by a small detail of troops from Fort Reno.

Early that winter white horse-thieves stole Indian ponies valued at two thousand nine hundred dollars, repeating the act that had goaded the Indians into war in 1874. Somehow the natives resisted retaliation, and had two years of improved conditions, due to their determination to become self-sufficient.

The winter of 1877, and the summer of 1878, however, were terrible for the Cheyennes.Their fall hunt was unsuccessful, and they straggled home, destitute and hungry. The usual horse stealing by Whites became bolder. Their Government rations were cut to insufficiency, but these were only the beginnings of their troubles.

The summer was unusually hot. Extreme heat, chills and fever, aggravated by lack of food, brought on terrible waves of sickness. There was no malarial treatment for them, and at least two thousand were gravely ill on the reservation.

Early in the Autumn, a band of some three hundred Northern Cheyennes took the desperate step of running off and attempting to make their back to Dakota. They fought desperately when pursued, but finally overpowered, they surrendered on the condition that they be taken to Dakota. They said they would rather die by bullets than go back to Indian Territory and die of chills, fever, and starvation.

They were made prisoners of war at Fort Robinson, Nebraska. They were ordered back to the Indian Territory, and the local Commander tried to starve them into submission. He stopped feeding them, and cut off their fuel while the mercury froze at Fort Robinson. After two days he said that the women and children could come out he would feed them. Not a woman emerged.

On the fourth night, or some accounts say on the sixth, the starving, freezing Indians broke out, overpowered the guards, and fled into the winter night with their women and children. For several days they held pursuing troops at bay. They made their final stand in a frozen ravine, and all were killed.

Fifty Cheyenne women and children, and some seven men, who had been held in a different part of the fort, did not have the good fortune to share in the outbreak meet a quick death in the ravine. All were sent to prison at Fort Leavenworth, the men to be tried for the deaths of soldiers they had fought on their way north.

Red Cloud, the great Sioux Chief, came to Fort Robinson immediately after the massacre, and asked to be allowed to take the Cheyenne widows and orphans into his tribe. The Government, in its kindness, permitted twenty-two widows, and thirty-two children, many of whom were orphans, to join the Oglala Sioux.

To his great shame, The Commissioner of Indian Affairs, said in his report of 1879 that the Indians were not starving at the time of their flight. The attempt only rebounded to his disgrace, and he was found guilty of absolute dishonest in his estimates, and that the quantity of beef issued to his Cheyene Agency was greatly less than he had reported. It was proven that the Indians, exactly as they had said, were indeed starving.

fifty native children starved to death on that reservation in 1877 and 1878, along with many young men and women, as well as the elderly.

As the century of great dishonor ended for the Cheyennes, there was not even warm clothing for them, let alone enough to eat. In the melancholy record of suffering of American Indians, a more glaring instance of confused multiplication of injustices can not be found. The Cheyennes, in their desperation, were pursued and slain for daring to leave the deadly reservation, which apparently, was not their reservation at all, they having had removed their legal right to any place on Earth. There are no adequate words to characterize such treatment of a handful of helpless people by a powerful, rich nation.

THE NEZ PERCES

Oregon: wide, healthful, beautiful, abundant, and inviting; no wonder it was coveted and fought for. When Lewis and Clarke visited it at the beginning of the 1800s, they found many tribes of Indians, numbering at least twenty to thirty thousand. Of all these, the Nez Perces were the richest, noblest, and most gentle.

To the Cayuses, one of the most warlike tribes, Lewis and Clarke presented an American flag, telling them it was an emblem of peace. The beauty and bright coloring of the flag, allied to its significance, deeply impressed the poetic minds of these natives. They set the flag up in a beautiful valley called the Grande Ronde,a fertile basin some twenty-five miles wide, surrounded by high basaltic walls, watered by a branch of the Snake River.

Around this flag they met their old enemies, the Shoshones, and swore to keep perpetual peace with them. The spot became consecrated to an annual sort of fair, where the Cayuse, Nez Perce, and Walla Walla Indians came every summer and traded their roots, skins, elk and buffalo meats, for salmon and horses, with the Shoshones. It was a beautiful spot, nearly circular, luxuriantly covered with grass, the hill wall around it thick with evergreen trees, chiefly larch. The Indians called it Karpkarp, which translates to "Balm of Gilead".

The life of these Indians was peculiar. Most had several homes, and as they lived only a part of the year in each, were frequently spoken of by travellers as nomadic tribes, while in fact they were as wedded to their homes as any civilized people. Their wanderings were as systematic as the seasonal moving of wealthy city people from town homes to country places. Each season had its duty and appointed place for the Nez Perce, and year after year the same month found them in the same spot.

In 1833 a delegation from these Oregon Indians went to Saint Louis, and through the artist, George Catlin, made known their object, which was "to inquire for the truth of what some white men had told them, that the American's religion was better than theirs, and that they would all be lost without it."

Two members of this delegation were Nez Perces; "Hee-oh'ks-te-kin" and H'co-a-h'co-a-h'cotes-min"; or "rabbit-skin leggings", and "No horns on his Head". Their portraits are found in "Catlin's American Indians". One of these died on the way back to Oregon, but the other told his tribe that the report which they had heard was true, and that good and religious men would soon come among them to teach this religion, so that they could all understand and benefit by it.

Two years later the Methodist Episcopal Society and the American Board both sent missionaries to Oregon. The efforts brought profound results among the natives. The Nez Perces became devout Christians.

The earliest mention of the Nez Perces in the official records of the Indian Bureau is in the year 1843. In that year an agent was sent to investigate the condition of the Oregon tribes, and he reported, "The only tribes from which much is to be hoped , or anything to be feared in this part of Oregon, are the Walla Wallas, Cayuses, and Nez Perces, inhabiting a district on the Columbia and its tributaries, commencing two hundred and forty miles from its mouth, and stretching four hundred and eighty miles in the interior."

The Nez Perces, living farther inland, "inhabit a beautiful grazing district, not surpassed by any I have seen for verdure, water privileges, climate, or health. This tribe forms an honorable exception to the general Indian character, being more noble, industrious, sensible, and better disposed toward the whites and their improvements in the arts and sciences; and though brave as Caesar (the Indians), the whites have nothing to dread at their hands in case of their dealing out to them what they conceive to be right and equitable."

When this agent arrived a the missionary station among the Nez Perces, he was met by a large body of Indians, with twenty-two of their chiefs. The missionaries received them, "with joyful countenances and glad hearts"; the Indians, "with civility, gravity, and dignified reserve."

He addressed them at length, explaining to them the kind intentions of the Government toward them. They listened with "gravity, fixed attention, and decorum". Finally an aged chief, ninety years of age, arose and said, "I speak today, Perhaps tomorrow I die. I am the oldest chief of the tribe. I was the high chief when your brothers, Lewis and Clarke, visited this country."

"They visited me, and honored me with their friendship and counsel. I showed them my numerous wounds, received in bloody battle with the Snakes. They told me it was not good; It was better to be at peace; and gave me a flag of truce. I held it up high. We met and talked, but never fought again. Clarke pointed to this day - to you and this occasion. ...I am glad to live to see you and this day."

At this council the Nez Perces elected a head chief named Ellis, and adopted a civil and just Code of Laws, except for the introduction, by the white agent, of punishment for certain crimes by whipping or flogging. The agent was written of by an historian of the period, as being, "a notorious blockhead". One cannot argue with his opinion, since the whipping-post was offered as a first installment of the United States' "kind intentions" towards these Indians.

A report by a Reverend Spauld, who had lived six years among the Nez Perces, says, "nearly all the principal men and chiefs are members of the school; that they are as industrious in their schools as on their farms. They cultivate their lands with much skill and to good advantage, and many more would do so if they had the means. About one hundred are printing their own books with the pen. This keeps up a deep interest, as they daily have new lessons to print; and what they print must be committed to memory as soon as possible."

"A good number are now so far advanced in reading and printing as to render much assistance in teaching. Their books are taken home at night, and every lodge becomes a schoolroom. Their lessons are Scripture lessons; no others (except the laws) seem to interest them."

The 1843 report of the Secretary of War reads, "The Nez Perce Tribe have adopted a simple code of laws that teach them self-restraint. ...It is remarkable that there should so soon be several well-attended, well-conducted schools in Oregon". It is not that remarkable, considering that the Congregationalists, the Methodist Episcopalians, and the Roman Catholics all had their missionaries at work there for eight years.

The Oregon Tribes, including the Nez Perces, disappeared in 1846 from the official records of the Indian Bureau. Congress decided to discontinue what had been a "temporary service" among the Oregon Indians. The missions were abandoned in 1847, after the Cayuse massacred the missionaries among them. Deprived of their teaching, The Nez Perces kept their faith and goodwill toward the whites.

A superintendent and three agents in 1851 were appointed for Indian service in Oregon. Treaties were negotiated, but not ratified and honored by the United States. "They have become distrustful of all promises made them by the United States", says the Oregon Superintendent. ...The settlement of the whites on the tracts which they regarded as secured to them by solemn treaty stipulations, ...augments bitter animosities and resentments."

Governor Stephens of Washington Territory wrote ,"These hitherto neglected tribes, whose progress from the wild wanderers of the plains to kind and hospitable neighbors, ...are entitled, by every consideration of justice and humanity, to the fatherly care of the Government." The Governor's opinion was ignored.

In 1855 there was a general outbreak of hostilities by the Oregon Indians. Tribe after tribe fell into the ranks of the hostiles. Terrified Oregon settlers, "were without discipline, without order, and similar to madmen", says one report.

"Every day they run off the horses and cattle of the friendly Indians. I will soon no longer be able to restrain them." It is difficult to do justice to the moral courage which is shown by those who remained friendly to whites under such conditions.

The hostiles then told the Nez Perces to join them against the whites or be wiped out. The Nez Perces had no ammunition, and the whites would give them none. The hostiles said, "we have plenty. Join us and save your lives." The defenselees Nez Perces were greatly alarmed, but were willing to make almost any sacrifice to obtain peace.

After sharp fighting, the outbreak ended with about equal losses on both sides. There was a sort of armistice, which left the Indians emboldened, confident that they could contend successfully against the whites. Failure to ratify previous treaties, and continued extension of white settlers, without consideration or compensation, was a constant source of hostile feelings among the natives.

An agent's report reflected truthfully, "Such a proceeding is not only contrary to our policy hitherto, but is repugnant alike to the dictates of humanity and the principles of natural justice." As expected, the armistice failed, and in 1848 the Oregon and Washington territories had another Indian war. The Nez Perces. along with the Flatheads, and Pend d'Oreilles, fought with the United States against the hostiles. One detachment of federal troops was saved by taking refuge with them.

When asked what they wanted, the Nez Perce said, "Peace, Plows, and Schools". In 1859 the Indians were considered conquered. The treaties of 1855 were ratified, and tranquility returned to the territories. Congress was implored quickly to grant the money stipulated in the treaties, to prevent another war. The Superintendents did not point out to Congress that had they lived up to the treaties, there most likely would have been no war.

The reservation granted to the Nez Perces was a fine tract, one hundred miles long and sixty wide, well-timbered, watered, and with great natural resources. The Indians immediately began cultivating and irrigating their fields, and developed large herds of horses.

In less than two years the peace of the Nez Perces was invaded by a deadly foe, the greed for gold. "To attempt to restrain miners would be like attempting to restrain the whirlwind," wrote the Washington Territory Superintendent.

For the next few years the Nez Perces were dismayed at the steady stream of settlers pouring into their country. That they did not resist by force can only be explained in the power of their religious spirit. In 1865 there land became part of the new Idaho Territory.

A powerful party arose among the Nez Perces, urging the formation of a league with the Crows and Blackfeet against the whites. The non-arrival of promised supplies and money, and the unchecked influx of miners on

281

the reservation, put strong weapons into the hands of the disaffected. Adding to the fervor was that the warriors who had fought so well for the United States in 1856 had still not been paid.

How many white communities would remain peaceable, loyal, and friendly under such a strain?

Also in 1866, The Governor of Idaho wrote to the Department of the Interior, "Could this loyal tribe have been kept aloof from the contaminating vices of white men, and had it been in the power of the Government promptly to comply with the stipulations of the treaty of 1865, there can be no doubt that their condition at this time would have been a most prosperous one."

The patience of the Nez Perces began to wear thin in 1867. The Idaho Governor again warns the federal Government, "...Serious trouble is imminent. It could all be settled by prompt payment by the Government of their just dues; but if delayed to long I greatly fear open hostilities. ...If neglected, war may be reasonably expected. If the Nez Perces strike a blow, all over our Territory and around our boundaries will blaze the signal-fires and gleam the tomahawks of the savages -- Kootenays, Pen d'Oreilles, Coeur d'Alenes, Blackfeet, Flat-heads, Spokanes, Pelouses, Bannocks, and Shoshones will be involved."

In spite of increasing disaffection, the Nez Perces remained industrious and prosperous. In 1869 their reservation was still unsurveyed, and when the Indians again claimed that whites were settling inside the lines, there was no way of proving it. In 1870, seven years after being promised, the reservation was surveyed, but the manner in which it was done proved to be a scandalous fraud.

The fence posts were not well set, much of the board lumber was deficient in width and length, and they were joined and nailed haphazardly, so that the entire structure soon fell down.

A commission was sent to hold council in 1873 with the Nez Perces in the Wallowa Valley, in Oregon, "with a view to their removal to the Nez Perce Reservation in Idaho." The relocation was reported as impractical, and the Wallowa Valley was removed from sale to settlers and set apart for the Nez Perces, by Executive Order.

The Commission's report quoted Chief Joseph's reason for not wanting schools and churches on his Wallowa Valley reservation. He said, "We do not want schools. We do not want churches. They will teach us to quarrel about God, as the Catholics and Protestants do. ...We do not want to learn that. We may quarrel with men sometimes about things on this earth, but we never quarrel about God."

White settlers greatly resented The Wallowa Valley being ceded to the Nez Perces, and in 1875 the Commissioner of Indian Affairs warned of great trouble if Chief Joseph could not be persuaded to join others of his tribe in Idaho. Only two years after officially setting apart the valley for them, the Department was planning on "compelling" them to leave.

The Indian Bureau recommended revoking the Executive Order, and President Ulysses Grant promptly did so, assuring that the Nez Perce would be subjected "merely to the same just and equal laws by which the President and all his people are ruled". Chief Joseph replied to the President that he asked nothing of him; that he could take care of himself; and that he no longer wanted the Wallowa Valley because it would subject his band to the will and laws of others. He wanted to move peaceably.

Government officials knew well the enormity of their lie about "equal and just laws", and that the instant Joseph and his band moved onto the Idaho reservation that they became subject to restrictive, totally different laws than those by which whites were bound. The Indians, as on all reservations, would be mere convicts in a prison without walls. For the sake of their own honor and integrity, it is amazing that four Government officials would sign their names to such a scurrilous document.

Of course, the Government had not fulfilled its treaty obligations to those already on the Idaho reservation. The Agent pointed out to the Government that continued failure to fulfill the treaty would add to the Indian's distrust in the faith of the Government. He was not heeded.

Facing the inevitable, Chief Joseph finally consented to move to the Lapwai Reservation. The chief's own words are recorded of the council, as were General Howard's, who negotiated for the Government. The General said he listened to the "oft-repeated dreamer nonsense of the chief, 'Too-hool-hool-suit' (An old chief under Joseph)," and finally said to him, "Twenty times over I hear that the Earth is your mother, and about the chieftaincy of the Earth. I want to hear it no more."

Joseph said, "General Howard lost his temper, and said, 'Shut up! I don't want to hear any more of such talk'".

Too-hool-hool-suit answered, said the General, "Who are you, that you ask us to talk, and then tell me I shan't talk? Are you the Great Spirit? Did you make the World?"

Joseph said, "General Howard replied, 'You are an impudent fellow, and I will put you in the guardhouse,' and then ordered a soldier to arrest him.

283

Too-hool-hool-suit made no resistance. He asked General Howard, 'Is that your order? I don't care. I have expressed my heart to you. I have nothing to take back. I have spoken for my country. You can arrest me, but you cannot change me, or make me take back what I have said.' ...Too-hool-hool-suit was prisoner for five days..."

Chief Joseph, as always, spoke with common sense as well as natural feeling, in saying, "I turned to my people and said, 'The arrest of Too-hool-hool-suit was wrong, but we will not resent the insult. We were invited to this council to express our hearts, and we have done so."

Consenting to move, Joseph said, "I said in my heart, that rather than have war, I would give up my country. I would give up my father's grave. I would give up everything rather than have the blood of white men upon the hands of my people." The young men wanted to fight, and Joseph had to ride among them brandishing a pistol and threatening to shoot the first of his warriors that resisted the Government.

Finally, they gathered all the stock they could find, and began the move. A storm raised the river so high that some of the cattle could not be taken across and were left behind with Indian guards. White men attacked the guards and took the cattle.

Joseph could no longer restrain his men, and two months of war followed, masterfully campaigned by the Indians. They were pursued by General Howard, they had General Crook on their right, and General Miles in front, yet not once were they hemmed in.

When they at last surrendered at Bear Paw Mountain, in the Montana Hills, it was not because they were beaten, but because as Joseph said, "I could no longer bear to see my wounded men and women suffer any longer. We had lost enough already. We could have escaped if we left our wounded, old women and children behind. We were unwilling to do this. We had never heard of a wounded Indian recovering while in the hands of white men."

On the fifth day, after having been promised by General Miles that they would be returned to Lapwai Reservation, Joseph said, "I went to General Miles and gave up my gun, and said, 'From where the sun now stands, I will fight no more.' My people needed rest; we wanted peace."

The terms of the surrender, as was routine, were shamefully violated. Joseph and his band were taken first to Fort Leavenworth and then to Indian Territory. While at Leavenworth they were placed in the river bottom, with only dirty river water to drink.

"Many of my people sickened and died, and we buried them in this strange land," said Joseph. "I cannot tell how much my heart suffered for my people while at Leavenworth. The Great Spirit Chief who rules above seemed to looking some other way, and did not see what was being done to my people."

Within a few months after arriving in Indian Territory, the sickness contracted while at Leavenworth killed at least a quarter of Joseph's followers. There the remainder languished till the end of the 1870s. Of the remainder of the Nez Perces, those on the Lapwai Reservation, the report of the Indian Bureau for 1879 said that they "support themselves entirely without subsistence from the Government."

As the Century of Dishonor ended for the Nez Perces, there was already a cloud on the horizon. The Lapwai Reservation was being lusted after by whites.

THE PONCAS

In 1803 Captain Lewis and Lieutenant Clarke, of the First United States Infantry, were commissioned by Congress to explore the Missouri River from its mouth to its source, to "seek the best water communication from thence to the Pacific Ocean," and to confer with all the Indian tribes on their route, with a view to the establishment of commerce with them.

They reported the "Poncars" as, "the remnant of a nation once respectable in numbers; they formerly resided on a branch of the Red River of Lake Winnepeg; being oppressed by Sioux, they removed to the west side of the Missouri, on Poncar River, where they built and fortified a village, and remained some years; but, being pursued by their ancient enemies, the Sioux, and reduced by continual wars, they have joined and now live with the Mahas (Omahas), whose language they speak."

They were numbered at about two hundred by Lewis and Clarke, but the count was probably low because most of the tribe was away on a buffalo hunt. In an 1829 census, they were listed at six hundred. The artist Catlin visited them a few years later and counted them a little less.

While painting the portrait of Chief Shoo-de-ga-cha (Smoke), Catlin wrote, " He related to me with great coolness and frankness the poverty and distress of his nation--and with the method of a philosopher predicted the certain and rapid extinction of his tribe, which he had not the power to avert."

285

"He told me he had 'once been powerful and happy; that the buffaloes which the Great Spirit had given them for food, and which formerly spread all over their green prairies, had all been driven out by the approach of white men, who wanted their skins; that their country was now entirely destitute of game, and even of roots for food, as it was one continuous prairie; that his people had foolishly become fond of firewater, and had given away everything in their country for it.'"

"He further said that it had destroyed many of his warriors, and would soon destroy the rest; that his tribe was too small and his warriors too few to go to war with the tribes around them; and that he was still more alarmed from the constant advance of the pale faces--their enemies from the east--with whiskey, and smallpox, which had already destroyed four-fifths of his tribe, and would soon impoverish and at last destroy the remainder of them."

The United State's first treaty with this handful of gentle and peaceable Indians was made it 1817, and was the usual "peace and friendship: prelude. In 1825 another was made, in which the Poncas admit that "they reside within the territorial limits of the United States, acknowledge their supremacy, and claim their protection." They also admit, "the right of the United States to regulate all trade and intercourse with them." The United States, on their part, "agree to receive the Poncar tribe of Indians into their friendship and under their protection."

For the next thirty years there was little mention of the Poncas in official Government records. The peaceable Poncas were left to shift for themselves because other tribes in the Upper Missouri region were so troublesome and aggressive. In 1846 the agent of the Upper Platte mentions incidentally that their lands were being fast intruded upon by squatters.

The Commissioner for Indian Affairs writes in 1858, "Treaties were entered into in March and April last with the Poncas and Yankton Sioux, who reside west of Iowa, for the purpose of extinguishing their title to all the lands occupied and claimed by them, except small portions on which to colonize and domesticate them. This proceeding was deemed necessary in order to obtain such control over these Indians as to prevent their interference with our settlements, which are rapidly extending in that direction."

In good faith, the Poncas abandoned their settlements and hunting grounds and were moved to their new home. Having been unsuccessful in their summer hunt, and having no crop to rely on, they were desperate and destitute. Since nothing had been done for them under the treaty, they conclude it was void and threatened to return to their ancestral home, el1ich in the meantime had been filled with white settler.

Because of Government delay, the Untied States had to "incur a heavy expense, to give enough food to keep the Poncas from starving. In 1859, under this pressure, the Senate finally ratified the treaty. The Poncas had lost all but a small tract between the Ponca and Niobrara Rivers. The treaty stipulated $20,000 in aid the first year (very little of which was actually received), plus diminishing annuities for thirty years.

The Agent had no money to feed them, so he induced the Ponca to go on a hunt. They straggled back in less than a month, begging for food for their women and children, whom they had left half-starved on the Plains. They had found no game, and only a few wild turnips. They had to trade away most of their blankets and other goods.

The reports are more pitiful for 1863. After the first hoeing of their corn, they went on a mostly unsuccessful buffalo hunt. Their crops withered before their return. The plains had been burned over and they could find no roots, berries, or anything else to eat. Through all these troubles the Poncas remained loyal and peaceable, and were "unwavering in their fidelity to their treaty" said the Indian Commissioner.

In December of the same year, a marauding group of soldiers at first taunted a small traveling group of Ponca women and boys. Then they destroyed their belongings and killed their ponies. As the Indians fled in terror, most were killed and mutilated by the men of Company B of the Seventh Iowa Cavalry. There was some correspondence between military authorities, but nothing was done.

The Poncas' reservation was extended down the Niobrara to the Missouri River in 1865, and the Government agreed to pay them $15,000 for their loss in the recent outrage and in others. Of course it took two more years to ratify this provision, and that, plus other promised money and goods fell far short, or didn't arrive at all.

In 1870, $5,000 was appropriated to resume the Poncas' school that had been discontinued due to non-receipt of promised funds. The Poncas were encouraged at this, and built many substantial homes despite being half-starved by lack of government-promised rations. The always peaceful, always loyal Poncas were digging wild roots to stay alive , and still did not complain when the saw wagons of food and herds of cattle being driven across their lands to feed the lately hostile Sioux, who continued to raid and drive off the little remaining stock of the Poncas.

They worked industriously for two years under these terrible conditions, but in 1873 the Missouri overflowed and entirely destroyed the Ponca village. The tribe worked around the clock for weeks to salvage what they could and move it further from the river. A year later they had recovered marvelously, having built new homes and put three hundred acres of land under cultivation.

The Poncas could not get through the year without more disaster. First came a drought; then three visitations of locusts, leaving nothing in the fields but straw. All newly planted trees withered and died.

The locusts came again in 1875, and destroyed all but the wheat crop. Much of the wheat was lost anyway, because there was only one reaping machine on the agency, and it could not do all the work. The Indians cut what could with knives, but much of it dried up and perished before it could be harvested.

1875 was also marked by a flagrant injustice of the helplessness of Indians in the courts. Two Poncas were waylaid by a party of Santees; one of the Poncas was murdered, the other seriously wounded. The courts dismissed the case, saying they had no jurisdiction over crimes committed between Indians.

The next year, in an absurd bit of reasoning, it was assumed that the Poncas would not mind being sent to Indian Territory in Oklahomas, since they had agreed to their earlier move. After much protest, the tribe at last gave what the United States Government called their "consent" to be moved.

The influences, deceits, and coercions brought to bear on these unfortunate creatures before this was brought about, is one of the most harrowing records of dealings with the Indians. A party of chiefs was induced to go with a United States Inspector to see that the new area would suit them. They were distinctly promised that if it did not suit them, they could go to Washington to consult with the President as to a suitable plan.

Chief Standing Bear, one of those who made the trip said they were suddenly approached by the Inspector who told them to pack up and move to Indian Territory immediately. They were told that the President would sell their land and give them the money after the move.

The Chief told him they didn't want to go, saying, "When a man owns anything, he does not let it go till he has received payment for it." The Inspector said that he would show them the land and if they didn't like they could see the President and tell him so.

He took ten chiefs to Oklahoma and showed them three poor tracts. He told them they had to choose one, and that they would not be paid for the land they left. When the chiefs told him he had lied, he angered, and told them that if they did not do as they were told he would leave them there, a thousand miles from home, without money or an interpreter. He did exactly that.

It was winter. They started for home on foot, sleeping in haystacks at night, barely keeping from freezing. Their moccasins wore out and they were barefoot in the snow, eating dried corn they found in harvested fields. Fifty days on the road, they were almost dead when they reached the Otoe Agency, leaving bloody footprints on the floor of the Agent's office when they told their story.

The agent had received a telegram from the cruel, deceitful inspector, saying the chiefs were runaways, and not to help them in any way. He was dismayed and sympathetic when her heard their plight. There they were fed and rested for ten days. The Otoes gave each a pony, and in seven days ride they reached the Omaha Reservation. They sent a telegram to the President, asking if he had authorized their treatment. There was no answer.

Four more days on the road and they reached their home, only to find the Inspector there. When the Poncas were alarmed at his arrival without their chiefs, he told them, "Tomorrow you must be ready to move. If you are not, you will be shot. Then the soldiers came to the doors with bayonets, and ten families were frightened. The soldiers brought wagons; they put their things in and were carried away", said Standing Bear. The rest of the tribe would not move.

"When we got there, we asked the inspector why he had done this thing, and he got very angry," said Standing Bear. "Then we said to him, 'We did not think we would see your face again, after what has passed. ...But here you are. This land is ours. Let us alone. Go away from us. You may take all the money that is to be paid to us for twelve years, if you will go and leave us our lands."

The Inspector called for more troops, but Standing Bear and his brother refused to go. Their families were driven across the river and the two men were jailed at a nearby fort. When the Commanding Officer heard their story, he said that they had done no wrong, but he was a soldier and had to obey orders.

The officer did send a telegram to the President about the affair. The President answered that he knew nothing about it. After ten days in jail, the chiefs, with their families and remaining tribal members were forced to begin the trip. Many died on the road, and most of their horses died after they reached the new land. The bad water killed all their cattle.

Standing Bear stayed until a hundred and fifty of his people died. He then he ran away with thirty men, women and children. Three months on the road, they were weak, sick and starved when they reached the Omaha Reservation. The Omahas gave them a piece of land and they were anxious to plow and put in wheat.

Soldiers arrived and arrested them, determined to return them to the Oklahoma. However, news of their arrest and the Government's intentions roused excitement in Omaha. An editor and two lawyers tested whether the Government had a legal right to do such a thing.

A Judge Dundy, whose name should stand with that of Lincoln in the matter of emancipation acts, considered the case several days and gave a decision that struck at the root of the whole matter, a decision which, when finally enforced throughout the Nation, took the ground from under the feet of the horde of unscrupulous thieves that robbed, oppressed, and maddened the Indians for so long.

When Standing Bear found that by the decision of Judge Dundy he was a free man, and could go where he pleased, he made a speech which should never be forgotten or left out of the history of the dealings of the United States Government with the Indians.

After he touchingly thanked his attorneys, he said, " Hitherto, when we have been wronged, we went to war to assert our rights and avenge our wrongs. We took the tomahawk. We had no law to punish those who did wrong, so we took our tomahawks and went to kill. If they had guns and could kill us first, it was the fate of war. But you have found a better way. You have gone into court for us, and I find that our wrongs can be righted there. Now I have no more use for the tomahawk. I want to lay it down forever."

Eloquently expr4essive, the old stooped down and placed his tomahawk at his feet. Then, standing erect, he folded his arms with native dignity and continued, "I lay it down. I have no more use for it. I have found a better way."

Stooping again, and taking up the weapon, he placed it in the hands of one of his attorneys, a Mr. Webster, and said, "I present it to you as a token of my gratitude. I want you to keep it in remembrance of this great victory which you have gained. I have no further use for it. I can now seek the ways of peace."

The first thing Standing Bear did with his freedom was to try to gain the freedom of his tribe, and to establish their legal right to their old home in Dakota. Accompanied by a young and well-educated Omaha girl and her brother as interpreters, and by Mr. Tibbles, the champion and friend to whom he owed his freedom, he went East, telling the story of the sufferings and wrongs of his tribe to large audiences in many of the larger cities.

Money was generously subscribed everywhere to bring suits to test the question of the Poncas' legal right to the lands which the United States had by treaty ceded to them in specified "townships," thus giving to them the same sort of title which would be given to any corporation or individual.

This movement of Standing Bear and his companions soon produced a strong effect on the community. This attracted the authorities in Washington, and letters were published contradicting Standing Bear's assertions. statements were circulated injurious to all members of the party. For some mysterious reason, the Department of the Interior was unwilling that the Poncas should be reinstated on their lands.

Discussions grew heated. The cruel Inspector involved with their forced move, published long letters attacking Standing Bear's veracity. The chief's pithy answers proved the falsity of many of the inspectors statements. What soon became clear to observers was that either the Secretary of the Interior or the inspector, or both, were liars.

Interest in the cas brought about a committee being appointed to represent the case in Washington, and to secure legislation on it. Standing Bear made a powerful impression on Congress. Once started on the subject, Congressional committees called for evidence regarding several other striking instances of injustices to Indians.

A bill was introduced in Congress to restore to the Poncas their old reservation in Dakota, and putting their houses, farms,and so on, in the same good condition they were at the time of their removal from them.

Damning to the Department of the Interior was the report of the agent who had superintended the forced move. Strangely, the Department made it part of its official record of the management of Indian affairs for 1877. It graphically documented the misery, horror, and wretched conditions the Poncas endured. Despite the official evidence in their own files, the Department of the Interior still contended that the Indians were not moved by force.

There was never any accusation brought against the military for brutality in this case. However, the very presence of the troopers was brutal and coercive. There was no doubt about the orders the "military force" would have carried out had the Poncas not finally submitted to the move.

"It is a matter of astonishment to me," said the Agent in charge in his report, "that the government should have ordered the removal of the Ponca Indians from Dakota to the Indian Territory without having first made some provision for their settlement and comfort."

"Before their removal was carried into effect an appropriation should have been made by Congress sufficient to have located them in their new home, by building a comfortable home for the occupancy of every family of the tribe."

"As the case now is, no appropriation has been made by Congress except a sum little more that sufficient to remove them, and the result is that these people have been placed on an uncultivated reservation, to live in their tents as best they may, and await further legislative action."

The Agent's journal is the best record that can ever be written of the sufferings of the Poncas in being taken from their homes. It cannot be discredited. It is an "official record", authorized and endorsed by being published in the Annual Report of the Secretary of the Interior.

In 1880, at the end of the hundred most shameful years in United States history, the remainder of the tribe was still in Indian Territory, anxiously awaiting the results of the efforts to restore them their old homes, and to establish their indisputable legal right to them.

THE WINNEBAGOES

The Winnebagoes belonged to the Dakota (Sioux) family, but were known as a naturally peace-loving people, and had no sympathy with their more warlike relatives. The Algonquins gave them the name of Winnebagoes, or "people of the saltwater", and as the Algonquin word for saltwater and stinking-water was the name, the French called them "les Puants," or "Stinkards." The Sioux gave them a more melodious and pleasing name, "O-ton-kah," which meant "The large, strong people."

Bancroft, in his account of the North American tribes, says, "One little community of the Dakota (Sioux) family had penetrated the territories of the Algonquins, The Winnebagoes, dwelling between Green Bay and the lake that bears their name, and preferred to be environed by Algonquins than to stay in the dangerous vicinity of their own kindred."

The earliest mention of this tribe in the diplomatic history of the United States, is in the council reports of July, 1815, at "Portage des Sioux", in Missouri, after the Treaty of Ghent. The Winnebagoes refused to send delegates, which was considered important. The Americans thought that British influence kept the Winnebagoes away, but it is more likely that they already had a general distrust of all white men. When visited later, one official observed, "There is no other tribe which seems to possess so much jealousy of the whites, and such reluctance to have intercourse with them..."

In spite of this reluctance, in 1816 they made a treaty "of peace and friendship with the United States," agreeing "to remain distinct and sepa-rate from the rest of their nation or tribe, giving them no assistance what-ever until peace shall be concluded between the United States and their tribe or nation."

In 1825 the United States Government, unable to endure the spectacle of Indians warring among themselves, and massacring each other, appears in the Northwestern country as an unselfish pacificator, and compels the Sacs, Foxes, Chippewas, and Sioux, including the Winnebagoes, to make a treaty of peace and friendship with each other and with the United States.

Treaty terms were precarious, especially as it was understood by all parties that "no tribe shall hunt within the actual limits of any other with-out their consent." The lands of the Winnebagoes at that time lay between the Rock and Wisconsin Rivers, along the shore of Winnebagoe Lake, and the six hundred member tribe claimed the whole lake.

The Winnebagoes signed a third treaty in 1827, along with the Chippe-was, and Menomonies, with the United States. This treaty completed the systems of boundaries of their lands, which had been only partially defined by the two previous treaties. Schoolcraft said, "these three conferences embody a new course and policy for keeping the tribes in peace, and are founded on the most enlarged consideration of the aboriginal right of fee-simple to the soil,... and contain no cession of territory (to the United States)."

They were the last such treaties, as by 1828, the people of Northern Illi-nois began to covet and trespass on Indian areas. Commissioners were sent to persuade the Indians to surrender their lands. The Indians refused, and the treaty was deferred. The United States then agreed to pay the four tribes $20,000, "in full compensation for all injuries and damages sus-tained by them in consequence of the occupation any party of the mining country."

293

In 1829 a benevolent scheme for the rescue of these hard-pressed tribes of the Northwest Territory was proposed that suggested the forming of a colony of them in the Lake Superior Region, stating, "The Indian is in every view entitled to sympathy. They are a political nonentity,.... with no vote to give. The whole Indian race is not worth one white man's vote."

Congressional appropriations were sadly behind. Promises made to Indians were unfulfilled simply because there was no money. Nonetheless, the all-engrossing topic of Congress in 1830 was "the removal of the Indians."

Meanwhile, the Indians were warring among themselves, and retaliating on white squatters on their lands. The inevitable conquest began in earnest, and in September of 1832 the Winnebagoes were compelled to make their first great cession of territory to the United States. In exchange for it they accepted a tract west of the Mississippi, and before June, 1833, most of those living on the ceded lands had crossed the river to their new homes.

Their title to this new area was not as good as supposed, for the treaty expressly stated that it was granted to them "to be held as other Indian lands are Held." In other words, they could again be evicted and moved at Government whim. With the recent cession, the United States had promised $10,000 annually for 27 years, plus buildings, teachers, and various allowances for stock implements, and so on, plus a doctor.

Five years later the Winnebagoes found the treaty scrapped, as they were forced to cede all their remaining lands east of the Mississippi, plus the right to occupy, "except for hunting," a portion of that which they "owned" on the west side. For this they were to receive $200,000, with a part of this sum to pay debts, part to pay for their removal from relinquished lands, and the rest "to be invested by the United States Government for their benefit."

This deceitful phrase, often appearing in one version or another in later treaties, merely meant that Indians received nothing.

The Winnebagoes were forced into another treaty in 1846, by which they ceded and "sold" to the United States "all right, title, interest, claim, and privilege to all lands heretofore occupied by them;" and accepted as their home, a tract of 800,000 acres north of Saint Peter's and west of the Mississippi River,with again the nullifying phrase, "to be held as other Indian lands are held".

For this third forced move they were to to be paid $190,000, $150,000 for the land they gave up, and $40,000 for relinquishing hunting rights on adjacent lands. As usual , part of this was to be spent in moving the Indians, with the remainder "left in trust" with the Government at five per cent interest. This of course translated to the Indians getting little or nothing.

The new reservation was totally unsuitable, and the tribe grew restless and discontented. Large numbers roamed back to their old homes in Iowa and Wisconsin. In 1855 another treaty was made, and they ceded all the land they had received in the 1846 treaty, in exchange for eighteen square miles on the Blue Earth River in Minnesota.

The improved lands they had been living on, including mills and buildings, were to be sold, and the amount received to pay for there forced move, some subsistence, and supposedly to help make them comfortable in their next home, which was to be "permanent". Since that false promised had not been used in prior treaties, it is presumed that the Winnebagoes took heart. Again, they went to work immediately, "Plowing, planting, and building."

Minnesota citizens did not like their new neighbors. Indignation meetings were held, and the move started to oust the Winnebagoes from their dearly-purchased land. All this tended to discourage the Indians from hoping to remain in their "permanent home." Nevertheless, they worked on, improving their area, and keeping good faith with the whites and their Government. However, they showed bad effects of repeated forced removals, and several hundred began roaming in Wisconsin.

They worked hard at farming, but were hampered by lack of promised horses and plows. Soon many asked to have their farms granted to them individually. The Government took advantage of this desire and devised the Treaty of 1859, that allotted lands to individuals, "in severalty," and the rest of the tribal holdings were to be sold, with the proceeds to be partly expended in farm improvements, and the rest held for them by the Government. This threw open hundreds of thousands of acres to white exploitation, and the greedy belt of civilization drew tighter around the natives.

To the Winnebagoes, however, prospects apparently brightened. With their farms supposedly given to them for their own, and with a promised sufficient sum of land sale money to help them improve their holdings, it looked like prosperity and comfort lay ahead for them.

In 1860 the Commissioner of Indian Affairs writes, "The Winnebagoes continue steadily on the march of improvement... The Indians were promised that new and comfortable houses would be built for them. The treaty not yet being ratified, I have no funds in my hands that could be made applicable to this purpose."

The next year he wrote that the funds the Indians were depending on, had still not been paid. "The Indians who have had their allotments made are clamoring for their certificates."

Drunkenness became a serious vice of the tribe. They were surrounded on all sides by whites that sold whiskey, and who were anxious to degrade the natives as much as possible, hoping to push them off their land. By 1863 the Winnebagoes were in trouble. The Sioux had massacred some white squatters, and Minnesota citizens demanded the expulsion of all Indians from the state. The Winnebagoes had refused to join the Sioux in their attack, and were threatened with death by the Sioux as well as by whites.

The Winnebagoe could not leave their reservation without fear of being shot. They never received their allotted farm implements. Game on their lands was exhausted, and their arms had been taken from them. They were starving. Somehow the tribe remained loyal.

The people of Minnesota triumphed in February, 1863, when Congress authorized the "peaceful and quiet removal of the Winnebagoe Indians from the State of Minnesota, and settling them on a new reserve, on the Missouri River, somewhere within a hundred miles of Fort Randall."

All their remaining weapons were taken, and the hostile Sioux were to be relocated to a reservation adjoining the new Winnebagoe location. Many Winnebagoe abandoned the Indian life, refused to go, and more or less "qualified for civilized life." Many enlisted in the military, and all tried to keep the homes allotted to them by treaty. The Government immediately sold the tribal lands and kept the money.

The bulk of the tribe was rounded up, uncomfortably transported at their own expense, and dumped on a sandy, inhospitable beach on the west bank of the Missouri River, at the Crow Creek Agency in Dakota Territory, at their own expense. The weather was harsh, the soil was sterile, and rather than face certain starvation, the tribe abandoned that barren spot. After a miserable trek, with several hundred starving or freezing on the way, they arrived at the Omaha Agency in a condition that aroused sympathy from most who learned of the wrong they had suffered.

In May 1863, the Winnebagoes were gathered at Fort Snelling to journey to yet another "suitable home". The tribe of about two thousand arrived at a wilderness along the Missouri River that was almost barren, with dry, hard, unplowable soil. A drought had parched the grass. There was no suitable timber, and the channel of the Missouri was so changeable,and the banks so low, that it was dangerous to get too near. They had to settle a half-mile from the river, and were understatedly reported as, "not pleased with their location."

They began making canoes to join the Omahas or others down the river. They were warned not to attempt to leave or they would be shot by troops stationed down-river. In spite of the threat, the dread of withering at the new location spurred the Indians to continue making boats and escaping in small groups, arriving at the Omaha Agency, begging for food.

By the autumn of 1863, over 1,200 of the 2000 destitute Winnebagoes had escaped and made their way to the Nebraska Omaha Reservation. The Government, in a moment of largesse, agreed to feed them until Spring.

Their stay in the totally unsuitable wilderness had left terrible effects on the tribe. They were spiritless and desperate from their sufferings, and were demoralized by again being forced into contact with their deadly, sworn enemy, the Sioux. They fought off attacks, and relapsed so far into the barbaric life that at one dance they roasted and ate the heart of a Sioux prisoner. Yet in less than a year, their hopes were rekindled for a "permanent home."

The long-suffering tribe made a new treaty with the Government in 1865, which by giving up all rights in the Dakota Reserve, they were to receive a tract of 128,000 acres in Nebraska, as the "future home of the Winnebagoe Indians forever". The promised land was a part of the Omaha Reservation that the Omahas agreed to sell.

The United States of course agreed to also erect mills, break land, furnish seeds, tools, guns, horses, oxen and wagons, and to feed the tribe for one year, "as some small reparation for the terrible losses and sufferings they had experienced." The Winnebagoes possibly took courage from the word "forever."

Showing much industry, The tribe was noted in 1866 to be improving, despite poor health resulting from their recently being hunted, herded and starved. Almost five hundred had died from being pushed out of Minnesota. It was totally unjust that the Indians themselves should have to pay for all they had been forced to endure. It was clearly a debt of the covetous people of Minnesota who were so vehement in forcing them out.

The stray Winnebagoes left behind in Wisconsin tried to claim their "allotted" lands and were to receive some Government allocations as they merged into local communities, becoming useful and productive citizens. Yet by 1872 the whites complained of them, and Congress approved their being gathered and shunted west of the Mississippi. They were not wanted anywhere. The Agent of the new Winnebagoe Reservation protested their being sent there, since "Nebraska does like Indians any better than Wisconsin or Minnesota..."

The tribal members in Nebraska began to fear anew that they would not get patents to their new lands, despite having lived on and improved them greatly for three years. In the winter of 1874, the discontented Wisconsin "strays" were herded and shipped to the Nebraska Reservation. In less than a year about half of them had wandered back to Wisconsin. The Government did little to recapture them, yet with a small weak tribe like the Poncas, whose thirty or so starving members ran for their lives from Indian Territory in Oklahoma, were hunted, arrested, and treated like thieves escaping with stolen property.

Only two hundred Wisconsin Winnebagoes were left in Nebraska in 1875. Meanwhile, the Nebraska portion of the tribe were praised as "being nearly civilized," with hundreds of new homes built and much of their land under cultivation. In 1876 they were "fast emerging from a condition of dependence upon their annual appropriations. The Winnebagoes once more were quietly established in comfortable, yet somewhat primitive homes.

How did the Government welcome this heroic triumph of a patient people over disheartening obstacles and suffering? It decided that all Indians should be concentrated upon a few reservations, "the fewer the better." In the federal wisdom, all Indians should be given 75 acres in the Indian Territory of Oklahoma. The true purpose of such a plan was that "most of the land now occupied as reserves reverting to the Government, would be open to entry and sale."

The Winnebagoes had been fleeing from this necessity to open Indian lands "to entry and sale" for thirty-eight years, 1815 to 1863. They were no safer in the 1870's. The Commissioner of Indian Affairs reliably stated, "with a fair degree of persistence, the removal can be secured," and no doubt it could. A barrage of such high-sounding, hypocritical phrases from the Government effectually hid from the American people the iron hand of injustice and cruelty which had grasped the Indians for a hundred years.

As part of the great injustice, in 1876 the Government cut funds drastically for Indian Agency operations, closing fine buildings, schools, and vital services. As usual, the Indians themselves received nothing for having all they owned taken from them.

In 1877 the Secretary of the Interior persistently recommended that the Indians be "gradually gathered together on smaller reservations," to the end that "greater facilities be afforded for civilization.

Since in 1878 "There is a vast area of land in the Indian Territory not yet occupied," writes the Commissioner of Indian Affairs, a bill was drawn "providing for the removal and consolidation of certain Indians in the States of Oregon, Colorado, Iowa, Kansas, Nebraska, Wisconsin, and Minnesota, and the Territories of Washington and Dakota... A reduction of twenty-five reservations and eleven agencies will thus be effected... There will be restored to the public domain 17,642,455 acres of land... Further consolidations of like character are not only possible, but expedient and advisable."

With the same ludicrous, complacent logic as before, he proceeded to give the reason for uprooting all these Indians from the home where they were beginning to thrive and take root, and moving them again, for the third, fourth, fifth, sixth, or seventh time. He forcibly argued, with great appeal to Congress, that the cost of uprooting and relocation would be met from the sale of vacated lands.

In continuing pompous, illogical reasoning, it was admitted that "the lands belong to the Indians", yet they would be compelled to restore over seventeen and half million acres of them "to the public domain." This statement perhaps is a high-water mark of the sophistry and dishonesty of the Department's position. The slyness continued: the Indians were "clearly entitled to receive the full value of the same when sold," but they would be compelled to expend that "full value" in moving them to a place they did not want to go.

The Commissioner concluded, "Every means that human ingenuity can devise, legal or illegal, has been resorted to for the purpose of obtaining possession of Indian lands." When news of such schemes reached the reservations, the Indians were greatly alarmed.

At the end of the most infamous hundred years of Government injustice to Indians, the Winnebagoes were anxious and desperate, facing the wicked inevitable. Citizenship was clamored for, in hopes of protecting what little they had.

THE CHEROKEES

The Cherokees were the original Eastern Mountaineers of America. Their country stretched along the Tennessee River, and into the highlands of Georgia, Carolina, and Alabama, the loveliest region east of the Mississippi River. Beautiful and grand, with lofty mountains and rich valleys fragrant with flower, and forests of magnolia and pine filled with singing birds and melodious streams, rich in fruits and nuts and wild grains, it was a country worth loving, worth fighting for, worth dying for, as thousands of its lovers have fought and died, white men as well as Indians, from 1780 to 1880.

When Oglethorpe came with this cargo of Madeira wine and respectable paupers from England in 1733, and lived in tents in midwinter on the shores of the Savannah River, one of the first conditions of safety for his colossal almshouse, in the shape of a new colony, was that all the Indians in the region should become its friends and allies.

The reputation of his goodness and benevolence soon penetrated to the fastnesses of their homes, and tribe after tribe sent chiefs and headmen to greet him with gifts and welcome. When the Cherokee chief appeared, Oglethorpe said to him, "Fear nothing. Speak freely." "I always speak freely," answered the mountaineer. "Why should I fear? I am now among friends: I never feared, even among my enemies."

The principal purposes of the Georgia English colony was to make a home for Englishmen who were "in decayed circumstances," and to "civilize the savages." In 1734 Oglethorpe took eight Indian chiefs to England. Nothing was neglected, we are told, "that was likely to awaken their curiosity or impress them with a sense of the power and grandeur of the nation." The tribes at home were gratified and impressed by the attentions paid to their chiefs.

When Wesleyian missionaries arrived in Georgia in 1736, they were met by some of the chiefs, bearing gifts of milk and honey, and one of them told Mister Wesley, "...we would not be made Christians as the Spaniards make Christians; we would be taught before we are baptized."

Wesley was enthusiastic, but intolerant and injudicious. He was unsuccessful with both Indians and whites. The same chief, when urged to become a Christian, said, "Christians get drunk! Christians beat men! Christians tell lies! Me no Christian!"

For twenty years Oglethorpe's colony struggled on . There were wars with France and Spain; tiresome squabbles with and among Methodist missionaries. At last the trustees of the Georgia Colony lost patience. Very bitterly they had learned that paupers, however worthy, are not good stuff to build new enterprises of. In June, 1752, the Georgia trustees resigned their charter and washed their hands of the colony.

The province was formed into a royal government, and soon had frightful Indian wars. Their old friend Oglethorpe was gone, and the new authorities neither understood nor kept faith with the Indians. The same scenes of treachery and massacre which took place up North, began to be repeated with heart-sickening similarity. Indians fought Indians, being allies with the French, and then with the English. Treaties made were broken immediately, and there was no peace or safety in Georgia.

At last a treaty was concluded in 1763 with the chiefs and headmen of five tribes, which promised better things. The Creeks and Cherokees granted the King of England a large tract of land, clearing their "debts to England" with the sum paid for it. Peace was destroyed several years later with the revolt of the American Colonies against Great Britain.

The British availed themselves of the Cherokees allegiance to the Crown. Atrocities were committed by all involved, disproving that innate cruelty is an exclusive Indian trait. The Cherokees had the worst of the fighting on the British side, as the British had no compunctions in throwing them on the front lines.

The first diplomatic relations of the United States Government with the Cherokees were in the making of the treaty of Hopewell, In 1785. The United States commissioners said to the Cherokees, "Congress is now the sovereign of all our country which we now point out to you on the map. They want none of your lands, nor anything else that belongs to you."

The chiefs complained bitterly of the encroachments of white settlers upon lands which had been by old treaties distinctly reserved to the Cherokees. They demanded that some of these settlers be removed. When the commissioners said that there were too many settlers for the Government to remove, one of the chiefs satirically asked, "Are Congress, who conquered the King of Great Britain, unable to remove those people?"

Finally, the chiefs agreed to accept payment for the lands which had been taken. New boundaries were established, and a general feeling of goodwill and confidence was created. In four years, the Cherokees had lost some 650 of their estimated 2650 people, mostly due to wars with frontier people. It was a deplorable situation for the tribe, and was an admitted "indispensable obligation of the United States to vindicate their faith, justice, and national dignity."

The Indians were charged with atrocities while evicting squatters for their lands, lands the Government had solemnly guaranteed that the Cherokees might "punish him or not as they please." Even the Secretary of the Interior reported that as a result of the bad faith of the Government, "The Indian tribes can have no faith in such imbecile promises, and the lawless whites will ridicule a government which shall on paper only make Indian treaties and regulate Indian boundaries."

The Treaty of Holston was made with the Cherokees in July 1791, establishing new boundaries and promising $1000 a year for the lands relinquished. The treaty reiterated the old, always broken promise that if anyone other than a Cherokee tried to settle on their land, they could punish him as they pleased.

The next year the Cherokees asked for an additional $500 a year. As a chief said, the $1000 a year, "would not buy a breech-clout for each of my nation". They got the $500, but not the promised plows, hoes, cattle, and so on, badly needed since "Game is going fast from among us."

White settlers continued to go where they pleased. Cherokees murdered them, as they were permitted to do. Whites retaliated by attacking friendly Indians, and the Indians retaliated again. Equally unjust to all parties, these miserable affairs continued for years.

At last the Government offered another treaty, but the Cherokees refused to cede any more lands, or let roads be built through their territory. After four more years of misery, the Indians acquiesced, giving up several large tracts and right of ways for several roads. In 1805 the United States took more land, and in 1816 they took all Cherokee lands in South Carolina.

In 1817, the Government promised six hundred and forty acres to each Indian that would become a citizen, and took even more lands from the tribe. So, in less than twenty years, the Cherokee Nation was found piteously pleading to be allowed to remain undisturbed on even a small portion of what had been theirs.

In the whole history of Government dealings with the Indian tribes, there is probably no record as black as its perfidy to the Cherokees. It would later seem almost incredible.

From the beginning of the 19th century they had been steadily advancing in civilization. There is no instance in all history of a race of people passing in so short a time from the barbarous stage to the agricultural and civilized. Yet, on December 19, 1829, the State of Georgia, by one high-handed outrage, made outlaws of the Cherokees.

They passed a law "to annul all laws and ordinances made by the Cherokee nation of Indians;" declaring "all laws, ordinances, orders, and regulations of any kind whatever, made, passed, or enacted by the Cherokee Indians, either in general council or in any other way whatever, or by any authority whatever, null and void, and of no effect, as if the same had never existed; also, that no Indian, or descendant of any Indian residing within

302

the Creek or Cherokee nations of Indians;, shall be deemed a competent witness in any court of this State to which a white man may be a party."

The doom of the Cherokees had been sealed on the day they declared, once and for all, that they would not give up another foot of land. Georgia demanded that the Indians should be made to vacate their lands, peaceably or otherwise.

The dignified and pathetic remonstrances of the Cherokee chiefs, and their firm reiterations of their resolve not to part with their lands, were called by the Georgia Governor, "tricks of vulgar cunning,... insults from the polluted lips of outcasts and vagabonds." He openly threatened the President that Georgians would make war if the Indians did not leave.

Earlier, President Jefferson had assured the Cherokees that they had a right to their lands and would be protected by the United States. General George Washington had told them that in the future they would not be defrauded of their lands. Yet thirty years later, they saw the United States uphold the State of Georgia.

Federal agents attempted all sorts of seductions of native leaders, but never did mountaineers cling more desperately to their homes than did the Cherokees. Year by year high-handed oppressions continued and multiplied. Military law reigned everywhere. The federal Government continued to say they couldn't protect the Indians, and kept offering them money for their country.

Nevertheless, they clung to their land. When the bill for their removal was before Congress, which to its credit must be noted that the bill passed the Senate by only one vote. Remonstrances poured into Congress from around the nation, all imploring the Government to keep its faith with the Cherokees.

As a last resort the Indians carried their case before the Supreme Court. The learned justices got out of it by declaring that the Cherokee Tribe was not a nation and could not bring the suit, although the court was manifestly sympathetic. This did not help the Cherokees.

Many were ready to remain and suffer death rather than give up. Wiser counsels prevailed, and in the last days of 1835 a treaty was made that relinquished all the lands claimed by them east of the Mississippi River. The United States did "guarantee to the Cherokee nation a perpetual outlet west, and a free and unmolested use of all the country west of the western boundary,... as far west as the sovereignty of the United States and their rights of soil extend."

A great part of the Indian Nation refused to sanction the treaty, saying it did not represent their wish, and hundreds refused money or supplies from the Government, lest they be considered thereby to have committed themselves to the treaty. For two years, with many near starvation, to the last moment allowed by the treaty, they clung to their homes, and at last were removed by military force. The Cherokee leaders had made no further protest against going, but simply asked to undertake the whole charge of the removal themselves.

The military commander quibbled with them about their estimated costs being too high, feeling for example, that sixteen cents a day for individual rations was too high. Since the costs were to be paid from tribal funds controlled by the Government, they were nobly liberal in finally agreeing to the small amounts requested.

To dwell here on the picture of the removal, the infamous "Trail of Tears", is not possible, and is dealt with better elsewhere. Hundreds and hundreds died on the midwinter trek over thirteen hundred miles west to the Indian Territory. No imagination so dull, no heart so hard as not to see and to feel, at the bare mention of such a forced emigration, what horrors and what anguish it must have involved.

For some years after this removal, fierce dissent rent the Cherokee Nation. Several of the signers of the treaty, influential members of the tribe, were murdered. The progress of the Cherokees in the following ten years, however, was almost beyond belief.

In 1860, agitation over slavery began, with stormy scenes also near the Kansas line. For several years white settlers had persisted in taking up farms there, and the Cherokees had in vain implored the Government to drive them away. An officer in charge finally forced a few out, burning their cabins over them.

In the first year of the Civil War a large number of Cherokees took up arms on the rebel side. The opportunity of fighting against Georgians could not but have been welcome to the soul of a Cherokee, but their defection to the Southerners was no doubt largely due to terror.

All United States troops had been withdrawn from their country. They were without any protection from the Government, and to leave them without any incentive to loyalty, the United States suspended the payment of their meager annuities.

The Confederate Government artfully promised to pay what the Northerners refused. Amazingly, thousands of Indians did remain loyal, and fled for their lives. Almost half of the Creek Nation, many Seminoles,

Chickasaws, Quapaws, Cherokees, and half a dozen other tribes, over six thousand in all, fled to Kansas. Their suffering there in the winter of 1862 was heart-rending.

The party feeling between the loyal and disloyal Cherokees ran as high as it did between the loyal and disloyal whites. It appeared impossible that opposing Cherokees could agree to live side by side, as it would to make discharged soldiers from Georgia and Maine settle in one village together.

However, after long and troublesome negotiations a treaty was concluded in 1866, by which all necessary points seemed to be established of a general amnesty and peace. The Indians were of course at great disadvantage in making these treaties. Government superintendents admitted that the rebel Cherokees had no choice in their loyalties, but were nevertheless, "at our mercy" and their treaty rights had been abrogated.

With a recuperative power far in advance of that shown by any small white Southern communities, The Cherokees at once began to rebuild their homes and reconstruct their national life. Thus a second time they recovered themselves, after what would seem to be well nigh their destruction as a people. Yet, the Indian's fate of perpetual insecurity, alarm, and unrest did not abandon them.

In 1870 they were said to be "extremely uneasy about the security of the possession of the lands they occupied. When asked why they had not re-established schools, and the like, the reply came, "we expect to have our lands taken away. What is the use of all that when our doom as a nation is sealed?"

When their delegates had gone to Washington in 1866 to make the new treaty, they were naturally alarmed to be told that the Cherokees, as a nation had forfeited its rights for having side with the Confederacy. It mattered not to the United States that only one third of the Cherokees had in any way aided the rebels, or that two Cherokee regiments had fought in the Union Army.

They could not refuse any conditions imposed upon them, and were intimidated into selling a large tract in Southeastern Kansas to white speculators at a dollar an acre. This fell into the hands of a railroad corporation. The Cherokees, also against their wishes, granted right of way for two railroad lines through their lands.

The rapacity of the railroad companies was as insatiable as their methods were unscrupulous. "Extinguishing Indian land titles" came to be associated with the prevailing attitude that extinction was the ultimate and inevitable fate of the Indian.

This is the only explanation of the unconscious inhumanity of many good men's modes of thinking and speaking in regard to the Indians being driven from home after home, and robbed of tract after tract of their lands.

Even though the Cherokees had been solemnly pledged seven million acres of land, and were entitled to them by the supreme law of the land, the Report of the Indian Bureau for 1876 stated, "By treaty the Government has ceded to the so-called civilized tribes--the Cherokees, Creeks, Choctaws, Chickasaws, and Seminoles--a section of country altogether disproportionate in amount to their needs."

The Department of the Interior in 1876 said the affairs in the Indian Territory are "complicated and embarrassing, and the question is directly raised whether an extensive section of country is to be allowed to remain for an indefinite period practically an uncultivated waste, or whether the Government shall determine to reduce the size of the reservation."

The phrase "whether the Government shall determine to reduce the size of the Reservation" sounded much better than "whether the Government shall rob the Indians of a few million acres of land." The latter phrase is truth, and the other is the spirit of lying.

The commissioner opined that "public policy will soon require the disposal of a large portion of these lands to the Government for the occupancy either of other tribes of Indians or of white people. There is a very general and growing opinion that observance of the strict letter of treaties with Indians is in many cases at variance with their own best interests and with sound public policy."

He then made the preposterously contradictory sentence, that it must not be understood from this recommendation that it was "the policy or purpose of this office to in any way encourage the spirit of rapacity which demands the throwing open of the Indian Territory to white settlement."

So it went for the Cherokees during Century of Dishonor. It is doubtful if their rapid progress to that of civilization and enlightenment has any parallel in the history of the World. What required five hundred years for the Britons to accomplish in this direction, the Cherokees accomplished in a hundred years.

THE SIOUX

The word Sioux is a contraction from the old French word "Nadouessioux," or "Enemies," the name given by French traders to this most powerful and warlike of all the Northwestern tribes. They called themselves "Dakota," or "many in one," because so many bands under different names were joined. At the time of Captain Carver's travels among the North American Indians, there were twelve known bands of the "Nadouwessies."

Nothing in the history of the earliest relations between the friendly tribes of North American Indians and the arriving Europeans is more pathetic than the accounts of their simple hospitality, their unstinted invitations, and their innocent desire to learn more of white men's ways.

Diplomatic relations between the United States Government and the Sioux began in 1815. In that year and the next, the Government made sixteen treaties of peace and friendship with different tribes, treaties demanding no cessions beyond the original grants made to these tribes by the French, English and Spanish Governments. "Perpetual peace" was promised, and "every injury or act of hostility committed by one or the other... shall be mutually forgiven and forgot."

Three of these treaties were made with bands of the Sioux: "Sioux of the Leaf, Sioux of the Broad Leaf, and Sioux who shoot in the Pine-tops." In 1825 four more treaties were made with separate Sioux bands. One of these treaties, that of Prairie de Chien, defined boundaries between the Chippewas and the Sioux, in hopes that their incessant feuds might end. The long-standing conflict had slowly driven the Sioux south and west.

A treaty couldn't keep peace between such ancient enemies, and fighting continued. White traders suffered almost more than the Indians. The Government couldn't stop the war, and merely hoped that the eventual loser would be lost as a separate power.

The next treaty, also at Prairie du Chien, in 1830, began boundary disputes that caused great misunderstanding and outbreaks by The Sioux for decades, compounded by unfairness on the side of the whites, and unwillingness on the part of the Indians.

All the early Government treaty-makers congratulated themselves on getting valuable land by the millions of acres for almost nothing, and as years went on, openly lamented that "Indians were beginning to find out what lands were worth."

Meanwhile the Indians, anxious, alarmed, hostile at heart, seeing themselves hard-pressed on all sides, driven "to provide other sources for supplying their wants besides those of hunting, which must soon fail them," yielded mile after mile with increasing sense of loss. They were powerless to prevent it, or the resentment it was unwise to show.

Soon after these treaties the artist George Catlin made his famous journeys among the Indians. He spent several weeks among the Sioux, and said of them, "There is no tribe on the continent of finer looking men, and few tribes who are better and more comfortably clad and supplied with the necessities of life.

Had the provisions of these first treaties been fairly and promptly carried out, there would have been living in Minnesota in the late 1800s, thousands of Sioux families, good and prosperous farmers and mechanics.

The Sioux were cheated out of their annuities by the Government. In 1836 Congress appropriated the puny sum of $2000 "for the purpose of extinguishing the Indian title between the State of Missouri and the Missouri River." This was the very land granted to the Sioux under the Treaty of Prairie du Chien, but the good people of Missouri wanted it. The Indians soon saw that they could not prevail and gave up the huge tract.

In 1837 The Government took a number of chiefs to Washington, D.C. to threaten them with the strength of the nation should the Indians "venture to attack our borders." Duly impressed with the show of might, the Sioux delegates, of the Medawakanton Band, reluctantly ceded to the United States "all their land east of the Mississippi River, and all their islands in the same." As usual, the Indians only got a fraction of what was promised.

For the next ten years affairs went badly with the Sioux; they were continually attacked by the Chippewas, Ottawas, and others, and continually retaliated. This was all fine with white authorities, as it seemed the best way to keep the whites safe. Whiskey traders and fur traders found it more profitable to deal with drunken Indians, and the Sioux rapidly grew demoralized.

Their government annuities were always in arrears, and in 1842 several bands were half-starved due to crop failure and Congressional failure to ratify a treaty they had made with the Sioux in 1841. The remaining buffalo had long since been driven far away, and most Indians were too poor to own a horse on which to hunt. The Government did see fit to keep most of them alive during the following winter, but in 1849, the "needs" of the white settlers on the east side of the Mississippi made it imperative that the Sioux should again be forced off their lands.

The commissioners were sent with absurd instructions: "Though the proposed purchase is estimated to contain some twenty millions of acres, and some of it no doubt of excellent quality, there are sound reasons why it is comparatively valueless to the Indians, and a large price should not be paid for it." Apparently it was "desirable, and absolutely necessary for white settlers," yet worthless to Indians.

"On full consideration,....it is the opinion of this office (The Department of the Interior) that from two to two and a half cents an acre would be an ample amount for it." Those same instructions rationalized that by giving the Indians practically nothing for their lands, The Government was doing the natives a favor since "it was a well-ascertained fact that no greater curse can be inflicted on a tribe so little civilized as the Sioux than to have large sums of money coming to them as annuities."

Apparently along those same "humanitarian" lines, the annual annuity to the Sioux was withheld from 1837 to 1850.

In plain English, the Government had in 1830 promised to let a band of men take out tracts of land, and settle down like other men on their home-steads. For ten years the men had begged to do so, and were refused. Then, thinking there was no hope of anything better, they sold the land back to the Government.

The United States did not pay, and nine years later congratulated itself, that since all these agreements had not been fulfilled, "the land was still held only in same manner as other Indian titles are held." In other words, it was not "held" at all, only used on sufferance of the Government, and could be taken back at the Government's pleasure.

The Government than took back another 143,000 acres apparently "of much less value than valueless," as the Indians got nothing from the deal but another eviction.

Meanwhile, the bands of the Medewakanton Sioux were occupying a large tract on the west shore of the Mississippi, while the Yanktons, San-tees, and other bands lived high up the Saint Peter's River. All these bands were almost always hungry. The Government supplied them little food, and none of the badly needed farm implements that they had promised.

Why did the United States Government keep on its obstinate way, feed-ing the Indian in gross and reckless improvidence with one hand, plun-dering him with the other, and holding him steadily down at the level of barbarism? No, forcing him below it by the newly added vices of gam-bling and drunkenness, and yet all the while boasting of its desire to en-lighten, instruct, and civilize him. It was as inexplicable as it was infamous; a phenomenon in the history of the world.

In the summer of 1851 the desired treaties were made. The Indians could see they had no choice, but held out for eight to nine cents per acre for their thirty five Million acres. Through usual Government chicanery,

Governor Ramsey was able to boast that the total of $3,075,000 to be paid actually came down to just $575,000 that might eventually make it to the tribes. Mills, schools, and farms were to erected for them, "as soon as practicable."

As expected, the Government view was that, "to the Indians themselves the broad regions which have been ceded are of inconsiderable value." Again we have a juxtaposition of thinking that defies logic, for the same writer also said that for the eight thousand people who, "have outlived in a great degree the means of subsistence of the hunter state," and must soon "resort to the pursuits of agriculture," nothing could have been more fortunate than to have owned and occupied thirty-five million fertile, well-watered acres such as those just taken from them.

Two years after relieving the Sioux of their worthless land, and having shoved the tribes into a supposedly worthless western fragment, the Government now wanted that land, also. The Indians were "induced" to agree, and part of the wording stipulated that the President could further relocate them, "if deemed expedient."

Whites poured into the ceded territories and on into the more or less temporary reservation. The reserve was poorly suited to sustain the Sioux anyway, and many agreed to be sent to the Indian Territory, but most desparately wanted the reservation confirmed to them. Added to this, the monies for removal of that portion that would abandon the area, "had been expended, their provision eaten up."

Here was a picture of a helpless people. Forced to give up what the Governor had said was "the garden spot of the State," and accept in its stead an "insignificant tract, on the greater part of which there is not wood, or timber, or coal sufficient for civilization;" and then, before the ink of that treaty had dried, told that even from this insignificant tract they must promise to move in five years.

What words could characterize such a transaction between a man and a man? There is not a country, a people, a community in which it would even be attempted. It was more the base, being between a strong government and a feeble race. Public outcry prevented the United States from this infamy, and the President decreed that the Indians remain "permanently" on their "insignificant tract."

While this went on, the Upper Missouri Sioux were still suffering and destitute. Among those peaceable and friendly bands a few half-starved groups started to raid whites. The Government in its maddening way, declared that all these Sioux had not "improved their condition", when they had nothing to improve it with.

The summer of 1857 was long remembered by Minnesotans. It opened with terrible massacres, the work of a wandering band of no more than fifteen Sioux outcasts. It started innocently enough, but the natives with pent-up fury lashed back at offending settlers, killing an entire small settlement.

The overwhelming majority of the Sioux, entirely innocent, were attacked by the Army. A group of loyal Sioux even pursued, fought, killed and captured some of the offenders. The hostilities came to an end, but the Sioux were not reassured, since the overwhelming sentiment among whites was to kill the entire Indian race.

The promised annuities were still greatly in arrears. More innocent tribesmen were killed by whites. Any further provocation by whites could suddenly throw the Indians into antagonism and hostility grossly disproportionate to the apparent cause. This was the condition of the Minnesota Sioux in the summer of 1862.

Starving Indians broke into a government warehouse. The Army retaliated, and the record of the resultant massacres of that summer is scarcely equaled in the history of Indian wars. Hostile Indians forced peaceable bands to join them, but many fled for their lives from their own tribesmen.

For three days the hostile bands, continually reinforced, went from settlement to settlement, killing and plundering. A belt of country some two hundred miles by fifty miles was abandoned by whites, who flocked in panic to towns and forts. Nearly a thousand of them were killed, and millions of dollars in property was destroyed.

The military quickly snuffed the outbreak, and a large number of Indians were captured. Three hundred of them were to be hanged, but all but 39 were reprieved. They endured sufferings worse than death for three years in a barren desert in Dakota Territory. The rest escaped to the Upper Missouri region or to Canada.

Minnesota, at a terrible cost to herself and to the United States, was at last free from of Indians, who were her enemies only because they had been treated with injustice and bad faith. Those that escaped to the North, joined the more or less hostile bands of Sioux in the Upper Missouri region.

In 1865, the Government having spent some forty million dollars on the campaigns, sent out a commission to treat with them, knowing well that the 14,000 Indians there had always wanted peace. The Government knew

311

well, also, that unless the tribes were reassured, there would be another formidable Indian war.

Nine treaties with nine tribes had the Indians pledging not to fight each other or the whites, in return for fifteen dollars per person each year, with twenty five dollars going to those who would become farmers. They kept faith during a bad winter, suffering from cold and hunger.

Still further treaties were made the next summer, seeing all Sioux pledged to peace. There was a bureaucratically bungled attempt to show some mercy to the thousand friendly old men, women, and children who were orphaned and widowed by Army actions.

Efforts were made to get reparations for friendly Indian farmers who had given all they had to help support and quarter Army troops during the conflicts. In 1866, in spite of strong protests of Nebraskans, these Sioux were settled on reservations of marginal land on the Niobrara River, in Northern Nebraska. In the Fall they were moved from that unsuitable area to the mouth of Bazile Creek, where they managed to stay alive during the winter.

They were cheered at having a delegation being taken to the Nation's capitol the next Spring, but all they got were promises of a commission to visit them the next year. They were told to move to Breckenridge, on the west bank of the Missouri River and plant crops there. If they liked it, they should have it "secured to them as a permanent home."

Before the new crops were harvested, the commission arrived and told them to move farther up the Missouri, where If they would farm like whites, they could keep the land and be assisted by the Government. The Indians gladly agreed to this treaty, but in 1868 the treaty had still not been ratified, and the appropriation was cut in half.

They were shuttled, abused, tricked, cheated on all sides, and starving half the time. There was never a tribe of all the persecuted tribes that endured a more piteous record than the Sioux. Nevertheless, by 1870 the Sioux somehow advanced in civilization. All were anxious to farm, as agreed to, but the promised equipment, seed, and assistance never came.

Chief Red Cloud led a delegation of chiefs to Washington in 1869, to plead their cause, receiving Government promises of good intentions. Red Cloud became an ardent and determined advocate of peace and loyalty.

Another important event in Sioux history occurred in 1870, when part of the Santee band withdrew from the tribe to take up farms under the Homestead Act, becoming independent citizens. These Indians, in taking up their homesteads, were required to renounce, on oath, all claims on the

United States for annuities. Without doubt, citizenship, and protection of United States Law, is worth a great sum, but was it right to require natives of this country to purchase, at a price of several thousands of dollars, that which was given free to every immigrant from Asia, Europe, or Africa, who asked for it?

The requirement of the Sioux to buy citizenship was appealed by friendly whites, who also argued for help for all the Sioux in establishing farms. In 1873 the Government yielded and sent out oxen, wagons, plows, and the like, enough to stock a whole thirty farms. The few who benefited were grateful, and apparently gave up hope of ever getting the money due them for the lands taken from them in Minnesota.

Also in 1873, a commission was sent to treat with some of the wilder bands of Sioux, for relinquishment of their right to hunt over a large part of their "unneeded" territory in Kansas and Nebraska. The Indians were coerced into yet another cession. By 1875 there were still about a thousand hostile Sioux roaming under their famous chief Sitting Bull, living by the chase when they could, and by depredations when they had to. Occasionally they appeared at Indian agencies, drawing rations among the other Indians unsuspected. The remainder of the bands were working their way toward civilization.

In the Spring of 1876, owing to failure of appropriations, the Indian Bureau had been unable to send supplies, and the Indians, being in "almost a starving condition", went north in large numbers to join the hostile camps of Sitting Bull. In Summer the same thing happened, and even more Indians left to Join the hostiles.

Companies of Army troops had to be stationed at reservations to prevent outbreaks among those who remained. Grasshoppers devoured the crops of many. Martial law was imposed. The natives faced starvation, and were constantly urged by friends and relatives to join in fighting the treacherous Government that had kept faith with nobody.

United States troops burned villages of friends and foes alike, including some encampments containing only women and children. Bands of friendly Indians living peacefully under Government protection at Sand Creek, in Colorado, were butchered in a surprise attack. Blood from The Sand Creek massacre will never be washed from the honor of Colorado and the United States Government.

It was at this time that Sitting Bull made his famous reply to Officials who wanted to treat with him, "Tell them at Washington if they have one

313

man who speaks the truth to send him to me, and I will listen to what he has to say."

The record of the military campaign against the Sioux in 1876 and 1877 is treated elsewhere, but another history, which can never be read, was written in the hearts of the widowed women in the Sioux Nation, and in the nation of the United States.

Before midsummer, the Sioux War was over. The indomitable Sitting Bull had escaped to Canada, the refuge of Indians and slaves. In the Fall a commission entreated him and his followers to return and be assigned to agencies, and to be treated "in as friendly a spirit as other Indians had been who had surrendered."

This was a strange invitation from a Government that knew that those who fled to Sitting Bull had been starving on the reservation. Secure on British soil, the Indians for once had freedom of speech, and replied with scathing sarcasm.

The commissioners returned from their fruitless effort, and the Interior Department simply recorded that "Sitting Bull and his adherents are no longer considered wards of the Government." The United States then went to work taking land from the Sioux that remained in the country, assigning them to the Indian Territory. Red Cloud and Spotted Tail were ordered with their bands to new agencies on the Missouri River.

The site chosen was the old Ponca Reserve that the Government had kicked that tribe out of earlier. The Commissioner said, " The removal of fourteen thousand Sioux Indian at this season of the year, a distance of three hundred miles from their old agencies in Nebraska to their new quarters near the Missouri River, is not a pleasant matter to contemplate."

The usual ill fortune attended the moving of these Indians. They were placed on more barren land, where there was no possibility of farming, no hope of becoming self-sufficient, and where they were kept as hopeless paupers. In hopes of placing them on arable land, they were hastily moved back to the Missouri River. The supplies for the coming winter had been delivered to the wrong agency, and owing to the lateness of the season, it was impossible to move them to where the needy Indians were. Accordingly, the Indians were compelled to travel in the midst of snows and storms, which had already set in.

This idiotic management of Indian affairs was enough by itself to call for an entirely new system. So many and such hasty, ill-considered, uninformed, capricious, and cruel decisions of arbitrary power could hardly be found in a seven year's record of any tyrant; and there is no tyrant whose throne would not have been rocked, if not upset, by the revolutions which would have followed such oppressions.

There is a sequel to the removal of the Red Cloud and Spotted Tail bands, who had consented to go the old Ponca Reservation only after being told that all their supplies had been sent to a certain point on the Missouri River, and it was to late to move all this freight northward again, and that they would starve if they stayed where they were.

Having a written pledge from General Crook that the Government would allow them to go back in the Spring, they most reluctantly consented to go the Ponca Reservation for the winter. In Spring, no orders came. March and April passed without orders. The chiefs sent word to their friend General Crook, who begged them not to break away.

Finally in May, the Commissioner of Indian Affairs went to them himself. When he rose to speak, Chief Spotted Tail sprang up, walked toward him, waving the paper containing the Government promise to return them to White Clay Creek, and exclaimed, "All the men who come from Washington are liars, and the bald-headed ones are worst of all!"

"I don't want to hear one word from you--you are a bald-headed old liar! You have but one thing to do here, and that is to give an order for us to return to White Clay Creek. Here are your written words; and if you don't give this order, and everything here is not on wheels inside of ten days, I'll order my young men to tear down and burn everything in this part of the country!"

"I don't want to hear anything more from you, and I have nothing more to say to you." He turned his back on the Commissioner and walked away. Such language would not be taken from unarmed and helpless Indians, but when it came from a chief with four thousand armed warriors at his back, it was another affair altogether.

The order was written. In less than ten days everything was "on wheels," and the whole body of these Sioux on the move to the country they had indicated. The Secretary of the Interior, in his report for 1878, naively said, "The Indians were found to be quite determined to move westward, and the promise of the Government in that respect was faithfully kept."

For the remaining two years of the Century of Dishonor, The Sioux showed rapid and encouraging improvement, despite for example, that the Ogallala Band had been moved eight times since 1863. It was a wonder that any Indians had any hope for the future.

That all this should be true of these wild, warlike Sioux, after so many hardships and forced wanderings and removals, was incontrovertible proof

315

that there was in them a strength of character, power of endurance, and indomitable courage.

WHITE MASSACRES OF INDIANS

When the English first entered Pennsylvania, Conestoga Indian messengers welcomed them with gifts of corn, venison, and skins. The entire tribe entered into a treaty of friendship with William Penn, which was to last "as long as the sun should shine, or the waters run into the rivers."

Pennsylvania historical records frequently mention this tribe in the early 1700s. The Governor, in 1705, sent a delegation to the Conestogas to meet for "purposes of mutual understanding and confidence." In the same year a party of Quakers were likewise welcomed by the tribe. The Governor himself visited the Conestogas the next year. Two nations were represented in the Conestoga band, the Senecas and the Shawanese.

Still preserved in records, this was said to him by an old chief, "Father, we love quiet; we suffer the mouse to play; when the woods are rustled by the wind we fear not; when the leaves are disturbed in ambush, we are uneasy; but when the rays appear, they give great heat to the body and joy to the heart. Treachery darkens the chain of friendship, but truth makes it brighter than ever. This is the peace we desire."

In the Spring of 1722, a Conestoga was killed by two white brothers. The Governments of New York and Pennsylvania conferred with the tribal chief as to what punish should be given. Surprisingly, the Indian king said, "One life, on this occasion, is enough to be lost There should not two die."

There were only twenty Conestoga left in 1763: seven men, five women, and eight children. They were miserably poor, living in their village on Shawanee Creek, and were wholly peaceful and unoffending. They had even named their children after kind whites, and strove in every way to show their goodwill.

At daybreak on December 14, a band of white "Presbyterians" from Paxton, attacked the little village, finding only six Indians at home; three men, two women, and a boy. The rest were away, working for whites or selling homemade wares. All six were shot, stabbed, or hatcheted to death. They were scalped and horribly mangled, and their huts burned.

When Lancaster magistrates heard the shocking news, they brought the remaining Indians into town for protection, harboring them in the town jail. The Governor ordered all lawmen to seek out the killers. The "Paxton Boys", fifty strong, broke into the jail and killed every Indian there with hatchets and bullets. With victory shouts, thee murderers rode off unmolested, after more horrible mutilations of the bodies.

The Governor offered a reward of $600 for the capture of any three of the ringleaders. The Paxton killers were like beasts that had tasted blood, and threatened to kill Quakers or anyone else befriending Indians. They openly mocked the Governor and announced that they would kill all the Moravian Indians who had been placed in protective custody in Philadelphia.

Along their route they acted like maniacs, terrorizing all they met. It is almost beyond belief that many people justified their acts. An Episcopalian clergyman in Lancaster vindicated them, "bringing scripture to prove that it was right to destroy the heathen." "The Presbyterians think they have a better justification--nothing less than the Word of God," said one of the writers on the massacre.

Horrid perversion of Scriptures to father the worst of crimes was nothing new. The wickedness was repeated often against Indians for the next Century--The Century of greatest dishonor in American History. What Pennsylvania pioneers did in 1763 to helpless and peaceful Conestoga Indians, was done in 1864 by Colorado pioneers to helpless and peaceful Cheyennes at Sand Creek, for but one example.

Soon after the Conestoga massacre, the earliest "removal" of Indians on record took place, one whose cruelty and cost to suffering natives well entitle it to a place in the gory narrative of genocidal exterminations. Everywhere in the Northern Provinces, fanatics renewed the old cry that the Indians were the Canaanites whom God had commanded Joshua to destroy; and that these wars were a token of God's displeasure with the Europeans for permitting "heathen" to live.

It was dangerous for the devoted Moravian Indians to be seen in public. There was a furious outcry all over the country at continued massacres of innocent Indians, which even included Christian Indians in its unreasoning hatred. The Moravian missionaries went along with the Governor's order that all baptized Indians from Nain and Wechquetank should be "brought to Philadelphia, and be protected in that city, having first delivered up their arms."

The aged, sick and little children were carried in wagons. The rest went on foot down roads heavy with November rains. The weary and heartbroken plodders were jeered, cursed, and abused on all sides. A threatening mob in Germantown taunted them with threats of tortures, burning, and hanging. A heavy storm reportedly prevented them such pleasure.

The four days of misery on the road was not over when they reached Philadelphia. Despite the Governor's order, the military commander refused to let them enter the barracks. They stood at the gates for hours as a riotous mob thickened. The brave accompanying missionaries tried in vain to protect the Indians, but drew the same threats and insults.

After five hours of this, the Governor, unable to compel the garrison to open the barracks, ordered the Indians be taken to Province Island, in the Delaware River, joined to the mainland by a dam. Six miles more, at increasing risk and terror, they passed again through the city.

They were settled in some comfortless unused buildings where they were confined for their own safety . Before they had been there a month, some of the villages they had left were burned, and the Paxton mob announced its intention of marching on Province Island to kill every Indian there. Public sentiment was so inflamed that the Government was practically powerless.

When the murderous mob moved toward the island, the Governor sent two sloops to take the Moravians to New York, to be placed under the protection of the English Army. Barely escaping the rioters, they made it to the ships, docked at Amboy, waiting to ferry them to safety. However, the Governor of New York had sent an angry order that not an Indian should set foot in that territory.

Greatly perplexed, the Moravian Indians were placed in the Amboy barracks, where they held daily religious meetings. The Governor of Pennsylvania had no choice, and ordered them back again to Province Island in the severest part of the Winter. Although the Indians set out with cheerfulness and trust in The Lord, the journey was hard. Elders had weakened from the repeated hardships, and the little children suffered pitifully. In crossing some of the frozen rivers, the feeble had to crawl on hands and knees.

Amidst molesting and threatening mobs, they reached Philadelphia on January 24. The Governor had eight heavy cannon installed and a rampart thrown up in front of the barracks. Good citizens were called to arms, and even Quakers took guns and hurried to defend the Indians. The Governor visited them with reassurances and promises of protection.

On February 4, rioters in large force approached Philadelphia. The whole city was roused in defense. Four more cannon were mounted, and the bullies wisely halted. The excitement subsided, and all through the Spring and Summer the Indians remained prisoners in the barracks. Confinement, unwholesome diet, and depression made their situation grave. To add to their misery, smallpox broke out among them, killing fifty-six over the summer.

At last, after a year of such imprisonment and suffering, on December 4, news of peace reached Philadelphia. A Government proclamation declared the "war" ended and hostilities should cease. The imprisoned Indians were joyous, but it was still unsafe to return to their old homes, which were thickly surrounded by white settlers who mere no less hostile at heart than they had been before.

It was decided, therefore, that they should make a new settlement in the Indian country on the Susquehanna River. After a touching farewell to those who had protected them for sixteen months, they set out on April 3 for their new home in the wilderness. For the third time their aged, sick, and very young were crowded into overloaded wagons, for a far harder and longer journey than any they had yet taken.

The inhospitable wilderness was worse than the curses and threats of riotous mobs. They struggled through snow storms, and camped in icy swamps, shivering around smouldering fires of wet wood. To avoid hostile whites they had to take great circuits through unbroken forests, cutting each foot of the path through the trees.

The men waded streams and made rafts for the women and children. Sometimes they had to camp while making canoes for deeper streams. Food gave out. They ate only bitter wild potatoes. They gave the sweet-juiced inner bark of chestnut trees to hungry, crying children. Their only water was often from shallow, muddy puddles. Once they were surrounded by blazing woods. Several died and were buried by the way.

On May 9 they arrived at Machwihilusing, forgot their pain, and "with renewed courage" started to build homes. They called their settlement "Friedenshutten" (Tents of Peace).

These natives had suffered all this persecution simply because they were Indians, and all would have been killed, were it not for the Government that kept the frontiersmen of Pennsylvania from driving them out or killing them. This would all be played out again in a hundred years, when the frontiersmen of Colorado and Nebraska would try to do the same to the helpless, hunted creatures that dared stand in their way.

Sixteen years after the Conestoga Massacre came the blackest crime on the long list, whose equal for treachery and cruelty cannot be pointed out in the record of massacres of whites by Indians.

The Gnadenhutten Massacre

In 1779 the congregations of Moravian Indians at Gnadenhutten, Salem, and Schonbrun, on the Muskingum River, were forced by hostile Indians to go north to the Sandusky River. The English instigated the move, convinced that Moravian missionaries were on the side of the colonies. These Indians had no part in the war, but The English found it easy to stir up hostile tribes to do their deeds.

The hostiles who escorted the forced march were commanded by English officers. "The savages drove them forward like cattle," said an old narrative. For a month these unfortunates were driven through the wilds, and then dumped on the banks of the Sandusky in the middle of October without game, provisions, utensils, weapons, or tools. They built huts of logs and bark, but had no blankets or beds.

The missionaries finally convinced the English that neither they nor their Indian congregations had aided the American colonists. They were told they could return home without attacks by the English-controlled hostile tribes. They faced a deadly, more insidious enemy, death by cold and starvation, while waiting to be able to return home in the Spring.

Some began to die of starvation, and they had almost no food left, so a group started to trek the 125 miles back to where their crop of corn, though withering in the fields and weatherbeaten, would still be a priceless store for them. On the way they were advised to go back openly in their deserted towns, assured that the the Americans were friendly to them now.

This they did, and spent several weeks gathering, husking, and storing corn to pack back to their families on the Sandusky. On the very day they were to have set off, some two hundred whites showed up, saying they were glad to see them and would take them to Pennsylvania where they would not be persecuted by hostile Indians or the English.

The Christian Indians believed them, and were advised to stop their work and go with the whites to Pittsburg, where they would be given all that they needed. The trusting Indians even showed them where they had been hiding their corn in the woods. The Americans helped them load everything up and even helped empty their beehives.

The whites also attracted the Salem Indians to join their "protective" caravan, all the while discussing spiritual matters with the Christian natives. In the meantime the defenseless Indians at Gnadenhutten were suddenly attacked, driven together, and bound with ropes. As soon as the Salem Indians arrived, they met the same fate.

320

By a vote, it was decided to kill all the Indians the next day. To the credit of humanity, a group of whites protested, declaring the Indians innocent and harmless, and should be set free. The majority were unmoved, and only disagreed on how to kill their victims.

Some preferred burning them alive. Others thought tomahawking and scalping would be best. The latter was agreed upon, and they told the Indians that since they were Christians, they should prepare themselves for death the next day.

The terrified Indians soon collected themselves and allowed the men to be separated from their families. Some whites wanted to start the killings immediately, but the natives begged a short delay to prepare themselves. As they prayed and sang to God, the impatient killers interrupted to ask if they were ready yet to die.

One of the killers picked up a cooper's mallet and killed fourteen with blows to their heads. He said his arm was tired and handed the mallet to a fellow murderer, saying, "I think I have done pretty well." In the women's house, an aged, pious old woman was first to be slain in front of the others.

Ninety-six patient Christians were slaughtered that day. Miraculously, two boys about fourteen years of age, managed to escape. One was scalped and left for dead, and the other had hidden in a cellar. At night he crept into the woods and met the other. The two, after incredible hardships, made their way back to Sanduskey.

A false account of the massacre was printed in the Pennsylvania Gazette, April 17, 1782: "The people greatly alarmed, and having received intelligence that the Indian town on the Muskingum had not moved, as reported, a number of men, properly provided, collected and rendezvoused on the Ohio, opposite the Mingo Bottom, with a desire to surprise the above towns."

"One hundred men swam the river, and proceeded to the towns of Muskingum, where the Indians had collected a large quantity of provisions to supply their war-parties. They arrived at the town in the night, undiscovered, attacked the Indians in their cabins, and so completely surprised them that they killed and scalped upward of ninety--but a few making their escape--about forty of whom were warriors, the rest old women and children."

"About eighty horses fell into their hands, which they loaded with plunder, the greatest part furs and skins, and returned to the Ohio without the loss of a man."

321

Massacres of Apaches

In less than a hundred years from the Gnadenhutten massacre, a United States Army officer, stationed at Camp Grant, in Arizona Territory, wrote to his commanding officer that he had allowed a some 525 destitute Apaches to make camp near the post, and had given the starving group rations after never receiving a reply from higher authority on what to do with them.

The young officer related how he had grown to admire the Indians and had done all he could to help them, including getting work on nearby ranches for them. The Apache were hopeful and anxious to hear from the distant General that they might stay there and build homes.

On April 30, 1871, the officer learned that a large party of Tucson citizens was enroute to kill all the Indians at his post. He sent a messenger to their camp to tell them to come immediately to the post for protection. The messengers found a burning village, strewn with dead and mutilated women and children. The soldiers formed a burial party, and later sent interpreters into the mountains to assure any surviving Apaches that the Army had nothing to do with the sacking of their village.

In two days, some 128 survivors and escapees straggled in, weary and gaunt from hunger. They kept faith with the Officer, but could not understand, since they were at peace and had no wrong intent, why they should be murdered. They asked for help in getting back their captured women and children, and that they be allowed to live here in their old homes, where nature supplied nearly all their needs.

This was not the only cruel outrage committed by white men on the Apaches. In the Report of the Board of Indians Commissioners for 1871, a letter was included from an Arizona pioneer who had spent 1840 and 1841 among the Apaches, a time when they were friendly to all Americans going among them.

Many American trappers were taking beaver on the headwaters of the Gila River at that time. The valleys were full of Apaches, whose closest enemies were the Mexicans, who feared them greatly and could not fight them man to man.

One of the trappers, a man named Johnson, went on a spree in Sonora. The Governor of Sonora offered him an ounce of gold for every Apache scalp brought to him. The trapper secured a small howitzer, and returned to his camp with supplies for his party. On approaching the valley he was welcomed back by the Indians who began preparing a feast.

While they were gathered in a laughing, chatting group near the fire, the trapper told some of his associates of the Mexican offer, easily overcoming the small supply of scruples among them. Since they were always armed with rifles and pistols, they needed no preparation.

The howitzer, which the Indians might have supposed was merely a small keg of whiskey, was placed on the ground and pointed at the group of warriors, squaws, and children around the fire, watching the roasting meal. Johnson gave the signal and fired the howitzer. All who were not killed by the blast were shot with rifles.

A very few escaped and fled to others of their tribe. The Apaches showed that they could imitate their civilized white brothers. A band immediately fell upon a group of trappers, killing almost all of them. The story then spread, of course, that the Apaches were cruel and treacherous, with no mention of what had first been done to them.

These are but four massacres out of scores, whose history, when fully known, proved that the Indian had not always been the aggressor, and that treachery and cruelty were by no means exclusively Indian traits.

CONCLUSION

There were about 300,000 Indians in the United States in the late 1870's, by best estimates, made up of nearly three hundred tribes and bands. There were, "In Minnesota and States east of the Mississippi, about 32,500; In Nebraska, Kansas, and the Indian Territory (present Oklahoma), 70,650; In the territories of Dakota, Montana, Wyoming, and Idaho, 65,000; In Nevada and the Territories of Colorado, New Mexico, Utah, and Arizona, 84,000; On the Pacific slope, 48,000."

Almost half were self-supporting on their own reservations, "receiving nothing from the Government except interest on their own moneys, or annuities granted them in consideration of the cession of their lands to the United States. Of the remainder, 84,000 were partially supported by Government monies due them, and by their annuities provided by treaties, being inadequate to their subsistence on the reservations where they are confined.

In many cases, those Indians furnished up to two-thirds of their support "by fishing and root-digging". Those facts should have disposed of the persistent accusation that Indians would not work. There were about 55,000 who never visited an agency, over whom the Government did not pretend to have either control or care. They lived, "by fishing, hunting, on roots, nuts, berries, and the like, and by begging and stealing." Some 31,000 were entirely supported by the Government.

All of the three hundred tribes or bands had suffered at the hands of the Government or of white settlers. The poorer, the smaller the group, the more helpless the band, the more certain the cruelty and outrage they endured.

This was especially true of the Indians of the Pacific Slope who were caught up in the tidal wave of gold-seekers. There was no time for Government treaties to be made, or even community laws. The tales of the wrongs to Pacific Slope Indians from 1850 to 1880 fills many volumes, and is too monstrous to at first be believed.

Wherever the record of Indian history is opened, every page and every year has a dark stain. The story of one tribe is the story of all, time and place making no difference in the facts. Colorado was as greedy and unjust in 1880 as was Georgia in 1830, and Ohio in 1795. The United States broke promises deftly throughout the period, with added ingenuity from long practice.

There are hundreds of pages of unimpeachable testimony on the side of the Indian, but they all went for nothing, tossed aside and forgotten. Presidential commission after commission contained eloquent statements of wrongs done by the Government, with recommendations to Tell the truth, keep promises, make fair bargains, ad deal justly in all ways and all things.

These reports were bound up in annual reports, and that was the end of them. Probably not one American citizen in 10,000 ever saw them or knew that they existed. The swamp of Indian affairs needed clearing, with the goal of making the Indians full citizens, with all rights and responsibilities. It was to be long in coming.

Cheating, robbing, and breaking promises were the three main things the Government needed to stop doing.

PICTORIAL
SECTION

BIOGRAPHY

William Penn Adair

Aripeka

Austenaco

Black Beaver

Black Fox

Elias Cornelius Boudinot

Billy Bowlegs

Joseph Brant

Dennis Wolf Bushyhead

Jesse Chisholm

Daugherty Colbert

Cornplanter

Crazy Snake

Alice Brown Davis

Frederick J. Dockstader

Hiawatha

Menewa

Mikanopy

Ninigret

Osceola

Pocahontas

Pleasant Porter

Powhatan

Pushmataha

Queen Anne

Red Jacket

Will Rogers

Sequoyah

PICTORIAL
SECTION

TRIBES & DAILY LIFE

Pennsylvania in 1775 is the scene of this attack on James Smith (left) on an Iroquois group.

An Apalchee Indian of the Fort Walton Period *(c. 1300-1650 AD)*. The reconstruction is based on archaeological and ethnographical data.

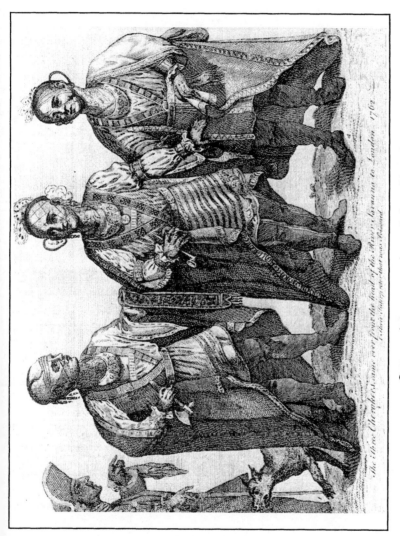

Copperplate engraving of the Cherokees.

The last Chickasaw Council House at Tishomingo, OK.

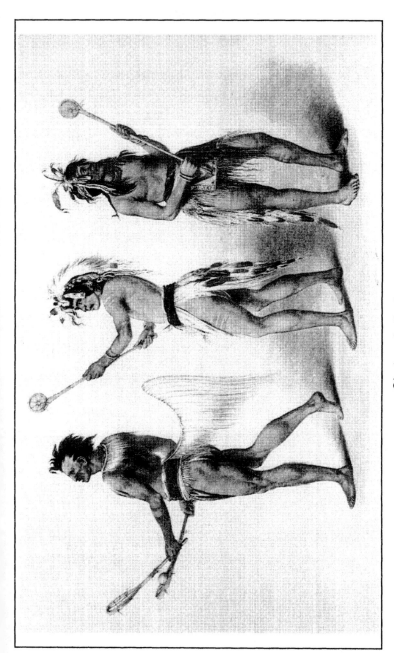

Chotaw ball players.

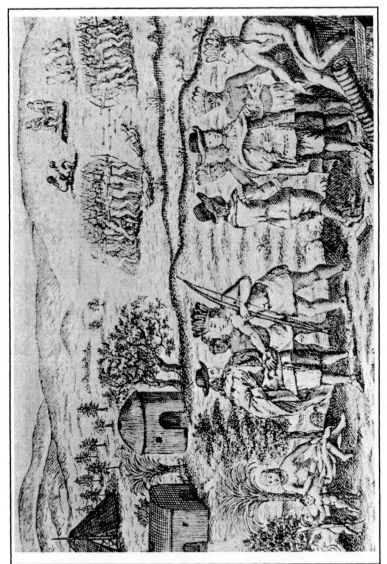

17th century sketch of trade between the Swedes and the Delawares.

Band of full-blooded Iroquios Indians in front of the Craigie-Longfellow House.

Engraving of Moravian Minister baptizing some Delaware and Mohegans.

Combat between the Ojibwas, Sacs and foxes on Lake Superior.

Onondaga town attacked by the French, led by Champlain in 1615.

Secotin Village

Seminole house.

Seminole house.

Seneca Eagle Dance.

An early Algonquin Village in 1585.

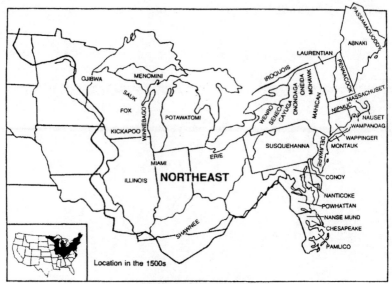

TRIBES OF THE NORTHEAST

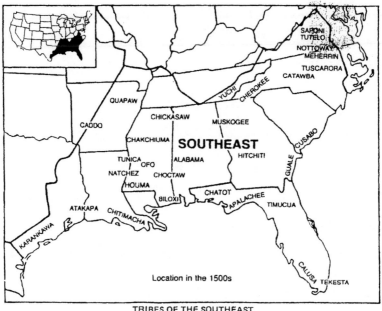

SOUTHEAST

QUAPAW

CADDO

CHICKASAW

MUSKOGEE

CHAKCHIUMA

TUNICA OFO

NATCHEZ CHOCTAW

HOUMA

ALABAMA

HITCHITI

SAPONI
TUTELO
NOTTOWAY
MEHERRIN

TUSCARORA
CATAWBA

YUCHI CHEROKEE

CUSABO

GUALE

ATAKAPA CHITIMACHA

KARANKAWA

BILOXI

CHATOT

APALACHEE

TIMUCUA

CALUSA TEKESTA

Location in the 1500s

TRIBES OF THE SOUTHEAST